AMERICAN LABOR UNIONS
AND POLITICS, 1900–1918

AMERICAN LABOR UNIONS

AND POLITICS

1900–1918

32247

BY *Marc Karson*

FOREWORD BY *Selig Perlman*

Southern Illinois University Press · Carbondale

1958

HD 8076
K18A
vol. 1

Foreword

WHEN, just about fifty years ago, the writer of these lines got thrown into the immediate shadow of him who has proved to be the greatest although the over-modest interpreter of American labor history, John R. Commons of the University of Wisconsin, he could choose but one of the following alternatives: either to remain basically true to the Marxism he had recently brought with him from his native Russia with its predetermined conclusions as regards the social trends leading to the inevitable proletarian revolution, or to compose himself to *listen* to a new though modest voice. It is, of course, not easy to account for a choice one has made at a time when all the voicing authorities insist otherwise, unless one attributes real significance to Commons' "American Shoemakers, 1648–1895," which appeared in the *Quarterly Journal of Economics* in the fall of 1909, an article of 11,000 words in which only the last five pages dealt with general ideas but which concluded with the words: "The Shoemakers have pioneered and left legible records. Their career is interpretative if not typical."

Now labor history is forever open to reinterpretation; it is a mental discipline that never stands still, and one into which each additional period gives rise to a multiplicity of considerations which govern the ultimate social result. So when recently the publisher of this volume asked for a brief introduction, my own present and past suddenly became merged into one. Commons' "Shoemakers" of five decades before as well as this writer's studied generalizations suddenly found themselves elevated into a position of judgeship over the conclusions advanced by one, who, while subject to a more modern training and conversant with a far more modern intellectual idiom, was not far behind in originality of thought and readiness to expand his field of investigation, as he has amply demonstrated in this volume, into that of the role of

v

the Catholic religion upon labor thought, which others have perhaps lacked the courage to accentuate fully.

The author has chosen the most significant stretch of time for his detailed analysis—the years between the end of the century and the end of World War I. These were the years in which the American labor movement under the leadership of Samuel Gompers had boldly struck out on its own and confronted America with its moderate program of collective bargaining *within capitalism,* despite the ever-growing menace of trustification, the constant accumulation of court persecution at the instigation of employers whose hold on public opinion, at least during the first half, seemed virtually unshakable, and a most uncertain attitude of the national government even under Theodore Roosevelt. Yet it also included the era of Woodrow Wilson, whose sympathy for labor was genuine enough to seem to render Gompers' hopes far from futile, especially during the year and a half of America at war. It was in these years when American organized labor boldly defied the intellectual prophets, who at the peak of their power had succeeded in penetrating up to two-fifths of the leadership of the American Federation and had rendered the role of Gompers one of the primary forces of history, as the author freely though sadly acknowledges.

The author, himself an unenthusiastic historical pluralist, does not deny that the victory scored by the apostles of moderation was a genuine majority victory, although he goes on to enumerate five or six principal causes. One cause he fails to list however, a cause which accounts for the intellectual self-confidence of Gompers and his confreres. This cause pertains to the sixty or seventy years preceding his period—the failure of American labor's basic aspiration during those decades to escape from the wage system into producer's co-operation, for which, under the Knights of Labor, a last but grandiose effort has been made.

Gompers' success in overcoming Socialist class-consciousness was not an immediate one—in fact Gompers had himself begun as a class-conscious Socialist under the influence of Marx's International Workingmen's Association with headquarters in London. It was the ideology-laden German immigrant who had come to these shores in the sixties and seventies as a Marxian trade-union Socialist, and who after many years found himself possessed of an ideology with its Socialist part already fallen into progressive disuse, that was able to face America and the world with something which to Daniel DeLeon and his industrial Socialists of the eighteen nineties appeared but as a labor faker's panacea. Thus labor history has partly avenged itself on the author of this excellent book as an historian who has spread his nets too late.

SELIG PERLMAN
John R. Commons Professor of Economics

The University of Wisconsin
June 26, 1958

Preface

THE AMALGAMATION of the AF of L–CIO in 1955 led many commentators of the mass media to declare that the labor unions would now possess the political strength to win control of the government. Such statements, designed to alarm the country and arouse antilabor feelings, implied that the participation of unions in politics was a new and threatening development. Actually, organized labor has always been in politics. Sometimes its only activity was lobbying for labor legislation and at other times this was combined with active participation in political campaigns. The greater the involvement of the modern American union movement in politics, the more the movement, its membership, and America gained. Labor in politics is as American as beans and baseball and Coca-Cola and corn.

The major purpose of this book is to examine and evaluate labor's political involvement as it developed in the years between 1900 and 1918. The future political development of American labor will be aided if people both inside and outside the unions acquire a deeper understanding of labor's political history. An examination of labor's political activity from the beginning of the twentieth century to the end of World War I reveals its political theory and political behavior in both war and peace. The political pattern in many ways—pragmatic in philosophy, opportunistic in method, and limited in goals—was typically American. Herein was its strength and weakness.

*

THE SUBJECT of this study was originally suggested by Professor Harold J. Laski in 1947 as we consulted about the topic of my doctoral dissertation which he was to supervise. When I told him that I was interested in exploring the relationship between the British

Trade Union Congress and the British Labor Party from 1900 to 1918, he replied, "Karson, we have enough papers on the British labor movement. I'd like to know what happened to the political development of the American union movement during this same period."

In seeking to answer Laski's question, I uncovered considerable unpublished material which suggested newer generalizations than those that have gained prominence among students of American labor history. For example, a recent book by Philip Taft, *The A.F. of L. in the Time of Gompers,* perpetuates the following beliefs: 1. that Gompers' leadership, by and large, was beyond reproach; 2. that the AF of L's traditional political policy was nonpartisan; 3. that religious influence was a negligible factor in the AF of L's opposition to independent political action and socialism; 4. that the AF of L's policy of Asiatic immigration exclusion was based on economic, not racial, considerations; 5. that the AF of L was opposed to discrimination against American Negroes; 6. that the AF of L was critical of American imperialism.

The data I regarded important enough to be written up, and which are not found in Taft's book, show the AF of L's adolescence to be somewhat different than now commonly understood. This version may not be as flattering to the AF of L as the one in Taft's book, but the skeletons in labor's historical closet are not so terrible that they should remain closed to reporting. The material reveals the limitations and shortcomings of Gompers' character and leadership as well as his strengths. It shows that the AF of L's political support from 1906 to 1918 was given to the Democratic party. It describes the AF of L's racialistic attacks on Asiatics and its toleration of discrimination against American Negroes. It notes the AF of L's indifference toward American imperialism in Latin America and Asia. It documents from Catholic sources the impressive anti-Socialist activity among workers undertaken by Roman Catholic churchmen and laymen.

The material is organized in the following manner. The first chapter introduces labor's nineteenth-century political history. It contains little not already covered by reputable works, but it will be helpful background to those unfamiliar with labor's nineteenth-century political origins. Chapters Two through Six tell of the AF of L's political thought and practice—its support of the Democratic party and its opposition to the Socialist minority in its ranks —during the years 1900–1918. Chapters Seven and Eight describe the ideology and political struggles of left wing unionism, represented during the period under study by the short-lived Industrial Workers of the World. Chapter Nine pioneers in exploring the principles and activities of the Roman Catholic Church and Roman Catholic clergy and laymen in their relationships with the American trade-union movement. The final chapter summarizes the AF of L's political character in 1918 and proceeds to interpret the reasons for the lack of Socialist strength in American unions and the absence of an American labor party.

The period from 1900 to 1918 is a particularly significant one in the history of the modern American labor movement because the present day union movement was developing its political traditions during this time. This was the period, too, when socialism, then at its height in American life, was intent on winning the unions to its cause. This was also the period when Roman Catholicism began its militant campaign to combat socialism within the unions and to propagate Catholic social principles.

The thesis of Chapter Nine, that the Roman Catholic Church in America has been a vital force accounting for the moderate political position of American trade-unionism, may gain a mixed reaction. Scholarly studies are sometimes exploited for purposes never intended by the authors. It would be regrettable if this chapter gives any comfort to anti-Catholics. My own position is as simple as this: the Roman Catholic Church works honestly, openly, and in moral ways for the social principles that are related to its faith. It ill behooves a non-Catholic, like myself, to be critical of catholicism's relationship with the union movement when its efforts spring from religious sources outside my frame of reference.

The responsibility of catholicism for the political character of the modern American union movement should not be overemphasized. Believing in multiple causation, I realize that a religious motivation alone has not determined the politics of American unionism. It seems to me, however, that the climate of opinion produced by catholicism's institutional and individual relationships with the labor unions helped influence unionism in the direction of political moderation. Even if a church took no formal position on the philosophy and activities of a social institution, the religious faith and training of the people connected with the institution would affect its philosophical position and practical work. The decisions that individuals make do not stem entirely from objective, rational considerations. Behavior is affected by value systems which are partly the outgrowth of forgotten subjective experiences. The effects of religious training in the family linger on in the conscious and unconscious life of the individual, producing a way of behavior that asserts itself in all areas of human activity.

A question may arise as to why there is a chapter in this book on catholicism and none on other religious faiths. The answer is that the search for early twentieth-century data about American unions and politics disclosed that the Catholic Church had a program for Catholic trade-unionists worth recording, while protestantism and Judaism were not similarly engaged with their people. As noted in several books on protestantism, the social gospels of the different Protestant denominations were at variance. Many Episcopalian and Congregational ministers often went as far as Christian socialism, while the Methodists, Baptists, and Presbyterians, except for a small number of individuals like Harry F. Ward, Charles Stelze, and Walter Rauschenbusch, were more moderate. But whether radical, moderate, or conservative, the Protestant social message was directly aimed at public opinion rather than at organized labor.

Judaism, as a religious institution, was, like protestantism, neither all pro-Socialist nor anti-Socialist, but contained rabbis of both persuasions. A larger ratio of Jews than Gentile workers were drawn to socialism, but their motivation was not of religious derivation. Quite likely some were attracted to socialism because they were unconsciously displacing their resentment of antisemitism onto the economic system. The needles trades and garment industries were often led by Jewish Socialists, but as their Americanization increased, their socialism decreased.

The generalization that the weakness of socialism in American unions is due, in part, to the successful anti-Socialist activities of the Roman Catholic Church within American unions may raise a question about the support unions give to left wing parties in countries such as France and Italy, the Catholic Church notwithstanding. The answer to this question is that a universal principle should not be inferred from my generalization. My generalization was drawn from a historical study of a particular period in a particular country. It may be that the Roman Catholic Church only succeeds in its purposes, as it did in America, when its opposition is just so strong but no stronger. Other cultural forces may have driven toward socialism more powerfully in those countries than in the United States. It may be, too, that those countries would today be completely Socialist or Communist had the Catholic Church not worked resolutely against that development.

The abundance of documented material on catholicism's anti-Socialist relationship with American trade-unionism may mistakenly give the impression that the Catholic social action movement in the early twentieth century was simply one of anti-socialism. Actually, even during this beginning period of its development the Catholic social action movement was also engaged in positive, Catholic socioeconomic-political reforms. For example, the Church propagated its concepts of social justice for its needy people through various kinds of charity and social work. It advocated a "just wage" and supported legislation for the protection of the weak and curbing of the strong under capitalism. However, it was outside the scope of this study to explore the broad field of Catholic social action. My task was to record catholicism's involvement with the labor union movement alone. Unlike its wider program for today's union movement, catholicism's contribution to early twentieth-century trade-unionism was notable primarily for its anti-Socialist interest and activities.

The role of the individual in influencing social development is often exaggerated, but it does have importance. The character of leadership, in particular, requires evaluation. Some readers may wonder if the behavior in the social struggle of some hard working, well-meaning leaders—Socialists, Catholics, IWW'ers, and AF of L'ers—was partly influenced by unconscious conflicts that produced fanaticism and compulsive behavior. In instances where this may be true, such leaders often hurt themselves, their own movement, and their fellow men. If they had weighed the possibility that their motivation was not all pure and noble they might have discovered its latent base and thereby reduced their need to manipulate causes and exploit other people. Social catholicism, democratic socialism, and trade-unionism each contain values that promote man's moral worth, cultural improvement, and economic welfare. But individuals who support these movements from faulty unconscious motivation can adversely affect essentially valid movements. Political behavior cannot be separated from human motivation; to consider the surface phenomena of any behavior without attention to the well springs of unconscious conflict overlooks the submerged, highly important, and often dangerous mass of the iceberg. If the aggressive leader often found in social struggles has deep-rooted love-hate needs, he may unconsciously project the central pattern of his own conflicts into his organization. Does not the history of Nazi Germany tragically illustrate the social havoc that leadership can help to produce? The examination of motivation and of the dynamic nature of unconscious conflicts should be a concern of all interested in the improvement of the quality of men's behavior and of their institutions.

One final comment: This book offers no specific answer to the question that has concerned generations of labor students, "Should labor form its own political party?" If I felt competent to answer this question, I would do so. But the facts upon which this book is based and the extent of my learning do not convince me that I possess the knowledge at this time to answer this question to my satisfaction. If I gave such an answer, I suspect it would not result from my understanding of the union movement and the needs of its members, but would be a projection of the value system produced by my own unconscious processes. I can only feel comfortable with myself if I use my professional skills to report and interpret social phenomena that are fairly clear to me. It is not clear to me whether the Democratic party can become the party to serve effectively labor's interests. Neither do I know whether America is approaching the stage of socioeconomic development where a labor party's presence is a vital necessity, nor, lastly, do I know whether a labor party could secure enough popular support for its necessary growth. Yet whatever the political structure within which American labor unions choose to function the data in this book suggest that constant and vigorous political action is necessary for the security of the union movement and for the welfare of its members.

*   *   *

I WISH to thank the following people: Arnold N. Tolles, of Cornell's Industrial and Labor Relations School, who taught me American Labor History at American University, Washington, D.C., in 1945 and as a sequel supervised a research credit course for which I wrote my first paper on labor politics; David Saposs for reading and commenting on the materials I discovered about the Roman Catholic Church's relationship to the American Federation of Labor; Monsignor George Higgins of the National Catholic Welfare Conference who read Chapter Nine and earlier helped me to understand that a non-Catholic may unintentionally arouse anti-Catholic sentiment; Dr. Harry Levinson, Director of the Division of Industrial Mental Health at the Menninger Foundation for encouraging my interest in the psychological motivation of union members and leaders; Dr. Orville Alexander, Chairman of the Southern Illinois University Government Department, for generously providing research time to complete the book; my colleagues in the Government Department, particularly Dr. Wesley Ward, for reading and advising me on my Preface and final chapter; the editors of the *Industrial and Labor Relations Review,* for permission to make use of my article, "The Catholic Church and the Political Development of American Trade Unionism, 1900–1918," published by them in July, 1951; and the staffs of the following libraries: The American Federation of Labor, The Catholic University of America, Columbia University, The German Catholic Central Verein, the University of Illinois, the Library of Congress, The London School of Economics and Political Science, the University of Michigan, The New York Public Library, St. Louis University, Southern Illinois University, The Tamiment Institute Library (formerly the Rand School of Social Science), the Wisconsin State Historical Society, the University of Wisconsin, and the Woodrow Wilson Memorial Library.

Naturally, I alone am responsible for the interpretations and for whatever errors the book contains.

MARC KARSON

Southern Illinois University
March 7, 1958

Contents

AMERICAN LABOR UNIONS
AND POLITICS, 1900–1918

1.

The Political History of the American Labor
Movement in the Nineteenth Century

> . . . poor men shall be able to become lords and masters
> and do-nothings; and oft will it be seen that they shall do so;
> and it shall be even for that cause that their eyes shall be
> blinded to the robbing of themselves by others, because
> they shall hope in their souls that they may each live to rob
> others: and this shall be the very safeguard of all rule and
> law in those days. . . . and those that see, and that have
> thus much conquered fear that they are furthering the real
> time that cometh and not the dream that faileth, these
> men shall the blind and the fearful mock and missay, and
> torment and murder: and great and grievous shall be the
> strife in those days, and many the failures of the wise, and
> too oft sore shall be the despair of the valiant; and
> backsliding and doubt, and contest between friends and
> fellows lacking time in the hubbub to understand each other,
> shall grieve many hearts and hinder the Host of the
> Fellowship.
>
> *William Morris,* A DREAM OF JOHN BALL

WHILE the American trade-union movement today is the lone
major movement in the democratic world not associated with a
labor or Socialist political party, the origins of the American union
movement tell of independent labor political action. Actually, the
United States produced the world's first labor party. The Philadelphia Mechanics' Union of Trade Associations gave America
this distinction when it established the Working Men's party of
Philadelphia in May, 1828. The following year a group of New
York City trade-union leaders created the New York Workingmen's party. These examples of workers' political parties were imi-

tated in other cities and by 1834 some sixty local labor parties in fifteen states had sprung up.

It was possible for American labor political parties to be founded ahead of those in other countries because American male workers in most states had gained the right to vote by the 1830's. American workers' decision to use their vote as an independent force was prompted by two factors. First, they were suffering from a number of political, social, and economic inequalities which the existing political parties refused to remedy. Second, many of the workers came under the reform influence of an energetic group of intellectuals led by Robert Dale Owen, Francis Wright, Thomas Skidmore, and George Henry Evans.

The most disturbing inequality in the minds of these early American workers was the lack of educational opportunity. Stimulated by the propaganda of Robert Dale Owen and Francis Wright for public education at government expense, the workers' political parties clamored for educational facilities for their children. An uneducated people, the workers reasoned, would not be able to realize the substance of democracy. The nation, too, would be impoverished if its people were unable to make the contribution of enlightened citizens.

Other evils protested by the labor political parties were the following: (1) the lack of government regulation of bank notes and credit; (2) imprisonment for debt; (3) compulsory militia service; (4) the issuance by the state legislatures of monopoly charters to corporations; (5) the absence of a mechanics lien law; (6) the lottery system; (7) heavy taxation; (8) excessive hours of work; (9) indirect systems of electing public officials; (10) expensive legal procedure.

This early period of labor political activity lasted until about 1834. Although the workers had only very limited success in electing their candidates, the movement was not a failure inasmuch as demands for free education, a mechanics lien law, and abolition of imprisonment for debt, received favorable attention in most of the states.

The collapse of these early workers' political organizations was due to the following factors: (1) The reformers who provided the intellectual leadership quarrelled among themselves about the principles and objectives of the movement. (2) This dissension was also reflected among the rank and file of the workers. (3) The established political parties incorporated in their platforms several of the prominent demands of the labor parties. (4) Because labor's voting strength by itself was not sufficient to win an election, workers' candidates often found it expedient to campaign on one of the old party tickets. Once this choice was made it led to the gradual acceptance of more and more of the principles of the old party. (5) The leaders of the labor parties were at a disadvantage in political campaigning against the experienced professional politicians of the older political parties. (6) The opinion-forming agencies in the community were hostile to the workers' political parties and exaggerated the radicalism of the movement by calling attention to the antireligious, antimarriage, antifamily and equal-division-of-property ideas held by its intellectual leaders. (7) Rising prices, beginning about 1834, caused the workers to lose interest in general improvements obtained through political activity and to seek instead immediate material improvements through the economic pressure of trade-union activity.[1]

A more general explanation of the failure of American labor's first political parties is that economic conditions in early nineteenth-century America were unfavorable to the perpetuation of workers' political parties. As long as cheap land was available, labor in short supply, and opportunity for self-advancement a distinct possibility, workers were not likely to question the wisdom of their indifference to politics or their attachment to the traditional parties. In fact, the economic forces in America had not yet made workers aware of the need for their own economic organization. The organization, educative influence, leadership, and financial strength of trade-unions are essential to provide the nucleus for a workers' constitutional political movement to take hold.

From 1833 to 1837, a period of increased prices and business prosperity, workers turned to the development and strengthening of trade-unions. In this period there arose the first federations of organized trades in the cities of New York, Baltimore, Philadelphia, and Boston and these city trades' unions took a further step in workers' solidarity by establishing the first National Trades' Union. Although for the most part the unions subordinated political activity to economic agitation, they conducted a lobbying campaign in the state and federal legislatures, and also urged the

President of the United States to press for the improvement of factory conditions; the ten-hour day in government work; safeguards
against the competition of convict, female, and child labor; the
repeal of laws under which trade-unions were declared illegal
combinations; a more just distribution of public lands; and universal education. The height of trade-union political activity in this
period occurred in 1835 in New York. Here the workers established a New York Equal Rights party in protest against the corruption of Tammany Hall, the monopolistic practices of business,
and the antilabor bias of Judge Swift who had denounced a tailors'
strike as a conspiracy and fined three of the union's officers. The
Equal Rights party's participation in the elections of 1835 split the
Tammany vote and enabled some Whig candidates to be elected
to the New York legislature. Because of this experience, Tammany
sought to attract the labor vote by adopting some of the principles
of the Equal Rights party. The Democratic party was establishing
the pattern of wooing the labor vote—a pattern that was to become
clearer over the years.

In Philadelphia the trade-unions entered politics in 1836 to
improve their chances of obtaining the ten-hour day. But in both
cities the young trade-union movement was not able to withstand
the disastrous effect of the financial panic of 1837. The panic grew
into a depression that continued until the gold discoveries of 1849
fostered business recovery. In this fifteen-year period the utopian
reformers attained the height of their power and prestige. Pro-
longed unemployment and the disintegration of the trade-unions
permitted middle-class thinkers like Arthur Brisbane and George
Henry Evans to win a sympathetic reception from the workers
never again equalled in later years. Brisbane, a disciple of Charles
Fourier, propagandized for social reorganization through Association—a utopian ideal of a small self-contained community
operating for the mutual benefit of all its members and based on a
division of labor harmonious with the human instincts expounded
by Fourier. Between 1843–1845 more than fifty phalanxes were
established in the northern states, the most famous one being the
reorganization of Brook Farm (the co-operative venture of Boston's transcendentalists) into a phalanx. By the end of the 1840's,
however, all the phalanxes had ended in failure. The various skilled
craftsmen and general laborers who had been members of the

phalanxes returned to capitalist society painfully aware of the difficulties inherent in the task of remolding the social order.

The land reform movement of George Henry Evans, although less idealistic in spirit and grandiose in objectives, nevertheless represented another attempt to escape from industrialism. Instead of accepting the inevitability of modern industrial development and determining methods and tactics whereby this development could be to the workers' immediate and long-range benefit, the land reformers devoted their agitation to the panacea of a wider distribution of land among the people. It was believed that if free land were given to actual settlers only, and if a limitation were placed on the amount of land an individual might possess, more people would gain the economic benefits of property owning. At the same time, the workers who remained in industry would be in a better bargaining position with their employers because of the decreased labor supply. To achieve this land reform objective, Evans, unlike Brisbane, regarded working class political action as essential. In 1844 he established the National Reform Association as a propaganda and political pressure agency. Workmen who joined the organization were required to sign a pledge that they would vote only for politicians who promised to enact their land reform program. This method of offering the votes of workingmen to any candidate of the established political parties who championed the workingmen's demands for land reform caused George Henry Evans to be named by twentieth-century labor historians as the founder of organized labor's non-partisan political policy.

On the central committee of the National Reform Association there were thirteen workmen, but mass workingman support was needed if the Association was to thrive. Therefore Evans attended a convention of New England workingmen's organizations which had been called by the Fall River Mechanics and Laborers' Association at Boston in October, 1844, for the main purpose of organizing a campaign that would get the New England workers the ten-hour day. In return for the convention's approval of a resolution in which it pledged itself to lobby for land reform legislation, Evans' Reform Association accepted the ten-hour demand as part of its program. The New England Working Men's Association, which arose as a permanent body from the work of the convention, quickly came under the control of the American Fourierists who gave priority to general social reforms rather than to political activity for the shorter workday. Nevertheless, the ten-hour day movement through legislative enactment was kept before the New England public through the activities of local workingmen's associations and female labor reform associations. The militancy exhibited by women textile workers in Massachusetts in their use of publications, strikes, petitions, and lobbying methods to promote the ten-hour day accounted for the appointment by the state legislature of special committees to investigate the workday situation. Dominated by leading businessmen, these committees until 1855 disapproved any shorter workday legislation. Thus, by the beginning of the second half of the nineteenth century, neither the idealistic aspirations of the utopian reformers nor the practical program of the overworked laborers was having much success. The humanitarian sentiment that had been at the root of the reformers' ideals now began to be absorbed by the slavery issue, while the revival of business prosperity following the gold rush of 1849 resurrected the trade-union as the laborer's instrument of protection and aid.

The labor unions of the 1850's hoped to obtain through economic methods the basic material improvements of higher wages, lower hours, and better conditions of work, and the union security measures of recognition, and trade agreements. Changing national economic factors such as the increase in industrial production, immigration, urbanization, and the improvements in transportation, widened the market to a national scope and increased the area of labor and trade competition. Consequently the skilled unions saw the need and value of expanding into national organizations to safeguard their skill against the invasion of cheaper labor and to match the growing territorial strength of the employer. In the 1850's, the Printers, the Stone Cutters, the Hatters, the Locomotive Engineers, the Cigarmakers, the Machinists, the Iron Molders, and the Blacksmiths established themselves as national trade-unions.

While for the most part the trade-unions were uninterested in politics, the 1850's saw the introduction of Marxian socialism in America. Joseph Weydemeyer, a German immigrant of 1851 and a friend and follower of Karl Marx, began publishing a Communist paper, *Die Revolution,* in 1851 whose title he changed the following year to *Die Reform.* He also organized in late 1852 a revolutionary society, the Proletarian League, whose major function consisted of sponsoring a conference of workers in 1853, that founded the American Labor Union. An English-speaking counterpart of the American Labor Union, the Workingmen's National Association, was formed in Washington in late 1853 by Sam Briggs. Although Weydemeyer hoped to see developed a single organization uniting German and American workers in a Marxist trade-union federation and a workers' political party, both organizations were unable to attract a mass following and died almost in birth. Marxian formulas applied in America with little modification had met their first failure, but certainly not their last. The depression of 1857 also shattered many established non-Marxist unions, and only a small number of the strongest locals and nationals were left at the start of the Civil War in 1861.

The attitude of Northern labor towards Negro slavery, slavery's expansion into the west, and the Civil War was an ambivalent one. In the 1840's and the early 1850's, most workers, except in organizations dominated by intellectuals like Robert Dale Owen, Albert Brisbane, and Horace Greeley, were indifferent to the situation of the Negro slave and to the moral and economic implications which slavery raised. Many workers had a traditional allegiance to the Democratic party and many, too, feared the competition in the labor market with emancipated Negroes. But Northern workers opposed the expansion of slavery into free territory because they saw slave labor as a real threat to free labor's living standards. The victory in 1860 of Lincoln and the Republican party, which opposed the further extension of slavery, was made possible by the votes of Northern industrial workers.

The secessionist movement of Southern states in February, 1861, aroused the opposition of many Northern workers who believed in the preservation of the union. A division did exist on the issue of whether compromise was preferable to war, but once the war began, organized labor loyally supported the Republic. In many instances entire local unions volunteered as a body for military service. The passage of the Conscription Act of 1863 did incite draft riots but these were among unorganized workers. The trade-unions, although objecting to the Act's provisions which allowed a draftee to avoid service by sending a substitute or paying the government $300, counseled their membership to campaign peaceably for amending these provisions. In some instances the trade-unions did engage in wartime strikes because wages did not keep pace with the doubled cost of living. But, in general, organized labor's support of Lincoln and the war continued. Prior to the election of 1864, trade-unionists in New York, Chicago, Boston, and Philadelphia organized a political body, the Workingmen's Democratic-Republican Association, to campaign for Lincoln's re-election and the prosecution of the war. A notable example of trade-union political action taken during the war for the immediate welfare of trade-unionism occurred when the trade assemblies of New York City, Brooklyn, Buffalo, Albany, and Rochester successfully warned their state legislators in 1864 that any legislator who voted for the Hastings-Folger antistrike bill would not be supported by labor in the next election.

The Civil War like the wars that followed in American history, had a favorable affect on trade-union growth. The national need for large-scale production of war materials, the decreased labor supply resulting from the induction of many workers into the military forces, and the enormous profits to employers from government contracts, vastly improved the trade-unions' bargaining position with employers. During wartime trade-unions have found it easier to organize many unorganized workers who wished to receive the benefits the union was obtaining for its members. Thus, the few trade-unions that had survived the 1857 depression grew stronger during the Civil War while in addition, many new locals arose, along with a noticeable growth in city trades' assemblies. By 1870 there existed about thirty national unions with about 300,000 members. Many of the city trades' assemblies had co-operative stores, free libraries, and legislative lobbies.

In this post-Civil War period, the National Labor Union, the first national labor federation in America, was created. William Sylvis, president of the Iron Molders' Union, was the guiding spirit of the new organization. Beginning with the first convention of the National Labor Union in 1866, the emphasis was on political activity. The convention declared itself in favor of the eight-hour day by legislative enactment, producers' co-operatives, public land reforms, the organization of unskilled workers and the early establishment of a national labor party. Conventions in the succeeding two years repeated the earlier position in these matters and went on to argue the questions of the acceptance of Negro workers in the union, of national currency reforms, and of co-operation with the international labor movement.

The debate on organizing Negro workers within the National Labor Union was unable to reach a permanent conclusion. Even those like Sylvis who argued for the admission of Negro workers into the unions did not believe in the moral right of Negroes to social and political equality.[2] Sylvis' view was that if they remained unorganized, they would be a potential threat to the economic standards of organized white workers. Of a total of 142 delegates who attended the 1869 convention, none were Negroes, and the convention urged that colored representatives from all states be sent to the next convention. A committee was also appointed to organize the Negroes in Pennsylvania.

The question of currency reform, however, became the dominating issue within the National Labor Union. The union emphatically announced its opposition to high interest rates, the national banking system, bank notes and tax-exempt government bonds, and advocated the government issuance of cheap paper "greenbacks" as legal tender. As for international relations, the National Labor Union was the first sizable national American labor organization to show a strong interest in the European labor movement. Correspondence of fraternal goodwill was conducted with the International Workingmen's Association, and, in 1869, A. C. Cameron represented the organization at a Congress of the International in Basle, Switzerland.

The national labor party contemplated by the first congress of the National Labor Union in 1866 did not immediately come into being, although a platform for the party was adopted at the second convention in 1867, and local nominations of workers for political office were recommended. The platform favored the eight-hour workday law, producers' co-operatives, workers' housing, a Department of Labor, government management of railroads, express, water transportation, and the telegraph system. Opposition was voiced to strikes, the national banking system, and monopoly in money and land. Initial organizational preparation for the new party started in 1870, when the convention appointed an executive committee for the national convention to nominate candidates for the party. However, by the time this convention got under way in

1872, most of the trade-unions had deserted the National Labor Union because they objected to its predominantly political nature and its preoccupation with currency reforms. The convention nominated Judge David Davis, who later refused the nomination when he learned that Horace Greeley had been nominated by the insurgent Liberal Republican party. Thus the political fate of the National Labor and Reform party without its original candidate and without trade-union support, was doomed. Its final candidate, Charles O'Conner, a New York Democrat and slavery defender, polled a meager 29,489 votes. The position of the National Union itself was equally dismal. In the next few years after 1872, it tried vainly to arouse the workers' interest and then completely collapsed, its more militant political figures turned to the Socialist movements and others to the Greenback party.

In Massachusetts a union move into independent party politics almost paralleled the rise and fall of the National Labor Union. A Labor Reform party was organized in Massachusetts in 1869 with particular trade-union support of the shoemakers' union, the Knights of St. Crispin. In 1869, the party elected 21 members out of 80 to the lower house of the Massachusetts legislature, but within a few years its strength was negligible. Its end was hastened by the general decline of the Knights of St. Crispin and by dissension between the renowned abolitionist, Wendell Phillips, who favored currency reforms, and Ira Steward, self-educated mechanic and national crusader for the eight-hour day.

The serious depression from 1873 to 1878 was a time of acute distress for workers and unions, and the worst period of labor violence ever witnessed in America. There were demonstrations of the unemployed in New York and Chicago and strikes among the textile workers in New England and the coal miners in Pennsylvania. Terrorism instigated by the secret Irish ring of "Molly Maguires" prevailed in the anthracite regions. During the nationwide railroad strike, in July, 1877, federal troops at Pittsburgh wantonly shot into a crowd of workers, killing twenty-six persons. The workers retaliated by destroying $5,000,000 worth of railroad property. For the most part the trade-unions were unable to withstand the effects of the depression. Only eight of about forty national unions, weakened in membership and finances, managed to survive this period.

A unique trade and labor organization that withstood the depression of the 1870's was the Noble Order of the Knights of Labor. Its first local assembly was organized in late December, 1869, by Uriah Stephens from the remnants of the Garment Cutters' Association of Philadelphia. In recognition of the employers' practices of lockouts and blacklists, and as a result of Stephens' early training for the Baptist ministry and his membership in the Masons, Odd Fellows, and Knights of Pythias, the Knights of Labor was constituted as a secret association with a mystic ritual. Its general purpose was a broad one dedicated to uplifting and improving the status of all laboring people—farmers and intellectuals, whites and blacks, skilled and unskilled, male and female. In fact, everyone was eligible for membership except bankers, stockbrokers, lawyers, gamblers, and liquor dealers, though it was stipulated that three-fourths of the membership of each assembly was to be composed of wage earners. During its three-decade existence the objectives of the Knights of Labor were modified by its leaders and by the composition of its membership but its advocacy of labor solidarity and its idealistic attitude toward reform remained as permanent characteristics. In contrast to the exclusiveness of the existing craft unions, its appeal was built around the motto "An injury to one is the concern of all."

The Knights of Labor, however, was not a proletarian, revolutionary organization in the Marxian image. Its national leaders neither preached the Marxian doctrines of the class struggle, nor did they believe in the use of the strike as a weapon to gain their objectives. Rather, they intended to rely on education and propaganda against the banking power, not against the employers. Believing that the economic system was not operating for the welfare of the people, they wanted to make the necessary corrections by law so that profitable self-employment in business or on the land would be available to all those who sought it. Like many humanitarian reformers that had preceded them in the century, their ultimate ideal lay in a co-operative society. Their contribution to advancing this ideal was in developing the solidarity of working people by organizing them in one big union and educating them to the need for economic and political reforms.

The Knights of Labor first achieved national stature in 1878 when they created a general assembly which had supreme central authority over the 100 local and district assemblies already functioning. The next year Terence Powderly was elected head of the Knights to succeed Stephens who had resigned. As an Irish Catholic it was easy for Powderly to understand that the growth of the organization was being limited among Catholic workingmen because the Church objected to secret societies. By 1882 he succeeded in having the general assembly revoke most of the secret ritual, particularly the oath in the initiation pledge, which was a major concession to the Church. In 1884, however, Cardinal Taschereau, Archbishop of Quebec persuaded the Vatican to condemn the Knights of Labor in Canada, and charged the Canadian bishops "to deter their diocesans therefrom." [3] Fearing that the Knights in this country might suffer a similar blow, Powderly undertook to prove to Cardinal Gibbons of Baltimore that the Knights was not a socialistic organization. The success of this move was evident when Cardinal Gibbons, on a visit in 1887 to receive the cardinal's hat in Rome convinced Cardinal Simeoni, Prefect of Propaganda, not to denounce the Order.[4]

The convention of 1878, which had established the general assembly, also adopted a platform emphasizing that legislation would correct the abuses of wealth and enable the Order to achieve its objective of elevating the people. The Knights' leaders also showed a personal active interest in politics. In the Congressional campaign of 1878, Stephens was an unsuccessful Greenback-Labor candidate, while Powderly, as a candidate of the same party, fared better and was elected mayor of Scranton and re-elected in 1880. Other leaders of the Knights, James L. Wright, Robert Schilling, Charles H. Litchman, John M. Davis, Ralph Beaumont, and George Blair also were Greenback-Labor candidates in 1878. Nevertheless, the Knights in principle did not at this time support any one party or urge the creation of a new party. The 1878 general assembly adopted no plan for political action to help it secure the laws its platform demanded. The next general assembly in 1879 agreed that the local assemblies could participate in political campaigns in whatever manner they felt was in consonance with the Order's interests. A resolution at the same convention to bar the general officers from engaging in politics was rejected. At the 1880 general assembly, Phillip Van Patten, secretary of the Socialist Labor Party, succeeded in having the policy of nonpartisan politics on a local basis recommended to the local assemblies. The recommendation carried the reservation, however, that no political action could be undertaken unless three-fourths of the local members were in favor of such political action; furthermore, no member was required to vote in political elections according to the preference of the local's majority. A motion at the same convention to submit a recommendation to the locals and district assemblies that they support the National Greenback-Labor Party was tabled after a lengthy discussion.

Although Powderly repeatedly warned the Order that politics should not be discussed within the organization, he agreed to the addition to the Preamble in 1884 which stated that most of the demands of the platform "could only be obtained through legislation, and that it is the duty of all to assist in nominating and supporting with their votes only such candidates as will pledge their support to these measures, regardless of party." [5] Legislative demands included in the platform at this time called for compulsory arbitration, a graduated income tax, the prohibition of the importation of foreign labor under contract, a postal savings bank, and government purchase and operation of the telegraph, telephone, and railroad systems. Succeeding general assemblies within the next decade adopted planks favorable to the restriction of immigration, the initiative and referendum, compulsory school attendance for children up to the age of fifteen, free school textbooks, the abolition of the militia, and the secret ballot.

In 1884 the Knights began the political technique of lobbying in state capitols and in Washington, D.C., as a means of securing their legislative demands. At that time they were a growing organization of over seventy thousand members frequently engaging in strikes which, although contrary to the principles of the Order and the wishes of its general officers, were nevertheless acknowledged by Powderly as aiding the movement's growth. The votes of the legislators on measures relative to labor also began to be recorded by the Order as a basis for precisely determining those politicians who were friendly and those who were harmful to the interests of labor. The Knights also had some success in having state conventions of the political parties incorporate demands of the Knights in their platform.

Around 1885 the Knights appeared to be the most successful

labor organization ever yet developed in America. They had 100,-000 members, their strike and boycott activities were meeting with considerable success, and when the powerful Southwestern Railroad magnate, Jay Gould, capitulated to their strike demands in 1885, their membership spurted in the next year to over seven hundred thousand.

The Knights' political activities in the campaign of 1886 were also very encouraging. In New York, Henry George, the Single-Taxer candidate of the United Labor party supported for mayor by the Knights, Socialists, and local trade-unionists, officially was credited with 68,000 votes to the winning Democratic candidate's 90,000. In Chicago, Milwaukee, St. Louis, Newark, and several smaller cities, labor candidates with the backing of the local Knights' organization made creditable showings. In a few of the smaller cities labor administrations actually were elected and a number of Knights were elected to state offices and to the national Congress, as candidates of the Democratic or Republican parties. The spring municipal elections of 1877 revealed that independent labor tickets with Knights' support were continuing to show sizable strength.

By the autumn of 1887, however, it was apparent that the strength of the Knights was waning. Independent labor candidates in spite of support by the Knights met with crushing defeat in their bids for political office. The Knights' membership itself showed a decrease in 1887 of 200,000 from the previous year but, worst of all, almost all of this loss occurred in the large industrial cities. In the next three years this decline steadily continued with some 300,000 additional members departing from the Order. Very likely many of the workers who had joined in 1885 and 1886 in anticipation of such benefits as the eight-hour day quickly grew disillusioned when they found that the Order neither fulfilled this expectation nor brought them any other remarkable material improvements. Other immediate factors responsible for the decline were increased opposition from the employers and their associations who had become alarmed at the Knights' sudden growth, unsuccessful strikes, the failure of co-operative enterprises, incompetent leadership, internal dissension over policies and politics, and the departure of skilled workers from the mixed assemblies into national craft unions.

Two incidents in 1887 may have scared many workers out of the Knights. One was the indictment, trial, and execution on November 11, 1887, of several anarchists for the Chicago Haymarket bomb affair of May, 1886. If the American community's hostility to social movements that threatened property interests was so keen that a belief in anarchism could be punishable by death, the more anxiety-ridden Knight concluded that it was safest of all to belong to no organization that in any way was looked upon critically by the propertied interests.

The other incident was the Vatican excommunication of a rebellious priest, Father Edward McGlynn, in June, 1887. In December, 1886, he had been deprived by his superior of his New York ministry because of his public support of the Henry George Single Tax movement. Since Father McGlynn was also sympathetic toward the Knights, some Catholics in the Knights may have assumed that they were running a religious risk in associating with a labor organization toward which their church had some misgivings.

A more fundamental explanation for the decline of the Knights is that it advanced idealistic postulates illogical in view of the conditions created by the industrial revolution. First, it considered that no conflict existed between employers and employees and that the inequalities in the social system were mainly caused by the "money power." Second, it considered that the interests of all workers were sufficiently identical to prompt all groups of workers to act unselfishly for the common good. Third, it gave its attention to ultimate and remote reforms before it had strong roots in the environment and before it was able to demonstrate that it could regularly secure immediate material returns for its supporters.

The membership of the Knights diminished so seriously that by the end of the 1880's control of the Order rested with a coalition composed of farmers and Socialists. Both of these groups were politically minded and, as a result, in 1889 the national leaders of the Knights took the first step toward political co-operation with the Farmers' Alliance. An agreement was reached whereby both organizations would lobby jointly before Congress for legislative demands that had mutually been decided upon. The following year the general assembly finally declared the need for national independent political party action. Powderly was instructed to call a

conference for the purpose of establishing an independent party
in time for the 1892 national campaign. Thus the People's Party
made its appearance. Its candidate for President was General
James B. Weaver, the Greenback candidate of 1880 who still represented agrarian discontent with monetary, land, and transportation conditions. In the election the People's Party polled more
than a million votes, predominently from the agricultural south
and west. The year after the election, Powderly was replaced
by James R. Sovereign, a farmer-editor from the midwest. The
Knights' steadily narrowing concept of its purpose as an organization mainly preoccupied with land reform had now become almost complete except for its retention of certain assemblies dominated by Socialist Labor party adherents. The latter clung to hopes
of reviving the Knights into an organization that would once again
gain a mass following among the industrial workers and then promote the ideals of labor solidarity and class emancipation.

During the period when the Order was in its ascendency, a
small number of independent national trade-unions of skilled
workers continued to function independently. A number of these
craft union leaders decided to cope with the development of industry's national expansion by uniting with other unions in a single
national federation. National federation could also provide a more
potent means of obtaining labor legislation from Congress than
was possible through independent action by individual unions.
Accordingly, in 1881 the Federation of Organized Trades and
Labor Unions of the United States and Canada was set up. No
secret was made that it was patterned after the British Trade Union
Congress which had been organized in 1868 particularly for the
purpose of influencing Parliament in the interests of the craft
unions. A five man legislative committee, including Samuel
Gompers of the Cigarmakers' Union (who became chairman of
the committee in 1883) was established, and its objectives were
outlined in the platform adopted at the organization's first convention. The platform requested laws providing for compulsory
education, the prohibition of child labor under the age of fourteen, the legal incorporation of trade-unions, abolition of the store
order system of payment to employees, the repeal of trade-union
conspiracy laws, a protective tariff, a national bureau of labor statistics, and mechanics lien protection. The platform also asked

for the enforcement of the national eight-hour law on government work, expressed sympathy with the people of Ireland struggling against British tyranny, and recommended "all trades and labor organizations to secure proper representation in all law-making bodies by means of the ballot." [6]

The progress of the Federation of Organized Trades and Labor Unions was threatened in a number of ways. The Federation lost the affiliation of the Amalgamated Association of Iron and Steel Workers when the Federation's second convention in 1882 rejected tariff protection; it failed to interest three-fourths of the trade-unions to affiliate; and its legislative committee's lobbying efforts went unrewarded. Two things, however, had a significant influence in keeping the idea of a national federation of trade-unions alive. One was the assumption of leadership by Samuel Gompers, British born Jew, who possessed tremendous energy, opportunistic character, psychic perception of the feelings of skilled workers, oratorical powers, and organizing ability. The other factor was the intense rivalry that existed between the Federation and the Knights of Labor. The conflict between these two derived mainly from their different philosophies. The Federation advanced a concept which looked to the immediate betterment of skilled unionists' conditions under the wage system rather than to far-reaching reforms of the capitalist system as envisaged by the Knights. Unlike the Knights, the Federation recognized the employer's power over his labor supply as the citadel which must be confronted if labor was to secure for itself immediate economic improvements. In line with this thinking, the trade-unions' main energy would be directed at acquiring control over the labor supply and, by the threat of withholding the labor force from the employer, the trade-unions would compel the employers to recognize labor's importance and to yield to labor's economic demands.

The result of the differences in philosophy, objectives, and tactics of the Knights and the Federation was that the leaders of each saw the other as a threat to its own purposes, and perhaps its very existence. When the Knights made their phenomenal growth in the year following their victory over the Jay Gould railroads, and many craft unionists (including entire local craft unions) joined the Knights, the officials of the national craft unions feared that the Knights might dominate, perhaps even absorb, the skilled trade-unions, unless the latter took action to prevent this.

In the spring of 1886 five national trade-unon leaders called a trade-union conference to consider the dangers to their movements posed by the Knights. This conference proposed a treaty which demanded that the Knights revoke the charter of its trade assemblies, refrain from organizing any further trade assemblies without the consent of the nearest local and international trade-union affected, cease interfering with trade-union strikes, and discharge any organizer who was restricting the growth of trade-unions. Since the acceptance of these provisions would have relegated the Order to a nonindustrial group primarily devoted to educational and political reform work, the Knights rejected the treaty. Consequently, the trade-union treaty committee called a conference in December, 1886, at Columbus, Ohio, which resulted in the establishment of the American Federation of Labor. The Federation of Organized Trades and Labor Unions, meeting simultaneously at Columbus, immediately merged with the new organization. Samuel Gompers was elected president of the AF of L and, except for his defeat at the 1894 convention, was annually re-elected to this office until his death in December, 1924.

Thus the AF of L evolved primarily for the protection of skilled labor, for the preservation of the autonomy of national craft unions, and for obtaining immediate economic advantages for its members. From the very beginning its leaders fully preferred the development of economic power over political power, although one of the original purposes of the organization, as expressed in its constitution, was to secure legislation essential to the interests of the skilled workers. While Gompers personally represented the AF of L before Congressional hearings from 1886 onwards, he constantly stressed to the Federation that workers should rely on trade-unionism and its economic methods instead of political activity and governmental aid. A proposal at the 1890 convention to establish a permanent lobby in Washington during Congressional sessions was defeated, but it was agreed that copies of all resolutions passed at the convention should be forwarded to every Congressman. The AF of L's growing interest in such measures as the eight-hour workday, seamen's aid, an anti-injunction bill, and further immigration restriction finally led the 1895 convention to provide for the setting up of a permanent lobbying committee. To make it clear, however, that the AF of L did not intend to exalt political action, the 1895 convention declared: "Party politics, whether they be Democratic, Republican, Socialistic, Populistic, Prohibition, or any other, shall have no place in the conventions of the American Federation of Labor." [7] Since lobbying was recognized as necessary, the AF of L tried to impress Congressmen with such announcements as approved in their 1899 convention that "Candidates of any party who openly declare themselves in favor of the AF of L platform of laws shall be endorsed." [8] But the Congress paid little attention to the Federation's legislative demands because the legislators knew that in actuality the AF of L leaders were undertaking no serious action that might conceivably swing labor votes to particular Congressmen.

The Socialist trade-unionists within the AF of L constantly argued against the idea of heavily concentrating on economic activity to the detriment of political activity. Their belief was that increased political activity would lead the AF of L to accept socialism as its political creed. This intention of permeating the trade-union movement with Socialist views was not an innovation in American labor history. In the early 1850's Joseph Weydemeyer was the first of the Marxian Socialists to propagandize the workers and trade-unions with the hope of converting them to Marxism and inspiring them to form a Socialist workers' political party. The National Labor Union in the 1860's under the particular urging of affiliated German Socialists, came close to joining the International Workingmen's Association. National Labor Union leaders were also given further encouragement to subordinating trade-union activity to political activity by a number of Lassallean Socialists within the labor unions.

In 1869, the General German Workingmen's Association of America led by F. A. Sorge joined Karl Marx's International becoming Section 1 of New York. A number of other sections arose, including an English-speaking one in New York. This section was notable for the presence of the eccentric, wealthy, and radical sisters, Victoria Woodhull and Tennessee Claflin, whose free love crusade shocked not only America but most of the other sections and resulted in the expulsion of their section from the International. The first national convention of twenty-two sections, comprising a membership of about five thousand, was held in New York in 1872, and the name, the North American Federation of the International Workingmen's Association, was selected. Three-fourths of every section's members were required to be wage workers and all sections were advised to establish cordial relations with trade-unions and aid in their formation and growth. However, the dissatisfaction of certain New York Socialists (largely Lassalleans) with an organization that refused to deviate from orthodox Marxist tactics and doctrines led to the withdrawal of some New York sections and the formation in 1874 of the Social Democratic Workingmen's Party of North America. Two years later a unity conference of Socialists representing the defunct International, the Social Democratic party, the Labor party of Illinois (Lassallean), and the Socio-Political Union of Cincinnati (German) merged into the Workingmen's Party of the United States. The second convention of this new party in December 1877 adopted the name of Socialist Labor Party of North America.[9]

Unity may have been achieved in name, but in actuality factionalism was rampant in the Socialist Labor Party. The various socialist elements—Marxian, Lassallean, and Bakuninean—that had divided and destroyed the First International, repeatedly clashed again in the Socialist Labor Party. The issues of political action versus trade-union activity, and revolutionary direct action versus gradual reform aims continued to plague the Socialist movement. Since the Socialist Labor Party at first devoted itself mainly to political action, either independent or in support of the Greenback party in 1878 and 1880, an anarchist wing within the party broke away and in 1881 organized the Revolutionary Socialist party. The influence of Albert Parsons and August Spies of Chicago on this new party accounted for its support of trade-unionism and acceptance of the ballot as an educational weapon. Two years later, however, the impact of a newly arrived member, Johann Most, was responsible for the party's changing its name to that of the anarchist international, the International Working People's Association. It then became a purely anarchist body, rejecting politics and trade-unionism in place of force and revolution. Its emphasis on propaganda by deed frightened middle and upper class property conscious America to the extent that seven anarchist leaders including Parsons and Spies were sentenced to death for the murder of several policemen from a bomb thrown in Chicago's Haymarket Square, May 4, 1886, although no real proof of their actual guilt was ever uncovered. This tragic incident resulted in the complete disintegration of anarchism as a movement in America, although scattered individuals like Alexander Berkman and Emma Goldman sought to keep it alive as a revolutionary force in later years.

With the separation of the anarchists from the Socialist Labor Party, it became a pure Marxist party disseminating Marxist propaganda among the trade-unions for the establishment of a Socialist commonwealth through the rise to economic and political power of the working class. In 1890 the party was joined by an aggressive, West Indian born, Jewish intellectual, Daniel DeLeon, who in a few years became its leader—a position he retained until his death in 1914. At the time DeLeon joined the SLP, the party was following a method which had been successful in a number of city central labor bodies—namely, "boring from within." In 1890 this SLP policy received a hard blow at the hands of the AF of L. Because a section of the SLP was affiliated with the New York Central Labor Federation, the SLP expected that it would be indirectly represented at AF of L conventions through its members who would be delegates of the New York Federation. But the Gompers administration, well aware of the infiltration plans of the SLP, convinced the convention participants that they should deny a charter to the New York Federation. The refusal was justified on the grounds that charters were issued to trade-unions, not political bodies, and that the New York Federation was not a pure and simple trade-union since it was linked with a section of the Socialist Labor Party.

In spite of this rebuff, the SLP through its individual members who were also members of unions affiliated with the AF of L, still continued its efforts to "bore from within." At the AF of L conventions of the early 1890's many resolutions were passed whose origins were clearly Socialist. At the 1893 convention, for example, the Socialists, aided by a nationwide depression, successfully introduced a resolution approving the then recent moves toward independent political action taken by some of Great Britain's trade-unionists. The resolution also contained the following eleven-point political program: (*1*) compulsory education; (*2*)

direct legislation; (*3*) a legal eight-hour workday; (*4*) sanitary
inspection of workshop, mine, and home; (*5*) liability of employers for injury to health, body, or life; (*6*) the abolition of the contract system in all public works; (*7*) the abolition of the sweating
system; (*8*) the municipal ownership of streetcars, gas, and electric
plants for public distribution of light, heat, and power; (*9*) the
nationalization of telegrams, telephones, railroads, and mines;
(*10*) the collective ownership by the people of all means of production and distribution; (*11*) the principle of referendum in all
legislation. All affiliated unions were asked to declare themselves by the next convention on each of these points and on the
question of an independent labor party. In the following year "a
majority of the international unions voting on the 'program' gave
it endorsement. Yet in the convention of the Federation in 1894,
Gompers succeeded in emasculating the 'program' by eliminating
the socialist plank and the recommendations for an independent
labor party." [10]

Gompers' anti-Socialist views, his pure and simple conception
of the role of trade-unions, his advocacy of immediate material improvements, and his relentless opposition to Socialist leaders
within the AF of L aroused DeLeon to frequently denounce him
and his administrative colleagues as traitors to the working class
and "labor fakirs." But these attacks solidified rather than endangered Gompers' rule of the skilled national trade-union officers,
who were largely Irish-Catholic and whose religious orientation
placed them in opposition to socialism. In addition, DeLeon's ti-
rades against Gompers, who was emotionally sensitive to criticism
only served to increase the AF of L leader's bitterness toward Socialists and socialism.

The DeLeon Socialists also tried to strengthen their influence
within the Knights of Labor, but their efforts fared no better. At
first, the Socialist Labor Party, which was particularly strong
among the United Hebrew Trades, succeeded with the latter's help
in gaining control, in 1893, of District Assembly 49 (the New
York City Assembly of the Knights of Labor). At the 1893 general assembly of the Knights, the Socialists, holding the balance
of power between the Powderly and Sovereign forces, decided to
give their votes—and thus the election—to Powderly. But at the
next year's convention, the DeLeonites switched their votes to

Sovereign in return for his promise that the editorship of the Knights' *Journal* would go to DeLeon's associate, Lucien Sanial. When Sovereign failed to keep this bargain and also refused to seat DeLeon as a delegate to the 1895 general assembly from District Assembly 49, the SLP leader despaired of the policy of "boring from within." He saw little hope of advancing the Marxist revolutionary aims of the SLP either within the AF of L or the Knights of Labor as long as these organizations were in the hands of and controlled by anti-Marxist leaders whose continued power was assured by a personal machine they had established. It seemed to DeLeon that any Socialistic progress that might result from "boring from within" would be severely limited because of the administration's opposition. Should "boring from within" at any time assume formidable proportions, the administration would certainly see to it that the groups from which Socialist influence emanated were expelled. So, if the mass organizations could not be captured by the DeLeon Socialists, the SLP would instruct its members to depart from those unions and create new ones. From the outset, the dual unions envisaged by DeLeon would be led by Marxian Socialists and consequently would develop a class-conscious, revolutionary organization waging an economic and political struggle against capitalism to ultimately overthrow the capitalist system and establish the Socialist Commonwealth.

Within the framework of this reasoning, DeLeon, in 1895, established the Socialist Trade and Labor Alliance, which was structurally patterned after industrial unionism and ideologically geared to Marxism as interpreted by himself. At the SLP convention in 1896, DeLeon introduced a resolution endorsing the formation of the Alliance which was overwhelmingly accepted. However, the Alliance not only failed to develop as a mass organization, but the controversies that it led to further weakened the Socialist Labor Party. A considerable number of SLP members deplored dual unionism as exemplified by the Alliance. Also they resented DeLeon's domination of the SLP and the Alliance and his uncompromisingly orthodox Marxist policies.

As this opposition came to the fore, DeLeon's vituperative attacks spread to his critics within the SLP, and his sense of party discipline and purity finally brought about the expulsion of these heretics. By 1899 the internal conflict within the SLP had rent the

organization into two factions, the DeLeonites and the anti-De-
Leonites. Each faction at that time banished the other from the
party and then claimed that it alone was the bonafide trustee of the
organization. When the right to retain the organization's name was
granted by the courts to the DeLeonites, the losing faction, led by
Morris Hillquit and Max Hayes, seceded and joined forces in
1900 with the young Social Democratic party of Victor Berger
and Eugene Debs, in support of Debs as a candidate for President
of the United States. The following year, at a unity convention of
the Hillquit-Hayes and Berger-Debs groups, the present Socialist
Party of America was founded. At that convention it was also decided to include immediate demands in the party's platform, a step
directly contrary to an action taken at the 1900 SLP convention
where the party withdrew all immediate demands from its platform because it was felt that the realization of immediate demands in no way aided the destruction of capitalism. DeLeon's
dogmaticism was also responsible for a decree issued at the 1900
SLP convention that any member of the SLP who accepted office
in a pure and simple trade-union would be expelled from the SLP.

Daniel DeLeon was probably the most intellectual as well as
the most stormy figure within the American labor movement of
this period. University educated, a former practicing lawyer, and
professor of international law at Columbia University, there was
no denying his brilliance. His authoritarian personality, however,
was a serious handicap for a left wing crusader already facing
many difficulties in the American environment. Morris Hillquit,
Socialist party leader who knew DeLeon intimately from their
early relationship in the Socialist Labor Party, wrote in retrospect
of DeLeon's personality:

> He never admitted a doubt about the soundness of his inter-
> pretation of the Socialist philosophy or the infallibility of his
> methods and tactics. Those who agreed with him were good
> Socialists. All who dissented from his views were enemies of
> the movement. He never compromised or temporized outside
> or inside the Socialist movement. "He who is not with me is
> against me" was his motto and the invariable guide of all his
> political relations and practical activities.[11]

Hillquit thought that DeLeon's "peculiar traits and methods were not due entirely to his personal temperament and character" but that "in part at least they were the logical expression of his social philosophy." [12] An astute labor scholar and commentator of today, Daniel Bell, notes, "The modern psychological temper, however, would reverse the emphasis of the two statements." [13]

DeLeon's political vocabulary was sprinkled with intemperate, exaggerated, and argumentative references. In social manner he was fiercely competitive, aggressive, and dominating. He could not maintain working relationships with those who would not make themselves and their minds subservient to him. He was constantly purging the Socialist Labor Party of any of his demonstrated or imagined critics. In other organizations, such as the Industrial Workers of the World, his inability to refrain from attacking the leadership's views and policies helped prepare his own ouster. His political philosophy was based on absolutes and he turned political discussions into polemics and individual disagreements into personal feuds. He saw institutions and people in terms of black and white, not grey. Gompers, for example, was nothing but a "labor fakir" and a "labor lieutenant of the capitalist class." There was a bitter class war going on, he averred, in which "the capitalists are refined cannibals." [14] Capitalist power could only be destroyed by working class power. "The issue between the two classes," he wrote, "is one of life and death; there are no two sides to it; there is no compromise possible." [15]

In the light of present day psychoanalytic evidence such extreme views and rigid behavior of DeLeon's, as noted above, suggests that to some extent he projected and displaced into the social struggle his own repressed, aggressive impulses. The implications dynamic psychology would infer from his political opinions and behavior is that his authoritarian personality was not a derivative of his political theory but rather that his political theory was the symptomatic superstructure his personality required to satisfy his unconscious conflicts.

By the beginning of the twentieth century in America the Socialist and the union movement stood as follows: DeLeon was the leader of the sectarian Socialist Labor Party whose 1400 members represented the isolated extreme left wing of America's workers.

The bulk of the union movement consisted of a half a million skilled workers in the politically moderate American Federation of Labor, a majority of whom were of the Roman Catholic faith. A new born Socialist party of reformist tendencies and a small 10,000 membership looked with hopeful eyes to socialism's growth in American life and in the AF of L. Within the following two decades the union movement was to go through a childhood of turmoil as it struggled to gain its political character. Out of its experiences it was to develop the insights and establish the patterns that would dominate its political behavior for much of its later twentieth-century adult life.

2.

Events Arousing the American Federation
of Labor's Interest in Politics

> Hunger and only hunger changes worlds?
> The dictate of the belly
> that gnawing under the navel,
> this alone is the builder and the pathfinder
> sending man into danger and fire
> and death by struggle?
> Yes and no, no and yes.
> The strong win against the weak.
> The strong lose against the stronger.
> And across the bitter years and the howling winters
> the deathless dream will be the stronger,
> the dream of equity will win.
>
> *From* THE PEOPLE, YES *by Carl Sandburg, copyright,*
> *1936, by Harcourt, Brace and Company, Inc.*

AMERICAN labor historians offer various interpretations of the history and behavior of the American trade-union movement. On one fact, however, they are in agreement. They all agree that 1906 was the year in which the American Federation of Labor made its first major move into the sphere of political action. The type of political activity undertaken, however, was quite compatible with established AF of L political theory, and was, in fact, simply the practical application of pressure group tactics on the two major political parties.

One of the AF of L's objectives stated in its constitution was to secure legislation in the interest of the working people. From the organization's birth in 1886, Samuel Gompers sought to use his presidential power to secure such legislation from Congress.

From 1886 until 1893 he arranged with the chairmen of the House and Senate Committees on Labor for hearings on measures affecting the AF of L's economic interests. In 1895, Andrew Furuseth of the Seamen's Union and Adolph Strasser of the Cigarmaker's Union were chosen by the AF of L to serve with Gompers as the legislative representatives of the Federation and instructed to remain in Washington during sessions of Congress for this purpose.

While lobbying was considered a proper AF of L activity, public support for a political party or candidate at the beginning of the twentieth century was considered unwise by most of the Federation officers. In a letter to John Lennon, AF of L treasurer, who was interested in campaigning for William Jennings Bryan in 1900, Gompers suggested that such behavior by an AF of L officer could be legitimately resented by "earnest republicans" in unions affiliated to the AF of L. He reminded Lennon that if some leaders came out for Bryan's candidacy it would prompt some unionists to campaign for other presidential candidates whom they preferred.[1]

At the same time the AF of L, in theory, supported the principle of workers' participation in the country's political activities. A resolution passed at the AF of L convention of 1897 was typical of the organization's political behavior steadily followed from 1906. This resolution read:

> Resolved that the A.F. of L. most firmly and unequivocally favors the independent use of the ballot by the trade unionists and working men, united regardless of party, that we may elect men from our own ranks to make new laws and administer them along the lines laid down in the legislative demands of the American Federation of Labor, and at the same time secure an impartial judiciary that will not govern us by arbitrary injunctions of the courts, nor act as the pliant tool of corporate wealth. Resolved, That as our efforts are centered against all forms of industrial slavery and economic wrong, we must also direct our utmost energies to remove all forms of political servitude and party slavery, to the end that the working people may act as a unit at the polls at every election.[2]

In terms of outright electoral campaigning, however, the AF of L made no systematic effort to adhere to this resolution until

1906. During Congressional sessions prior to 1906 it confined itself to lobbying activities and did not seriously try to influence the outcome of elections. Efforts of Socialist unionists to secure passage of resolutions at the annual conventions which would amount to an AF of L endorsement of independent political action were steadily unsuccessful. Various pronouncements by AF of L convention delegates and leaders underlined the AF of L preference for economic action and, wherever possible, its wish was to avoid rigorous and direct political activity.

Two legislative proposals before Congress, in which the AF of L was particularly interested before 1906, were a bill establishing an eight-hour workday and an anti-injunction bill. Of these, by far the more important one to the AF of L was the anti-injunction bill. Without achieving the passage of the eight-hour bill, the Federation could still thrive; in fact, it might even obtain the eight-hour day through collective bargaining with the employer. But failure to gain relief from court injunctions seriously threatened the Federation's very existence.

Of all the antilabor legal weapons, none so vividly illustrated property rights and the hostility of employers and government to unionism as the labor injunction. Simply defined, the labor injunction is a judicial order commanding an individual or a union to refrain from a strike or any other activity which the court considers injurious to the property rights of the employer. Indeed, Supreme Court Justice Brandeis criticized the injunction as not usually desired "to prevent property from being injured nor to protect the owner in its use, but to endow property with active militant power which would be dominant over men." [3]

The dependence of some judges on the few precedents set by earlier labor cases served as a severe handicap to the trade-unions, inasmuch as the earlier cases originated in a period in which labor had no part in forming the laws on property. Most judges, however, found that precedents were lacking and that statutory law defining legal activity of trade-unions was nonexistent. Therefore when confronted with labor-capital conflicts, they had to decide largely for themselves the legality of trade-union activities. In such instances the judges had to enter the field of purpose, intent, and motive. To arrive at decisions, they often had to decide whether the purpose of a strike was injury to the employer's business or the attainment of certain working conditions which the employer had not been willing to grant through the process of collective bargaining. Being men of property themselves and former lawyers who often had defended corporation interests, it was undoubtedly as difficult for judges to understand the position and aspirations of labor, as it was easy for them to attribute motives and purposes and then rationalize their own standard of values. It should be remembered that once injunctions are issued, compliance with their terms usually follows. Trade-union leaders and the rank and file realize that disobedience can mean fines and prison sentences for contempt of court. In addition they recognize that the strength marshalled against them by virtue of the issuance of the injunction has become enormous. On such occasions they may face not merely the opposition of their employers, but also sanctions by the courts, federal attorneys, the Supreme Court of the United States, the governor of their state, the President of the United States, the state militia, federal troops, and an unfriendly public opinion.

From 1894 on, when the American Railway Union strike led by Eugene Debs against the Pullman Company was broken by a government injunction, the trade-unions suffered increasingly from scores of injunctions issued by both state and federal courts. Preoccupation with obtaining injunction relief from Congress became the AF of L's main political interest.

For more than a decade before 1906, the AF of L Legislative Committee patiently lobbied at each session of Congress for passage of an anti-injunction bill. The AF of L convention proceedings repeatedly refer to Gompers' reports of these vain lobbying efforts.

Apparently by 1904 the situation looked quite hopeless to the AF of L. Furthermore, the attitude of President Theodore Roosevelt on this subject was no more encouraging than that of Congress. In his message to Congress on December 5, 1905, he said, "There has been a demand for depriving courts of the power to issue injunctions in labor disputes. Such special limitation of the equity powers of our courts would be most unwise." [4] Concerned as the AF of L was about obtaining legislative relief from the injunction menace, but unable through its lobbying committee to persuade the government to grant this relief, the Federation was obliged to conclude that its existing methods were not adequate for its legislative needs. Several other factors also probably influenced the AF of L's decision in 1906 to enlarge its field of political activity.

In any attempt to uncover why a trade-union took a particular position at a particular time, the attitudes and practices of the employers in the same period are worth examination. The relationship between the employer and the union can often influence the attitude of the union towards political action. For example, if unions are able to secure from employers certain working conditions, such as higher wages or shorter hours, they do not seek such benefits for themselves from the government. Conversely, where they are unable to compel employers to satisfy certain wants they may turn to the government for help in the matter.

Around 1905 the general attitude of employers towards trade-unions had become one of increasing hostility. Professor Selig Perlman writes that the "new anti-union pattern that came to be the model for the American employer . . . was developed by the United States Steel Corporation. The board of directors of that corporation took what amounted almost to an oath to extirpate unionism." [5] The broad antiunion movement revealed itself particularly in judicial injunctions and damage suits against unions, their leaders and members, and in the open-shop campaign. Although employers claimed that the open shop's purpose was to protect the right of nonunion workers to a job, in reality, this open-shop campaign was designed to keep the union and its members from the employer's plant, so that his authority would be unchallenged. Antiunion tendencies of the employers around 1905 led them to such aggressive actions as employing spies, *agents provocateurs,* and strike breakers; and using city, state, and federal troops, privately paid deputies, local police officials, and company guards. Less aggressive methods used to maintain the open shop included the dissemination of propaganda which insisted that the union leaders were corrupt officials existing parasitically from the dues paid by duped workers, that unionization was "un-American," that unions denied the individual his sacred right to work, and that an identity of interest existed between the employer and his workers. Perhaps the most effective method used by the employers to prevent workers from joining unions was the dismissal of the more militant workers who were the leading advocates of

unionization and even, in some instances, the dismissal of many
rank-and-file workers who had joined the union.

In addition to already existing employers' organizations' growing more aggressive against labor, a number of employers' associations were created at this time primarily for combatting the
unions. The National Association of Manufacturers changed its
policy about 1902, from a group to promote trade expansion to
one openly dedicated to opposing organized labor. In Congress in
1902 it effectively lobbied against such bills as the AF of L supported anti-injunction and eight-hour day measures. The following
year "its agents tried to cut off labor's influence at the source by
defeating Congressmen and Senators favorable to labor." [6] On
August 23, 1905, the *New York Daily Tribune* reported that the
board of directors of the National Association of Manufacturers,
composed of "twenty-one well-known manufacturers from different parts of the country" incorporated their organization "for the
principal purpose" of furthering anti-union activity. Other prominent antiunion employer associations of this period were the Anti-
Boycott Association, which was established in 1902; the National
Metal Trades Association, which broke with the Machinists' Union
in 1901; the National Founders Association, which refused to deal
with the Molders' Union after 1904; the National Erectors' Association, which began at this period its warfare with the Bridge
and Structural Iron Workers' Union; the Citizens Industrial Association of America, created among business men soon after 1903;
the Stove Founders' National Defense Association, which had
periods of antiunionism; and a portion of the United Typothetae.

The creation of the Industrial Workers of the World in 1905
also spurred the AF of L to enter actively into politics. The IWW
claimed that one reason for its origin was the AF of L's failure to
protect adequately the interests of the workers. No doubt, the
AF of L planned to meet the threat imposed by this new dual movement by embarking on a program of political activity to hold the
interests of the workers and offer them a solution to some of their
outstanding grievances.

In addition to the advent of the IWW another left wing development gave the AF of L leadership cause for worry. This added
source of concern was the Socialist party, founded in 1901 largely
from among secessionist ranks of the Socialist Labor Party, and

controlled by a moderate element that advocated "boring from within" the AF of L. At the annual AF of L conventions Socialist leaders like Max Hayes, Victor Berger, Duncan McDonald, Adolph Germer, J. M. Barnes, and many others criticized the AF of L's narrow political program and weak political activities and sought to undermine the delegates' confidence in the officers responsible for these policies. This newly born Socialist party appeared to have some appeal for working people, as Eugene Debs, the party's candidate for President of the United States, increased his vote from 96,116 in 1900 to 402,321 in 1904.

Both the rise of the IWW and the growth of the Socialist party were reminders to AF of L leaders of a fast-developing leftist discontent which openly voiced its opposition to established AF of L union tactics. One way for the AF of L leadership to counter this leftist challenge to its rule was to make some concession to the demand for political action which many Socialist trade-unionists had been urging upon the AF of L for a number of years. The AF of L leadership, faced with a growing internal and external radical movement, decided to reassess and alter its political policies.

The figures on membership and financial receipts for the years immediately prior to 1906 also offered a blunt warning to the AF of L officers that the organization's policies needed investigation. Membership and finances are the two major indices of the strength of most organizations. A downward trend in one or both of these requires immediate attention. The AF of L's total receipts had started to decline in 1904, when for that year they were listed as $220,995.97, compared with $247,902.96 for the previous year. In 1905 this decline continued, with receipts reading $207,-417.62. Returns from the per capita tax in 1904 were revealed as $136,941.74, and in the succeeding year they dropped to $113,-978.32.

As noted, the decrease in AF of L membership and finances by 1905 was bound to be of serious concern to its officials. Apparently the increased opposition the Federation encountered among employers, in Congress, in the state and federal courts, and among left wing elements, was having a directly adverse effect upon AF of L membership and financial strength. A feeling was cropping up among certain segments of organized labor that the AF of L was not equal to the task of protecting its members against the organized power of modern capitalism. A union, like a government, in order to maintain the loyalty of its people, must satisfy their material and psychological needs and give them a feeling of confidence in the future. AF of L officers were practical and intuitive enough to recognize these fundamental obligations of leadership. They decided that to fulfill these obligations more than their customary emphasis on economic action was required.

The antilabor bias which the AF of L felt was characteristic of American courts also prompted the AF of L's decision to enlarge its political activities in 1906. The significant Danbury Hatters case with its dangerous implications for union security caused the AF of L to consider improving its political effectiveness for protection from the persistent onslaughts of the courts. This case was an outgrowth of the United Hatters' Union's efforts to organize itself nationally in the hat industry. One of the main weapons which the union found effective in accomplishing its purpose was the boycott. One hat company, D. E. Loewe of Danbury, Connecticut, started a law suit in August, 1903, not against the Hatters' Union but against individual members of the Hatters' Union in Danbury. This suit, initiated under the terms of the Sherman Antitrust Law, called for triple damages in the amount of $240,-000. Such legal action against individual union members posed a new threat to American unionism. Union supporters were accustomed to the appearance of labor injunctions but to learn suddenly that employers could sue individual rank-and-file union members was an unexpected blow. Successfully prosecuted suits could impoverish union members, and even if the suit were only partially successful, or ultimately unsuccessful, the unions would be involved in time-consuming and costly legal proceedings that could wreck the union treasury and cripple the union. Furthermore, during the period in which the case was pending before the courts, the union was restrained by the injunction from those activities which it had originally initiated as necessary for its membe.. welfare.

In response to the complaint against them in the Circuit Court for the District of Connecticut, the officers of the Hatters' Union contended that their boycott did not involve a violation of the Sherman Law, inasmuch as there was no interference with the physical transportation of the hats between states. The AF of L was greatly dismayed and alarmed when the Court, on December 13, 1905, declared the complaint was sufficient for the case to be tried.

Union leadership now began to fear that the final outcome of the Danbury Hatters case might be a crushing one for unions. Had not the Amalgamated Society of Railway Engineers been fined £20,000 by the British Law Lords for business losses suffered by the Taff-Vale Railway during a strike? This material blow led the British unions to found a labor party in the hope that it would secure them legislation making such court decisions impossible. The fear of the AF of L that the American courts might inflict financial punishments on unions caused the AF of L, like its British cousins, to see the need for extending its political activities also.

Another injunction blow descended on American labor in the winter of 1906 during a strike of the International Typographical Union for the eight-hour day. The periodic nemesis of trade-unions made its appearance in a judicial order issued against the Chicago Typographical Union by Judge Holdom of Chicago. In addition to prohibiting "peaceful picketing, any moral suasion whatever," it forbade any "attempt by the printers to induce non-union printers to join the union." [7]

Gompers was enraged by the injunction against the Chicago union and by the facts that two of its officers were sentenced to jail and that the union was fined $1,500 for contempt of the injunction. The AF of L leader pointed out in the *American Federationist* of March, 1906, that even such conservative newspapers as the New York *Sun* and the Chicago *Record-Herald* had paid tribute to the high regard for law and order exhibited by the strikers. He wrote that "the injunction violated every fundamental right of citizenship" and that "such 'law' no self-respecting defendant will obey for a moment. Judicial usurpation and anarchy are not 'law' and American labor is too intelligent and courageous to submit to the 'law' as laid down by bigoted or ignorant tools of plutocracy."

Gompers' vituperative language suggests how serious he viewed the injunction against the Chicago printers. The injunction disturbed him far more than previous injunctions had, as, for example, those against the American Railway Union in 1894 and the Western Federation of Miners between 1899 and 1904. These latter two unions were not affiliated with the AF of L and had radical and Socialist reputations which hardly endeared them to the AF of L officers. Injunctions against some other AF of L unions may have been justified because of the violence and lawlessness involved in the laborer-employer conflict. Yet none of these explanations could be offered as the reason for an injunction against the International Typographical Union. The printers were not only an AF of L union, a mainstay of the Federation, a model of conservative unionism supposedly immune from insecurity because of their economic strength, but, in addition, they had gone on strike for a reasonable objective and conducted themselves soberly during the strike.

For many years Gompers had justified his opposition to the AF of L Socialists' agitation for an independent political party by maintaining that the Socialists were incorrect in their criticism of society—a criticism especially based on class consciousness and the class struggle. In 1903 he sharply reproved the Socialists at the AF of L convention who had submitted ten different resolutions urging further political activity by the AF of L:

> I want to tell you, Socialists, that I have studied your philosophy; read your works upon economics, and not the meanest of them; studied your standard works, both in English and German—have not only read, but studied them. I have heard your orators and watched the work of your movement the world over. I have kept close watch upon your doctrines for thirty years; have been closely associated with many of you and know how you think and what you propose. I know, too, what you have up your sleeve. And I want to say that I am entirely at variance with your philosophy. I declare it to you, I am not only at variance with your doctrines, but with your philosophy. Economically, you are unsound; socially you are wrong; industrially you are an impossibility.[8]

Gompers had confidence in his own non-Marxist evaluation of capitalism and American institutions. As AF of L president, his moderate economic policies and his rejection of independent political party action stemmed, in part, from the belief that not only were American capitalism and its property relations immutable fixtures, but that class consciousness was a Socialist myth that would never become a reality in the minds of the mass of American workers. At one time he wrote that he had come "to the conclusion many years ago that it is our duty to live our lives as workers in the society in which we live, and not to work for the downfall or the destruction or the overthrow of that society, but for its fuller development and evolution." [9] Labor's only practical recourse, therefore, was to maintain and increase the trade-union's economic strength so that the union could secure what the capitalist employer was able to give and what the workers wanted— namely more and more material benefits. Collective bargaining, accompanied by the closed shop, and, if necessary, the strike, was the method by which labor would gain more and more. As labor improved its material welfare, the Socialist crusader would discover that his appeals were even more meaningless to the worker. A wage earner who had a property stake in capitalist society would not take to revolutionary ideas which carried a threat to property rights, Gompers reasoned. Orderly and overt economic bargaining methods and the avoidance of radical doctrines would give the workers respectability in the community's eyes, and even the employers would become more conciliatory to labor as they recognized that their rights of ownership were not being threatened.

Gompers' anger about the injunction against the Chicago Typographical Union certainly did not make a Socialist of him or essentially change his economic philosophy. However, it did remind him to not minimize the number of employers who still would fiercely resist unionism whenever unions made demands which, if satisfied, would sizably decrease employers' profits. The lesson learned from this Chicago injunction probably dispelled much of the complacence the AF of L leaders had felt about the security of the *conservative* core of the Federation. Plainly, conservative unions, as well as the radical ones, were still open to attacks by employers and the courts.

Around the time of the injunction against the ITU Gompers began to make public intimations of a needed change in the AF of L's policy. In March, 1906, he wrote for the April issue of the Federation journal:

> Whatever one may think of the general question of 'labor in politics' is there any reason why workmen should give their

votes to 'injunction judges', to men who glory in such arbitrary and unconstitutional orders as Holdom and capitalistic tools like him are issuing?

.   .   .   .

We hope and expect that Holdom will be taken care of by the organized workmen of Chicago when he again presents himself at an election as a candidate for the bench.

.   .   .   .

Yes, legislation checking judicial usurpation, and safe-guarding the rights of citizenship, the rights of labor, will, and must be obtained. The way to secure such legislation is to or-ganize against the injunction outrage, to defeat every bigoted, ignorant or class-serving judge, and every legislator who is not willing to pledge himself to oppose the destruction of lib-erty and the acquiescence of legislatures, national and state in judicial tyranny and judicial insolence.[10]

This editorial suggests that the Holdom injunction was the final factor surrounding the AF of L's decision in 1906 to revise its political practice and begin to participate in political elections. The "reward your friends, punish your enemies" political slogan, which was later formally adopted as the cornerstone of the AF of L's political practice, was apparently well formulated in Gompers' mind early in March, 1906, as he pondered the serious implications of the Chicago injunction.

Once again history revealed that man is most often driven to action not by the dreams he has but by the blows he receives. The AF of L went into political action in 1906 for the reasons previ-ously discussed: (1) The court's issuance of injunctions and its curtailing of strikes, picketing, and the boycott, (2) the imprison-ment of union officials, and levying of fines against unions for contempt of injunctions, (3) the increased hostility of employers' organization, (4) the challenge posed by the appearance of the IWW and a growing Socialist party, and (5) the decline in AF of L membership and finances.

Although for many years Gompers had warned the Socialists in the AF of L that the trade-unions would be ruined if they entered politics, by March, 1906, it became clear to him that labor must enter politics or be ruined by the ruthless manner in which the employers were utilizing the state against trade-unionism. Political action was no longer an issue to be fought over between the Socialist trade-unionists and the "pure and simplers," but it was a vital, practical requisite necessitated by the elementary principles of self-defense and self-preservation. What was left to the AF of L to determine, however, was the precise type of political action that it would employ. To adopt independent political action would be admitting that the Socialists were correct in their diagnosis of labor's political needs. The establishment of such a political course might also mean that eventually Socialist leaders would be likely candidates for the new party. Therefore, in consonance with its philosophy which accepted the postulates of a capitalist society and which preferred immediate results to ultimate ends, the AF of L leadership agreed on a political method which it hoped would obtain the union security sought without, at the same time fulfilling the Socialist desire for an independent labor party.

3.

The American Federation of Labor's Political Activity under Republican Administrations, 1906–1912

> The weakness in the approach of American labour to politics is the vital one that it has taken its theory of the State from the employers and asked only for concessions and adjustments on the ground that the American government, as the agent of the State power, is a neutral and mediating force among the different elements in society. And implied in this outlook is the doctrine that the property relations of the United States are eternal and that all labour can do is to persuade the State power to act rationally and objectively. There is not an atom of serious evidence to justify this position. The business of the American government in a capitalist democracy, especially a capitalist democracy moving ever more swiftly to the stage of organized monopoly, is essentially to see that those who own the monopolies are assured of that law and order which maintains the continuity of access to profit.
>
> *Harold J. Laski,* THE AMERICAN DEMOCRACY

ON MARCH 21, 1906, the presidents of all AF of L-affiliated unions met with the Executive Council at the AF of L headquarters in Washington, D.C., for the purpose of reformulating the Federation's political program. A document drafted by Andrew Furuseth and Samuel Gompers, "Labor's Bill of Grievances," was submitted and approved by the 117 union representatives. The group on the same day submitted this document through separate audiences to President Theodore Roosevelt, President of the Senate William Frye, and Speaker of the House Joseph Cannon.

The "Bill of Grievances" complained in general about the government's failure to pass outstanding labor legislation which the AF of L had requested for many years. The particular legislative items now requested of the government were an anti-injunction bill, an effective eight-hour bill, a bill to safeguard the AF of L from the competition of convict labor, a bill to prevent the violation of the Chinese Exclusion Act, a bill restricting immigration, a bill to free seamen from involuntary servitude, a bill to provide additional ship safety for seamen, and a bill making the antitrust law more stringent. Two nonlegislative items requested recession of the Presidential order prohibiting the right of petition to government employees, and the reorganization of the membership of the House Committee on Labor so the Committee would be more sympathetic toward labor. The "Bill of Grievances" concluded by declaring that the AF of L had adopted this method of petition since the unionists, as citizens, had the right to expect their political representatives to grant them legislation necessary for their welfare. Congress was warned that if it gave no attention to labor's plea, the AF of L would "appeal to the conscience and the support of our fellow citizens." [1]

The "Bill of Grievances" did not elicit a favorable response from administration leaders. President Roosevelt agreed in general with the items on immigration, Chinese exclusion, and the eight-hour workday, but he differed radically on some other points. Speaker Cannon would not accept the AF of L contention that the House Committee on Labor was antagonistic toward labor. *The Nation,* March 29, 1906, quoted him as bluntly telling the AF of L delegation that "Union labor is not the whole shooting match. There are the workmen to be considered who refuse to wear the shackles of unionism." [2]

The following day the AF of L Executive Council met to discuss the cool reception "Labor's Bill of Grievances" had obtained from the Republican leaders. The group decided that their next step would be "to take an active part in the impending Congressional election and to defeat or elect candidates for Congress that the Federation cannot or can pledge in advance to its bidding." [3] Having received no satisfaction from the presentation of "Labor's Bill of Grievances" to the officials of the Republican administration, the AF of L now intended to carry out the threat in the close of that document—"to appeal to the conscience and support of our fellow citizens." [4] The *New York Daily Tribune* of March 25, 1906, reported in a page one column one story that the AF of L was throwing "a gag of defiance to Congress."

On April 7, 1906, the AF of L leadership bought the entire matter to the attention of its membership by distributing a leaflet containing "Labor's Bill of Grievances" and the unfriendly attitude the Bill had provoked from the three Republican party figures. The leaflet concluded with the political method which the AF of L would now bring into practice.

> Let the inspiring watchword go forth that—
> We will stand by our friends and administer a stinging rebuke to men or parties who are either indifferent, negligent or hostile, and, wherever opportunity affords, to secure the election of intelligent, honest, earnest trade unionists, with clear, unblemished, paid-up union cards in their possession.[5]

There was nothing new or startling in this political announcement. Its basic theory of "reward your friends and punish your enemies" was traditional AF of L political thought that had been uttered many times before 1906. In practice, however, little had ever been done to translate these words into reality. Would the AF of L this time use means to implement its threat?

On April 26, 1906, the Federation made another gesture suggesting aroused political interest when it sent each Congressman a copy of "Labor's Bill of Grievances" together with a letter requesting that Gompers be supplied with a statement of the Congressman's views upon the items contained in that document. In June, Gompers wrote in the *American Federationist* that if any person authorized by his organization to request information about the labor attitude of a Congressman would write to the AF of L an answer would be given. He also stated that the replies which the Congressmen made to the letter of April 26 would be published in the AF of L journal.

On July 22, 1906, the Executive Council of the AF of L issued a leaflet which explained the political philosophy, the need for political participation, and the Congressional campaign plans of the Federation. This leaflet, entitled *A. F. of L. Campaign Programme,* was addressed "To all Organized Labor and Friends in the United States" and was mailed to all local AF of L unions with instructions that it be read at the next local meeting. This leaflet announced the creation of a "Labor Representation Committee" composed of Samuel Gompers, James O'Connell the AF of L vice-president, and Frank Morrison the AF of L secretary, to provide the leadership for the ensuing campaign. The legislative branches of the government were attacked because "in their frenzied rush after the almighty dollar" they had been "indifferent or hostile to the rights of man." Consequently, the time had "arrived for labor and its friends to raise their voices in condemnation of such de-generacy, and to invite all reform forces to join with it in relegating indifference to the peoples' interests, corruption and graft, to po-litical oblivion; to raise the standard of legislation by the election of sincere, progressive and honest men, who, while worshipping money less, will honor conscience, justice, and humanity more." [6]

The *A. F. of L. Campaign Programme* made no mention what-soever of support for the Socialist party or of the possibility of establishing a labor party. The leaflet simply repeated the "reward your friends, punish your enemies" policy with the proviso that, in a district where the AF of L had no friend in either the Demo-cratic or Republican candidates, "a straight labor candidate should be nominated." [7] Affiliated local unions and central bodies were asked to promptly elect delegates who would prepare the political strategy for labor's success in the November national election.

Accompanying the *A. F. of L. Campaign Programme* to the local union was another leaflet entitled, *Appeal for Labor's Cam-paign Fund.* This leaflet appealed for funds to carry on the cam-paign since AF of L financial receipts obtained from the per capita membership tax could not be used for political purposes. Con-tributions would be accepted from the local unions or from the members as individuals, and contributions however small were welcomed. Because the response to this appeal was insufficient, another leaflet of a similar nature was issued on September 4, 1906, requesting every trade-union member to contribute $1 to the campaign fund. This plea also was largely unheeded, for the Fed-eration later listed the total funds received from its two appeals as $8,225.94 of which $8,147.19 was spent during the course of the 1906 campaign.

In addition to "Labor's Bill of Grievances" and the *A. F. of L.*

Campaign Programme, the Federation published its political views and position in another leaflet called *Textbook of Labor's Political Demands.* About two thirds of this thirty-eight page pamphlet discussed the history of labor injunction cases while the remainder was a résumé of the organization's political philosophy and practice. Each issue of the *American Federationist* from May, 1906, moreover, gave attention to politics on a scale unprecedented for the AF of L journal. Gompers' editorials in the *American Federationist* were focused regularly on politics, and other AF of L leaders contributed articles to arouse the interest of the workers in the forthcoming Congressional elections. The September issue of the Federation journal was the largest issue ever published, with almost fifty pages alone devoted to the answers received from Congressmen on "Labor's Bill of Grievances." To many of these replies the journal's editor, Samuel Gompers, added his comments. Of 50 Democratic Congressmen's letters received, Gompers judged 47 as satisfactory answers to "Labor's Bill of Grievances," but of the 73 Republican replies he considered only 23 as acceptable.

In the actual conduct of its 1906 political campaign the AF of L strove more for the defeat of Republican Congressman Charles E. Littlefield of the Second District of Maine than for any other member of Congress. The first meeting of the AF of L's campaign to defeat Mr. Littlefield was held in Lewiston, Maine, August 18, 1906. Gompers was the chief labor speaker, and for two and a half hours he presented labor's case for Mr. Littlefield's defeat.

From the time of his August 18 speech until the balloting one month later, Gompers delivered about nine other addresses against Congressman Littlefield in the latter's district. Apart from Gompers' efforts, public addresses were also made by more than a dozen well-known labor leaders in this area, and other addresses were also delivered in union meetings and at social gatherings.

Several reasons explained the preoccupation of the AF of L in Congressman Littlefield's campaign. First, Littlefield's hostility to AF of L legislation was well known. His position in the important House Judiciary Committee enabled him to balk injunction relief bills desired by the Federation and to propose bills providing for even stricter application of the Sherman Law to trade-unions. Secondly, since the election in Maine took place on September 10

—almost two months before the nation's general election—the AF of L had the opportunity to utilize its strength and concentrate its campaign efforts on a limited area. Furthermore, an AF of L triumph in Maine would mark an auspicious beginning for its revised political program and would not only vindicate the leadership who had initiated the program but would also increase labor's prestige among the existing political parties. Finally, the AF of L leaders were encouraged to test their political strength against Congressman Littlefield because they had 3,000 union men in his district. This number might conceivably account for his defeat, since he had won his previous election by only 5,419 votes.

When the ballots were tabulated it was found that Mr. Littlefield had been re-elected, although his 1904 plurality had been reduced to 1,362 votes. Gompers asserted that labor's efforts had gained a moral victory, but he failed to mention that the issue of prohibition had hurt all of the Republican candidates in Maine. In three other Congressional districts where the pluralities of the Republican candidates suffered reductions similar to the one incurred by Littlefield, the AF of L had made no direct campaign.

The political method and technique that the Federation henceforth practiced duplicated its Littlefield campaign activities. The AF of L would enter into political contests where it desired to unseat labor's outstanding enemies. To achieve this objective, it would compile the antilabor political records of Congressmen and would disseminate this information through addresses and printed material to affiliated workers in the voting areas of these legislators. In essence, the Federation would conduct a form of educational campaign for labor's political advantage by acquainting the public and its membership with the functioning of the American political process, the power residing in the people's use of the ballot, the laws passed by Congress, the bills desired by labor and labor's broad aspirations, the attitudes and decisions of the courts, the influence of business interests on the three branches of government, and the hostility of business toward the purposes of unionism. Working people once presented with this knowledge, would, it was hoped, be likely to use their ballot to support labor's political friends and to defeat labor's political enemies.

The AF of L president noted in the *American Federationist* of May, 1908, that "in innumerable instances a large number of our citizens for years have gone on blindly voting for either one of the two great parties, and could give no other reason for doing so except that their father or grandfather had voted that way and they continued in their practice." This custom had two serious shortcomings. First, the workers' voting behavior was not based on an objective appraisal of candidates' and parties' attitudes and actions toward labor. Second, the labor vote was split between the two parties, and thus rendered ineffective as a political bargaining weapon. By publicizing labor's legislative aims and by informing the working people of the opinions and deeds of Democratic and Republican candidates and their respective parties toward these aims, Gompers hoped to weaken the workers' inherited allegiance to political parties. Since both parties contained legislators who did not always follow the position of their party, Gompers stressed that the phrase "reward your friends and punish your enemies" was not limited to parties, but could be applied to individual politicians within a party. For example, if the Democratic platform was more favorable to organized labor than the Republican one, this did not mean that AF of L trade-unionists were to be unswervingly partisan and support all Democratic candidates. In an instance where the labor legislative records or public utterances of two opposing candidates revealed that the Republican candidate was friendlier to the AF of L, he would receive the Federation's official endorsement.

Since Federation leaders recognized that American political parties were less based on ideologies than on opportunism and willingly bargained for votes to win office, they proposed to attempt to keep labor's vote "independent" and thus induce the two parties and their candidates to vie with each other for "labor's vote." Naturally, the party or candidate which promised to satisfy the largest number of labor's legislative demands would be the one that the AF of L would recommend to its membership.

The probable effectiveness of the Federation's political practice evolved in 1906 was a moot question. Since the AF of L limited its legislative demands to the grievances of organized labor and did not include the grievances of those outside the fold of unionism, the latter had little reason to vote for the AF of L's suggested candidates. Yet the trade-union vote by itself was not large enough in 1906 to insure the election of any candidate endorsed by the AF of L. Actually, the AF of L faced the formidable task of getting its own membership to follow its recommendations and vote for those candidates, irrespective of party, who appeared to be labor's friends. The slogan "reward your friends and punish your enemies" was mere verbiage unless the trade-unionist strictly would follow this dictum. In view of workers' inherited attachment to party and the fact that many local unions were frequently involved with the dominant political machine in their locality it was doubtful whether the AF of L could swing the labor vote in its first attempts.[8] It was also questionable whether both parties would bargain for the labor vote, as Gompers hoped, or if doubting the AF of L's ability to deliver the labor vote they saw no value in pledging themselves to labor's legislative demands. Furthermore, how would the AF of L face the dilemma of maintaining a "reward your friends and punish your enemies" philosophy in the light of situations where it could not be distinguished if either candidate were a friend of labor?

As far as the national results of the 1906 Congressional elections were concerned, the Republican majority in the House of Representatives was decreased from 112 members to 56 and many of the Republican incumbents were returned with a smaller plurality than in 1904. Although the AF of L's campaign throughout the nation could not be compared to the vigor it had exhibited in Congressman Littlefield's district, nevertheless Gompers asserted that the AF of L could take credit for the majority party's losses and could be confident of the practicability of its new political activity.[9] Some satisfaction was felt also because six Congressmen elected held trade-union cards. Apparently, however, the Federation's political debut was not of such magnitude as to sufficiently alarm its enemies or impress its friends, for the Republicans, in the main, continued to show hostility and indifference while many of those legislators who had pledged themselves to labor's cause forgot their pledges once in office. The House of Representatives from 1906 to 1908 was even less sympathetic to trade-unions than hitherto.

Throughout 1907 there was almost complete silence by the AF of L on the subject of political action. The Federation journal, in contrast to the attention displayed in 1906, made little reference to the continued need for political activity and Gompers, in his presidential report to the 1907 convention was silent on this issue.

Certain court decisions however, compelled the revival of the AF of L's interest in politics. These were the Buck's Stove and Range, Danbury Hatters', and Adair decisions. Factors of somewhat lesser influence that also contributed to awakening the Federation to political action in 1908 were the continued indifference of Congress toward "Labor's Bill of Grievances," the appeal of the National Association of Manufacturers for a fund of $1,500,-000 to be distributed over three years "to fight industrial oppression," and the preparations of the Republican party to nominate William Howard Taft, regarded by the AF of L as "The Injunction Standard Bearer," for President of the United States.[10]

The incident which precipitated the conflict between the Buck's Stove and Range Company and the International Molders' Union began when the foundry employees and metal polishers of the company would not accept an increase in the hours of their labor. The company responded by dismissing the recalcitrant men. When negotiations between the union and the company failed to adjust the matter, the Molders' Union got the AF of L to include the Buck's Stove and Range Company on their "We Don't Patronize" list in the *American Federationist* beginning with the May, 1907, issue. This, in turn, stirred James W. Van Cleave, the president of the company and president of the National Association of Manufacturers, to serve notice upon the AF of L, August 19, 1907, that the business of his company had been seriously lessened and was threatened with ruin because of the *American Federationist's* boycott against his goods. Van Cleave's legal action, far from causing a cessation of the boycott, produced instead an AF of L circular to all affiliated unions asking them to intensify their boycott activities.

Van Cleave's next move was to request an injunction from Justice Gould of the Supreme Court of the District of Columbia against the AF of L, its officers, and the Electrotype Molders' and the Finishers' Union No. 17. On December 18, 1907, Justice Gould issued a temporary injunction prohibiting labor from referring to its dispute with the Buck's Stove and Range Company and from interfering with Van Cleave's factory or business. On March 26, 1908, the injunction was made permanent.

President Gompers at once labeled this injunction as "the most sweeping ever issued," because *"It is an invasion of the liberty of the press and the right of free speech."* [11] The Federation decided to make a test case of this injunction in the hope that a victory would restrict the issuance of further injunctions against trade-unions. To implement this intention, the Executive Council retained the services of several lawyers, including Alton B. Parker (former Chief Justice of the New York State Court of Appeals and Democratic candidate for President in 1904), and appealed the permanent injunction to the District of Columbia's Court of Appeals. Although Gompers gave orders to discontinue the publication of the "We Don't Patronize" list, he continued to discuss the principles involved in the controversy between labor and the Buck's Stove and Range Company. To secure funds for the legal battles that lay ahead, a circular was distributed on January 25, 1908, appealing "to all unions and union members, and the friends of justice to contribute as generously as they can." [12]

In July, 1908, a petition was presented by the Buck's Stove and Range Company and the Supreme Court of the District of Columbia that ordered AF of L officials Samuel Gompers, John Mitchell, and Frank Morrison to show why they should not be held in contempt of the court's injunction decree. Gompers did not deny that AF of L officers had editorially discussed both the suit which the St. Louis company had brought against them and had also discussed the principles involved in the injunction issued by Justice Gould; but he did not consider such action indicated contempt of the court order. Perhaps Gompers was inclined to optimism because the AF of L appeal against the injunction itself was before an appellate court, and therefore he imagined that the contempt decision would be deferred until the higher court had rendered its decision. This assumption proved unfounded, however, as on December 23, 1908, the three AF of L officers were declared guilty of contempt by Justice Wright of the Supreme Court of the District of Columbia and sentenced to jail. [13]

The Buck's Stove injunction and contempt decision were not the only blows that trade-unionism received in 1908. On February 3, 1908, the Supreme Court issued what Gompers labeled as "the most dramatic and far-reaching decision which had ever been handed down" affecting organized labor. [14] The highest court of the United States considered that interference with the physical transportation of an article was not necessary to cause a violation of the Sherman Law. The Hatters' Union of Danbury, Connecticut, was liable for damages, according to the complaint of the Loewe Company, because the Hatters' Union boycott showed an unlawful conspiracy in restraint of trade. The court declared that the "defendants were members of a vast combination . . . 'engaged in a combined scheme and effort to force . . . the plaintiffs, against their will . . . to unionize their shops, with the intent thereby to control the employment of labor and the operation of said factories . . . and to carry out such scheme, effort and purpose, by restraining and destroying the interstate trade and commerce of such manufacturers, by means of . . . boycotting them . . . until such time as, from the damage and loss of business resulting therefrom, the said manufacturers should yield to the said demand to unionize their factories.' " [15]

The fears created in the trade-union world by the reasoning of the Supreme Court were enormous. Although the decision applied to the Hatters' Union, now that the legal precedent was established that the intent of certain economic activities of unions was to impair the employer's business, all unions were endangered. They might find that their striking, picketing, and boycotting measures classified them as conspiracies and made them liable to dissolution because of the damage suits brought against them by employers eager to see their organizations wrecked. The Buck's Stove and Range Company injunction and the Danbury Hatters' damage suit were milestones in the history of the political life of American trade-unionism, for they dramatically registered the simple point that organized labor must obtain legislative relief from the Sherman Act and injunctions.

Another severe court decision against trade-unionism had been given in the Adair case on January 27, 1908. The U.S. Supreme Court declared unconstitutional section 10 of the Erdman Act of 1898. This section had made it unlawful for an employer to discriminate against, or discharge any employee because of the latter's membership in a union or to require any person to enter into an agreement not to join a union. In the case before the court a worker had been discharged because he would not give up his union membership. Justice Harlan's majority opinion said, "The right of a person to sell his labor upon such terms as he deems proper, is in its essence, the same as the right of the purchaser of labor to prescribe the conditions upon which he will accept such labor from the person offering to sell it. So the right of the employé to quit the service of the employer, for whatever reason, is the same as the right of the employer, for whatever reason, to dispense with the services of such employé. . . . In all such particulars the employer and the employé have equality of right, and any legislation that disturbs that equality is an arbitrary interference with the liberty of contract which no government can legally justify in a free land." [16] This decision, in effect, gave constitutional sanction to yellowdog contracts and the blacklist.

These several severe setbacks from the courts did not budge the Federation from its established political policy of seeking legislative relief within the framework of the two-party system. These reversals, however, did have the effect of forcing the AF of L to pursue its political pressure methods with more effectiveness. If the state power left the AF of L alone, the organization was content to pay little attention to politics and to rely instead on the potentialities of economic power. When governmental behavior was such, however, as to seriously threaten trade-union security, the Federation resorted to pressure politics on the two major parties. Thus, a short time after the Buck's Stove and Range Company's temporary injunction and the Supreme Court decision in the Hatters' case, Gompers suggested that the AF of L would be renewing its political activity in the forthcoming presidential campaign along the methods followed in 1906. Gompers said that Congress would have the opportunity to act upon certain bills before it which would amend the Sherman Law and exempt labor from further court decisions like that in the Hatters' case. If Congress would not meet this request, he threatened that the AF of L would renew its political activity by taking the matter to the people in the national presidential campaign of 1908, as it had in 1906.

On March 3, 1908, Gompers took the first step in preparation for the AF of L's 1908 political activities. He wrote the AF of L Executive Council that many affiliated bodies had informed him that they wished the AF of L to adopt a political course for protection against court reverses recently suffered. He disclosed that already "a number of central bodies have under consideration resolutions declaratory in some form or another of a movement wholly independent and divergent, while others have taken actions declaring that the Executive Council shall call a mass convention to take action for the creation of an independent political party, and in the event that this is not done by a specified time, that they themselves will inaugurate such a movement." Of course, he was opposed to any independent party movement and was pleased that "others have shown their intelligence and devotion to the cause of labor by expressing themselves as willing to fall in line with the course laid down by the Executive Council." [17] In view of this situation, Gompers' letter asked the Executive Council to a meeting on March 16, 1908, in Washington, D.C. A few days later the AF of L leader addressed a similar letter to the presidents of each national and international union affiliated to the Federation inviting them to meet with the Executive Council on March 18 to formulate labor's political program. Gompers knew it would be wise for the AF of L to extend its political efforts not only because of recent court decisions but because unrest among the workers intensified by a business depression might crystallize into support for an independent labor party or the Socialist party.

This meeting, known as Labor's Conference of Protest, approved two political documents entitled *Protest to Congress* and *Address to the Workers*. A labor committee led by Gompers presented the *Protest to Congress* to the president of the Senate, Charles W. Fairbanks, and to the Speaker of the House, Joseph Cannon. As its title suggests, this document was a protest but unlike the 1906 "Bill of Grievances," it mainly expounded on a single item—the application by the courts of the Sherman Law against trade-unions. The *Protest to Congress* registered labor's indignation over the treatment it was receiving from the courts. In consequence of what labor had already suffered and might continue to suffer, this document asked Congress to amend the Sherman Law so as to exclude trade-unions explicitly from its provisions. Congress was warned that labor would hold the party in power responsible if legislative aid to labor was not forthcoming.

Gompers probably did not expect the Republican party to heed labor's most recent appeal and pass the amendment to the Sherman Law. Since the Republican administration had consistently been oblivious of the AF of L's legislative requests, and since it had failed to act upon "Labor's Bill of Grievances," which was of a similar spirit to the *Protest to Congress,* there was little reason to suppose that the administration's attitude of indifference toward the AF of L had changed. Speaker Cannon, a constant foe of legislation sought by labor, was still the majority party leader in the House. And no overtures had been made by the Republican party after the AF of L participation in the 1906 election campaign to suggest that the party leaders were impressed with the display of labor's political power.

In view, then, of the small likelihood of the Republican Congress assenting to the request contained in *Protest to Congress,* why was the document prepared and presented to the Republican leaders in Congress? The answer may be that it was neither actually intended for the Republican party, nor was it expected that its request would be granted by Congress. It probably was a tactical stroke planned by Gompers in the hope that it would later enable him to justify to the AF of L membership an endorsement of the Democratic presidential candidate in the 1908 election. The expected Republican Congress' indifference to the document would bolster his case when he asked the AF of L rank and file to vote for most of the Democratic candidates rather than the Republican ones. It was necessary for this appeal to be well made if it was to be successful, for many workers were known to be regular Republican party voters.

Never before in the history of the AF of L had a major attempt been made to swing the vote of its rank and file to a political candidate for President of the United States. As this would be the first effort at so big a task, its significance was certainly appreciated. If it were reasonably successful, labor's political bargaining power would be enormously increased. But if little success were obtained in influencing the membership's vote, any future political threats by the Federation leadership might be regarded with equanimity by the major political parties. The importance, therefore, of the new AF of L political move made it imperative for the AF of L leaders to devise methods which would strengthen their position when they faced the task of persuading many habitual Republican voters within the Federation to end their allegiance to that party. The *Protest to Congress* was designed to meet the difficulties inherent in this problem. Once the Republican Congress rejected this document, as was certainly foreseen, the AF of L leadership could, in effect, say to the rank and file that it was utterly impossible for the labor movement to gain from the Republican party the legislative relief needed. For many years that party had been in control of the executive and legislative branches of the government and throughout these years they had neglected repeated requests for help. The AF of L leaders could plead that no other alternative remained open under the democratic process but to attempt to turn the Republicans out of power and replace them with the other major party, in order that the latter might be given the opportunity to show if they would fulfill the AF of L's legislative requests.

It may seem that the AF of L had sufficient reason to ask its membership to vote against the Republican party presidential candidate and legislative candidates in 1908 without having to use the Republican rejection of the *Protest to Congress* as an argument. But Gompers was not one to underestimate the difficulties of changing the loyalty of people to a tradition—in this case, the loyalty of many Federation members to the Republican party. Furthermore, one of Gompers' passions was to maintain himself as the president of the Federation. To achieve this ambition it was necessary for him to be extremely careful not to do anything which would cause the powerful leaders of affiliated unions to grow angry and withdraw their support of his annual candidacy.

The *Address to Workers,* written at the same conference which produced *Protest to Congress,* was a leaflet explaining to the workers why the Conference was called, the meaning of the *Protest to Congress,* and the lobbying that could be done to gain the passage of an amendment to the Sherman Law. All local unions, city, central, and state federations, were instructed to hold mass meetings throughout the country on April 19 and 20 to protest against the recent Supreme Court decision in the Danbury Hatters' case and to pass resolutions warning Congress that labor was holding it responsible for not passing an amendment to the Sherman Law. The individual worker was also told to write a personal letter to his political representatives asking that they cast their votes for labor-desired legislation or risk the consequence of losing labor's vote.

Several million copies of labor's *Protest to Congress* and *Ad-*

dress to Workers were printed and distributed by the AF of L and a discussion about the Hatters' case decision accounted for thousands of extra copies and a special edition of the *American Federationist*. Besides additional printed circulars, mass meetings were held throughout the country, as designated by Labor's Conference of Protest. In spite of this labor agitation for legislative aid, Congress adjourned in May, 1908, without passing any of the legislation desired by labor. Apparently, the Republican party was not worried about the threat made by the AF of L in the *Protest to Congress* that labor would hold the party in power responsible for the failure to grant legislative relief. The *American Federationist* of July, 1908, quoted the majority leader on the floor of the House, Mr. Payne of New York, as having openly declared on May 9, 1908, "We are doing this business; we are legislating; we are responsible for what we do, and we are responsible for what we do not do, and we propose to assume the responsibility for it from beginning to end." [18]

The AF of L took one further step in solidifying its case preparatory to urging its membership to vote against the Republican party. The Executive Council decided to appear before the platform committees of the two national political conventions to lobby for the labor planks it wished inserted in the party platforms.

A few days before the Republican convention in Chicago, Gompers and AF of L secretary Morrison talked with the expected Republican candidate for President, Secretary of War William Howard Taft, about labor's grievances, but the AF of L leader was not at all satisfied that anything had been achieved by this meeting. Then the two AF of L leaders joined the AF of L Executive Council in Chicago to hear their recently enlarged Legislative Committee report on the current action of Congress on all subjects concerning labor. Following this briefing, Gompers and two of the AF of L vice-presidents, James Duncan and Daniel J. Keefe, were chosen to present to the Republican Committee on Platform the labor planks drawn up by the AF of L Executive Council. Duncan and Keefe were selected because they were commonly known to be followers of the Republican party. The planks which the AF of L proposed for insertion were eight in number. They asked the Republican convention to pledge that it would seek the passage of the following measures: *(1)* a bill guaranteeing that trade-unions would not be regarded as combinations in restraint of trade; (2) a bill limiting the use of the injunction in labor disputes and providing for trial by jury when contempt punishment was being considered; (3) an amendment extending the existing eight-hour law to all persons employed on government work irrespective of whether they were employed by contractors or sub-contractors; (4) a bill, as far as federal jurisdiction extended, providing for general employers' liability coverage; (5) a bill creating a Department of Labor with a Secretary at its head having a seat in the President's cabinet; (6) a bill establishing a federal bureau of mines and mining; (7) a bill establishing United States government postal savings banks; (8) a bill submitting a constitutional amendment to the states which would seek the ratification of suffrage for women.

The Republican Committee on Platform refused to grant the AF of L leaders a hearing before its entire committee and instead arranged for a hearing with a subcommittee. In the room with the subcommittee Gompers noticed the presence of the political agents for the National Association of Manufacturers, James Emory and Martin Mulhall, and the NAM president himself, James Van Cleave. Businessmen were to contribute over two million dollars to the Republican party's 1908 campaign.

Ignominious failure was the only result of the AF of L's efforts to have the Republican party insert labor's legislative requests in the party's platform. The Republican convention completely omitted planks on seven of the eight items which the AF of L had recommended. The lone AF of L proposal included in the convention platform—the injunction item—was denounced by Gompers in the August, 1908, *American Federationist,* as "a flimsy, tricky evasion of the issue. . . . *It is a pro-injunction, not an anti-injunction declaration."* [19] In evaluating the position taken by the Republican convention toward the AF of L, Gompers tersely wrote: "Labor asked the Republican convention for bread, and it gave it a stone." [20] What further distressed the Federation leadership was that the Republican "convention nominated as its standard bearer, William Howard Taft, known as the 'injunction judge.' "

The AF of L Executive Council next appeared at the Democratic party convention held in July at Denver. Here the Council's presence was more cordially acknowledged than it had been in

Chicago. Its members were given a hearing before the full Platform Committee, chaired by Judge Alton Parker who was also
the AF of L's appeal counsel in the Buck's Stove and Range Company injunction case. The Council members presented the Committee with the identical planks submitted to the Republican convention. Then they entered into an earnest discussion with the
committee in defense of the planks. The hearing was a success, as
the Committee's recommendations to the convention were reasonably similar to labor's requests. Of the eight items of legislation requested by the Federation, the Democratic platform
pledged the party to all but those on woman suffrage and government postal savings banks. Gompers was very pleased with the
outcome of the Executive Council's trip to the Democratic convention.

The *American Federationist* of August, 1908, contained an
editorial by the AF of L president, entitled "Both Parties Have
Spoken—Choose Between Them." It gave a résumé of the Executive Council's activities and accomplishments at both party conventions and carefully brought out the point that while the Republicans had been indifferent, if not supercilious, the Democrats
had sincerely befriended them. With this as his final indictment to
the lengthy list of offenses committed by the Republican party
against trade-unions, Gompers had completed his case for asking
the AF of L membership to repudiate the Republican party at the
polls. For the first time in the history of the AF of L, the workers
were asked during a presidential election to give their vote to a
specific political party.[21] The editorial stated:

> We desire to repeat here that we believe that the whole
> mass of the workers of the country will respond in hearty sym-
> pathy with the Democratic party in the coming campaign as a
> result of its action in the labor planks of its platform. They will
> be of practical benefit to the workers.
>
> We have no hesitation in urging the workers and our
> friends throughout the country to support the party in this
> campaign which has shown its sympathies with our wrongs
> and its desire to remedy them and to see that the rights of the
> people are restored.
>
> We say this not necessarily because it is the Democratic

party which has done this. We would urge the workers to support any party which had incorporated our demands into its platform and promised to work for their fulfillment.[22]

Gompers, as the AF of L spokesman, was not only continuing his organization's practice of participating in elections which had begun in 1906, but he was seeking to steer the trade-union vote to the Democratic party. Although he boasted that the AF of L was nonpartisan, for all practical purposes the AF of L in 1908 showed that it was partisan—it favored the Democratic party.

The AF of L's campaign methods in 1908 followed the same general pattern established in 1906. Extensive use was made of the Federation journal, circulars, leaflets, and press statements to inform the workers of the records and attitudes of candidates toward labor's legislative demands. Again and again the need for voting against those who were responsible for endangering labor's security was stressed. The September and October issues of the *American Federationist* carried more than thirty articles by outstanding AF of L union leaders all of whom explained why the Federation was participating in the ensuing political campaign and why the Democratic party was going to receive their votes. These publications also featured a considerable number of letters and resolutions from trade-unions affiliated with the AF of L that endorsed the AF of L's political campaign and support of the Democratic party.

In addition to using its press to arouse and influence the vote of its membership, Gompers and many other AF of L leaders delivered political addresses at mass meetings sponsored by union bodies affiliated with the Federation. Throughout August, September, and October of 1908, Gompers' speaking tour took him into the industrial areas of Pennsylvania, Michigan, Ohio, Indiana, Illinois, and New York.

While leaving no doubt in his speeches that he hoped to see the Republican party defeated, Gompers, mindful of the Republican sentiments of many unionists, frequently emphasized the AF of L was not politically partisan. In view of the disdain the Republicans had shown for labor, he informed the press that "the interests of the wage earners would be furthered by the success of the Democratic party, not because it is the Democratic party, nor that the workers are Democrats but because that party has adopted a platform" compatible with labor's legislative needs.[23] The unionists were warned by Gompers in the November issue of the Federation journal that the Republican presidential candidate, Mr. Taft, was a believer in injunctions, a candidate sponsored by big business, and had "always been the active and energetic servant of the corporations as against the unions, as his judicial record proves." [24] Any workers who might be considering casting their vote for the Socialist party or for William Randolph Hearst's newly created Independent party were reminded of the importance of recognizing that "a vote for the Socialist or Independent Party is one lost to the Democratic candidate." Furthermore, Gompers argued, since these minor parties had no chance of wining the election, it would be no "immediate practical use" for a worker to give them his vote.[25]

The political liaison established between the AF of L and Democratic party is apparent in a letter of August 28, 1908, written by Gompers to Mr. Norman E. Mack, chairman of the Democratic National Committee.[26] The AF of L leader referred to the meeting of the AF of L Executive Council with Mr. Mack on August 27, 1908, at which time a fourteen-point agreement was reached on the kind of aid that the AF of L would lend to the Democratic party and the type of co-operation that the AF of L expected in return. The AF of L Executive Council had consented to having a representative of their organization and the Democratic party in the Democratic headquarters in Illinois, New York, Indiana, and Maine. Gompers was to recommend to the Democratic chairman the names of the trade-union leaders who could be assigned to different sections of the country as speakers at labor meetings to arouse workers' support for the Democratic party. Mr. Mack agreed to have printed and distributed at the Democratic party's expense three million eight-page pamphlets and other relative material which Gompers submitted to him. Mack also agreed that the Democratic party would make a special effort to publicize Speaker Cannon's antilabor record and would bear the expense of any general printing which Mr. Cannon's opponent, Mr. Bell, wished done. The AF of L itself, or its officers, were not to receive any remuneration whatsoever from the Democratic National Committee. Despite this agreement on finances,

Gompers later wrote in his autobiography that Mr. Mack, just before the campaign ended, offered him twenty-five hundred dollars for personal expenses incurred, but he refused to accept any remuneration. Mr. Mack told him, Gompers also wrote, that he was the only one whom he knew in the campaign who had refused any offer of compensation.

William Jennings Bryan, the Democratic presidential candidate, held several conferences with Gompers on the campaign. Bryan and Gompers also communicated with each other by mail and wire in an effort to further the co-operation between the Democratic party and the AF of L, and on several occasions during the campaign Gompers had printed in the Federation journal the speeches made by Bryan which were favorable to labor. At a Labor Day banquet in Chicago for Bryan, according to Gompers' autobiography, the Democratic nominee announced that if he became President he would appoint Gompers to his cabinet, but the Federation leader replied that although he "urged and hoped for the election of Mr. Bryan, under no circumstances, if he were elected, would I accept any office either in his Cabinet or in any other capacity." [27]

While the AF of L's support of the Democratic party in 1908 received the endorsement of most of its affiliated bodies and their officers, as indicated by the publication of resolutions and letters in the *American Federationist* during the few months before the election, exception to the organization's policy was taken by a few unions and union officers. Tom Lewis, president of the United Mine Workers, formerly announced that the UMW would remain neutral without, however, challenging or antagonizing the AF of L's policies. However, most of the trade-unions that differed with the AF of L were local unions where the Socialists possessed a controlling influence. Gompers' correspondence of this period reveals letters of disagreement written by the Bakery and Confectionary Workers of Brooklyn, the Cigarmakers of Brooklyn, the Cabinet Makers of Norfolk, the National Brotherhood of Potters of Trenton, and the International Union of Steam Engineers. These unions refused to contribute to the appeal made by the AF of L for funds to carry on its political campaign. The unions that supported the appeal, however, donated a total of $8,469.98.

The most prominent non-Socialist trade-union leader who differed with the organization's support of the Democratic party was Daniel Keefe, AF of L vice-president and president of the International Association of Longshoremen. As the AF of L's political campaign unfolded in the months prior to the election, it became obvious that Mr. Keefe was maintaining his lifelong affiliation with the Republican party in preference to following the AF of L's endorsement of the Democrats. His deviation from the Federation's position was welcomed by the Republicans and the press who publicized it as an example that there were labor leaders who would not relinquish their political independence to satisfy Gompers' wishes. At the 1908 AF of L convention after the elections, Mr. Keefe refused to run for re-election to the Executive Council because he felt that the pro-Democratic position of Gompers' presidential report restricted "members of the Council as to what they shall do or shall not do in political contests. I have voted the Republican ticket in national affairs for thirty years and will continue to vote the Republican ticket." [28] Shortly before Mr. Taft was sworn in as President of the United States, President Roosevelt appointed Mr. Keefe as Commissioner of Immigration.

The attitude of John Mitchell, AF of L vice-president and former president of the United Mine Workers, toward the Federation's political campaign was one of polite inconsideration. He was known to be an admirer and friend of President Roosevelt, and most likely this personal friendship made him feel an obligation to not campaign against the Republican party and become known as a supporter of the Democratic party. The Labor Day issue of the *American Federationist* which carried articles by more than twenty leading AF of L officials on "Labor's Political Duty" revealed that the articles of Mitchell and Keefe, unlike those of their colleagues, offered but a cursory treatment of the subject and conspicuously avoided any castigation of the Republican party or any approval of the Democrats. Gompers had also been unsuccessful in persuading Mitchell to give a campaign speech against Republican Congressman James Watson, a long-time foe of labor who was seeking election as Governor of Indiana. Since the miners' union had considerable strength in Indiana, Gompers believed that Mitchell's talk would have a strong influence on the vote of many miners. Mitchell, however, declined a speaking engagement on the grounds of poor health. From the tone of Gompers' letter to Mitchell it appeared that the AF of L president was aware of the miners' leader's physical condition but believed that the speaking engagement should be undertaken.[29] Nevertheless, though Mitchell did not actively participate in the Federation's pro-Democratic campaign, neither did he openly oppose it, as did Daniel Keefe. In fact, when Mr. Taft claimed that Mitchell dissented from the AF of L's support of the Democratic party, the miners' leader telegraphed to the Federation his denial of this statement and reaffirmed his loyalty to its announced political policies.

The election resulted in defeat for the Democratic party. Taft won 321 electoral votes to Bryan's 162, and both houses of Congress remained in control of the Republican party. The Socialist candidate, Eugene Debs, polled 424,483 votes, a slight increase over his 1904 total, notwithstanding the fact that Bryan, because of certain radical tendencies, attracted some votes that would have gone to Debs. It was particularly humiliating to the AF of L that a large popular vote for Taft was concentrated in the northeastern states, the very area where the Federation had its greatest membership. In a statement to the press on the day after the election, Gompers announced: "Though temporarily defeated, labor is not conquered." [30] As in 1906, through the Federation journal the AF of L ruler consoled the membership and justified the organization's political efforts by claiming that it had educated the public to labor's mistreatment. Gompers also bragged of a letter he had received from Bryan thanking him for the "powerful support" which he had given the Democratic party.[31]

In surveying the AF of L role in the 1908 campaign, it is evident that labor leadership was unable to deliver the labor vote. The fact that the membership did not follow the political advice of their leaders becomes an interesting subject for speculation.

First, it is important to remember that in 1908 the AF of L consisted mainly of skilled workers in craft unions with its primary objective to secure immediate improvements in the material comforts of life for its members. In order that the AF of L's support of the Democratic party in 1908 should have a practical effect it was necessary for the Federation leadership to enlist the cooperation of all its affiliated unions in support of the Democratic party. Here the AF of L officers met a stumbling block inherent in the very form of business unionism which they advocated and followed. Immediate results attractive to business unionism were being secured by individual unions having favorable positions with their employers rather than through the combined effort of many unions. Therefore well established unions within the AF of L were not necessarily concerned about court decisions against other unions unless these decisions directly threatened their own ability to conduct their economic activities. Concepts of working class loyalty and solidarity were as unfamiliar to many of these unions as they were in contradiction to the business union methods and philosophy they followed. Nor did they particularly care to seek any help from Congress when they were satisfied that their own economic power could always be utilized to take care of themselves.

In brief, many AF of L craft unions had created a select spot for themselves under the capitalist system and were loathe to risk this advantage for the mere purpose of aiding unions less strong than themselves. There is a certain irony in the fact that while in 1908 Gompers desired the AF of L unions to protect their business unionism concepts by uniting behind the Democratic party, business unionism in political action as in economic action retarded successful united action of the labor union movement.

Even in the cases where the leaders of international unions agreed with the Federation's 1908 political policies, they apparently had little success in convincing the part of their membership who were Republicans to change its party affiliation. And, again, the business union philosophy of immediate gains worked to the disadvantage of the AF of L's hopes. A worker could easily rationalize his Republican vote by giving himself this pragmatic test: which party's victory would more likely mean continued employment and good wages for him immediately following the election? Since an overwhelming number of employers desired a Republican victory, the success of that party at the polls would mean immediate business confidence and expansion which would rebound to the workers' immediate material advantage.

The AF of L also reaped an unsatisfactory political harvest in 1908 because of the political tradition the organization had long nurtured. From the inception of the AF of L, Gompers had made political action a heresy, so that many unionists had grown as accustomed to "no politics in the union" as many Americans were to "no politics in the church." When events convinced Gompers by 1908 that it was necessary for the AF of L to enter party politics in the national field, he found himself in the awkward position of urging the unionists to assume a role he had always deprecated.

The behavior of unionists, like that of most people, is rigid in its adherence to traditions. The process of destroying loyalty to a tradition is slow and difficult. Unfortunately for the AF of L leadership, the plight of the Federation in 1908 called for quick political action that would result in the election of a Democratic administration pledged to granting the AF of L relief from the Sherman Law. To their regret, the Federation's officers discovered that the membership clung too well to the antipolitical dogma which they had been responsible for introducing into the organization.

The ingrained belief of the native-born skilled workers in the middle class traditions of natural God-given rights was another handicap to the AF of L's political objectives in 1908. In politics this was applied by many workers as their inviolate right to vote as they chose and not as any authority was pressuring them to vote. The Republican party, many employers' organizations, and the press were quick to make the point that Gompers was destroying the workers' liberty by attempting to deliver their vote. This Republican tactic was effective for it was necessary for Gompers many times during the campaign to deny this allegation in addresses and writings.

The fact that William Jennings Bryan was considered part of the left wing of the Democratic party may have further weakened the AF of L's political cause in 1908. Many AF of L skilled workers thought of themselves as middle class because of their wages, property, political rights, and social status. They neither felt nor exhibited any solidarity with unorganized unskilled labor. Throughout the campaign the Republicans emphasized the dangers that would exist to holders of property and believers in liberty if a man of radical tendencies like Bryan were elected. Bryan himself added to the fears of property-minded workers by announcing during the campaign that the inherent monopolistic character of railroads inevitably would lead to their eventual nationalization.

The newspapers capitalized on this remark to headline "Bryan Out for Government Ownership!"

Although many of the AF of L rank and file did not vote as their leadership urged in 1908, it is significant to recognize that the AF of L at its top level became an adjunct of the Democratic party without incurring internal repudiation from its membership for its new political behavior. At the same time the AF of L debut in the national elections was not sufficiently impressive for the major political parties to conclude that labor could deliver the vote.

A lull in AF of L political activity in 1909 followed the disappointment in the organization's 1908 political effort. However, the circumstances that had motivated the AF of L toward increased political activity in 1906 and 1908 were still prevalent. The Republican Congress had continued its resistance to the Federation's legislative requests, the courts were still issuing injunctions against trade-unions, the Socialist party strength was increasing, and the Buck's Stove and Range Company injunction and contempt charges and the Danbury Hatters' damage award were pending legal appeals. At the 1909 convention Gompers admitted that the need for labor legislation was as great as ever, but he offered no further concrete plan or method that would enable the legislation to be gained than the policy of "reward your friends and punish your enemies" already in existence. Convention delegates were urged to participate in the primary elections with a view to nominating men on both tickets who were friendly to labor. The affiliated unions were advised "to begin agitation and to organize so as to be prepared to take action in the next Congressional campaign." [32]

Actually this advice was not strictly followed by Gompers himself. The AF of L political activity the following year was subdued and almost reminiscent of the period before 1906. Although a Congressional election was to be held in November, 1910, the Federation journal made little reference to the subject of politics in the months preceding the balloting. One issue, the March, 1910, issue, did carry an editorial by Gompers entitled "A.F. of L. Political Policy." But in this editorial the AF of L president seemed to be seeking to avoid saying anything that would bind the organization to a fixed and definite political policy. At the same time the editorial suggested Gompers was seeking to credit the Federation with a political policy. Stripped of its ambiguous verbiage the editorial made only two specific declarations. One was a typical Gompers' phrase—the kind of mumbo-jumbo characteristic of Fourth of July orators: "The American labor movement is not partisan to a political party; it is partisan to a principle, the principle of equal rights and human freedom." The other statement, which endorsed the "spirit of Democracy," as represented by the advent of "the initiative, referendum, and direct nominations" in many states, was more explicit, but could not be acclaimed for its profundity.[33]

The reluctance of the AF of L to engage in a strong political campaign in 1910 is further evidenced by the lack of administrative pronouncements for political action at the organization's 1910 convention. Gompers merely cautiously advised the organization "to trust all the time to definite and time-tried trade union economic methods, and to the ballot only in so far as results are to be foreseen to a positive certainty." [34] At the same time, however, the Federation did continue its practice of publicizing the legislative voting records of the Congressmen and urging its membership to vote. Several pamphlets were published and distributed to affiliated unions. The most important one entitled "Record Vote of Congressmen For and Against Labor" had a circulation of one quarter of a million. The voting record of any individual Congressman was also furnished to anyone requesting such information and some speaking engagements were undertaken. The AF of L Legislative Committee reported that it had collected $3,488.48 for the campaign and had spent $3,148.73 of this amount.

While the AF of L's restrained political pressure on its affiliated unions in the 1910 elections may have pleased the "pure and simplers" and solidified Gompers' position with the conservative elements who either opposed political participation entirely or opposed the organization becoming an adjunct of the Democratic party, such a policy would not overcome the serious problems of judicial hostility and Congressional inconsideration still very much evident. Congress in session in 1910 defeated the AF of L-supported Hughes amendment to an appropriations bill which would cut off any funds to the Justice Department that could be used to prosecute unions. This continued opposition which the AF of L encountered from the government was a serious threat to union security and, unless alleviated, could also arouse a rank-and-file dissatisfaction with its leadership.

Thus Gompers was confronted with a serious dilemma around 1911. If he took the Federation into politics despite the fact that it was not wholeheartedly in favor of such a policy, and if this resulted in no more immediate gains than in 1906 and 1908, his supporters might begin to waver in their loyalty to him. Yet, if the organization avoided political participation, thereby allowing the court and congressional abuses which labor was suffering to continue, the rank and file would be displeased with his leadership for not safeguarding their interests. The Socialists in the AF of L who were always ready to discredit the administration's policies might take advantage of such rank-and-file discontent and possibly succeed in ousting the administration. Of course Gompers had already shown himself to be a wily politician in defending himself against Socialist attacks and in cleverly playing up to these attacks for the purpose of rallying the support of the conservative, often Catholic, factions to him as their martyr and defender. Nevertheless, the problem of assuring the rank and file of union security in the face of the persistent hostility of courts and Congress to unionism could not be solved by Socialist baiting. Fortunately for the AF of L leader, forces outside the AF of L, known in American history as the "Progressive Revolt," eased the impasse confronting the AF of L leadership.

Around 1910 the AF of L was not alone in suffering from the policies of big business and of the government. Many people outside the labor movement were disturbed by the disparity between the great wealth of the few and the poverty of the many. A further critical spirit was evoked by the revelations of the muckrakers who particularly exposed the evils of large-scale business and machine politics. Since the late nineteenth century a reform movement against economic and political abuses had been gaining momentum. Out of a growing desire to place honest, humane men in public affairs who would increase governmental control over monopoly, restore competition in industry, and reopen opportunity to small business, the concept of the positive state was emerging in America. The negative state had shown its inability to protect workers, consumers, and small business men against an acquisitive individualism supported by the doctrine of laissez faire. As a result, the desire had arisen to see the precepts of the American dream restored for all. This dream included the essential assumptions of capitalism but the system's destructive and sordid features would be regulated by a benevolent state power.

The first definite indication of the "Progressive Revolt" in national politics occurred in the Congressional elections of 1910 when the Republican party—the party more commonly understood to be associated with big business—was unseated in the House of Representatives, and the Democrat party gained control. The session of Congress which followed passed more labor-desired legislation than any previous Congress. In number, the AF of L listed twenty-seven pro-labor measures that became law between March 4, 1911, and March 3, 1913. In addition the AF of L took pride that the new chairman of the House Labor Committee was the Democratic Congressman from Pennsylvania, William B. Wilson, former secretary-treasurer of the United Mine Workers.

The pro-labor legislation that AF of L was beginning to obtain from a Democrat-controlled House of Representatives was considered a pleasant foretaste of what it might expect if both legislative houses and the executive branch of the government were in Democratic party hands. In opposition to the socialist sentiment which was at its height in the nation, Gompers warned the AF of L rank and file in the June, 1912, *American Federationist,* "Don't be deluded by fanciful political programs that assume to transport the labor movement to some Utopian land of promise. Strive for the better day TODAY. Material and actual results constitute the ethics of trade unionists." [35]

The AF of L president recognized that the Democratic party's chances of winning the executive branch in 1912 were going to be better than in previous years because of the liberal reform tide stirring the nation. Since that party demonstrated by the bills it had passed in the House that it would show greater consideration to labor than the Republican party had shown, Gompers intended to use his influence in the Federation to secure the labor vote for the Democratic party. However, to maintain the so-called nonpartisan policy of the AF of L, he made the nominal gesture of affording the Republican party the opportunity to bid for labor's vote by submitting the AF of L's 1912 legislative demands to the Platform Committee at the Republican party convention.

The nine measures which the Federation asked the Republicans to pledge themselves to pass were as follows: (*1*) a bill eliminating the possibility of labor associations being regarded as combinations in restraint of trade, (*2*) a bill prohibiting the issuance of injunctions in cases arising out of labor disputes and a bill providing for jury trials in contempt actions arising out of injunction cases, (*3*) a bill safeguarding labor from the competition of the products of convict labor, (*4*) a bill restricting immigration, (*5*) a bill providing that seamen shall not be compelled to endure involuntary servitude, (*6*) a bill creating a Department of Labor with a Secretary at its head having a seat in the President's cabinet, (*7*) a bill stating that government employees shall not be dismissed or demoted for petitioning Congress for the enactment of laws to improve their condition, (*8*) a bill providing, as far as federal jurisdiction permitted, for workmen's compensation coverage, (*9*) a proposal of a constitutional amendment for the ratification of suffrage for women.

Of these nine labor-desired measures, the Republican party platform pledged itself to a workmen's compensation act, an immigration restriction act, and an act ending the involuntary servitude of seamen.

At the Democratic party convention which Gompers next attended he hoped to have most of labor's legislative demands incorporated in the party's platform, and he also hoped to see Champ Clark, Speaker of the House of Representatives, whom he considered a friend of labor, nominated as the presidential candidate. Gompers' platform objectives were fulfilled when the Democratic convention platform repeated its labor planks of 1908 which had included the major demands of the AF of L. He was disappointed, however, when his friend and choice, Speaker of the House Champ Clark, was deserted by William Jennings Bryan, and lost the nomination on the forty-sixth ballot to Woodrow Wilson.

The Progressive party, established by a group of insurgent Republicans led by Theodore Roosevelt who were dissatisfied with the conservative policies of the Republican party, nominated Roosevelt and Hiram Johnson of California for President and Vice-President respectively. While their platform called for a multitude of reforms relating to government, labor, currency, social legislation, taxes, and conservation, the party's heavy dependency on the impulsive, erratic character of Roosevelt and on the financial contributions of George Perkins, a director of the monopolistic International Harvester Company, weakened its progressive appeal. Although it made a strong bid for the labor vote by inserting more pro-labor planks in its platform than did the two major parties, the AF of L leadership largely ignored the presence of the Progressive party in 1912.

At an Executive Council meeting in August, 1912, the Federation decided to reaffirm its political position taken in 1906, 1908, and 1910. This meant the repetition of the "reward your friends, punish your enemies" slogan with the implicit suggestion that the Democratic party had proved itself the "friend" and the Republican party had been the "enemy" of labor. Unlike 1908, and more like 1910, the AF of L leadership and the Labor Representation Committee did not intend to take a very active part in the campaign. In addition, Gompers planned to not engage in many political addresses because the experience gained in the 1908 campaign when he was attacked for vigorous participation led him to conclude that discreet counsel was preferable to overt action.

The general tone of the articles and editorials in the *American Federationist* during the late summer and early fall preceding the 1912 election was more restrained than they had been in 1908 in its attacks on the Republican presidential candidate and its eulogizing of the Democratic nominee. But the AF of L did emphasize that it considered the Democratic party worthy of labor's vote.

The October, 1912, issue of the *American Federationist* officially announced the 1912 political position of the Federation agreed upon by the Executive Council. This article was also published in the AF of L *Weekly News Letter* as the "Special Campaign Issue, 1912." [36] The labor planks of the Republican, Democratic, and Progressive parties were reproduced and were commented on. The Republican party was charged with having a labor platform that ignored labor's demands while the Democratic and Progressive parties were praised for writing planks desired by labor. The Republican party was further derided for having been unfriendly to labor during the many years it controlled the government. It was also shown that the Democratic-controlled House of

Representatives, which convened in March, 1911, had passed twenty-eight measures desired by labor, but the Republican Senate had rejected seventeen of these bills.

The November issue of the Federation journal distributed to the AF of L membership shortly before the election summed up the leadership's outlook on the political campaign. Gompers stressed the animosity of Taft and the Republican party toward labor in contrast to the friendliness of the Democrats. Endorsement, however, was given to Republican Senator Borah of Idaho because of his outstanding pro-labor record. A letter was addressed to the "Officers and Members of All Local Unions and Central Bodies in Idaho" which gave a detailed account of Borah's friendship for labor. The Progressive party and its candidates received no mention in the November, 1912, AF of L journal.

The election returns showed that the reform movement in the nation was at its highest peak. Taft received only three and a half million votes out of a total of over fourteen million. Wilson received over six million votes, Theodore Roosevelt received over four million votes and the Socialist candidate, Eugene Debs, received the largest vote ever yet won by a Socialist candidate for President in America—901,062 votes. This increased vote particularly satisfied the Socialists, inasmuch as they had been handicapped in their campaign by the reforms that both Wilson and Roosevelt promised the electorate. What especially pleased the AF of L leadership, however, was that it had at last supported the winning candidate. Its chances of attaining the legislative measures sought for many years were additionally promising because the Democratic party had also captured control of both Houses of Congress.

4.

The American Federation of Labor

During Wilson's First Administration, 1912–1916

> But American union leaders are still considered inter-
> lopers in the political field, special pleaders for a single-
> interest group. Americans who have only recently come to
> swallow, and have not yet digested, the idea that collective
> bargaining is not treason are likely for some time to view
> labor political action as a compact with the Devil and an
> agreement with Hell. The legislature and Courts will
> continue to block union efforts to raise campaign funds
> from member contributions. Although the strongest political
> group in the nation, labor is still a political outsider. The
> prevailing attitude in the major parties is that, like a
> mastiff, it must be kept tolerably content, but under no
> circumstance admitted into the house.
>
> *Max Lerner,* AMERICA AS A CIVILIZATION

BETWEEN the time of Wilson's election in November, 1912, and his inauguration in March, 1913, Gompers asked for and was granted several meetings with Wilson. At one meeting Wilson told Gompers and AF of L secretary Morrison that "they would not be disappointed with the labor program he would outline in his inaugural address." [1]

One of the first indications that the AF of L had a friend in the White House was Wilson's appointment of William B. Wilson to his cabinet as Secretary of Labor. Wilson, a Democratic Congress-man from Pennsylvania, was a former secretary-treasurer of the United Mine Workers. *The New York Times* of March 9, 1913, commented that the appointment had been made at "the instiga-tion of Samuel Gompers." One of William Wilson's major accom-

74

plishments during his cabinet period was the establishment of the federal mediation service, known as the Division of Conciliation.

In March and April of 1913 Gompers wrote President Wilson two very lengthy explanations of labor's desire to obtain relief from prosecution under the Sherman Antitrust Law. Wilson was urged to sign the sundry Civil Appropriations Bill which contained the Hughes amendment preventing the use of any government appropriated funds to prosecute labor under the Sherman Law. Wilson each time answered Gompers politely that he was grateful for the letters and they would help him "in thinking things out." [2] Because Gompers at this time was ill with mastoiditis he had Frank Morrison and AF of L vice-president James O'Connell visit Wilson in late May to persuade him to sign the bill containing the Hughes amendment.[3] Labor's long lobbying for the passage of the bill and its faith that the Democratic party would be more responsive to its requests was finally rewarded in June, 1913, when the Democratic Congress and President approved the Hughes amendment.

The real test of the intentions of the Democratic party to meet its pledges to labor, however, was to be its attitude toward a wider measure that would give trade-unionism complete relief from prosecution under the Sherman Law. The amendment of the Sherman Antitrust Law so that injunctions, contempt proceedings, and damage suits would not continue their long-time threat to the security of trade-unionism was the much desired and much needed legislative redress of the AF of L. The courts were showing no evidence of proceeding slower in the matter of issuing and upholding injunctions under the provisions of the Sherman Act. The memorable Danbury Hatters' and Buck's Stove and Range cases had been before the courts for about a decade, and, while the Federation had gone to the expense of appealing the decisions of inferior courts, it was not securing more favorable decisions from the higher courts.

On May 5, 1913, the Court of Appeals of the District of Columbia sustained a lower District Court in finding Gompers, Mitchell, and Morrison guilty of contempt of the Buck's Stove and Range Company injunction. On December 18, 1913, the United States Circuit Court of Appeals for the Second Circuit in a hearing on the Danbury Hatters' case affirmed the findings of the Hartford, Connecticut, trial court that a conspiracy in restraint of trade was entered into as alleged in the complaint. This decision resulted in a judgment of $252,130.90 being upheld against the 197 Hatters' unionists.

Another antilabor court decision was one delivered on December 23, 1912, against the United Mine Workers' efforts to organize the coal miners of West Virginia.[4] On this date Justice Dayton of the Federal District Court of the Northern District of West Virginia issued an opinion which made permanent a temporary injunction of 1907 restraining the United Mine Workers from organizing activity among the employees of the Hitchman Company. By contending that the United Mine Workers was an illegal combination under the Sherman Law, Justice Dayton was in effect making the joining of a union a crime. Gompers angrily denounced him because he had "autocratically forbade free workers to unite for organization, to induce others to make common cause in strikes, to walk along public highways or private for the purpose of picketing." [5] Since the Hitchman Coal Company only hired workers who agreed not to join a union, Judge Dayton's decision sanctioned the right of an employer to protect his property interests by this method of employment. This right of the employer, according to the West Virginia Justice, furthermore, could be maintained against union organizers, by a request from the courts for an injunction.[6]

This steady court hostility toward unionism certainly gave the Federation sufficient reason to insist that the government pass a bill excluding trade-unions from the provisions of the Sherman Law. When the Federation learned that the 1914 Congress intended to revise the Antitrust Law, the AF of L decided to lobby for the inclusion of labor sections in the law instead of attempting to have separate anti-injunction bills passed. The Democratic party's measure was sponsored in the House of Representatives by Congressman Clayton of Alabama and the sections of the bill which applied to labor were to become famous as section 6 and section 20.

At a regular meeting of the AF of L Executive Council in May, 1914, the pending Clayton Bill in Congress was discussed. A resolution was adopted expressing dissatisfaction with the wording of the sections that applied to labor, because they contained "language which is indefinite, ambiguous and liable to an interpretation by the courts inimical to Labor's rights and interests." [7] Where the section read, "Nothing contained in the anti-trust laws shall be construed to forbid the existence and operation of labor organizations," members of the Executive Council voted to advise their friends in Congress that this phrase be stricken out and amended to read, "Nothing contained in the anti-trust laws shall be construed to apply to labor organizations." [8]

The Federation noted in its journal of July, 1914, that if section 6 was changed in this way, "the section would definitely and clearly exempt the organizations of laborers and producers from the civil as well as the criminal sections of the Sherman anti-trust law." [9] British unions had already secured this protection by the British Trade Disputes Act of 1906 which unqualifiedly stated that no civil action could be brought against a trade-union for any wrongful act committed by it or on behalf of it.

Gompers wrote to each member in the House condemning the wording of section 6 of the Clayton Bill and urging the adoption of the AF of L's substitute sentence. However, because of considerable Congressional opposition to the AF of L's suggested change in wording, the Federation's leaders gave up their advocacy of it. A compromise was reached which read, "The labor of a human being is not a commodity or article of commerce," and a concluding clause that read, "nor shall such organizations, orders of associations, or the members thereof be held or construed to be illegal combinations or conspiracies in restraint of trade under the anti-trust laws." [10]

As later court decisions were to show, the AF of L president was overly optimistic in believing that labor had won "a momentous victory" and that "The opening statement of this section of the bill gives it strength and virility." [11] Gompers wrote in the *American Federationist* of October, 1914, that "This declaration removes all possibility of interpreting trust legislation to apply to organizations of the workers and their legitimate associated activities." He prematurely boasted that "The workers of America have won a great victory for themselves and for all humanity. The principle and the rights incorporated in labor provisions of the Clayton anti-trust bill will be the foundation upon which the workers can establish greater liberty and greater opportunity for all those who do the beneficent work of the world." [12]

In contrast to Gompers' elation the Socialists announced that labor merely had received meaningless phrases. The Socialists in their party press service, the *Washington Letter* of June, 1914, wrote that "astute legal minds in Washington completely realize that the amendment will not exempt the unions, but the politicians are delighted with the success of the game they have put across." Many public newspapers, like many Congressmen, were in disagreement about the meaning of the bill. Some thought it would exempt labor from the Sherman Act and others said it merely stated labor's right to exist.

On October 15, 1914, President Wilson signed the Clayton Bill. A year later Gompers still enthusiastically wrote in the *American Federationist* of September, 1915: "We proclaim as one of the great legislative declarations of all the ages this sentence in the Clayton Anti-Trust Act: The labor of a human being is not a commodity or article of commerce." As American historian, Harvey Wish, wrote in his book, *Contemporary America,* this sentence was "In language suggestive of the famous papal encyclical *Rerum Novarum."* [13]

While the Clayton Bill was being formulated in Congress, the activities that the AF of L undertook to assure its passage illustrate the Federation's lobbying methods. Gompers and the AF of L legislative committeeman Arthur Holder visited Congress regularly to keep in touch with the progress of the bill. Personal conferences with Congressmen who were staunch friends of labor were held so that strategy and tactics could be discussed which would facilitate the passage of the kind of bill the AF of L desired. Officially, AF of L representatives presented their views on the Sherman Law and on injunctions to both the House and the Senate Judiciary Committees whose task was to recommend legislation in this area.

Besides using its own persuasive efforts on Congressmen, the AF of L leadership utilized its membership in its lobbying campaign for the passage of the Clayton Bill. Since most Congressmen wished to assure themselves of re-election, they had to take into account the wishes of their constituents on pending legislation. Well aware of this, Gompers urged the AF of L rank and file in the AF of L *Weekly News Letter* of June 6, 1914, to petition, wire and write Congress for immediate and favorable action upon the labor provisions of the Clayton Bill. When opposition to the labor provisions of the Clayton Bill developed in the Senate, he informed the membership that they should impress "upon their respective members in the Senate the imperative necessity for taking immediate and favorable action upon labor's needs and demands. Demand the bill as it passed the House." [14] Many special circular letters sent out during the summer of 1914 requested members to write to certain Senators who could be influenced if subject to significant pressure. Gompers also wrote a number of times to the AF of L Executive Council informing them of the latest developments. In addition, he wrote all AF of L organizers to hold meetings with unions and leaders that would result in Congress' hearing from labor throughout the country.

AF of L lobbying activity, which was already well developed by 1914, has continued through to the present as the basic political method used by the AF of L to gain its legislative needs. But for the AF of L's lobbying to be effective labor had to demonstrate that it could deliver the vote at the polls. For example, if a Congressman has reason to believe that the unionists in his district have a greater loyalty to a political party than to the political exhortations of their union leaders, he will act in Congress according to his conscience, or according to the dictates of the political machine, or according to the pressure from special interests whose support does insure his continued presence in congress. But if he suspects that his re-election depends on labor's votes on election days he will be more likely to meet the requests of labor's lobbyists.

The AF of L took little part in the Congressional elections of 1914. True, the Executive Council meeting in Washington, D.C., in July, 1914, authorized the Labor Representation Committee to conduct a campaign for electing trade-unionists to Congress. But this action seemed little more than a verbal gesture, for not much of an active campaign was undertaken. The Federation journal had little to say about politics in the months preceding the November, 1914, elections. Probably the AF of L's political arm was not strong enough to give attention to a Congressional election at a time when its energies were engrossed in lobbying for the passage of the labor provisions of the Clayton Bill. Perhaps, too, it was hoped that the publicity given to the Clayton Bill and its reception in Congress would of itself alert affiliated unions to the value and need of rewarding labor's friends and punishing labor's enemies.

Furthermore, within the context of the AF of L leadership's political thinking, there was less need to participate strongly in the Congressional election of 1914. The AF of L's political practice was largely a negative affair of seeking to defeat those outstanding political enemies (generally Republicans) who were strongly opposed to its legislative objectives. Both houses of Congress in 1914, however, were in Democratic hands and Republican members did not hold the chairmanship of committees that could disturb the AF of L. Also, the AF of L originally had entered political campaigns in 1906 primarily to secure legislative relief from the Sherman Act and injunctions issued under it. But when it appeared to AF of L leaders that the Clayton Bill would answer their legislative need, the original incentive for influencing political elections subsided.

As to the matter of lobbying, however, the Federation officers' activities continued. On October 16, 1914, Gompers wrote to Woodrow Wilson that a Congressional session was drawing to a close and the Democratic party had not yet passed a Seamen's Bill, as its platform pledged. Wilson replied that other legislation had been given precedence, but he was glad to receive Gompers' letter. President Wilson also wrote Andrew Furuseth, Seamen leader, that he favored legislation to promote seamen's welfare, but that he feared that such legislation might disrupt our relations with many countries with whom we had treaties on the subject of seamen. Through the help of Senator LaFollette who was sponsoring the Seamen's Bill, Furuseth gained an audience with both Secretary of State Bryan and with President Wilson. In both instances, the seamen's leader moved the government leaders deeply as he described the terrible conditions of employment existent in the merchant marine. On March 3, 1915, the seamen's bill that Furuseth had persistently labored for since the AF of L's beginnings was signed into law.

Lobbying activity did not come to an end when a bill became a law. Inadequate enforcement of a law could destroy its effectiveness. The AF of L learned that the Secretary of Commerce was interpreting the LaFollette Seamen's Act too narrowly for it to achieve its purposes. Hence in February, 1916, the AF of L Executive Committee sent a resolution to President Wilson and Commerce Secretary Redfield voicing their complaint. President Wilson answered Gompers that he regretted the Commerce and Justice Department's interpretations and hoped that in time the Act's administration would improve and meet their approval.

When the Democratic-controlled session of the Sixty-third Congress ended in March, 1915, the AF of L evaluated the results of their lobbying during two years of the Wilson administration. AF of L Legislative Committee Chairman Arthur E. Holder declared the Democratic-controlled session had shown labor more consideration than had any previous Congress. The AF of L listed twenty-six measures of interest to labor which the sessions of Congress had passed. The more important of these provided that: *(1)* labor organizations would be taken from the purview of the Sherman Act; *(2)* injunctions would be more limited in their use; *(3)* contempts of injunction writs would cover a more limited sphere and punishment for contempt would be less severe; *(4)* the Department of Justice would be prohibited from using antitrust appropriation funds to prosecute labor organizations under the Sherman Act; *(5)* seamen's contractual rights, working conditions, and welfare would be improved; *(6)* the eight-hour law would be extended to women and children workers in the District of Columbia.

A number of measures on the AF of L's legislative program had failed to be enacted. The more important of these were: *(1)* an immigration restriction bill with a literacy test; *(2)* a bill protecting labor against the competition of domestic or foreign convict labor; *(3)* a bill against child labor; *(4)* an employers' liability bill and a workmen's compensation bill for government and railroad employees; *(5)* a bill establishing a Bureau of Safety in the Department of Labor. Nevertheless the AF of L knew that their legislative program had been more successful under the Wilson administration than under previous Republican administrations.

In addition to appreciating the Democratic administration's passage of pro-labor legislation, the AF of L felt that this administration also showed a friendliness for labor in other ways not typical of previous Republican administrations. The AF of L learned during Wilson's years in the White House that they could write to him and receive prompt and friendly replies and could call on him for various kinds of help and find a sympathetic ear. In early January, 1916, Gompers asked Wilson to write a statement that would be placed on the cornerstone of the new AF of L building. Wilson sent his congratulations to the AF of L for their new building and declared "I think you know how genuinely I am interested in the fortunes of the Federation and how earnest and sincere a hope I entertain that its leaders will be crowned with the best sort of success in the promotion of the best interests of the working men of the country." [15] On July 4, 1916, President Wilson, the Vice-President, and several cabinet members attended the dedication ceremonies of the new building. In the principal address of the day, President Wilson declared that "No man ought to suffer injustice in America. No man ought in America to fail to see the deep dictates of humanity." [16] The President also remarked that it was obvious to him that "a man's labor is not a commodity but a part of his life" and he was "sorry that there were any judges in the United States who had to be told that." [17] Statements such as these from the President of the United States and the President's willingness to confer, write, and visit with labor carried tremendous weight with Gompers. Apropos of Wilson's July 4 dedication speech, Gompers wrote, "nowhere in the pages of American history" could a "clearer and more definite pronouncement in behalf of real, genuine, human liberties" be found.[18]

The AF of L also was pleased with the Wilson administration for the consideration it gave labor in the matter of appointments. President Wilson's appointment of William B. Wilson, a man of definite union background, as Secretary of Labor, gave the AF of L leadership a feeling of acceptance and importance. President Wilson's nomination of AF of L officers James O'Connell and John Lennon to the Commission on Industrial Relations investigating the causes of labor-management difficulties was equally gratifying to the AF of L officials. Like most people, the AF of L leaders needed recognition and status. They had suffered years of rebuffs and rejections from Republican office holders, business leaders, and newspaper publishers, and it was psychologically satisfying to be treated at last with consideration and sometimes even with approval.

Another illustration of the Wilson government's generally

sympathetic attitude toward labor was its reaction to the "Ludlow Massacre." In April, 1914, a tent colony of striking miners' families were burned and the families shot by Colorado Militia during an organizing strike of the United Mine Workers against the Rockefellers' Colorado Fuel and Iron Company. President Wilson ordered federal troops to Colorado and these troops showed as much concern for the miners' rights as for the company's rights. They did not act as strikebreakers, as troops had been known to do. They earned the miners' gratitude by their behavior and James Ford of the AF of L Mining Department visited President Wilson in October, 1914, to request that the troops remain until a settlement was reached. The UMW at a special convention also approved Wilson's proposals for ending the strike a number of months before the operators accepted a settlement.

With the approach of the Presidential election of 1916 the Federation officials favored the re-election of Wilson and the Democratic party for objective and subjective reasons. The AF of L leadership's problem, however, was one which they had had to face since their entry into politics in 1906. How could they urge their membership to support the Democratic party generally without arousing some union and worker resentment against their Democratic partisanship? One of the first techniques used that could produce little risk for its initiators was the publication and wide distribution of a pamphlet, *Legislative Achievements of the A.F. of L.* This pamphlet described the legislative gains of the AF of L in each Congress since the 1906 "Labor's Bill of Grievances." Only one conclusion could be reached by a reading of this pamphlet—that the Federation had far greater success in securing the legislation it desired when the Democrats were in power rather than the Republicans.

In spite of evidence by mid-1916 that the Federation leaders were partisan to the Democratic party, the custom was continued of the AF of L Executive Council and the Labor Representation Committee extending tacit support to non-partisanship by presenting the AF of L's legislative demands to the conventions of the Democratic and Republican parties.

The principal requests made by the Federation to the Democratic and Republican conventions were as follows: (*1*) the maintenance and enforcement of the Clayton Law and Seamen's Act;

(2) the enforcement and extension of the immigration law; (3) the passage of a measure providing adequate assistance to public educational institutions offering industrial education and vocational training; (4) the enactment and enforcement of a federal child labor law; (5) the passage of legislation excluding the products of convict labor from interstate commerce; (6) the enactment of a workmen's compensation bill; (7) the observance and enforcement of all federal eight-hour laws and their extension to all departments of federal government; (8) the creation and maintenance of a Bureau of Safety in the Department of Labor; (9) the exclusion of "speeding up systems" in work where the federal government was involved; (10) the bestowal of American citizenship on the people of Puerto Rico; (11) the submission of a constitutional amendment to the states for ratification of woman suffrage; (12) the passage of legislation providing for federal government ownership of telegraphs and telephones.

Before the Democratic Platform and Resolution Committee, Gompers expressed the AF of L's desire to continue its established friendship with and support of the Democratic party. "To you are turned the political hopes of the toilers. We have not been disappointed in your declarations of the past; let us not be disappointed in the declarations of the present and of the future. We believe with you, we can work with you, if you give us but the opportunity to work with you further. When the time shall come and you turn your backs upon us and ignore us, gentlemen, we must look elsewhere for redress and for right." [19]

Unlike previous conventions, the Republican convention of 1916 adopted in its platform several of the AF of L legislative demands, but these still fell far short of the number incorporated in the Democratic platform. The reproduction in the July, 1916, issue of the *American Federationist* of the labor planks of the platforms of the two parties gave the AF of L members an opportunity to compare and contrast them.

Following the political conventions Gompers had Furuseth aid the Democratic National Committee in writing a pamphlet, *Wilson and Labor*. This pamphlet which was published by the Democratic National Campaign Committee intended to show the pro-labor record of the Wilson administration. On the cover page of the pamphlet dated August 25, 1916, Gompers wrote that he had

never experienced "anything like the fine spirit toward labor . . .
pervading all the branches of the Wilson administration. . . . This
fundamental right spirit has guided the Wilson administration to
wise and righteous labor legislation. Because of that spirit and its
results in definite laws and policies, how can liberty-loving Americans, loyal to the Republic and its ideals, fail to sustain an executive who has done so much for their realization?" Gompers'
reference to the Republican candidate was that Hughes was an
antilabor judge and injunction supporter.[20]

In August, 1916, the AF of L Labor Representation Committee
printed and distributed a *Circular Letter* to the AF of L affiliated
unions containing both President Wilson's position on labor measures during his incumbency and the Republican candidate Charles
E. Hughes's attitude to labor measures during his period as a Supreme Court Judge. Wilson's loyalty to labor was shown by the
fact that he had initiated or signed thirty-seven pro-labor bills,
that he had appointed as Secretary of Labor to his cabinet Congressman William B. Wilson former secretary-treasurer of the
United Mine Workers, and that he had approved the creation of a
Commission on Industrial Relations to probe the field of industrial
unrest, as well as appointing AF of L officers John B. Lennon and
James O'Connell to the Commission. As a Supreme Court judge,
Hughes was condemned by Gompers for concurring in the United
States Supreme Court decision in 1914 which had declared the
Danbury Hatters guilty of violation of the Sherman Law, and for
a decision in the case of *Truax* v. *Raich* upholding the injunctive
process against labor.

Wilson's prestige with labor further increased during the campaign months because of his signature of two pro-labor bills. In
August he signed the Keating-Owen Child Labor Bill which
barred the products of child labor from interstate commerce. In
September he signed the Adamson Bill which established, according to his recommendation, the eight-hour day as the basis
for computing overtime wages for railway workers.

As the pre-election contest between the two parties increased
in intensity, the AF of L leadership dropped any pretense of nonpartisan activity and went all out for Wilson's election. About a
month before the election, the AF of L exclaimed in its annual convention that "the issue is represented in the campaign by the con-

flicting interests represented by labor and Wall Street." [21] Wilson and the Democratic party, it was stated, were the proved friends of labor but the Republican party had not been, and could not be the friend of labor because its candidates were the friends of the "interests of Wall Street and their satellites" who seek to "continue their activity to retain the special privileges and power that they have secretly and corruptly stolen from the people." [22]

The AF of L leadership stated at its 1916 convention that actual count and importance of labor bills enacted into law during the first session of the Sixty-fourth Congress, adjourning before the 1916 elections, proved that the Democrats co-operated more closely with the AF of L than had previous Republican administrations. The delegates were told that twenty labor-advocated measures had become law during the most recent session of the Democratic Congress. One law cited in particular was the Keating-Owen Child Labor Law which prohibited from interstate commerce the factory products of children under the age of fourteen. In seeking credit from its members for its lobbying efforts with the Democratic Congress the AF of L officials did not acknowledge that some legislation had been secured because of the support of nonlabor organizations and individuals also interested in such legislation. The Seamen's Act, the Immigration Act, and the Child Labor Act are examples of measures owing their existence to combined labor and nonlabor lobbying efforts.

At the 1916 AF of L Convention Gompers said apropos the coming national elections, "It is an obligation that the members of the organized labor movement owe to those who have done so much to make possible the splendid humanitarian legislation that has been enacted, and to the spirit of administration mindful of humanity and justice, that our support should be given them that they may retain their positions in which they are able to accomplish so much for the movement."

In a letter to all officers of the AF of L on October 14, 1916, Gompers requested them to do everything in their power that would help bring about the election of Woodrow Wilson.[23] He himself set the example for labor political campaigning by engaging in a number of partisan speeches for Wilson and Democratic Congressional candidates. At a political rally in Indianapolis, he spoke in terms which left no doubt that the Federation leadership desired union workers to vote for the Democratic party. After reviewing the antilabor legislative record of James Watson, Republican candidate for United States Senator from Indiana, he remarked, "if the working people, the liberty loving people of Indiana, care to have as their Senator a man of the caliber of Jim Watson, may the Lord have mercy upon them." But Gompers thought the wise workman would realize that "in this campaign we cannot help but be just to ourselves and support the platform and candidates nominated on the platform of the Democratic party." Concluding on a note of disapproval for the Republicans, he said "If the men of labor have to depend upon what is promised by the Republican party and candidates in this campaign, God save them. That is all." [24]

Addressing a mass political meeting in Chicago a few days later, the AF of L president emphatically approved of the Democratic party and announced: "Brothers and sisters, in this great struggle men and women of Illinois, I have but one vote to give . . . and that vote which I possess and control . . . will be cast for Woodrow Wilson for president of the United States." [25] Always sensitive, however, to possible Republican unionists' resentment of his Democratic party sentiments, he defended himself by saying "when we went to both Republican and Democratic parties asking them to relieve the working people of America from that gross injustice, the misinterpretation of the Sherman anti-trust law to apply to voluntary association of the working people, the Republican party turned their backs upon us, and the Democratic party declared it would put Labor's demands in their platform and they did. What were we going to do after that—turn our backs on the Democratic Party?" [26] One of the AF of L's final campaign appeals to its membership was a Gompers' editorial in the November issue of the *American Federationist*. The AF of L president counselled:

> It is up to the workers, the masses of our liberty loving citizenship, to decide whether President Wilson, with his clear vision and courageous heart and mind, shall be supplanted by the reactionary candidate of predatory wealth—Mr. Hughes. President Woodrow Wilson has advocated, urged and signed legislation protecting the welfare of the workers and all of the masses of the people. . . . It lies with the working people—

the masses—on Election Day to determine by their vote
whether the policy of progress, justice, freedom and humanity
shall prevail in the re-election of Mr. Wilson to the presidency
of the United States or whether the pendulum shall swing back-
ward and the policy of reaction be enthroned.

Three days before the 1916 election an AF of L circular letter
was issued. It advised the workers not to be influenced by the fact
that "Wall Street coffers have been opened like a flood-gate in
the effort to publish mis-information, and to mislead and corrupt
the electorate, wherever possible." [27]

By the late hours of the election night it appeared that Hughes
would be the victor for he had won the industrial states of the
northeast and many of the midwestern states also. However, later
returns from the Rocky Mountain and far western states improved
Wilson's chances and finally California's electoral votes enabled
him to squeeze out a victory. The electoral vote was 277 to 254
and the popular vote gave Wilson 9,129,600; Hughes, 8,538,200;
and Allan L. Benson, the Socialist party nominee, 585,100. Although the Democrats retained control of both houses of Congress, the Democratic majority had dropped considerably, the result thus foreshadowing the coming Republican return to power
in the 1918 Congressional elections.

Could the AF of L rightfully take partial credit for the Democratic party victory by claiming that it had induced its rank and
file to vote for the Democratic party? Many industrial areas in
the east that usually voted Democratic had deserted Wilson. The
Catholic and the Irish had been especially critical of Wilson because of his Mexican policy and his attitude to Irish independence.
Apparently religion and nationality had had a greater influence
on the workers' voting behavior than economic factors. On the
other hand, vigorous political campaigning done by the San Francisco Central Labor Union and by Secretary of Labor William B.
Wilson for the Democratic party of the west coast was of tremendous help in putting California and Washington in the Democratic
column.

Political victories also sometimes occur because of the mistakes of the opposing party. Undoubtedly the Republican party's
inability to end a rift between the national party and California's

Republican, Senator Hiram Johnson, also contributed to the loss of California's decisive electoral vote in 1916.

Newspaper editorials of the time were not in agreement on the effectiveness of labor in the 1916 campaign. Some, like the New York *Tribune,* wrote that the labor vote had not gone heavily for Wilson, but others, like the New York *Sun,* pointed out that the labor vote in Ohio and California had given the victory to the Democratic party in those states, and thus had produced the necessary electoral votes for Wilson's victory.

Samuel Gompers wired Wilson on November 9, 1916, that "Despite the desperate efforts of intrenched power as represented by wealth alone with its blinded followers, the common people have stood the test and have proven true. The cause of labor, justice, freedom, American patriotism and humanity has been vindicated. The people and our Republic are to be congratulated on your re-election as President." [28] Gompers, rarely modest and always compulsively driven to justify his actions, wrote later in his autobiography that he was phoned on November 10, 1916, "by the secretary to Postmaster-General Burleson to convey the message that to me more than any other one man was due the re-election of President Wilson." [29] On the same day Gompers and the AF of L Executive Council called upon President Wilson and, according to *The New York Times* of November 11, 1916, congratulated him on his re-election and promised him their support in his next administration.

5.

The American Federation of Labor

and Political Problems of World War I

> The trade union movement in this country can make
> progress only by identifying itself with the State—by
> obeying its just laws and by upholding the military as well
> as the civil arm of the government.
>
> *John Mitchell,* ORGANIZED LABOR

ALTHOUGH the foreign policy of President Wilson's administration was popularized by his campaign managers in 1916 with the slogan "He kept us out of war!" five months after his re-election America was at war with the Central Powers. The AF of L attitude toward militarism and war was typical of social reform groups in the United States. In the years before the outbreak of hostilities, various Federation conventions favored the International Court of Arbitration at The Hague, the principles of international arbitration, a limitation on armaments, and a world assembly. At the war's outset, the Federation wanted America to stay neutral and for the fighting to come to an early end. As the war continued, however, the AF of L became openly sympathetic to the Allied nations, and interested in an Allied victory. Finally, on the eve of America's entry into the conflict and after Congress' declaration of war, the AF of L demonstrated unmistakable loyalty and active support of the government.

Prior to World War I, Gompers considered himself a life-long pacifist. He had written articles for international peace, was a vice-president of the National Peace Conferences in New York (1907) and Chicago (1909) and participated in the International Peace Meeting held in connection with the Conference of the International Secretariat of Trade Unions in Paris in 1909. In 1913 he successfully supported a resolution in the AF of L convention which approved a universal naval construction holiday proposed by Winston Churchill. The resolution also instructed the AF of L Legislative Committee to "use every honorable means to prevail upon the present administration of the United States to use its best offices to encourage this movement for international peace and disarmament." [1]

Less than a year before the European war began, the *American Federationist* in October, 1913, contained an editorial entitled "Militarism Must Not Prevail." It expressed Gompers' disagreement with the American government's plans to establish military camps for college youths during their summer holidays. "The whole scheme to improve the army," Gompers declared, "has the appearance of an attempt to foist militarism upon the people of our free country." The United States "should arouse herself to this danger and defeat militarism before it fixes its clutches upon the people." The workers should "inform themselves, and act—not in behalf of military and naval forces but of justice, right thinking and right living." [2]

Immediately following the outbreak of war, Gompers still gave evidence of his pacifism. He wrote that he was horrified at the inhumanity and economic waste of the conflict. He blamed the war on autocratic governments who preferred war to democratizing their own governments. Such governments, he argued, should be abolished. The people should be educated to war's tragedies and a world organization should be founded to promote peace and prevent any future wars.

In the early days of the war, Gompers' feelings were not as markedly anti-German as they become later. In concluding a letter (September 30, 1914) to the German trade-union leader, Carl Legien, he said, "In sadness, and yet in hope for the best I send fraternal greetings to you and your fellow trade unionists of Germany." [3]

In the autumn of 1914 the AF of L Executive Council announced through the October issue of the *American Federationist* that it was willing to assist or lead a movement for a negotiated peace:

The European war must not be permitted to become a war of extermination. Human lives are too precious to be sacrificed to passions of greed or revenge which might prolong the war indefinitely. Now is the time for the humanitarian, peace-loving men of the United States to inaugurate a movement that shall be able to do constructive work for peace and civilization at the first opportunity.

The Executive Council of the American Federation of Labor holds itself in readiness either to initiate a movement for peace at the opportune time or to assist in any effort to bring the terrible war to a close. Work along this line is already in progress. The working people of America will do all in their power to protect their fellow workers of all nationalities.[4]

A year later the Federation was still somewhat receptive to the opportunity to effect peace between the countries at war. Gompers wrote to W. S. Appleton, secretary of the General Federation of Trade Unions in Great Britain: "It is possible that the American government may be in the best position at the appropriate time to act as the mediator between the countries now at war, and of course in that effort the American Federation of Labor will put forth its best efforts." [5]

At its 1915 convention, the AF of L Executive Council urged that strict neutrality be maintained by the American government in the war. The statement was made, "After all, deep down in the hearts of all real trade unionists lies that fraternal spirit and world-wide brotherly love, genuine sympathy, and kindly regard, for the welfare of our fellow workers, regardless of place and of nationality." [6]

But other evidence was not lacking that Gompers' pacifism was seriously waning. For one thing, he refused to send any trade-union delegates to a Conference of the Emergency Federation of Peace Forces, in Washington D.C., January 10, 1915, under the chairmanship of the prominent social worker, Jane Addams. Further, he remained aloof from Labor Peace Councils that were formed in several large cities, and, as he writes in his autobiography, visited many labor men who had been attracted to these Councils and "explained to them what was involved in the situation and induced practically all of them to sever relations with these Peace Councils." [7] When the Labor Peace Councils and several Irish and German national organizations were preparing for a national conference in Chicago in September, 1915, he made use of his office to warn the trade-union movement not to allow itself to be used by German and Socialist propagandists. At the 1915 AF of L convention Gompers also successfully opposed a resolution which not only protested against the introduction of military propaganda in the public schools but also urged workers not to join the armed forces.

About the time when Gompers made his first public preparedness speech, in January, 1916, before the annual meeting of the National Civic Federation, he was being approached by various people representing the Allies and those interested in an allied victory. Some of these people included the two British labor emissaries, James Seddon and Albert Bellamy, his friend and secretary of the National Civic Federation, Ralph M. Easley, Herbert Hoover, and President Woodrow Wilson. He was also visited by representatives of the House of Morgan and House of Rothschild, who like the other-mentioned visitors sought to persuade him of the righteousness of the Allied cause and urged him to use his influence to prepare American labor sentiment for the eventual declaration of war. Some of these visitors shrewdly exploited Gompers' well-known narcissism and anti-Socialist bias to ingratiate themselves with him and gain his support for their mission.

By 1916 it was apparent that Gompers' addresses were of a different nature than earlier ones. Either he was bewildered and not fully convinced within himself of the position he should follow on this subject, or, in opportunistic fashion, his periodic declarations were tempered by the type of audience. To the National Civic Federation, in January, 1916, he declared: "Men worthy of the name will fight for a scrap of paper when that paper represents ideals of justice and freedom." [8] But in Washington, D.C. on May 26, 1916, before the League to Enforce Peace, Gompers announced: "No class renders such sacrificial service during war as does labor. In war labor sees the results of years of struggle for wider justice swept away." [9] In October, 1916, he confessed to the Wilson Eight-Hour League: "I was willing to go to the limit to stop war or prevent war. But when I found that the people responded to their colors, whether for Kaiser, Czar, president or king, I made up my mind that I had been living in a fool's paradise, and that after all it is necessary for men to be prepared to defend themselves." [10] Like many people, Gompers—finding it increasingly difficult to maintain an unpopular opinion—rationalized his new position as insight and growth on his part.

The completion of his conversion from pacifism to military preparedness came when he accepted an appointment by Wilson in October, 1916, as labor's representative to an advisory commission of a council of national defense, and became chairman of a labor committee established under this commission to advise the government upon labor policies. Not long afterwards he assured his friend, Speaker of the House Champ Clark, that the workers could be counted on to not "fail in the performance of duty and to give service for the safety, integrity and the ideals of our country." [11] To gain support for his involvement with business leaders in the defense program and to back up his promises to government leaders of labor's wartime support to the government, Gompers explained to the AF of L Executive Council on February 28, 1917, that if the union movement wanted better treatment from the government, it must support the national preparedness program. He argued that war was imminent and therefore defense plans were going to be adopted. The question was, in his opinion, would labor partake in the formulation of these plans or would it sit back and let these plans be drawn by people "out of sympathy with the needs and ideals of the workers." [12]

Following Gompers' advice, the Executive Council issued a call for a conference of the representatives of affiliated unions with a membership slightly over two million. The purpose of the conference was to promulgate labor's position toward the defense emergency. For three days before the conference convened, the Executive Council met and prepared a statement for the conference containing labor's position on the war situation. On March 12, some 148 representatives of seventy-nine affiliated unions, representatives of four unaffiliated unions, the National Window Glass Workers, and five departments of the AF of L presented themselves for the conference. Important AF of L international unions that sent no representatives were the International Ladies Garment Workers, The Mine, Mill and Smelter Workers, the Typographical Union, The Journeymen Barbers, the Cloth, Hat and

Cap Makers, the Steam Engineers Union, the Papermakers Brotherhood, the Photo Engravers, the Pulp, Sulphite and Paper Mill Workers, the Railway Carmen Brotherhood, and the Theatrical Stage Employees Alliance.

For one day delegates debated the declaration which the Executive Council had prepared for them and finally, without a dissenting vote, adopted it exactly as it had been submitted to them. The declaration requested the government to recognize the trade-union movement as the representative of organized as well as unorganized workers and to grant labor representation on national defense boards. The government was asked to limit employers' profits, to observe trade-union standards in all defense work, and to accept the principle that women receive equal pay for equal work. The declaration concluded with a patriotic pledge:

> But, despite all our endeavors and hopes, should our country be drawn into the maelstrom of the European conflict, we, with these ideals of liberty and justice herein declared, as the indispensable basis for national policies, offer our services to our country in every field of activity to defend, safeguard and preserve the Republic of the United States of America against its enemies whosoever they may be, and we call upon our fellow workers and fellow citizens in the holy name of Labor, Justice, Freedom and Humanity to devotedly and patriotically give like service.[13]

Undoubtedly the United States government and business leaders had some apprehension over the support that labor would extend in the event of war. It was known that many Americans of Irish or German extraction were anti-English or pro-German or doggedly neutral. Both these nationalities were important blocs in rank-and-file numerical strength as well as in leadership position in the AF of L. In addition, a sizable section of the Socialist element within the AF of L and most of the membership of the IWW held outspokenly antiwar views.[14] Thus the AF of L's assurance of co-operation with the government, as announced in the March 12, 1917, declaration, reassured government and business leaders at a critical time when war was almost imminent. The prestige of Gompers, who in their eyes had successfully manipulated the passage of labor's declaration of loyalty, was considerably increased—a fact which gave great pleasure to the AF of L leader who throve on social approval.

On April 6, 1917, Congress declared that a state of war existed between the United States and the German governments, and in a fortnight's time was debating the merits of the conscription of men for military service as against the method of voluntary enlistment. Consistent with its tradition of opposition to laws resting on compulsion by the State, the AF of L Legislative Committee appeared before the House and Senate Military Affairs Committees and opposed the passage of a military conscription bill. The Congressional Military Committees also received communications from Gompers stating that the AF of L favored the voluntary principle to that of compulsion. But in the latter part of May, when conscription was enacted, the AF of L at its 1917 convention "accepted the action taken by Congress as necessary in carrying out the purposes for which this country had entered the war." [15] The AF of L officials felt better when they secured the War Department's approval for a representative of wage-earners on the five-man District Exemption Boards which had appellate jurisdiction over all exemption cases and direct jurisdiction of all industrial conscription cases.

A number of the Federation's officers and international union officers were also appointed to some of the newly created government boards dealing with wartime problems. The year 1917 saw labor members placed on the Emergency Construction Board, the Fuel Administration, the Special Committee on War Savings Certificates, the Women's Board, the Food Administration Board, and the War Industries Board. A frequent visitor to the White House during this war period, Gompers complained to Wilson, however, that labor felt it was entitled to further representation on boards than it was securing.

Gompers recognized that AF of L leadership which had traditionally opposed government interference in economic matters was now co-operating with government in such matters. He condoned this reversal of thought and practice because of the exigencies of war. One thing was paramount—the winning of the war—and to this end peacetime concepts of voluntarism could be abandoned. Such a patriotic view he considered was also in accord with the wishes of labor's rank and file. "American workers," he declared, "felt that the War was their war." They did not see it, like the Socialists and the IWW did, as a capitalist war. AF of L trade-unionists, "have never felt that their identification with organized labor has built up any class lines that separate them from other groups of citizens. Organized labor realized that the most valuable service it could contribute to winning the War was to help maintain and raise production levels." [16]

As Chairman of the Labor Committee to the Council of National Defense, Gompers invited a group of trade-union officers, businessmen, financiers, technicians, and publicists to aid him. Subcommittees were organized on Wages and Hours, Mediation and Conciliation, Women in Industry, Information and Statistics, Press, Publicity, Cost of Living and Domestic Economy, Industrial Safety, Sanitation, Vocational Education, Housing, Recreation, Public Education in Health Matters, and Standard Guides for Employers. To benefit from the experience and advice of workers in Allied countries who had already been confronted with these same problems, the Federation leader cabled Prime Minister George of Great Britain, Premier Ribot of France, and Prime Minister King of Canada asking them to send representative labor men to counsel his committee. Great Britain and Canada were able to comply with this request and sent trade-union representatives who informed the Committee on Labor of their governments' experiences in meeting wartime labor problems.

The work of the Committee on Labor had mixed results. It drew attention to the need for increased compensational and government insurance for military personnel. A bill of this nature drawn up by the Committee was approved by the Council of National Defense and by President Wilson and became law. The inadequacy of housing for workers in war production was also disclosed by the Committee, and the information secured on this subject was supplied to the Housing Corporation of the Department of Labor.

On the maintenance of union standards and collective agreements with the government covering war production, the Federation leader had his greatest difficulty. In April, 1917, the Council of National Defense, upon Gompers' recommendation, declared that employer and employee were to continue to observe existing standards rather than seek new agreements. This produced a decided hardship on workers, since the cost of living was rising daily. The Council of National Defense declared that labor was justified in seeking to maintain its standard of living but would not be justified in striking to gain union recognition. For the adjustment of labor disputes, Gompers presented a plan to the Defense Council which proposed a national board of adjustment, an eight-hour day as the standard for all war production work, and a wage standard based on the wage level established by the trade-unions in the area of the dispute. But the Defense Council considered these proposals too favorable to labor and consequently rejected them. The AF of L president was more successful in concluding agreements in the summer and autumn of 1917 with the War and Navy departments establishing Adjustment Boards and union scales of wages, hours, and conditions in force on June 1, 1917, in the locality in which work was being done.

During the summer and autumn of 1917 a number of strikes (mainly IWW led) occurred in the West. Alarmed because war production was being interrupted by the strikes, President Wilson appointed a Mediation Commission to investigate the causes of the strikes and to make recommendations for a government war labor policy. Acting, in part, upon the Commission's report of January 8, 1918, the President authorized Secretary of Labor William B. Wilson to assume charge over war labor problems. The Labor Secretary shortly announced a plan for founding a conference board to prepare a program for dealing with industrial relations affecting war production. This board, known as the War Labor Conference Board, consisted of five representatives of employers nominated by the National Industrial Conference Board, and five representatives of employees nominated by Gompers. Each of these nominated groups selected one representative of the public who served as chairman on alternate days.

On March 29, 1918, the War Labor Conference Board issued its recommendations to the Secretary of Labor. The Board suggested the creation of a National War Labor Board similar in number and nominated in the same way as itself. Its primary function would be to mediate industrial disputes so production would continue uninterrupted. The main principle governing its arbitration function was: "There should be no strikes or lockouts during the war." To facilitate acceptance of this principle the following points were agreed upon. Workers were to have the right to organize trade-unions and bargain collectively through their representatives. Employers were neither to discharge workers for membership in trade-unions, "nor for legitimate trade union activities"; but the workers were neither to use "coercive measures of any kind to induce persons to join their organization, nor to induce employers to bargain or deal therewith." Where labor had unionized an establishment "the same shall continue" and the union standards maintained.[17] The government, however, would not provide automatically for the closed shop where it did not exist. In establishments where both union and nonunion workers were employed, and where the employer's policy was to refuse to meet with union representatives not in his employment, the continuance of such a condition would not be considered a grievance. As later events showed, the latter provision led many employers to establish company unions.

The other principles enumerated in the War Labor Conference Board's recommendation included equal pay for equal work for women; the application of the basic eight-hour day wherever existing law required it; the discouragement of "methods of work and operation on the part of employers or workers which operate to delay or limit production" or artificially increase production costs, and the right of all workers to a "living wage." [18] In a letter to the members of the AF of L Executive Council on March 29, 1918, Gompers referred to these recommendations as a "wonderful achievement." [19]

On April 8, 1918, President Wilson announced the establishment of the War Labor Board and the government's support of the principles recommended to govern the permanent body. He reappointed the members of the Conference Board to the new Labor Board and he urged employers and employees to make use of this new board.

A centralized arbitration board and a policy for arbitration had been created in the War Labor Board. This board had jurisdiction in all cases of war production not served by previously established arbitration agencies as well as appellate jurisdiction over these existing agencies. Although no penalties were provided to compel acceptance of the board's principles, its authority was usually accepted since many war contracts had clauses compelling submission of disputes and obedience to decisions. Agreements on union recognition also often included similar clauses.

The AF of L officials accepted the no-strike policy as enunciated in the principles of the War Labor Board because they believed the principles had strengthened labor's position in other ways. Labor had secured acknowledgement of the rights of workers to organize into trade-unions and to bargain collectively, and had obtained a declaration against lockouts and against the discharge of workers for union activity. The recognition by government and industry of these long-sought-for labor principles marked the greatest advance unionism had made so far in gaining acceptance on the American scene. Functioning under these principles the AF of L conducted organizing drives in many defense industries, and was successful except in the steel industry. While the AF of L hoped that a new era of labor-management relations was beginning, the postwar period and the return to normalcy showed that labor's war time gains had not secured deep enough acceptance. The New Deal era under another Democrat, Franklin D. Roosevelt, saw the resurrection of labor's World War I rights— the right to organize and the right to bargain collectively.

The IWW and many Socialist trade-unionists bitterly maintained that the no-strike policy agreed to by the AF of L leadership during World War I constituted a complete departure from fundamental trade-union principles. This criticism became the standard interpretation of extreme left wing groups and later of the American Communist party who alleged that the AF of L leaders were more interested in personal advancement than in protecting workers' interests. But Gompers wrote in the *American Federationist* of August, 1918, that labor's policy of co-operation was the result of "broad-minded leadership in the various trade organizations, and loyal, clear-thinking on the part of all workers" who realized "at least during the war, that labor's interests and welfare are a part of that larger problem represented" in the establishment of "world democracy and human freedom." [20] To the workers directly, the AF of L president had counselled in the May issue of the Federation journal that "No strike ought to be inaugurated that cannot be justified to the men facing momentary death" on the battlefields.[21] Gompers' seriousness on this score is apparent from a personal letter to William Hutcheson, president

of the Carpenters, on April 2, 1918, in which he sought to persuade the carpenters' leader to have a number of shipyard strikes
called off.[22]

The report of the Executive Council to the 1918 convention
also urged the members to avoid strikes which would interrupt the
war production effort. The report stated:

> The workers in the war production industries are practically
> a part of the fighting force, the Army and Navy. They cannot
> stop work without interfering with the whole program. The
> whole campaign from production to where munitions are used
> in the field must be so precise, so well articulated, that nothing
> shall interfere with any forward movement if we are to check
> and defeat the best organized war machine the world has ever
> seen. No action should be taken in the shops or on the field
> not in harmony with the purposes of the war.
>
> .   .   .   .
>
> Organized labor, true to its traditions, had proffered its full
> and comprehensive support to the Commander-in-Chief, and
> it will not now be paralyzed by infirmity of purpose or action.
> . . . We advise the organized labor movement that in this
> crisis it must prove its loyalty to our Republic and to our
> fellowmen, and demonstrate its capacity to deal with big prob-
> lems and big needs in a constructive manner.
>
> .   .   .   .
>
> . . . No strike should be inaugurated which cannot be justified
> to the man risking his life on the firing line.[23]

Declarations such as these left no doubt that the Federation
leadership was doing its utmost to convince its members to give
their complete support to the government's war effort. The same
Gompers, who for decades had voiced an extreme suspicion of
government, now regularly declared that the war aims of the
American government converted this war into a crusade for world
democracy and human freedom. The former pacifist announced
to a London trade-union audience in September, 1918, "If ever
there was a war in which the vital interests and the rights of the

masses of the people of our democratic countries were involved, this is the war." [24]

A number of groups and individuals connected with the labor movement did not share the prowar views of the Federation leadership. Within the ranks of organized labor, opposition or indifference to the war existed, particularly among the IWW, the left wing Socialists, some German-American and Irish-American workers, and among some Russian-Jewish workers attracted by the Russian Revolution and its peace proposals. On May 30, 1917, representatives of these groups met in New York City in the First American Conference for Democracy and Terms of Peace. After endorsing the peace terms of the Russian Revolution, the defense of civil liberties, and the maintenance of living standards, and hearing denunciations of the AF of L for its support of the war, the Conference proposed the establishment of a permanent national People's Council. After the conference, branch organizations, known as local Workmen's Councils, were created preliminary to the calling of a constituent convention on September 1, 1917, which was to mark the beginning of a national organization. By the end of June, the People's Council claimed that 284 organizations were affiliated with it and of these almost a hundred were trade-unions, while the rest were local Socialist, peace, and fraternal organizations.

Gompers grew steadily alarmed over the origin and development of the antiwar, anti-AF of L, People's Council. The New York Workmen's Council, an especially active branch of the People's Council which had the support of a few trade-union organizations in its area, particularly antagonized the AF of L leader by announcing that workers should look to the Council for the protection of their interests during the war. Gompers interpreted this statement as a rebuke to his leadership and his policy of co-operation with the government. Therefore he held several conferences with the Central Federated Trade Union of New York City and with a number of Socialist party members who were displeased with the official antiwar position adopted by their party. The results of these conferences led to the formation of the American Alliance for Labor and Democracy in New York City on August 16, 1917.

A loyalty pledge to support the United States government was adopted as a declaration of one of the purposes of the American Alliance for Labor and Democracy. Gompers' next move was to present the Americanization and loyalty objectives of the Alliance to the Council of National Defense, and to George Creel, head of the Committee on Public Information. As a result, the Alliance gained the government's official approval and secured funds for its operation from the Creel Committee. At its outset the work of the Alliance was limited to New York City, but as the activities of the People's Council spread to many parts of the country, the Alliance decided to counteract this situation by extending its coverage nationwide. The Alliance's routine function was to increase working-class enthusiasm for the war. Therefore it specialized in such publicity work as serving the labor and left wing press with loyalty material and organizing public meetings to hear loyalty addresses by its own members, by distinguished Americans, or by visiting representatives from Allied nations.

Since the first national convention of the People's Council was to be held September 1, 1917, at Minneapolis, the AF of L leader saw the opportunity to publicize the difference between the two organizations by having the Alliance convene nationally at the same time and in the same city. Organizers of the AF of L were notified by Gompers to give their full energy to making certain that labor men and unions would be strongly represented at the Alliance Conference. A little more than half of the 170 delegates who attended were trade-unionists, while the remainder were prowar Socialists, or represented various types of patriotically animated social reformers.

In essence, the declarations adopted at the Alliance Conference pledged support to the United States government and its allies until complete military victory was gained. The Conference delegates resolved that anyone who publicly disagreed with this view was taking undue advantage of civil liberties and "should be repressed by the constituted authorities." [25] Loyalty to the government, however, did not preclude the right to agitate for reform. Necessary reforms as enumerated at the Conference were the conscription of wealth, the right of the workers to bargain collectively, labor representation on important government war agencies, universal suffrage for women, and government action against speculative interests raising living costs. In separate declarations relating to international affairs, the Conference pledged its support to the democratic leaders of the new Russian government, condemned the Russian Bolsheviks, approved President Wilson's avowal of self-determination for small nationalities, requested labor representation on postwar peace commissions and urged upon President Wilson "and the international congress which will negotiate terms of peace, the legitimate claims of the Jewish people for the reestablishment of a national homeland in Palestine on a basis of self-government." [26]

Following the Minneapolis conference, a number of local Alliances were organized by affiliated bodies of the AF of L, but progress was limited by internal dissension between the trade-unionists and the leftist intellectuals. The former were interested in trade-union objectives, the control of war profiteering, the Americanization and loyalty of the workers, and opposition to bolshevism. On the other hand, the intellectuals were concerned with traditional left wing political legislation, the formulation of a political program for the reconstruction period, and the establishment of a new progressive political party.

The growing disparity between the AF of L and the pro-war Socialists on the principles of the Alliance was evident at the AF of L 1917 convention. Gompers and the Executive Council's request that full endorsement be given to the American Alliance for Peace and Democracy produced a lengthy debate. The opposition to such approval mainly came from Socialists who complained that the workers were being exploited in the name of patriotism, that free speech was being unwarrantly suppressed, and that business was making exorbitant profits from the war. As one critic of the Alliance put it, "the real patriot, when he performs a patriotic deed or act, does not parade his patriotism in the newspapers." [27] The great majority of the delegates, however, agreed with the Alliance's purposes and efforts. Flattered also because they had been addressed by President Wilson—the first time in the AF of L's history that they had received this recognition from an American President—the delegates' patriotism was at a high ebb and they approved the work of the Alliance by an overwhelming vote. In fact, their emotional fervor was so great that a resolution was easily passed favoring the induction of allied aliens (including workers) into the armed forces or their deportation. The delegates' patriotism carried over into the next AF of L convention when they endorsed the extremely severe Espionage Act (June, 1917) and Sedition Act (May, 1918).

Until early in 1919 the Alliance continued to operate, although it found it increasingly difficult to obtain adequate funds from the Creel Committee. Probably its most notable single accomplishment was the staging in 1918 of a country-wide labor loyalty program during the week of George Washington's birthday. The Alliance, through Gompers, arranged for four British Labor representatives to tour the industrial centers of the United States. The main purpose of this tour was for American workers to learn of British labor's thought and purpose in regard to the war and to the problems produced by the war. Knowing that segments of British Labor were showing signs of war weariness, Gompers cabled George Barnes, Labor Minister in the British War Cabinet, to send a "small group of true British trade unionists." [28] What the AF of L president apparently meant by "true British trade unionists" were anti-Socialists and ones against a negotiated peace. Critics of Gompers alleged that the men who were chosen such as W. A. Appleton, conservative president of the British General Federation of Trade Unions, were unrepresentative of a British trade-union movement which was leaning more to the left. These particular British union leaders were accused of being incapable of creating American understanding and sympathy for the latest developments in the British Labor movement. Gompers, however, telegrammed Appleton in early January, 1918, expressing his pleasure that "representative British Labor men" had been chosen for the trip.[29]

When the United States entered the war in 1917, the AF of L leadership was enthusiastically patriotic while many of the labor leaders of the Allied countries at war were understandably weary of the sacrifices and burdens of three years of fighting. The war weariness of some European trade-union leaders was intensified by their Socialist analysis of the imperialistic nature of the struggle. To this attitude the first Russian Revolution and its ensuing peace proposals inspired many of these labor leaders with hopes of an early peace. To the AF of L officers, however, such hopes were seen as impractical and as German propaganda. Gompers continuously asserted that while the German army remained undefeated in the field, any peace proposals launched by international labor conferences were merely German-created tactics to weaken Allied fighting spirit.

The peace proposals that began to reach the AF of L president after America's entry into the war evoked his opposition, not his encouragement. The first of these proposals was contained in a letter from Karl Durr, Secretary of the Schweiz Gewerkschafts-bund. It stated that the French trade-unions had indicated willingness to participate in a conference to be convened by the Schweizerisch Gewerkschaftsbund of the International Federation of Trade Unions, at Berne, on September 17, 1917. The purpose of the conference would be to consider the continuance and domicile of the International Federation of Trade Unions, the publication of the IFTU's *Weekly News Service,* and the labor measures for the peace treaty suggested by Allied labor representatives at the Leeds conference of July, 1916.[30] No reply to Durr's invitation was published in the Federation journal, but at the following AF of L convention in 1917 Gompers criticized the Leeds proposals for advocating the enactment of comprehensive state social legislation. He said it was "inexpedient, so far as our country is concerned, to have these subjects included in the terms of an international peace treaty." [31]

Throughout the war Gompers maintained a steady correspondence with W. A. Appleton, president of the British General Federation of Trade Unions, and co-operated with that organization much more on matters relative to international conferences than he did with leaders of the British Trade Union Congress. Yet, the British GFTU never represented more than 30 per cent of British trade-unionism. Writing of this war period in his autobiography Gompers expressed his friendship for Appleton "in whose integrity" he said he had "implicit confidence and in whose mind he had found most gratifying congeniality." [32] These two federation presidents were drawn together by their agreement on pure and simple unionism, their hostility toward Socialists and socialism and their disapproval of a negotiated peace with Germany.

When Appleton informed Gompers that the British General Federation of Trade Unions would aid in the arrangement of a conference of allied trade-unions affiliated to the International Federation of Trade Unions for September 10, 1917, in London, the AF of L Executive Council authorized its fraternal delegates to the British Trade Union Congress to also represent the AF of L at the London Conference. At the Conference, the AF of L delegates agreed with President Appleton's opening address opposing any international labor conferences which intended to include the Central Powers. A previous invitation from the British Labor Party through its secretary, Arthur Henderson, to attend an international conference of allied labor and Socialist parties in August, 1917, had been rejected by AF of L leaders. The expected presence of the American Socialist party, the lack of representation of the British General Federation of Trade Unions, and the negotiated peace aspirations of Henderson made this conference unacceptable to Gompers.

The AF of L's sweeping antagonism to any international Socialist peace movement was reflected in Gompers' action to one arranged for Stockholm, August, 1917, by the International Socialist Bureau, a Dutch-Scandinavian Socialist Committee, and the Petrograd Soviet. He cabled the Petrograd Workmen's and Soldiers' Council of Deputies on May 6, 1917, that they should disregard the movements for peace because these were in the interest of the Kaiser. Two days after sending this cable, the AF of L president released similar cables to the French Confederation of Labor, the French Socialist Party, and the British Labor Party. He informed these groups that

As you know the most insidious influences are at work not only to create a pro-Kaiser propaganda but also to divide and alienate from one another the nations and people fighting for the freedom and democracy of the world. It is your duty as it is the duty of all to impress upon all labor organizations of European neutral countries the truth about the pretended international socialist congress called to be held at Stockholm. It should be emphasized that it does not represent the working class of America, England, France or Belgium, but was called by the German socialists and certain other notoriously pro-German agitators in other countries either to bring about a Kaiser-dictated peace under the deceptive catch-phrase 'no annexations, no indemnities,' or in the hope of deceiving the Russian Socialists into betraying the great western democracies into consenting to a separate peace.[33]

Throughout the spring and summer of 1917, the Federation refused many invitations to attend international trade-union conferences in Europe for the purpose of discussing the claims that trade-unions should make at the future peace negotiations. The AF of L convention of November, 1917, upheld the attitude and actions of the AF of L leadership concerning the international invitations which had been received, and the convention agreed that labor should not call a peace conference because such a responsibility belonged to the government. A labor peace conference, it was claimed, would undoubtedly make the mistake of declaring particular peace terms which might, at a later date, bind the government's terms.

In an address before a Canadian Victory Loan Rally in Toronto, November, 1917, Gompers again reiterated his disapproval of an international conference to discuss peace terms. Once more he alleged that "when these invitations to international conferences were sent out from Petrograd or Stockholm or Berne, they were already more or less tainted with German militarist sympathies." [34]

In an early January, 1918, cable to his British friend W. A. Appleton, Gompers reminded Appleton that the AF of L would not attend any international conference which included delegates from Germany. The message stated that before the AF of L appeared at a conference, it first desired to see German autocracy and militarism overthrown either by the German people or by the Allied armies.[35]

It is equally clear, however, that the Gompers' hostility toward socialism made the conference invitations from Socialist leaders or organizations even more objectionable for him. In fact his anti-Socialist feelings sometimes made his remarks quite extreme and contrary to historical data. Speaking before the Canadian House of Commons on April 27, 1918, he argued that the Socialists of Germany had been in league with the imperialist and war ambitions of the German government. Ignoring the antiwar position of Karl Liebnecht and other German Socialist leaders and their actual imprisonment at this time for their opposition to the war, Gompers stated, "There is no question but what there was understanding between the Socialist political leaders of Germany and the German Imperial Government to carry out its policies." But he himself, he claimed, "never was fooled by the sophistry and pretenses of the socialists. As a matter of fact, there is not in England, France nor America a Socialist party of these countries. In America we have a German branch of the German Socialist Party. . . . The Americans have left the party since the perfidy of the Socialist Party in the United States, when it revealed its true colors, when it showed itself to be a German agency in the United States." [36] Again the truth was somewhat different than Gompers' remarks for many Socialists of distinct American nationality like Eugene Debs, Norman Thomas, John Reed, Algernon Lee, Scott Nearing, Kate Richards O'Hare, Max Eastman, Roger N. Baldwin, H. W. L. Dana, and Floyd Dell were against the war and supported the Socialist party's opposition to the war. German-American members of the Socialist party were a small number in 1918, for the total membership figure of all foreign federations in the Socialist party in 1918 was 25,000 out of 81,000 party members.

In his autobiography, Gompers recorded his increasing anxiety because "the executives of the Labor Party and the British Trade Union Congress under the leadership of Henderson were advocating the Stockholm idea." The AF of L's nationalism and lack of class consciousness made it impossible for it to assimilate what Gompers termed, "British Labor's 'liberal' concept of international relations." Gompers classified this concept as a move to "connive with wage-earners of other countries to forge a club against our own republic." International working class unity, he felt, was not "characteristic of the individualism of America expressed in genuine absence of class stratification" where "financiers, industrialists, farmers, wage-earners, and every group were solidly behind the president" and where "allegiance to the government took precedence over all other relations." [37]

Nine prominent representatives of the AF of L in March, 1918, proceeded to England and France to present the AF of L position on war policies, aims, and peace conditions. Their primary purpose was to make known that the American trade-union movement opposed any conference with German representatives while Prussian militarism remained intact and her armies in Allied lands. The AF of L representatives hoped to head off a growing British Socialist peace movement, evident in the adoption of "War

Aims" on September 28, 1917, by British Labor, in the work of the British Labor Party's Conference at Nottingham, in January, 1918, and of the Inter-Allied Labor and Socialist conference in London in February, 1918.

AF of L fears of a Socialist-inspired negotiated peace continued to grow during the spring of 1918 and provoked the organization to further efforts against this possibility. Gompers decided to challenge the Socialist peace drive in England and France by personally visiting these countries. His objective, as stated by the official AF of L history book, was to drive "into the hearts of the war-ridden people of France, Italy and Great Britain that there were no 'quitters' in America and that a peace by agreement would be considered a defeat." [38]

On this European tour Gompers addressed the delegates of the British Trade Union Congress, and told them that American labor would be unwilling to shorten the war "one hour if it meant that the German military machine remained unbroken." [39] Later, at a joint conference of the Parliamentary Committee and the Executive Committee of the Labor party, in reply to Henderson's announcement that the French Labor and Socialist bodies regretted that the Socialist Party of America had not been invited to the forthcoming Allied Labor and Socialist Conference, Gompers answered, "There was no such thing as an American Socialist Party but a German adjunct in America of the German Socialist Party." [40]

The AF of L delegates were displeased by the influence of European Socialist representatives at the Allied Labor and Socialist Conference. At one point Gompers insisted that John Frey, secretary of the Conference's War Aims Committee and an AF of L leader, write and read his committee's report instead of its being done by Sidney Webb, the Committee's chairman and British Socialist. The Conference confirmed Gompers in his opinion that the workers in the European labor movement were "at the mercy of the intellectuals who had largely seized and dominated the movement." [41] To the delegates he said:

> Socialism holds nothing but unhappiness for the human race. It destroys personal initiative, wipes out national pride—the hearthstone of a people's culture—and finally it plays into the

hands of the autocrats. One had only to watch its ravages on the human soul—the soul without a country—to know that Socialism is the fad of fanatics, the sophistry of so-called intelligentsia, and it has no place in the hearts of those who would secure and fight for freedom and preserve democracy.[42]

Gompers states in his autobiography that he gave the delegates the following advice: "Socialists, the world over are of the same mental calibre—there is only one way to deal with them—don't argue, just tell them." [43]

The AF of L delegation approved the report of the Conference's War Aims Committee which supported the text of Wilson's fourteen points, labor representation at the peace conference and the inclusion of industrial standards in the peace treaty. However, the AF of L delegation opposed a resolution recommending a labor conference of all warring countries and instead offered an unsuccessful amendment for a meeting only with enemy people in revolt against their governments. The American labor leaders also did not support a resolution criticizing governments that withheld passports of labor people wishing to attend a peace conference.

Following the conference and several receptions, the AF of L group visited France and Italy where they transmitted their anti-Socialist peace ideas to workers, trade-union officers, and government leaders. Back again in the United States, Gompers told an American Alliance for Labor and Democracy audience which had gathered in Chicago to honor the AF of L's labor mission that his group had impressed upon all whom they had met the need for continuing the war until German militarism was beaten. He noted that in all the Allied countries they had visited they had been met by the opposition of the Socialists. He concluded that the trouble with the European labor movement was that it "is usually dominated by some professor, some failure in public life," who in molding it to his theories, "usually poisoned it." [44] The more the delegation had seen of Europe the more they were convinced that in all matters, government and trade-union, "America is the apotheosis of all that is right." [45]

Gompers at the Inter-Allied Conference in September, 1918, had been appointed to a committee to plan a world labor conference to be held at the same time and place as the peace treaty would be written. Although Gompers at first accepted the appointment, he later decided against participating in the conference when it was called by Henderson. Apparently it looked to him too much like a Socialist gathering. Moreover, he did not wish to meet with labor men from enemy countries until the representatives of these enemy countries had signed the peace treaties.

A request was made by Jan Oudegeest, the acting chairman of the IFTU, on October 20, 1918, for the AF of L to appoint delegates to an international trade-union conference, to be held while the peace treaty was being prepared. The purpose of the trade-union conference would be to consider the peace program of the Leeds and Berne Conferences and to reorganize the International Federation of Trade Unions. The AF of L rejected this invitation. The AF of L Executive Council maintained that several recent AF of L conventions had instructed it to convene such a conference, and, furthermore, the AF of L was opposed to both the Leeds and Berne peace programs as being too lenient to Germany. In January, 1919, Gompers sailed for Europe with the intent of convening an Inter-Allied Labor Conference before some European Socialist leadership took the initiative. The AF of L leader, however, was unable to secure the support of any country other than Belgium for the conference.

Gompers was bitterly disappointed when Wilson did not appoint him to the American Peace Commission in Paris in 1919, but this disappointment was somewhat softened when he was appointed to represent the United States on the International Labor Legislation Commission that drafted the labor clauses of the peace treaty. The report of the Commission, Part XIII of the Versailles Treaty, provided for the creation and operation of an International Labor Organization with two component parts—an International Labor Office and an Annual International Conference. A Bill of Rights for Labor was largely modelled on the labor peace terms relating to trade-unionists, as approved by the 1917 AF of L convention and the September, 1918, Inter-Allied Labor Conference in London.

At the meeting of the International Labor Commission, Gompers was elected chairman; writing of this experience in his autobiography, Gompers said that he had to continuously oppose the "Old World" desire of "dealing with labor problems through legislation" and of developing "a super-government that would develop standards for the workers everywhere." [46] He wanted labor problems met by the economic power of unionism and he also "was not in favor of giving an international labor bureau mandatory powers." [47]

In August, 1919, Gompers, and AF of L leaders Daniel Tobin and John Haynes, attended the International Trade Union Conference at Amsterdam which was to re-establish the International Federation of Trade Unions. Gompers as a supporter of the Versailles Treaty had many arguments at the conference with the German delegates who he demanded should admit Germany was guilty for the outbreak of the war. As customary, he was also at odds with the Socialist trade-unionists who were dissatisfied with the conservative provisions of the labor charter in the Versailles Treaty. The Socialist strength in the IFTU worried Gompers but the election of W. A. Appleton of England as president of the new International lessened the AF of L leader's anxiety. However, the Socialist influence in the IFTU which showed itself to be stronger than the conservative influence of the AF of L, eventually accounted for the AF of L's withdrawal from the organization in 1921.

In addition to the AF of L's hostility to socialism, the rise of communism after 1917 gave the Federation leaders a new foe to denounce. Shortly after the first Russian Revolution, Gompers' cable on April 2, 1917, to the Russian Duma revealed the beginning of fear which was to assume larger proportions in the succeeding months—the fear of the growth of communism. In his cable he advised that "it is impossibile to achieve the ideal state immediately for freedom cannot be established by revolution only—it is the product of evolution." [48] Many other cables were sent in an effort to influence the Russians to move moderately and to avoid the Communist type of government. As Gompers later wrote in his autobiography, "All our efforts to prevent the second Russian Revolution failed. . . . The Bolsheviki seized control. These pirates ran up the black flag over helpless Russia and declared war upon the established order about which the fabric of civilized life had been woven." [49] At the London Inter-Allied Labor and Socialist Conference in September, 1918, the AF of L delegation unsuccessfully proposed a resolution approving the Allied armed intervention in Russia.

The AF of L leadership, for years at odds with the Socialists, now saw new enemies—the Soviet Union, the Communist party, and the Communists. Gompers proclaimed that the AF of L was the greatest bulwark against communism. In a May Day speech in Boston in 1918 he declared: "If there had been a bona fide labor movement in Russia, something like the American Federation of Labor, you would never have had the Bolsheviki in Russia. If it had not been for the American Federation of Labor during the war, you would have had the Bolsheviki in the United States." [50]

While exaggerating the internal Communist menace in America had its value for the AF of L, there were a number of more imminent and realistic dangers facing the Federation in the immediate postwar years. The unity that had existed between capital and labor in order to fulfill the common war effort could not be expected to endure once the external threat to national survival had ended. The protection and consideration which the government had extended to trade-unionism during the war was a wartime expedient, not a permanent attitude. A steady increase also in the cost of living was going to work hardships in workers' families. Finally the hopes excited in the leftist elements within the Federation by the reconstruction program of the British Labor party and by the Russian Revolution would lead to increased agitation for a left wing AF of L program.

An AF of L Reconstruction Committee in late 1918 was given the task of drawing up a program to meet the problems the AF of L faced in the postwar world without basically changing the AF of L's political thought and practices. On December 28, 1918, the Committee rendered its report to the Executive Council which was meeting in New York City. The Council endorsed the report and recommended it for adoption to the following annual convention. At the convention, the Committee on the Report of the Executive Council advocated approval of the reconstruction report "not because of its idealism, but because of its practicability, not because of its novelty, but because it is founded on experience and justice." [51]

The Secretary of the Reconstruction Committee was Matthew Woll who in 1919 began a long tenure as AF of L vice-president lasting until his death in 1956. Woll, often labelled the "crown prince of the AF of L," was also a very dedicated leader in the Knights of Columbus.

American labor's Reconstruction Program, as adopted by the convention, spelled out the rights and proposals which the AF of L wanted the government and industry to concede to it. On matters directly affecting trade-unionism, the Federation called for the right to organize into trade-unions; a living wage; an eight-hour day; a further extension of workmen's compensation laws; equal pay for women; a child labor law; the right of public employees to organize and bargain collectively; a two-year suspension of immigration and its further restriction thereafter.

The remainder of the program called for the following:

(*1*) the right of farmers to co-operative efforts and of consumers to co-operative buying and selling

(*2*) government ownership, operation, or regulation of public utilities

(*3*) a graduated tax upon all usable land above the acreage cultivated by the owners

(*4*) low government interest rates for working people who desire to purchase land

(*5*) further government regulation of corporations; and also an increased graduated income and inheritance tax

(*6*) government financing and building of low cost homes for workers

(*7*) state subsidization of general education, and an extension of state colleges, and labor representation on all industrial education boards

(*8*) the reintroduction of freedom of speech, press, and assembly

(*9*) a constitutional amendment enabling the people or Congress to override court decisions declaring congressional acts unconstitutional

(*10*) avoidance by the government of militarism and large standing armies.

On the question of the political practice of labor, the Reconstruction Program declared that labor should participate in politics only for the purpose of seeking legislation covering conditions and provisions of life unobtainable through collective bargaining with employers. Political participation was to be conducted on the basis of the established "non-partisan political policy of the American Federation of Labor," the policy which within the framework of the two major political parties stood for electing those politicians who favored, and defeating those who opposed, the AF of L's legislative demands.

In contrast to the postwar reconstruction programs of workers' movements in other democratic lands, the AF of L program for its almost three million members was a limited one. The British Trade Union Congress, for example, was giving its support to the British Labor party, a party which formally labelled itself a Socialist party in 1918. The AF of L Reconstruction Program viewed, however, within the perspective of the meager political origins of the Federation, was a program that showed the AF of L was growing up— growing up slowly—but growing.

6.

American Federation of Labor

Social and Political Thought, 1900–1918

MR. HILLQUIT. Mr. Gompers, what I ask you is this: You say you try to make the conditions of the workers better every day. In order to determine whether the conditions are better or worse you must have some standards by which you distinguish the bad from the good in the labor movement, do you not?

MR. GOMPERS. Certainly. Well, is that . . .

MR. HILLQUIT (*interrupting*). Now just . . .

MR. GOMPERS (*interrupting*). Well, one moment. Does it require much discernment to know that a wage of $3 a day and a workday of 8 hours a day in sanitary workshops are all better than $2.50 a day and 12 hours a day and under perilous conditions of labor. It does not require much conception of a social philosophy to understand that.

FINAL REPORT AND TESTIMONY OF THE COMMISSION ON INDUSTRIAL RELATIONS.

THE moderate political position of the AF of L is as old as the organization itself. It began its existence in 1881 when the Federation of Organized Trades and Labor Unions, the AF of L's direct precursor, was born as the reaction of practical men to the unsuccessful idealistic-reform precepts of the Knights of Labor. In 1883 Adolph Strasser, president of the Cigarmakers' Union, close friend of Gompers, and one of the AF of L founders, while testifying before the Senate Committee on Education and Labor, replied in answer to a query on labor's long range goals, "We have no ultimate ends. We are going on from day to day. We are fighting for immediate objects—objects that can be realized in a few years." The Senator's further probing led Strasser to declare,

"We are opposed to theorists. . . . We are all practical men." [1]
This practical and materialistic outlook wove its way deeply into
the fabric of the AF of L, its affiliated unions, and their rank and
file. Not only was it expounded year in and year out at union meetings and conventions and in union newspapers and journals, not
only were the Socialist conceptions of "ultimates" constantly berated and held in derision but it was regularly practiced in day-to-
day activities, through the media, particularly, of trade agreements
with employers. The emphasis on pure and simple unionism and
the rejection of any political considerations which implied a reconstruction of social institutions were positive indications that the
capitalist system was accepted and that trade-unionism was simply
concerned with bettering the economic conditions of its own skilled
membership under that system.

The majority of men who led the international and local unions
affiliated with the AF of L were not men of social ideas, well read
or schooled. They were practical, unimaginative union leaders
who had risen from the workers' ranks and whose trade-union
philosophy was evolved from their everyday experience, not from
intellectualizing. They had the uneducated workers' cynicism toward politics and were especially hostile to left wing ideas because these ideas were often advanced by foreign-born workers
or American intellectuals, whose presence in the labor movement
they resented as threats to their own rule. A majority of the leaders
were Roman Catholics and mindful that their church was opposed
to revolutionary unionism and Socialist thought. They rationalized
their rise to power and the growth of skilled, craft unions as due
to facts which they, not left wing theorists, correctly understood.
The facts to these "Men of Power" were that in America personal
and social progress came from self-interest, not collective sacrifice,
from attention to materialism, not idealism, and from resort to
reforms, not revolution. From their limited grasp of the history
of organized labor in America they generalized that its involvement in politics had always been disastrous to its future. For the
most part they neither believed in nor were capable of inspiring
the imagination of the rank and file of the trade-unionists with
visions of a more moral society; neither did they seek to nor did
they have the faculty for penetrating the workers with theoretical
explanations of a more planned economic system. Their appeal

could only be a reflection of their own lives and standards: it was an appeal to self-advancement, in Carl Sandburg's phrase, to the "dictates of the belly." Truly, it was for "more, more, now," as they expressed it themselves.

The rank and file were not only susceptible to the philosophy of their leaders but were actually grateful for the practical leadership supplied and for the officers' willingness to look after all the dull but necessary routine tasks of building up and maintaining a union. Most workers were more than willing to trade "pie in the sky bye and bye" for some real and immediate material gains. In this striving for speedy material progress the worker's wage consciousness inevitably increased, as whatever class consciousness he may have had receded. It was difficult for the workers to feel any class consciousness when their cultural heritages, languages, social backgrounds, nationalities, religions, political affiliations and trade skills were often different. When, in addition, they saw that the social scale in America was not rigidly stratified, and then found that the wage gains they secured helped them to climb in this scale, their attachment to immediate gains increased.

The AF of L's economic philosophy of business unionism and its depreciation of politics was a pragmatic solution to the conditions and forces in American life. Its philosophy was an affirmation of the aspirations of its rank and file. Craft unionism and wage consciousness rested on a philosophy which was in accord with the individualist philosophy of the AF of L unionist, and this philosophy of both the Federation and its membership was an outgrowth of the dominant materialist American mores of money making and self-interest.

The Socialists within the AF of L took exception to the political policies of the organization, and were consistently the chief source of opposition encountered by the Gompers administration. On all fundamental political questions, they were at odds with the administration. Convention after convention resolved itself into clear cut battles between the AF of L leadership and the Socialist faction. Three Socialist proposals in particular were often the cause of constant argument. These were the following: the establishment of an independent political party, the approval of social legislation, and the cessation of affiliation of AF of L officers with the National Civic Federation.

The 1906 AF of L convention illustrated the recurring debates that took place on the question of a workers' political party. The Socialist element within the AF of L hoped to see the Federation's political action momentum which had begun in that year's Congressional elections accelerated further until it resulted in the creation of an independent labor party. Shortly before the convention began, Max Hayes, Socialist party national committeeman and leader in the AF of L International Typographical Union, wrote in the *International Socialist Review* of July, 1906, that "pure and simpledom has heard its death knell in the Federation, the bars are down and the political issues must be discussed, and the Socialists who have steadfastly fought in conventions in favor of political action have been vindicated. It is now up to the Socialists to make their principles known in the local unions, and then it won't take long to completely down reaction and fossilized conservatism." [2] But the AF of L leaders were convinced that their political campaign of 1906 was essentially correct in its philosophy and methods, and they did not want to see the organization become any more involved with politics in the future than it had in this past campaign. Therefore they were determined to thwart Socialist political ambitions for the AF of L. Gompers was quick to point out in his opening address at the convention that the Federation's 1906 political activities had not deviated from its traditional concept of regarding economic power as more important than political power. He exhorted the delegates to not establish any rule impairing economic power, for the ability of economic power to "accomplish tangible results" was unsurpassed.[3]

One week later the assembled delegates had the opportunity to show their attitudes on the question of labor and politics. The Committee on the President's Report endorsed the organization's 1906 political campaign and indicated its agreement with that part of Gompers' opening day address which stressed that labor wielded the most effective power through its economic power. Frank K. Foster, the chairman of the Committee, stated that, among the various resolutions received from the delegates, some asked the Committee to recommend AF of L participation in a labor party, while others asked the Committee to determine the most effective plan of political organization for the Federation. It was the Committee's opinion that the organization should not "indorse any

political party or any plan for the formation of a political party."
Political movements had proved they were ephemeral, they endangered the solidarity of the trade-union movement and "violated the minority right of the humblest man to vote where he
pleases." The Committee believed that the AF of L should "carry
on an aggressive educational campaign" to furnish the workers
with the records toward labor of candidates for political office. In
this way the workers would recognize the individuals and political
parties hostile to labor and would oppose them at the polls. The
political method followed by the AF of L in the recent campaign
was designated as the proper manner of political action for labor.[4]

The Committee's report inaugurated a lengthy debate which
basically resolved itself into the administration's supporters who
did not want to see the organization extend its political practice
any further than it had gone in the past campaign, and the Socialist-
minded delegates who wished to see a further increase in political
activity. The first speaker to oppose the Committee's report, delegate Lavine, declared that the AF of L's 1906 political efforts were
"a miserable failure compared with what could be done." Even
if a few men were to be elected who were friendly to labor they
would have little influence on their parties, since capitalist parties
could not function for labor's benefit. Working class legislation,
Lavine declared, could only originate from a working class party.
A labor party would unite all the workers, organized and unorganized, at the polls and gain them control of the government.[5]

Delegate Victor Berger, Socialist party national committeeman, who was elected to Congress from Wisconsin in 1910, also
spoke critically of political action within the framework of the
existing two parties. He charged that the AF of L's policy of applying pressure on the two parties was wasted effort because he
had "never known a Republican or Democrat who would not
promise anything before election, but they have never kept these
promises after election." [6]

William B. Wilson, prominent United Mine Worker, Democratic Congressman from Pennsylvania, and later Secretary of
Labor in Woodrow Wilson's first cabinet, took exception to Berger's remarks and hastened to inform the delegates that trade-
unionism had accomplished a great deal by the political pressure
it had applied upon the two nonlabor parties. As specific examples

of legislative gains made by labor, Wilson mentioned legislation that ended child labor in the mines, improved sanitation in industry, and provided for a better school system with free text books.

Another trade-unionist of Socialist convictions, delegate Finger, reminded the convention of the remarks of the visiting fraternal delegate from England, Mr. Bell, who had told the convention a few days before that the British trade-unions had found it possible to launch a successful political party of their own. Delegate Finger then gave his reasons for a labor party:

> . . . if we are going to continue the policy of each one voting for his own party . . . the result will be as it has been in the past. New York is now represented by a scab employer and other parts of the country are represented by scab employers. They entirely ignore us between elections, and merely consider us when the election is on. . . . I fail to see how any in the trade union movement can presume that my interests are identical with the interests of the great corporation lawyers who are elected year in and year out by the working class? . . . If we find that our trade union movement does not progress politically because of the men elected to office, I fail to see it from any other point of view than we have elected men who do not represent us and who apparently care naught about the votes of the workers. The reason we are organized into trade unions is because we recognize our interests as a class; and having recognized that we must subserve our interests as a class economically, does it not stand to reason that we must also recognize the fact that we must get our rights politically by organizing as a class. The time is ripe when we should cease this method of taking action individually.[7]

Andrew Furuseth, Seamen's leader and veteran AF of L lobbyist, sided with the AF of L administration in favor of the Committee's report. He rejected the idea of a labor party because, he said, the working class was not a majority party. Labor could most effectively utilize its strength by "defeating somebody, not particularly by electing anybody." [8] What labor had secured in politics had been gained by making the party in power responsible for legislation. The threat of retribution at the polls was a powerful weapon that labor could use on politicians. For this labor did not need any party machinery but merely an understanding of what was wanted.

The vigor of the Socialist argument for an independent labor party stirred the Socialist critics to impassioned replies. William D. Mahon, president of the Street Railway Employees and a later vice-president of the AF of L Executive Council, answered the Socialists that:

> We have been told about Great Britain, Germany and different parts of the old world, yet I notice they are still coming to America. . . . I believe my country is yet the best one upon God's footstool. I want to resent the criticisms that come from those who come here, take a glance at our American conditions, and then tell us all about them. We will compare Chicago, as far as the hungry people are concerned, with London, Liverpool, or any other place in the world. . . . We must follow the same careful policy that had always led us— not so fast as our friend Berger would have us go—but one that has led us safely. The trade unions have lost nothing. From some of the remarks one might have imagined that we have been standing still. When we began to organize our railroadmen twelve years ago we were working 14 and 16 hours a day with a maximum pay of fourteen cents an hour. Thousands of our men today are working nine hours a day with a maximum pay of thirty cents an hour. Such people have an idea that everything is going to come from legislation.[9]

Committee chairman Frank Foster again gained the floor and concurred with the administration chastisement of the Socialists. He said that the economic power of trade-unionism was its strongest weapon and had gained practical reform. The fact that European labor in some instances had their own political parties was no reason for the AF of L to discontinue its "policy of guarding the constitutional freedom of our members to vote how they pleased." The AF of L would never survive if it identified itself with a political party based on the class struggle. If labor was to gain support for the legislative aid it desired, its appeal, Foster said, had to be extended not to the "class spirit of hatred and bitterness" but to the "principles of justice and equity in the minds of a broader citizenship." [10]

The incumbent AF of L leadership was determined to have the convention cast its vote for the Committee's report. Such an action would have the effect of keeping the organization's political policies unchanged and of rejecting the Socialist-led agitation for an independent labor party. Therefore many outstanding administration leaders, including Executive Council officers and international union presidents, had spoken in praise of the Federation's political policies and had warned of the danger of independent political effort to the economic strength of trade-unionism. To this clique, AF of L vice-president and Machinists' president James O'Connell, who with Gompers and AF of L secretary Morrison comprised the organization's Labor Representation Committee, added his voice.[11] He said that, unfortunately, he could not inform the convention of certain information he possessed, but if the delegates could know these things as he did, they would be bound to agree with him that the organization's past political campaign had been an outstanding success. If the delegates would have but patience with the present political policies of the Federation the results would before long amply reward their faith.

O'Connell's enigmatic plea was followed by a passionate outburst against the Socialists delivered by delegate Maloney:

> You will find that from the time the Social Democratic Party was first organized in Germany a record of miserable tactics, lying insinuations, and foul blackguardism has stamped the Socialist parties of the world as professional character assassins. I have read papers published by these organizations and have yet to find one kind word on behalf of the tried and true labor leaders representing the American Federation of Labor. . . . I have just these words to say, Mr. President, that it is time we aroused ourselves. We should have the good common sense and courage to stamp this political party once and for all as an enemy of the trade-union movement. That party it is that discredits our movement. Their leaders are a wrangling gang of peanut politicians, and their stock in trade is a tirade of abuse and vilifications against the leaders of other movements. I hope you will not . . . give them a chance to go into our organizations and try to have adopted the principles of the bitterest enemies organization has in America today—the

principles of the Socialist Party and the principles of the Socialist Labor Party.[12]

The last speech of the afternoon before the vote on the Committee report was that of Samuel Gompers. Like several speakers who had preceded him, he aroused opposition to an independent labor party by inflaming the latent anti-Socialist feelings of many delegates. He quoted from an article by Victor Berger, the editor of the Milwaukee *Social Democratic Herald* in which Berger had attacked him as "an empty self-complacent old fool." [13] Having demonstrated that the Socialists considered him as their principal enemy in the Federation, and thereby suggesting that he and his policies safeguarded the Federation from socialism, the AF of L leader re-emphasized that politics was secondary to economic power in the trade-unions. Politics was necessary on a limited scale, but only to gain "the things that we cannot secure ourselves." [14] As for labor's foes in Congress, Gompers declared that the AF of L's recent campaign in the 1906 Congressional elections would mean that antilabor Congressmen would "not be so arrogant toward the representatives of labor as they had been in the past." [15]

A few moments later the voting began which resulted in the triumph of the Committee's report. As usual, the AF of L administration had distinctly proved that it could successfully defend itself from any Socialist-led challenge to its established policies. The convention made it clear that the organization's increased political activity during the 1906 election campaign was not to be interpreted as the prelude toward still greater political activity. It was equally clear that the AF of L's tried method of lobbying activity followed up by seeking the defeat of legislators who had exhibited unfriendliness would remain as its political practice.

Another issue on which the AF of L administration and the Socialists in the AF of L clashed was the National Civic Federation. The debate on the National Civic Federation in the 1911 AF of L convention was a high mark in the Socialists' efforts to discredit the lack of class consciousness of the AF of L leadership. The Civic Federation, a private organization, was created in 1900 through the efforts of Ralph M. Easley, secretary of the Civic Federation of Chicago. The National Federation's major function, contrary to the Chicago group, was to apply itself to labor problems. The avowed purpose of its Conciliation Department was "to do what may seem the best to promote industrial peace and prosperity, to be helpful in establishing rightful relations between employers and workers, by its good offices to endeavor to obviate and prevent strikes and lockouts and to aid in renewing industrial relations where a rupture has occurred." [16] To achieve this purpose the Civic Federation said it aimed "to bring together the three great interested forces of capital, labor, and the general public to work out industrial problems through evolutionary rather than revolutionary processes . . . to bring into cooperation the sane and patriotic leaders of the forces of employers and employed, and of the . . . general public." [17]

At the first meeting of the Civic Federation in December, 1901, representatives of these three groups accepted appointment to its Executive Committee. Representatives of the public included Oscar Strauss, Archbishop Ireland, C. F. Adams, Grover Cleveland, and C. W. Eliot; representatives of the employers included C. M. Schwab, John D. Rockefeller, Jr., and Marcus H. Marks; and representatives of labor included Samuel Gompers, John Mitchell, James O'Connell, and James Duncan. Inasmuch as these divergent groups intermingled at the organization's annual meetings, dinners, committee and conference sessons, Gompers was of the opinion that it aided in removing that "suspicious bred of isolation in which class conflict has its roots." [18] The Socialists, on the other hand, alleged that AF of L affiliation with the Civic Federation not only propagated the idea of class collaboration, but that AF of L leaders who attended Civic Federation functions replete with the figures, ideas, and interests of capitalist society gradually lost the point of view of the workers whom they were elected to represent. Labor historian Norman Ware has written that the National Civic Federation "united A.F. of L. officialdom and powerful financial interests against all aggressive labor leadership in the United States. The A.F. of L. became a 'Morgan partner' in attacking radicalism wherever it appeared." [19]

The Committee on Resolutions at the 1911 AF of L convention announced that it had received three resolutions which declared the Civic Federation to be "hostile to the interests of organized labor" and which requested the convention to express its "unqualified disapproval of any member or officer of the labor unions of this country holding membership in the National Civic Federation." [20] The Committee declared it did not concur in these resolutions for the following reasons: (*1*) the purposes of the Civic Federation were not antagonistic toward organized labor; (*2*) the actions of the Civic Federation had not been unfriendly toward organized labor; (*3*) the Civic Federation was disliked by the antitrade-union employers' associations; (*4*) "the trusted and capable officers" of the AF of L and its affiliated unions "would have been the first to sound a note of warning if any of them had discovered that the National Civic Federation was in any manner inimical to the welfare" of trade-unionism; (*5*) it was unwise to "not meet and discuss the grave problems which affect the wage-earners' standard of civilization with an association whose membership may include some whose vision has not yet been sufficiently broadened." [21]

Many of the delegates, the Socialists in particular, were not of the same opinion as the Committee, and a long debate took place on this subject. Duncan McDonald, United Mine Workers delegate and prominent Socialist, echoed a phrase of Eugene Debs when he said that the Civic Federation was conceived " 'to chloroform the labor movement into a more submissive mood.' " [22] McDonald reminded the delegates that among the Civic Federation's officers and members there were directors and controllers of the United States Steel Corporation, the organization that had "resorted to the vilest and most brutal methods in its treatment of workingmen." Such corporations, McDonald said, "the most bitter, heartless enemies labor has ever had . . . are the ones who are putting up the money to run the Civic Federation, and at the same time they are taking it out of the life blood of our people at home." [23]

The AF of L administration had many supporters at the 1911 convention who defended the officers' membership in the Civic Federation. AF of L vice-president Denis Hayes maintained that when labor leaders met with capitalists the former were able to educate the latter in the just purposes of unionism and to dispel their prejudices toward unions. He personally had overheard Gompers and Mitchell "meet the very men referred to here, Andrew Carnegie, Belmont and others, and they put the cause and objects of organized labor so thoroughly and impartially before them, that they made friends for our cause." [24] AF of L vice-president O'Connell argued that it was not proper for the AF of L to "curtail the liberties, the rights" of AF of L officers to belong to any organization of their choice. O'Connell warned that "To-day you say your officers cannot belong to the National Civic Federation. Next time you may say they have got to be Catholics or Protestants. Then the next time you will say they have got to be democrats or socialists. And the next time you may come back and say something else, and after a while you will have rebellion in your ranks." [25]

The next to last speaker in the Civic Federation debate was Samuel Gompers. In a long speech he claimed that the Civic Federation debate was a Socialistic tactic to disrupt the trade-union movement. The Socialists rejected trade-union activity, he alleged, for a philosophy that said, " 'Vote right and you will vote yourself into glory and salvation!' " The trade-unions' practical objective, however, was for higher wages and shorter hours. Meetings with employers in the Civic Federation gave the AF of L officers, Gompers said, an opportunity "to drive home the claims of labor." There could be "no greater mistake made in the labor movement" than a ruling barring its officers from the contacts with employers available in the Civic Federation. The roll call vote on the Committee's report provided the administration with a 11,815 to 4,924 victory.

Eight-hour day legislation was a frequent controversial matter between the AF of L supporters and the Socialist-oriented delegates. The action of the 1914 AF of L convention in declaring against legislation for the eight-hour day was made a major issue by the Socialists who were always eager to promote support for and gain converts to the idea of social legislation. In the year following the 1914 convention the Socialist members of unions affiliated to the AF of L assailed the AF of L leadership for sponsoring the view that the eight-hour workday should only be sought through economic action. At the same time the Socialists spread their reasons among the rank and file why this measure should not be rejected, if it could be obtained by law. Consequently, when the 1915 convention assembled, the Socialists had prepared the groundwork for a hectic argument on this matter. Debate was set off when the Committee on the President's Report concurred with

Gompers in urging that efforts to secure the eight-hour day be limited to economic action. The Socialist-led opposition produced a lengthy criticism of this view. One delegate argued that since the organization advocated legislation for a shorter workday for women, consistency demanded that it adopt the same position toward men. Another delegate alleged that an eight-hour measure could have been enacted in his state by means of the initiative which was in operation, if it had "not been for the fact that the enemies of labor availed themselves of the declaration of the American Federation of Labor that it is not in favor of the eight-hour day for men." [26] When the administration supporters maintained that the eight-hour day could be obtained through the exertion of labor's economic power, the Socialist answer was that the majority of workmen were not organized and therefore unable to secure the eight-hour day in this manner. In rebuttal Andrew Furuseth contended that if the eight-hour day for men was obtained through legislation "you will waste all the effort you have been making because the courts will knock it out." [27]

William Green, Mine Workers and AF of L vice-president and president following Gompers' death in 1924, expressed his disagreement with the administration's position. He was of the opinion that the workers should make use of all legitimate methods to obtain the eight-hour day. "Is there any one here," he asked, "who believes that the man who enjoys the benefit of the eight-hour day through the strength of his economic organization, appreciates and enjoys it more than the man who secured the eight-hour day through legislation?" [28]

The debate concluded with a wordy Gompers defense of the AF of L leadership's position in the matter. He charged that the Socialists had initiated the agitation in the AF of L "to secure the eight-hour day by law. It was predicted upon the notion of ballot box mania and it was for the purpose of injecting into the conventions and into the labor movement of America such questions as may tend to divide us so that we can scarcely work in harmony upon the non-controversial questions of wages and hours and conditions of employment." [29] Workmen were jeopardizing their liberty if they depended on the government to advance their welfare for, Gompers said, "There never was a government in the history of the world and there is not one today that when a critical moment came, did not exercise tyranny over the people." [30]

The Committee's report endorsing the securing of the eight-hour day through economic action alone was approved by a convention vote of 8,500 to 6,396 with 4,061 votes not being cast. The pure and simplers had won a victory, as customary—by a smaller margin this time, but a victory nevertheless.

The eight-hour controversy had served to demonstrate once again that the AF of L leadership wished to discourage trade-unionists from turning to the state for relief of any problems which the economic power of the union might conceivably remedy. The purpose of law, Gompers wrote, in the *American Federationist* of February, 1914, should be to "free people from the shackles and give them a chance to work out their own salvation." Legislation also meant an increase in state power and organized labor's treatment at the hands of the state had not always been a sympathetic one. The AF of L leaders who had struggled through many vicissitudes to develop their organization believed in building up the power of trade-unionism, not a power outside trade-unionism. The main legislation which the Federation desired was of a kind restraining the state from limiting the economic power inherent in trade-unionism.

The Socialist strength within the AF of L was never strong enough to win a majority of the votes of the convention delegates. It was at the peak of its power in the AF of L in 1912, as it was in the nation at large. Max Hayes, Socialist leader in the printers' union, received 5,073 votes for president of the AF of L in 1912, compared to 11,974 for Gompers. For a vice-presidency position, the Socialists did better with their candidate, William Johnston of the Machinists, getting 6,200 votes to James O'Connell's 10,800. In January, 1911, the United Mine Workers (whose vice-president, Frank J. Hayes, was a Socialist party member), passed an amendment to their constitution forbidding their officers to be members of the National Civic Federation. A few months later Gompers' union of his craft, the Cigarmakers, elected several of his regular Socialist opponents to office. In the same year, James O'Connell, first vice-president of the AF of L was deposed of his office as president of the Machinists' Union by the Socialist, William Johnston. The Socialist element within

the AF of L was also increased by the return in 1908 of the indus-
trial-organized Brewery Workers, and in 1911, of the militant
Western Federation of Miners. The Hat and Cap Makers, Painters, Boot and Shoe Workers, Glass Workers, Bakers, Metal
Workers, Cigarmakers, Textile Workers, Fur Workers, Boiler-
makers, Tailors, and Iron Shipbuilders also contributed to the
Socialist strength in the AF of L. Although the AF of L administration at the 1913 convention was able to secure the defeat of a
resolution for the establishment of an independent labor party, it
found it necessary to make some verbal concessions to the Socialist-inspired third party convention feeling. The Committee on
Resolutions declared that "the time has not yet arrived" for labor
to be old and strong enough to found a "distinct labor party." The
resolution added that when the AF of L's "present political activities have suitably materialized, a new political party will be
the logical result." [31]

While the AF of L leadership remained a constant foe of the
Socialists, nevertheless the latter's influence caused the AF of L
to give convention approval to many progressive resolutions.
Whereas the resolutions adopted during the first twenty years of
the Federation's existence were limited almost entirely to subjects that applied to trade-unionism, the 1914 convention expressed approval of an agricultural credit bill, extended felicita-
tions to the new Carranza government in Mexico, urged the
conservation of natural resources, supported the extension of the
parcel-post system, requested national legislation to aid the unemployed, asked for citizenship for Puerto Ricans, recommended
a presidential primary law, favored an easier method of amending
the United States Constitution, and demanded of the states free
and uniform text books in the public schools. The convention also
went on record for the abolition of child labor, a general campaign
of education for an old age pension law, the improvement of the
conditions of employees in state hospitals and institutions, further
legislation for the prevention and cure of tuberculosis, and government loans for municipal and private ownership of sanitary
houses. It also declared it would support any plan which could
bring about disarmament, expressed its hopes of an early cessation of the European war, and proposed that world organized labor meet at the same time as the general peace conference.

Actually, most matters which did not directly affect trade-unionism received little more than convention endorsement and were not followed up by a strenuous lobbying campaign in Congress. Gompers, himself, more than once expressed his reluctance to letting the organization become involved in social controversies other than those which sought to "secure higher wages, more reasonable hours and better conditions of work" for trade-unionists. Writing in the *American Federationist* in November, 1915, in regard to the efforts that were made "to secure the co-operation and endorsement of the American Federation of Labor for various purposes, schemes, theories and organizations," he felt that "the labor movement is ready and willing to render such assistance as it can, but it is not willing to subordinate its necessary and distinctive work for any of these purposes and it will guard carefully lest any representative of these presume upon any favor or any recognition that has been given or endeavor to use any relationship in an effort to force the labor movement to render greater assistance." Thus the AF of L did not become involved by itself, or with others in mass meetings and demonstrations to focus attention on unemployment. In the *American Federationist* of March, 1915, Gompers rejected requests "to permit our movement to be used for any such purpose." Nevertheless, it was apparent by 1914 that the AF of L was at least often giving verbal comfort to the aspirations and grievances of people outside its movement.

At a hearing before a United States Senate Committee investigating Industrial Relations in New York City, May 21-23, 1914, Gompers had the opportunity to outline at length the position of the AF of L on matters of political and economic significance which directly or indirectly affected trade-unionism. His testimony revealed that, on matters not directly affecting the AF of L, the organization favored the legislative fixing of the maximum number of hours of work for women and children, unrestricted and equal suffrage for men and women, the initiative, referendum, and recall, the direct election of the United States President and Vice-President, and further government efforts for general education. Under cross-examination from Socialist leader Morris Hillquit who asked whether the AF of L was guided by a general social philosophy, Gompers declared that it sought "to work along the lines of least resistance to accomplish the best results in improving the conditions of the working men, women and children today, to-morrow, and tomorrow's tomorrow, and each day making it a bet-ter day than the one that went before. That is the guiding principle, philosophy and aim of the labor movement." [32] The same commit-tee was assured by John Mitchell, AF of L vice-president, that he was not antagonistic toward capitalism nor did he hold any ideas of "ownership of industry by the people, or that they may own stock in any industry, or that they may share in the profits of in-dustry." He thought that "capitalism and capitalists ought not to be condemned as a class because some of a number commit the most atrocious acts." He believed in "democracy in industry" but this term simply meant "the freedom of workingmen to belong to their unions, the right of the workmen to sell their labor collec-tively." The collective bargaining process itself, he testified, "deals with no other question except wages and hours of labor and their conditions of employment. There is absolutely no attempt to con-trol the business end of the industry." [33]

About the same time as the government's hearings on indus-trial relations, John Lennon, treasurer of the AF of L, in reply to the question sent to the AF of L by a group of educators, "What kind of an American nation would your group make if it could?" answered, "We want a world where every man and every woman who does useful work will receive for that work ample to enable them to live up to their best ideals as to morals and their social life." He also wrote that the AF of L wanted to see a shorter day, safety legislation, an improved public school system, and the safe-guarding and promotion of the personal rights of the individual.[34] One of the most concise expressions of the objectives of the AF of L was stated by Gompers in the *American Federationist* of Au-gust, 1916. The statement declared that the AF of L's goals were based "upon the right of the workers to a larger and constantly growing share of the production."

The AF of L administrators were no theorists; in fact, they were almost contemptuous of theory. Gompers caustically re-marked to the AF of L convention in 1911 "that if the lesser and immediate demands of labor could not be obtained now from so-ciety as it is, it would be mere dreaming to preach and pursue the will-o-the-wisp, a new society constructed from rainbow material

—a system of society on which even the dreamers have never agreed." [35]

Interestingly, the AF of L leadership of the early twentieth century held a social philosophy in many ways similar to that of the American businessman. It was, in part, based on the eighteenth-century concept of liberty and the nineteenth-century belief in individualism. But it was distinctly American, too, because it stressed the practical rather than the theoretical, the material rather than the spiritual, opportunism rather than principles. Could not the businessman approve such Gompers statements as "the socialists have a concept of government in which there is no individual liberty. The concept of government of which the socialist dream is a government of governmental control, of governmental regulation." Such a theory would "stress the state" and would "devitalize the individual." [36] Like the businessman, the AF of L not only rejected the tenets of socialism, but it resented the interference of government legislation in the economic areas that it considered its private domain. In 1919 the AF of L's official history book disclosed that the AF of L "has consistently opposed the fixing of a minimum wage for men." At the 1913 convention a report of the Executive Council was endorsed which read, "If it were proposed in this country to fix by law wages for men, labor would protest by every means at its power. Through organization the wages of men can and will be maintained at a higher minimum than they would be if fixed by legal enactment." [37] During the hearings before the 1914 Industrial Relations Commission, Gompers registered the Federation's opposition to minimum wage legislation for men as well as for women, to the legal establishment of a maximum workday for men, and to state insurance of the unemployed. He informed the Commission that he "was very suspicious of the activities of government agencies" and apprehensive "as to the placing of additional powers in the hands of the Government which may work to the detriment of the working people." Furthermore, the increase in governmental powers was a "curb upon the rights, the natural development of the individual." [38] Consistent with its distrust of government, authority, and regulation, and its approval of laissez-faire and individualism, the Federation pitted itself against compulsory state health insurance. Gompers wrote in the *American Federationist,* April, 1916, on this matter:

Compulsory sickness insurance for workers is based upon
the theory that they are unable to look after their own interests
and the state must interpose its own authority and wisdom and
assume the relation of parent or guardian.

There is something in the very suggestion of this relationship and this policy that is repugnant to free-born citizens.
Because it is at variance with our concepts of voluntary institutions and freedom for individuals, Labor questions its wisdom.[39]

At a Conference on Social Insurance held in Washington, D.C.,
in December, 1916, the AF of L president again reiterated his organization's opposition to government health and unemployment
insurance:

The introduction of compulsory social insurance in cases of
sickness, or compulsory social insurance in cases of unemployment means that the workers must be subject to examinations,
investigations, regulations and limitations. Their activities
must be regulated in accordance with the standards set by
government agencies. To that we shall not stand idly by and
give our consent. . . . My hope is that we shall be enabled to
sing as we hope that generations that follow us shall be able
to sing,

"My Country 'tis of thee,
Sweet land of liberty."

For a mess of pottage, under the pretense of compulsory social
insurance, let us not voluntarily surrender the fundamental
principles of liberty and freedom, the hope of the Republic of
the United States, the leader and teacher to the world of the
significance of this great anthem chorus of humanity, liberty.[40]

The 1916, 1917, and 1918 conventions of the AF of L went on
record as opposing the Socialist trend as exemplified by state
old age pensions. In fact it was not until 1929 that the AF of L
openly came out in support of old age pensions by the state. As an
alternative to government unemployment insurance Gompers
suggested in the *American Federationist* of April, 1914, that "The
way out lies not through flamboyant agitation, fads, or utopian
dreams but through practical policies whose worth has been dem-

onstrated. If the unemployed would but resist reductions in wages, enforce the eight-hour workday, and under no circumstances work overtime, except to save life or property, much would be accomplished to eliminate unemployment." [41] Testifying in May, 1916, before the House Committee on Labor investigating the subject of social insurance at the instigation of the lone Socialist Congressman, Meyer London of New York City, the AF of L spokesman critically berated compulsory government social insurance. He expressed his fear of the extension of government regulation of the life and activity of the individual; he condemned the Socialists as inspiring the action on this subject, and he affirmed his belief in the eventual ability of the trade-union movement to provide voluntary social insurance for the workers of America. Not until 1932 did the AF of L endorse state unemployment insurance.

Since the AF of L was in favor of securing legislation for workers' needs when the union's economic power alone could not satisfy these needs, immigration restriction was a task which the Federation consistently proposed that the government meet. The majority of immigrants during Gompers' period of AF of L leadership came from eastern Europe where considerably lower standards of living prevailed. Most of these immigrants on their arrival lacked industrial skill and adequate finances. Inevitably their competition in the labor market threatened the wage scale, employment conditions, and the unions' control of the labor supply. The availability of abundant, cheap, immigrant labor tempted the profit ambitions of employers and encouraged businessmen to resist both the employment demands and the organizing efforts of trade-unionism. So from its very origin the AF of L placed an immigration restriction law high on the list of its legislative requests. Of the eight items demanded of the government in "Labor's Bill of Grievances" in 1906, two concerned immigration—one for a general law restricting immigration and the other for a law to prevent violation of the Chinese Exclusion Act. In arguing for laws that would keep foreign workers from entering America the AF of L not only took the view that these workers threatened the standards of organized labor, but held the "principle that maintenance of the nation depended upon the maintenance of racial purity" and that "national interests" would not be "furthered" by the arrival of "cheap labor that could not be Americanized and could not be taught to render the same intelligent efficient service as was supplied by American workers." [42] The AF of L was striving, Gompers wrote in the January, 1911, *American Federationist* for "the maintenance of American institutions as they are and only immigration restriction could make this possible."

The verbal and written attacks made by the AF of L on the Chinese people were extremely vehement ones stressing Caucasian superiority. Those who befriended the Chinaman, Gompers wrote in the *American Federationist* in 1901, were either "dilettante sentimentalists," profit-greedy businessmen, or "degenerate politicians" scheming "to Chineseise the American people." [43] At the 1901 convention the Committee on Resolutions denounced the Chinese as "people of vice and sexual immorality who were incompatible with our moral concepts," and were of "inferior social standards." [44] At this convention Gompers read from a lengthy anti-Chinese pamphlet of which he was the coauthor. He compared them to the American Negroes and said that the Negro "slaves of the south were as a race kind and faithful" but the "Chinese as a race are cruel and treacherous." Chinese immigrants, Gompers said, mean "so much more vice and immorality injected into our social life." [45] An AF of L "Memorial" to Congress, printed as an appendix to the pamphlet, declared that any offspring of Asiatic-American marriages "has been invariably degenerate" and possess neither "the virtues of either but develop the vices of both." [46] Before a National Civic Federation Conference on Immigration in 1905 Gompers remarked that the AF of L was "opposed to the Chinaman coming to the United States because his ideals, his civilization are absolutely in antagonism to the ideals and civilization of America." [47]

The 1914 Federation convention approved a report urging "State and city central bodies in the Pacific and inter-mountain states to be vigorous and energetic in their efforts to secure the enactment of such legislation that will do away with the abhorrent condition of the employment of white women by Asiatics under any circumstances." [48] Regularly the AF of L conventions requested of Congress the extension of the Chinese Exclusion Act so as to exclude permanently from the United States and all its insular territories "all races native to Asia." This action was asked

by the 1914 convention not simply for the protection of the economic position of trade-unionists but also because "the racial in-
compatibility as between the peoples of the Orient and the United
States presents a problem of race preservation which it is our
imperative duty to solve in our favor, and which can only be effectively solved by a policy of exclusion." [49]

The Federation also singled out the Japanese people for racialistic discriminatory attacks. Writing in the *American Federationist*
in 1905 that the Japanese should be barred from the United States,
Gompers insisted that they were difficult to assimilate into the
American culture. The difference between the two nationalities
were emphasized by the allegation that the American God was
not the God of the Japanese. Gompers wrote in his autobiography
that he extended approval when Mayor E. Z. Schmitz of San Francisco, "a labor candidate and elected on a labor platform, began
the work of segregating Japanese children from white children in
the public schools." [50] An editorial in the February, 1907, *American Federationist* testifies to Gompers' support of the school
board's action.

The outbursts of the AF of L president against the Japanese
were sometimes extremely vicious. Mr. Katyama, a Japanese Socialist who visited the United States in 1905, was referred to in
the May, 1905, issue of the Federation journal as a "presumptuous
Jap" with a "leperous mouth whose utterances show this mon-
grel's perverseness, ignorance and maliciousness. . . . Perhaps
this Japanese Socialist may be perturbed by the fact that the
American workmen, organized and unorganized, have discovered
that the Japanese in the United States are as baneful to the interests of American labor and American civilization as are the
Chinese, and that workmen in the trade unions, and even the unorganized, have declared and about made up their minds that the
Japanese as well as the Chinese must be excluded from coming
into the United States."

The American Negro, too, felt the sting of Gompers' tongue
and the discrimination of organized labor. Because business had a
tendency to hire Negroes to replace white workers on strike, Gompers criticized the American Negro for accepting employment at
such times. In the *American Federationist,* April, 1901, Gompers
editorialized that "the colored workers have allowed themselves

to be used with too frequent telling effect by their employers so as to injure the cause and interests of themselves as well as of the white-workers. They have too often allowed themselves to be used as 'cheap men.' " He advised that Negro workers should "become affiliated with the organizations of white wage earners or form colored workers' unions" for whom the AF of L would "grant charters to separate local and central bodies of colored workers." Although the AF of L was in favor of "the complete organization of all workers," Gompers wrote, "it does not necessarily proclaim that the social barriers which exist between the whites and blacks could or should be obliterated; but it realizes that when white and black workers are compelled to work side by side, under the same equally unfair and adverse conditions, it would be an anomaly to refuse to accord the right of organization to workers because of a difference in their color." [51] The AF of L leader wrote in the Federation journal for September, 1905, that organized labor desired no controversy with Negroes, but he warned that "if the colored man continues to lend himself to the work of tearing down what the white man has built up, a race hatred far worse than any ever known will result. Caucasian civilization will serve notice that its uplifting process is not to be interfered with in any way." While it was not the customary policy to practice racial equality, it was not the policy of the AF of L to make such official threats. Between 1881 and 1895 the Federation attempted to adhere to its constitutional principles of racial equality but this policy was concluded in 1895 when it was realized that its equalitarian practice was making the organization of white workers more difficult. Henceforth, international unions were accepted for affiliation even when it was known that they barred Negroes from membership by constitutional restrictions. Furthermore there was no evidence that the Federation leadership in the first half of the twentieth century gave more than occasional lip service opposition to racial discrimination within the union movement. After 1900, in cases where Negro workers were refused admission to an affiliated AF of L union, the Federation adopted a policy of organizing them into separate locals or directly affiliated "federal" labor unions. This policy was sanctioned by Article XI, Section VI of the AF of L constitution which read, "Separate Charters may be issued to Central Labor Unions, Local Unions, or Federal Labor Unions,

composed exclusively of colored members, where in the judgment of the Executive Council, it appears advisable and to the
best interests of the Trade Union movement to do so." Negro delegates to AF of L conventions during the years 1900–1918 frequently petitioned the conventions for the appointment of colored
organizers. Although such recommendations were adopted by the
1902, 1907, 1917, and 1918 conventions and referred to the Executive Council, little action was taken in this area.

In 1917, the wartime need for labor resulted in the migration
of thousands of Negroes to northern industrial cities. The unions
did little to either organize the Negroes or to take any effective
action against the rising tension between the races. According to
a House investigating committee, "the bringing of Negroes to break
a strike which was being peacefully conducted by organized labor"
against the Aluminum Ore Company helped bring on a race riot
in East St. Louis on July 2, 1917, causing the death of thirty-nine
Negroes and eight whites.[52] At the AF of L convention in 1917
following this incident, a delegate from the San Francisco Labor
Council offered a resolution to the Committee on Resolutions and
later, apologetically, explained to the convention delegates that
he was compelled to present it because he was under obligation to
the International Negro League. The resolution listed a number of
offenses suffered by Negroes such as disfranchisement, segregation
laws in regard to transportation, schooling, housing, hotels, thea-
ters, restaurants, and other public places, the lack of voice in local
and state affairs, and enormous extra-legal punishments for crimes.
The resolution further stressed that the President of the United
States had declared that the war was being fought for democracy
and therefore, since colored soldiers were fighting abroad under
this slogan, the time had come for democracy to extend to America's Negroes at home. The convention was asked to direct the Executive Council to influence the President and Congress of the
United States "to the end that all the political, civil and economic
disabilities so offensive and destructive to the rights of negroes as
human beings and American citizens be removed." The Committee
on Resolutions presented the resolution to the convention without
approval and with the specific announcement that it accepted no
responsibility for any of the statements in the resolution. But this
did not satisfy the Southern trade-unionists who were disturbed

at the presence of a Negro-rights resolution in the convention. After the resolution was denounced on the floor of the convention, an amendment was attached to the committee's report of nonresponsibility which "rejected the statements contained in the resolution." [53] This amended report of the committee, in effect countenancing inequality and discrimination against the Negroes in America, was adopted by the convention.

Negro efforts to gain the AF of L support against discrimination continued. A number of prominent and distinguished Negro leaders secured a meeting with the AF of L Executive Council in early 1918 and expressed their opposition to the discriminatory practices encountered by Negroes within unions. Gompers' partial defense of this situation was to point out "the limits of the Federation's power." [54] Six months later Eugene Kinckle Jones, secretary to the National Urban League, presented several proposals to Gompers on behalf of the Negro committee. The Council reported that "it could find no fault with the past work of the Federation" although "it was pleased with the report of these race leaders." Nevertheless "no further action was taken upon the proposition." [55] It was not until the post-World War II period that the AF of L undertook activity and made progress against racial discrimination in its organization.

In labor's history there occur a number of sensational murder trials of workers that aroused national passions and revealed the biases and emotional feelings many people had towards labor and capital. The vigorous supporters of the accused often saw a case as symbolic of capitalistic injustices toward those threatening property rights and profits. The accused workers, said these supporters, were being framed and persecuted, not for the crime contained in the indictment, but because they were aggressive and effective trade-union organizers. Antilabor sentiment, on the other hand, believed trade-unionists had no respect for law and order and considered labor organizers as capable of any crime to person or property. Thus charges of robbery, violence, and murder against militant trade-unionists were taken almost as synonyms for actual guilt by labor's critics.

The reaction of the AF of L to controversial cases of this kind seemed to depend on whether the accused's political views were in accord with the AF of L or with socialism. The McNamara case was an instance where the defendants, members of the AF of L Bridge and Structural Iron Workers, received strong financial and morale support from the AF of L. The McNamara brothers were charged with the death of twenty-one persons following the dynamiting on October 1, 1911, of the Los Angeles *Times,* owned by General Harrison Gray Otis, a notorious open shop exponent. Clarence Darrow, famous for his championing of the oppressed and his ability as a criminal lawyer, was hired by the AF of L for the defense. In recognition that the prosecution had adequate evidence of the accused's guilt, Darrow went along with journalist Lincoln Steffens' plan of a "Christian" application of justice and mercy. An agreement was obtained with the McNamara brothers, prominent businessmen of Los Angeles, the employers—National Erectors Association—with whom the McNamaras' union had been involved in years of militant struggle, and the prosecution, that the McNamaras would plead guilty as the condition for their lives' being spared. When Gompers heard that the guilty plea had been entered, his fear that the public mind might henceforth associate violence with the AF of L put him into a depressed state for several days. When he recovered, he sought to publicize the fact that the AF of L deplored the crime and should not be blamed for the unauthorized criminal activity of crazed individuals like the McNamaras. (Victor Berger declared at the Socialist convention in 1912 that the McNamaras were members of the Militia of Christ.) [56]

In several other celebrated murder trials during the period 1900–1918, where the defendants were trade-unionists of Socialist political convictions, the AF of L did not get itself as involved as it did in the McNamara case. The kidnapping-arrest in Denver, Colorado, in 1906 of Western Federation of Miners' leaders Charles Moyer and William Haywood for the murder of Governor Steunenberg of Idaho, caused Gompers merely to editorialize in the *American Federationist* against the illegality of the seizure of the Miners' leaders from Denver, Colorado, by Idaho state police. He referred to the abduction of the miners' leaders as "a total . . . disregard . . . for both life and liberty." [57] To the AF of L Executive Council Gompers did state that the kidnapping aroused his suspicions that a plot existed to find the Miners' officials guilty of murder.[58] But when William Mailly, National Executive Committeeman of the Socialist party presented Gompers with the signatures of almost two dozen officers of AF of L unions petitioning for the convening of an AF of L national conference to aid the imprisoned miners, a majority of the AF of L Executive Council, with Gompers in agreement, ruled against taking such action. Nor is there any other evidence to show that the AF of L undertook any major activity in this labor case.[59]

One of left wing America's popular figures who died in 1915 as a labor martyr was Joe Hill. The IWW songwriter and organizer was arrested in Salt Lake City for the holdup-murder of a grocer in January, 1914. The extent of the AF of L's exertions did not significantly stand out in the total defense campaign conducted in the nation by Joe Hill's supporters. Following Hill's conviction, the AF of L convention of 1915 took a stand favoring clemency for him. Gompers transmitted this message in writing to the Utah State Board of Pardons, as well as wiring President Wilson to do what he could to prevent Hill's death. But when consideration is given to the pressure that progressive groups and individuals exerted upon the AF of L administration to aid Hill, and the need of the AF of L for its own interests to not appear indifferent to possible employer schemes of destroying labor, the AF of L efforts in Joe Hill's behalf do not appear unusually magnanimous.

The Tom Mooney case was a further example that the AF of L's political philosophy precluded action any more forceful than the passages of resolutions and the appeals to government authorities. Mooney, a radical California labor leader, was sentenced to death, and Warren Billings of the Boot and Shoe Workers' Union was given life imprisonment for responsibility in the bombing of a San Francisco (war) Preparedness parade in July, 1916, that killed eight spectators. Beginning in 1917 AF of L conventions spoke out for the prisoners. The 1917 convention asked for a new trial because the reliability of the prosecution's witnesses was open to suspicion as perjury. In the following months the AF of L Executive Council also requested the state of California to accept the findings of President Wilson's Mediation Commission that justice had not been done by the conviction of Mooney and Billings. The AF of L 1918 convention urged President Wilson "to exercise such power vested in him to prevent the execution of Thomas J. Mooney, so that the widespread suspicion that a gross and flagrant

miscarriage of justice has occurred with the knowledge of authorities may be allayed." [60] Additional pronouncements of such nature as well as for pardons continued to go out from the AF of L
to governmental authorities. But the AF of L leadership gave no
comfort to the anarchist International Workers Defense League,
or even for that matter, to several AF of L city centrals, like the
Chicago Federation of Labor, which was holding demonstrations
and suggesting the calling of a general strike in the prisoner's behalf. Mooney's sentence was commuted to life imprisonment by
Governor Stephens in 1919 and about twenty years later he was
pardoned by Governor Olson.

Although the AF of L was less internationally-minded than
European trade-union organizations, it did maintain and develop
relations with the union movements of other countries. From 1894,
except for the war years of 1914 and 1915, its representatives
were annually elected to attend the British Trade Union Congress.
At the congress it was customary for the American fraternal delegates to make an address on the developments in the American
labor movement for the preceding year. This meeting with British
labor was a reciprocal arrangement with the British Trade Union
Congress also sending its accredited representatives to the AF of
L convention each year. Periodically the *American Federationist*
carried articles on the development and activities of the British
labor movement. Although these articles usually refrained from
commenting on Socialist and Labor party permeation of the British trade-unions, Gompers himself was less discreet when he referred to the British labor movement. Typical of his approach
were his remarks at the 1919 AF of L convention declaring that
it was the American trade-union movement which "has brought
more hope and encouragement, more real advancement to the
working people" than any other "movement economic or political, in any country on the face of the globe." [61] The British trade-
union movement, Gompers wrote in the same year, had made
the mistake of adopting a political course which now meant that
the "Labor Party of England dominates the labor movement of
England." [62]

Nationalist sentiment was well entrenched in the AF of L. The
fraternal relations with the labor movements of other nations never
lessened the keenness of the Federation's nationalism. After attend-

ing a Conference of the International Secretariat in 1909 and visiting many European countries, Gompers concluded: "The Old World is not our world. Its social problems, its economic philosophies, its current political questions are not linked up with America. All the people of the globe may be on the broad highway to social justice, peace among men of all tongues, and universal brotherhood, but all the nations and governments have not reached the same points on the road. In the procession, America is first." [63]

The AF of L's position toward the nation's foreign policies changed at the beginning of the twentieth century from one of anti-imperialism to one passively or actively supporting imperialist activities. In the late 1890's the AF of L opposed the annexation of Hawaii, criticized the movement for war against Spain, and, immediately following the Spanish-American War, denounced any forcible annexation of Cuba, Puerto Rico, Guam, and the Philippines.[64] Within a few years, however, the AF of L was no longer condemning the acquisition of these islands, and had begun silently accepting, sometimes even approving, further American expansion. At the 1902 AF of L convention Andrew Furuseth, Seaman leader, introduced a resolution that the AF of L should oppose the building of a canal by the United States or "any encroaching upon the independence of any Latin American state . . . which must lead to war, bloodshed and hatred, in and through which workers must be the chief sufferers." [65] The Committee on Resolutions would not recommend this resolution for convention adoption and the delegates voted to table it. The following year Furuseth offered a resolution of a similar nature which the Committee on Resolutions again refused to support. Instead, the Committee substituted a resolution merely urging Congress to use Italian-American workers on the proposed canal and the delegates adopted this substitute resolution. Although President Theodore Roosevelt recognized the government of Panama on November 6, 1903, a mere three days after the revolt had begun against Columbia, the AF of L offered no criticism. A treaty negotiated a few weeks later guaranteeing the United States the right to construct a canal across the isthmus also produced no AF of L disapproval.

Toward the entire "dollar diplomacy" of the Roosevelt and Taft administrations in Latin America and Asia the AF of L was almost as silent as the general American public. The most significant instances of American imperialism in Latin America during these administrations were the Venezuela affair of 1903, the seizure of the customs house of Santo Domingo in 1905, the interference in Cuban disorders in 1906, and the break-off of relations with Nicaragua in 1907. Philander C. Knox, Taft's Secretary of State, also followed an Asiatic policy designed to extend American influence in Peking and Manchuria and aid American business enterprises in the Far East.

American imperialist policies in Latin America were evident, too, under Wilson's administration and brought no reproach from the AF of L. In April, 1914, American naval forces bombarded Vera Cruz and occupied the city. In July of 1915 American marines landed in Haiti, imposed a military occupation to safeguard and extend American business interests, and did likewise in Santo Domingo in November, 1916.

The AF of L's sympathy for Puerto Rico's and Mexico's struggle for democratic reform was one of the more progressive aspects of the AF of L's international policies. Beginning in 1904, AF of L conventions approved of political privileges for the Puerto Rican people and finally by 1914 demanded American citizenship for them. As for Mexico, at first the 1910 Madero Revolution received no word of greeting from the AF of L. But when American business interests began a campaign for American military intervention to protect their property and profits in Mexico, the AF of L convention in 1912 passed a resolution offered by Furuseth extending greetings to the Madero government and opposing any American intervention. Gompers wrote in his autobiography that he hoped to see the revolution succeed because he recognized "an identity of interest in helping Mexican workers to establish standards that would not undermine standards across the border." [66] He probably also was friendly to the Mexican revolution because otherwise Socialist and IWW prestige might increase in the Mexican labor movement. Through correspondence and in person he urged upon President Wilson the recognition of the new Carranza government which was granted in 1915. In addition, previous to this, he had championed the right of Mexican revolutionaries to find political asylum in the United States and he claimed that it was no "exaggeration to say that the American Labor Movement was the most potent single agency in inducing President Roosevelt and President Taft to refuse to permit the United States government to hunt Mexican refugees." [67]

At the 1913 convention Socialist pressure in particular was responsible for a resolution which was passed that read:

> The American Federation of Labor condemns the attempts being made by American and foreign corporations, and certain jingo newspapers, to force armed intervention by the United States government in Mexico, and urges upon the president of the United States the continuance of the policy looking to a peaceful adjustment of the conflict among the Mexican people, and that the president and secretary of the American Federation of Labor be instructed to transmit the position of the Federation upon the matter to the president of the United States.[68]

The Pan American Federation of Labor was established largely through the efforts of Samuel Gompers. Besides seeing the value to the AF of L's workers of the introduction of higher economic standards among Latin American laborers, the AF of L president also considered that a Federation of the workers of the western hemisphere would give the AF of L the opportunity to propagate its economic and political philosophy in the Latin American labor movements. Gompers acknowledged in his autobiography that he was disturbed because "Most of the labor movements in these countries were either Socialist or Anarchistic. There was little understanding of the trade union movement as we know it. Most of their literature came from Europe and was prejudiced against the American Federation of Labor." [69] Another factor, according to Louis Reed, one of Gompers' biographers, which led Gompers to create the Pan American Federation of Labor was his own ambition to be the head of a labor movement of all the American countries. Reed says his ambition extended as far as desiring to achieve the leadership of the International Federation of Trade Unions. With the approval of the 1915 AF of L convention, Gompers did the preliminary work that resulted in a number of labor representatives of Latin American countries assembling in Laredo, Texas, in November, 1918, and establishing a Pan American organization. According to the *American Federationist* of August,

1916, the new organization would make it possible for organized labor in the western hemisphere to co-operate through economic action in improving its conditions of work and standards of living. Gompers served as the president of the Pan American Federation of Labor until his death in December, 1924.

The AF of L's relations with a European International trade-union federation dated from the year 1909. After having rejected invitations to the 1905 and 1907 conferences, Gompers, as an observer, attended the sixth Conference of the International Secretariat of Trade Unions in 1909 in Paris. He was not very well satisfied with the conference because of the presence of many Socialist and syndicalist delegates whose theories on trade-unionism differed with those held by the AF of L. But since by temperament he was always eager to be connected with vital social events, and since the AF of L's position was safeguarded by the conference's declaring that the trade-union movement of every country was free to decide its own policies and that all decisions of the Secretariat must be unanimous to be valid, he successfully recommended to the 1909 AF of L convention that it join this international body. AF of L affiliation with the Secretariat, he told the 1909 AF of L convention, also might promote the development of an International Federation of Labor. At the next Conference of the International Secretariat in 1911, James Duncan, AF of L executive vice-president, made a proposal to this effect and the succeeding conference in 1913 accepted the proposal and the name of the organization was changed accordingly.

At the 1911 Budapest Conference, Duncan, under instruction from the AF of L, made it known that the AF of L was against the antipatriotic and antimilitary proposals of the French Confédération Générale du Travail. The principles which the AF of L announced itself in favor of at the Budapest Conference were the prevention of the exportation of international strike breakers, more uniform legislation among countries concerning maximum hours of labor in dangerous trades, and the prohibition of child labor under the age of fourteen. Duncan was also successful in opposing the efforts of William Z. Foster to have the conference approve the affiliation of America's Industrial Workers of the World to the International Secretariat. Thus, at the outbreak of

World War I, the AF of L was a member, although a lukewarm supporter, of the existing international trade-union body.

To summarize, then, the AF of L's political thought in the early twentieth century was far more conservative than that of trade-unions in other major countries. It was almost as fearful of social legislation as were the business pressure groups. It was unequivocally opposed to socialism and to a labor party. While its conventions increasingly passed resolutions putting forth the grievances of nonunion groups, the only legislation it would actively lobby for was legislation which could secure it results beyond the attainment of collective bargaining. Nationalism also had roots deep in the Federation, Catholic social principles were apparent, evidences of racialism were all too obvious, and imperialism, too, often found support. Above all, its political thought was of a kind that placed great practical importance on gaining union security and immediate material rewards for its own members rather than on seeking any fundamental changes of the social system.

7.

The Industrial Workers of the World
and Its Early Ideological Conflicts

> . . . while there is a lower class I am in it; while there is
> a criminal element, I am of it; while there is a soul in prison,
> I am not free.
>
> *Eugene V. Debs*

THE history of the Socialist movement in nineteenth-century Europe showed that socialism was preoccupied by doctrinal differences which bitterly divided its followers. These differences were partly the outgrowth of varying national temperaments, traditions, and institutions among European countries. They also were caused by the theoretical disagreements originally expounded by the Communists Marx and Engels, the anarchists Proudhon and Bakunin, the social democrats Lassalle and Bernstein, and the syndicalists Pelloutier and Lagardelle.

One of the basic conflicts in the Socialist movement centered on the role of trade-unions and political organizations in the struggle against capitalism. Should trade-unions entirely concentrate on developing their economic strength or should they also wage their fight along political lines? Should Socialists seek to make trade-unions the primary instrument for securing the overthrow of capitalism and the establishment of socialism, or should they seek to accomplish these objectives through the strength of a political party? The right wing German Social Democrats, the French Ministerialists, and the British Fabians stressed that socialism could be achieved through an emphasis on political organization and activity. This view which also proposed the tendency to accept immediate legislative results partly to attract a broad electorate necessary for political victories earned for its advocates the title of opportunists or reformists. Another group of Socialists, particularly strong in France, Spain, and Italy, rejected political action as incapable of destroying the capitalist order and maintained that this objective could only be accomplished by the working class through direct action in the economic sphere. A third group, more orthodox followers of Marx and Engels, held that both a class-conscious workers' political party and a trade-union organization should be used to conduct the revolutionary class struggle against capitalism.

In the United States these three groups were in evidence within the Socialist party and the dual trade-union organization, the Industrial Workers of the World. The American Socialist Party created in 1901 was largely under the influence of those who tended to parliamentary opportunism, while the IWW in its first three years contained the more left wing Socialists and anarchists. After 1908, however, the IWW repudiated political action and stood as an organization upholding revolutionary industrial unionism based on the class struggle. It advocated solidarity among the entire working class so that capitalism could be abolished and working class industrial control instituted. Its main tactic to realize its revolutionary ends was direct action of the workers—a method which was believed would increase their class consciousness, educate them to the reality of the class struggle, train them in class warfare, and awaken their sense of importance and power in the economic system.

Of the IWW's brief and dramatic role in American labor history two generalizations may be made: (*1*) The IWW's history suggests the difficulties encountered by those who challenge the power of an established order when the character of the age suggests that such an effort will be unable to muster the strength necessary to success; (*2*) The inaccurate evaluation of the strength of social forces by the IWW leaders suggests that their sense of social reality was a poor one, determined not by external facts but by their need to see external facts in the way they did. Thus the field of social controversy apparently may be an attractive area for the talented but emotionally disturbed who make use of the social opportunity to externalize the conflicts raging within themselves.

The need for an industrial organization of all wage earners

founded on the precepts of the class struggle was particularly felt
by the Western Federation of Miners, a radical industrial union,
unaffiliated with the AF of L after 1897. From 1899 to 1904, the
WFM was engaged in tumultuous strikes, the violence of which
were an outgrowth of an indigenous frontier situation where a
middle class was lacking as a buffer between the militant workers
and aggressive employers. In 1904 the last of the strikes in Cripple
Creek, Colorado, was broken by the Mine Owners' Association,
Citizens' Alliance, and state military forces. The lessons from this
conflict and defeat convinced the WFM that unionism needed
greater strength if it hoped to survive in the face of a powerful and
antagonistic employer class.

Since unity is one way to strength, the Miners' Federation convention gave its executive board authority to prepare plans for
uniting all American workers in one organization. In furtherance
of this instruction, discussions were conducted with Dan Mac-
Donald of the American Labor Union, George Estes of the United
Railway Workers, and Clarence Smith, secretary of the American
Labor Union, which led to an agreement for staging a secret conference on January 2, 1905, in Chicago. On November 29, 1904,
invitations to the conference were sent to some thirty labor leaders
asking their participation in the formation of a Socialist labor
organization built on the structure of industrial unionism. The
letter of invitation expressed the hope that the working people
united politically and industrially could take possession of the nation's industries.

The January conference's major accomplishment was to draw
up a "Manifesto" which criticized existing craft unionism and suggested one great industrial union "embracing all industries" and
"founded on the class struggle." Its regard for class consciousness was apparent in its statement that craft unionism

> offers only a perpetual struggle for slight relief within wage
> slavery. It is blind to the possibility of establishing an indus-
> trial democracy wherein there shall be no wage slavery but
> where the workers will own the tools which they operate and
> the products of which they alone will enjoy. It shatters the
> ranks of the workers into fragments . . . dividing their class
> at the ballot box, as well as in the shop, mine and factory. . . .

Craft divisions hinder the growth of class consciousness of the Workers, foster the idea of harmony of interest between exploiter and employed slave.[1]

All workers who agreed with the Manifesto's principles were asked to attend a convention on June 27, 1905, in Chicago to establish a working class economic organization.

An ominous forewarning of what was to be a serious weakness of the IWW—the lack of Socialist party support—was evident in the absence of the moderate wing of leaders of the Socialist party at the Manifesto's inception. Both Max Hayes and Victor Berger, members of the National Committee of the Socialist party, rejected invitations to the January conference. In a letter published in the IWW's 1905 proceedings, Hayes explained his refusal to attend the January conference. Hayes declared that he would not permit himself "to be dragged into any more secession movements or fratricidal wars between factions of workers because they are not of one mind at this juncture." Instead he preferred to "agitate on the inside of the organizations now in existence to dump conservatism overboard." This could be done for "the rank and file of the trade union are awakening as never before, and as soon as even a good-sized minority become thoroughly class conscious, the fossilized leaders will 'go up in the air.' " It was also superior strategy, Hayes wrote, to remain "inside the fort and take chances to secure the adoption of my plans than to be outside and regarded as an enemy." [2]

The lone prominent Socialist party leaders who attended the January conference were Eugene Debs and A. M. Simons, editor of the *International Socialist Review*. But both participated in an unofficial capacity and not as spokesmen for the Socialist party; nor were they considered representative of the political thought of the majority of the Socialist party. Debs and Simons were a part of the party's left wing element, and at the 1904 convention their trade-union views had been formally repudiated. In spite of Debs and Simons' urgings, the 1904 Socialist party convention had refused to denounce the AF of L for its craft unionism and conservative political policies and had not declared itself solely in favor of industrial unionism. Against the opposition of Debs and Simons the Socialist convention had passed a resolution on trade-unionism which urged workers to join the existing AF of L movement. The resolution disapproved dual unionism contending that "neither political nor other differences of opinion justify the divisions of the forces of labor in the industrial movement." [3] While a radical minority including Debs and Simons voted against this resolution, nevertheless it was the official position taken by the Socialist party. Thus Socialists who wished to be in accord with their party's pronouncements, were, in this particular instance, obliged to support "boring from within," rather than dual unionism.

After the January conference's decision to hold a convention in June to found a dual union organization, Max Hayes lost little time in publicly disavowing Socialist responsibility for this maneuver. Hayes not only disapproved of the tactic of dual unionism, but he also was annoyed at Gompers' remark that "The Socialists have called another convention to smash the American Trade Union movement." [4] Hayes retorted in the March, 1905, issue of the *International Socialist Review* that Gompers "deliberately misrepresented the Socialist Party." He also warned any Socialists who intended to join the new organization that they were making a serious mistake. Once more he expressed his persistent belief that "The trade union question will be fought out within the present organization." [5]

At the IWW's first convention, 43 unions and 60,000 workers were represented. The political ideas of the delegates who convened in Chicago in June, 1905, stemmed principally from socialism, anarchism, and revolutionary industrial unionism—or syndicalism, as it later was called. Delegates representing these varieties of left wing political thought were able, temporarily, to reconcile their differences because they were united on two points: (1) their dislike of the American Federation of Labor's craft unionism, conservative leadership, and nonclass-conscious policies; (2) their desire to create a revolutionary labor organization on industrial lines that had for its ultimate purpose the overthrow of the capitalist system. Despite agreement on these points, the presence of dissimilar ideologies produced factional strife from the outset of the first convention which persisted throughout most of the IWW's history.

In opening the first IWW convention William D. Haywood, Western Federation of Miners' leader, avoided the areas of disagreement and more prudently touched on the unifying factor—the revolutionary ideal—which inspired the delegates. He referred to the convention as "the Continental Congress of the working class" and said its purpose was "the emancipation of the working class from the bondage of capitalism," through securing control of the instruments of production and distribution. The organization being created, unlike the AF of L, he declared, would be a working class organization "based and founded on the class struggle, having in view no compromise and no surrender." [6]

Eugene Debs's address to the delegates showed that he was in accord with the revolutionary spirit of the convention. Like many other speakers, he considered that the AF of L was totally inadequate as a working class organization. He alleged that it had "long since outgrown its usefulness" and had "become positively reactionary, a thing that is but an auxiliary of the capitalist class" and was under capitalist class control. He saw it as "preaching capitalist economics" and extinguishing the revolutionary spirit of the working class.[7] His criticism did not spare elements within the convention itself. Addressing himself to DeLeon and the delegates who were members of the Socialist Trade and Labor Alliance, he admitted he had long disagreed with their tactics. He did not berate their principles or theory but contended that their inability to increase their membership suggested that their tactics could stand improvement. Specifically, their fault lay in their dogmatic approach, for they failed to "appeal to the American working class in the right spirit" and "are too prone to look upon a man as a fakir who happens to disagree with them." Their sin was fanaticism and "fanaticism is as fatal to the development of the working class movement as is fakirism." Nevertheless, Debs felt the convention's conflicting factions could find a middle ground and he was ready "to take by the hand every man, every woman that comes here, totally regardless of past affiliations." [8]

This bid for harmony earned a friendly response from the man to whom it had been mainly directed—Daniel DeLeon. DeLeon replied that he had come to the convention with an open mind and without any past grudges, except toward the capitalist class. He was ready to work with all those who would "plant themselves squarely upon the class struggle and will recognize the fact that the political expression of labor is but the shadow of the economic organization." In social struggles there was "nothing more silly than Right without Might to back it up. And the ballot box . . . is the biggest fraud on earth if it is not backed up by the Might to enforce it." In addition, he announced, the convention would be wise not to conceal the revolutionary aims of the economic organization it contemplated. It should state "what it was there for and state it frankly." It should make known "that they had to capture the public powers" for it was not possible to "first take the men into the union under the false pretenses that you were going to raise their wages, and afterwards indoctrinate them." [9]

Remarks by other figures at the convention continued the revolutionary tone of the speakers already noted. William E. Trautman, editor of the *Brauer Zeitung,* official organ of the United Brewery Workers, emphasized that the organization "must be based on the class conflict." [10] Its objectives must be to gain for the workers control of the means of production and distribution that would then be operated "not for the benefit of the few, but for the common good of all." [11] A. M. Simons wanted to see "that the proletariat of America has left no weapon out of its reach in the armory, that it stands ready to grasp the ballot, the strike, the bullet if it should be that we are driven to it." [12] Delegate Elemensic added to the Marxist sentiments expressed by declaring that "All wealth is produced by labor and it belongs to the producers thereof. That is the program we want and that is the program we will stick to and that we will carry out to the letter." [13]

It was the reading of the political clause in the preamble to the constitution that provoked considerable debate and revealed the divergent views of the heterogeneous left wing elements of the convention. This clause, the second paragraph in the preamble, was presented by the Committee on Constitution as follows:

> Between these two classes [capital and labor] a struggle must go on until all the toilers come together on the political, as well as the industrial field, and take and hold that which they produce by their labor through an economic organization of the working class, without affiliation with any political party.[14]

The inclusion of the precept that the workers must "come together on the political . . . field" was objected to by Clarence Smith because it did not "represent the principles and purposes of industrialism but represents a toadyism to three different factions in this convention," the pure and simple trade-unionists, the Socialists, and the anarchists.[15] A. M. Simons agreed with Smith that the appeal made by the political clause was too vague but where Smith wanted all references to political action deleted, Simons favored "the principle of independent political action" and wanted to see it included.[16] Herman Richter also desired a preamble clearly endorsing political expression and he offered an amendment which read, "the workers must unite and organize as a class on the industrial, as well as the political field." [17]

The wishes of such delegates as Simons and Richter, who were important members of the Socialist party and Socialist Labor Party, respectively, for stronger emphasis on political action aroused the suspicions of other delegates not affiliated with either of these two political parties. These suspicions rested on the fear that the two Socialist parties would seek to permeate the IWW with their doctrines and ultimately gain the endorsement of the IWW in order to become its political adjunct. For delegate Gilbert this apprehension was overcome by the political clause in the preamble because he considered that it plainly stated that "this is primarily an economic organization based upon the conflict of classes . . . as individuals you are perfectly free to take such political action as you see fit [but] we do not stand committed to any organization in existence." [18]

The anarchist position, which in later years was to merge into syndicalism and become the dominant philosophy of the IWW, was expounded at the first convention by delegate Bartlett who declared:

All the voting that you fellows have to do is among yourselves as to what plan of action you will take against this capitalist class, and time will reveal to you fellows the rank nonsense of voting at a capitalist ballot box. You can vote better probably with machine guns and hand grenades in the course of time. I am in favor of referring that resolution back to the committee in order that they can strike out all of that confusing language about political action at the capitalist ballot box and all that stuff, and bring back in place of that clause a plain statement, of what the working class is going to do on the economic field.[19]

The longest argument in favor of the political clause was made by Daniel DeLeon. In answer to Clarence Smith's objections that the clause was a sop to different factions, DeLeon said that it was less political than the Socialists desired and more political than the anarchists and pure and simple trade-unionists wished it to be. In reply to delegates like Bartlett who championed physical force, the SLP leader urged that political action was a civilized method of seeking progress. Since America had an established political tradition and since the ballot box was available to the male workers, DeLeon advised the workers to utilize this opportunity and to "proceed along the lines that make peace possible." [20] He did not, however, argue for an unlimited faith in political action under capitalism. It was necessary, he said, to "gather behind that ballot, behind that united political movement, the Might which is alone able, when necessary to 'take and hold.' " The real "Might" then of the workers was in a disciplined, class-conscious industrial organization. Its ultimate power would be held in abeyance but "if the capitalist should be foolish enough in America to defeat, to thwart the will of the workers as expressed by the ballot," then would be the time for the working class through their industrial organization "absolutely to cease production and thereby starve out the capitalist class, and render their economic means and all their preparations for war absolutely useless." [21]

When this controversial political clause finally came to a vote, the Constitution Committee's work and DeLeon's argument were sustained by a sizable majority. Yet the heated debate had clearly disclosed the delegates' conflicting political feelings—feelings which later were to lead to major cleavages in the IWW.

The IWW's revolutionary aim and class-conscious spirit was reflected in its constitution and in various resolutions that it adopted. Race, creed, color and sex were made no bar to membership. Convention chairman "Big Bill" Haywood declared that although unions affiliated with the AF of L discriminated against a worker who was a Negro or foreign born, to the IWW it "did not make a bit of difference whether he is a Negro or a white man. It does not make any difference whether he is American or a foreigner." [22]

A resolution was adopted that an Educational Bureau composed of a literature and a lecture section be established, as the

IWW was to be "primarily an educational movement to show the workers that their interests are common in every part of the world . . . that the earth and all that the earth holds are theirs." [23]

Initiation fees and dues were made very low in order to facilitate, in one delegate's words, "the up-lifting of the fellow that is down in the gutter." [24] Under the IWW plan of organization, the industries of the United States were divided on the basis of the products manufactured into thirteen main industrial groups and all workers were classified into one of these groups. By this method of organizing all the workers in any of the thirteen groupings into one union, the IWW would have control of the workers who participated in the different phases of a particular manufactured product. Such control would increase IWW bargaining power and, if necessary, also would increase the effectiveness of strikes. Where workers learned the value of industry-wide strikes, they would see the value, too, of community general strikes and national general strikes.

In a further move to wield the united strength of workers against the owners of industry, the IWW General Executive Board was given the authority to call any union out on strike during the period when any other IWW union was involved in a strike situation.

Time contracts in the trade agreements negotiated with employers were rejected because they prevented the workers from striking at any moment that appeared favorable to them and unfavorable to the employer. The presence of time contracts was also resented because such agreements restricted the calling of sympathetic strikes. The general strike was recommended as the most effective final weapon against capitalism.

The convention further decided that only wage earners were eligible for IWW membership, and any immigrant with a valid union card was qualified for immediate membership. Militarism was condemned and membership denied to any one who joined the state militia or police.

Eugene Debs delivered several propaganda speeches and wrote some articles for the IWW in the autumn of 1905. He stressed that the supreme need of the working class was to unite economically and politically and to abolish capitalism. He saw AF of L unionism as the enemy of the workers because it brought them into conflict with each other, subscribed to a harmony between employer and employee, and was content to accept the wage system as final. Any efforts to progressively influence the "rotten graft infested" AF of L craft unions, Debs wrote in a letter to the *Chicago Socialist,* December 23, 1905, were as "wasteful of time as to spray a cesspool with attar of roses." The IWW, Debs proclaimed in an address in New York City on December 10, 1905, was the workers' great hope for emancipation from the tyranny of capitalism. It fostered industrial unionism not craft unionism; it was class conscious not wage conscious and it believed in increasing workers' discontent against capitalism rather than pacifying it.

In Chicago on November 23, 1905, Debs succinctly explained why he approved IWW objectives as set forth in its preamble.

> You will find it written there that the workers and capitalists have nothing in common; that there are a few who have all the good things in life, while the millions writhe in poverty and cry out in despair; that those who do nothing and produce nothing are rich, while those who do everything and produce everything are poor; that these two classes consist of capitalists who own tools they do not use, and of workers who use tools they do not own; that the capitalists who own the tools have it in their power to take and do take from the workers what they produce, and that the workers must organize both their economic and political power to take and hold that which they produce by their labor.[25]

The leaders of the craft unions were severely denounced by America's leading Socialist. He charged that one reason they fought revolutionary unionism was because its success would mean the loss of their jobs. For the most part he saw them as defenders of capitalism, although earlier in life, as workmen themselves, they had been devoted to the working class. But after ascending to office their character altered. Noticeable changes occurred in their dress, habits, and associations. They begin to meet with employers and at this stage, Debs told his Chicago audience, the labor leader often betrayed his class. He became flattered by his association with capitalists and by the praise they shrewdly lavished on him. He began to think that his personal experience had enabled him to see that capitalists were not as inhuman as he once thought they were. Opportunities developed for him to meet some "distinguished person he had read about, but never dreamed of meeting, and thus goes on the transformation. All his dislikes disappeared and all feeling of antagonism vanished. He concluded that they were really most excellent people and now that he had seen and known them, he agreed with them that there was no necessary conflict between workers and capitalists." [26]

Before another Chicago audience two days later, Debs also mocked the craft unions' leadership for their slogan of "a fair day's pay for a fair day's work." This slogan, he said, was based on the mistaken view that an identity of interests enabled both the employer and employee to obtain justice. A fair wage for the worker would be nothing less than the entire profit netted by the product. The industrial worker, Debs declared, says, " 'I want all I produce by my labor.' " [27]

Repeatedly, Debs informed his working class audiences that they were worthy of the best which life had to offer and that it was within their power to end a system where their labor provided capitalists, not themselves, a life of plenty. To those Chicago workers who had assimilated the capitalist-created fantasy that by hard work every one would improve his position in life, the Socialist crusader announced, on November 24, 1905, "As an individual worker you cannot escape from wage-slavery. It is true that one in ten thousand wage-earners may become a capitalist, to be pointed out as a man worth a million who used to be a clerk, but he is the exception that proves the rule. The wage worker in the capitalist system remains the wage worker." [28] The only escape from wage slavery, Debs affirmed, was in the path provided by the IWW. When sufficient numbers of class-conscious workers joined the IWW, the organization could take control of industry and operate it for the welfare of all. All men would have the right to work, the workday would be steadily lessened as machinery increased productivity, and the profits of an industry would be shared by its workers.

Although throughout his life Debs continued to believe in revolutionary industrial unionism, his specific agitation for the IWW itself subsided in less than a year after its establishment. One explanation for this lies in the influence that certain moderates of the Socialist party—Victor Berger, in particular—had over him. To them, DeLeon's presence in the IWW and the radical tendency he represented was particularly obnoxious. In addition, they placed their emphasis on securing socialism through the ballot and legislative action rather than through economic action, as stressed by the IWW. Believing that the Socialist party's voters were mainly recruited from the existing trade-unions, these moderates considered it essential that the Socialist party do nothing to seriously offend those unions. Their responsibility, as they saw it, was not to antagonize the AF of L by extending Socialist party support to a dual union movement, but to bore steadily from within and transform AF of L members into Socialists. To Max Hayes, writing in the *International Socialist Review* in September, 1905, the progress of socialism was "a matter of education, and workers who are unacquainted with the principles of Socialism must be reached by those in whom they have confidence." [29] He warned his fellow Socialists not to join the IWW since this organization would not succeed in enrolling the majority of workers. The place for Socialist infiltration, he advised, was the AF of L which was strongly established as an organization and already had a substantial number of the working people affiliated with it.

While in 1905 the leaders of the Socialist party were not completely united about their relationship to the IWW, no division existed within the Socialist Labor Party. Under DeLeon's dominance it firmly supported revolutionary industrial unionism. Following the organization of the IWW, DeLeon's daily and weekly *People* took up its cause with great vigor, and SLP leaders became enthusiastic IWW members. In an effort to gain members for the IWW and, at the same time, to implant his concepts of revolutionary Marxism within the IWW, DeLeon gave talks in a number of cities.

At Minneapolis, in July, 1905, in answer to those who at the IWW convention had opposed the political clause of the preamble, he explained that the political movement was a valuable trade-union weapon because it enabled the masses to be propagandized. The suffrage was firmly rooted in the American tradition and should not be circumscribed, but, instead, should be utilized for the pursuit of socialism. The ballot "is so bred in the bones of the people that, notwithstanding it has become a gravel in the shoe of the capitalist, he, powerful though he is, dare not abolish it outright. Among such a people, chimerical is the idea of expecting to conduct a great Movement whose palpable aim is a Socialist Revolution to the slogan of 'Abstinence from the Ballot-box!' The proposition cannot choose but brand its supporters as freaks." [30]

Even though DeLeon upheld the need of political action in the revolutionary movement, he did not regard parliamentary socialism as the panacea for the working class, because he saw in it some serious limitations. For one thing, he told his Minneapolis audience, labor politicians often failed to work for the overthrow of capitalism once they entered Congress. To guard against such betrayal there was the need of a direct action working class economic organization. The economic power of the workers would keep labor's political representatives from compromising their revolutionary objectives in parliament. A revolutionary industrial organization not only needs its "Might against the capitalist tyrant to put the quietus upon him; it also needs that Might," DeLeon reasoned, "to prevent the evil consequences to which in this corrupt atmosphere of bourgeois society, the political Movement is inevitably exposed." [31]

Before it had been in existence one year, the IWW was badly torn by a factional struggle for leadership. At the 1906 convention it was charged that Charles O. Sherman, United Metal Worker leader and IWW president, and all general officers and executive board members except William E. Trautman and John Riordin were unsympathetic to the organization's revolutionary objectives and content with establishing conservative industrial unions. Since most of this incumbent group leaned toward the Socialist party, and since DeLeon was allied with the more left wing faction, the clash in the 1906 convention saw the SLP and the SP on opposite sides.

The net result of the 1906 IWW convention argument was a victory for the revolutionary elements. Sherman was deposed from his office, the office of General President abolished, and the 27,000 Western Federation of Miners, less Haywood and St. John left the IWW. Speaking to the convention delegates after his ouster, Sherman charged that DeLeon and the Socialist Labor Party "controlled this convention" and "their tactics are suicide to the movement." What he had learned during the past year as

president of the IWW convinced him that his friends were correct
who had warned him that the SLP and "DeLeon would control
the next convention." [32]

In the *Industrial Workers of the World Bulletin* of December
1, 1906, DeLeon justified his support of Sherman's ejection on the
same ground advanced by St. John and Trautman—that the IWW
had to be purged of its nonrevolutionary elements so that it could
"continue its work as the revolutionary economic organization of
the working class of America." [33] The defeat of the Sherman
forces, DeLeon said before the 1906 convention delegates, was the
defeat of a "conspiracy to squelch the revolution in this convention, and to start over again another American Federation of
Labor." [34]

Attempts were also made at the 1906 IWW convention to
eliminate the political clause from the preamble. DeLeon's opposition to such efforts, however, influenced the Constitution Committee to recommend that the preamble remain unchanged.
Therefore delegate Moore introduced an amendment calling for
the deletion of the words "political as well as" from the second
paragraph in the preamble. The amendment, if adopted, would
mean that economic unity without political unity was desirable.

In answer to DeLeon's argument that political action gave
dignity to the labor movement because it showed that the workers
would follow lawful means of fulfilling their aspirations, delegate Moore countered that "the capitalist class knows what you're
doing whether you hide behind one button or another." It was
best for the IWW to center all its efforts on economic activity without political abstractions which avail nothing because "all politics
outside of this organization is capitalist politics." He unequivocally favored an economic method like a "general lockout of the
capitalist class and no high sounding phrase like democracy is
going to turn my brain into following a man otherwise." [35]

The attack on political action provoked DeLeon's colleague,
Richter, to enter the debate. He argued that "to claim that participation in politics means to acknowledge and recognize capitalism is ridiculous." The trade-unionist possessed a dual power—
power as a worker and power as a citizen. The worker exercised
his power in the economic field when he went on strike, why then
should he not use his power in the political field and participate

in politics? The pure and simple trade-unionist by not engaging in politics was actually abandoning "the power he possesses as a wage working citizen over to the capitalist class so that it may be used against him." [36] Richter was supported by delegate Foote who made the Aristotelian observation that politics could not be avoided in modern society for "every action of every man in a political society is a political act." [37] The propolitical statements aroused one delegate to comment that it was futile to vote at capitalist-controlled ballot boxes because the totals released for the candidates "do not comply with the votes that you put in the ballot box." [38]

Although there was a strong feeling among many delegates against political action, this element was not numerous enough to defeat DeLeon and his followers. St. John and Trautman were unwilling openly to side with and lead the antipolitical group against DeLeon at this time. Instead, the anarcho-syndicalists chose a compromise with DeLeon on the political action controversy which satisfied them that the IWW was to be no political arm of DeLeon's or of any Socialist party. They agreed to support the Constitution Committee's recommendation that the preamble remain unaltered in return for DeLeon's support of a resolution submitted by St. John on behalf of the Mining Department which resolved

> that the second annual convention of the Industrial Workers of the World shall adopt and submit to a referendum vote of the membership for their ratification so that it may become a part of the preamble of the Constitution of the Industrial Workers of the World the following: 'That the Industrial Workers of the World does not desire the endorsement of any political party, neither will the Industrial Workers of the World endorse any political party.' [39]

This resolution was approved by the convention, delegate Moore's antipolitical amendment was defeated by a 367 to 243 vote and the Committee's report was approved by a vote of 359 to 241. Thus the only change made in the preamble at the 1906 convention was the inclusion of a statement that the IWW would not endorse nor desire the endorsement of any political party. But, as further conventions would show, and as the convention debates had already suggested, antipolitical action feeling within the IWW was strongly held among the more aggressive and embittered workers.

On the matter of IWW endorsement of any political party, the convention, in addition to passing the resolution just noted, also approved two resolutions censuring a candidate and a political party, respectively. Denver Local Union 125, which had recently endorsed the candidacy of William Haywood for Governor of Colorado on the Socialist party ticket, was advised "to withdraw its endorsement and keep within the provisions of the Preamble and the Constitution of the Industrial Workers of the World." [40] *The Miners Magazine*'s editor, J. M. O'Neil, who had endorsed the Socialist party of Pennsylvania in his journal's issues of June 7, 1905, and August 31, 1905, was rebuked as guilty of "insubordination" against "the objects and aims of the IWW in general and the Mining Department in particular." [41] However the delegates did acknowledge the importance of political indoctrination by approving the passage of a resolution recommending that the Good and Welfare Committees in local unions give at least ten minutes of each meeting to discussing economic and political questions.

Several other matters discussed at the 1906 convention showed the IWW's philosophy was turning more radical than the previous year. The Convention Resolutions Committee refused to recommend the adoption of sick and death benefit funds because such features were incompatible with the IWW's purposes. Any reformist measures which lessened the worker's class consciousness, blocked his recognition of the class struggle, and dimmed "the fact that unless he overthrows the system of capitalist exploitation he will always be a wage slave" were declared unacceptable by the Resolutions Committee.[42]

On the question of strikes, the secretary-treasurer's report to the convention said, "No strike of wealth producers, whatever the circumstances, is unjustified, is without a motive cause, as long as such a strike is aimed against the citadels of the employing class and their outposts." Since working class solidarity was a cornerstone of IWW political thought, a strike was further looked upon with favor because it was "as much a thermometer upon which to measure the growing spirit of solidarity of the working class, as any other medium, that may be advocated by those who are striving for the better order of things." [43]

The ideological conclusions reached by the 1906 IWW convention showed that the decrease of the Socialist party influence in the IWW would remove the brake on the organization's left wing tendencies. As already observed, Socialist party moderates like Max Hayes and Victor Berger, and the Socialist press, had from the first exhorted Socialists to avoid the IWW. When A. M. Simons and Eugene Debs were no longer identified with the IWW by 1906, and the Socialistic Western Federation of Miners withdrew its affiliation after the IWW's second convention, many other rank-and-file IWW members of Socialist party tendencies or membership quit the IWW. The effect of the Socialist exodus was to leave the organization in the hands of the more extreme revolutionaries whose position became strengthened and whose influence less open to successful challenge.

These militants had a number of reasons for believing that the policies of the Socialist party were inimical to those of the IWW and not genuinely revolutionary. For one thing the speeches and writings of the moderates in the Socialist party frequently attacked the IWW for its radicalism. Most Socialist party leaders also urged their own members to bore from within the AF of L rather than to join the IWW. Furthermore, socialism as expounded by America's Socialist party, tended to a greater advocacy of immediate demands and reforms through parliamentary action than did nineteenth-century Marxist parties. Finally, it was recognized that the Socialist party convention in May, 1908, had sought to destroy the IWW's influence within the Socialist party and to make plain that the Socialist party favored peaceful parliamentary action as opposed to the IWW's direct action theories. One amendment that passed at the 1908 Socialist party convention made it mandatory that anyone joining the party sign a pledge acknowledging, among other things, his acceptance of political action. Another successful amendment provided expulsion for any members of the party who opposed political action. A resolution was also adopted that urged the working class "to refrain from violence and from works inciting to violence." [44]

Displeased by Socialist party ideology and by its policies toward the IWW, and suspicious of the political emphasis and doc-

trinaire fanaticism of the Socialist Labor Party, the direct action
IWW leader Vincent St. John declared that the "two camps of socialist politicians looked upon the IWW only as a battleground
upon which to settle their respective merits and demerits." [45] The
estrangement of many Socialist party members within the first two
years of the IWW caused the anarcho-syndicalists to hope, however, that the IWW might be enabled to exist unfettered by the
ideas of Socialist political theorists. But in 1907 Daniel DeLeon
still stood as a serious obstacle to the realization of this hope. His
unflagging efforts to indoctrinate the IWW with his interpretation of Marx's doctrines were bound to irritate the St. John-Trautman leadership—a leadership critical of political action, over-
sensitive to theorists, and having its own aggressive needs to assert
its will on the organization.

DeLeon's use of the SLP paper *The People* in early 1907 to
carry on a discussion on the question of political action provoked
the nonpolitically minded IWW leaders. His inability to restrain
himself from viciously attacking those in the IWW who opposed
political action intensified their fears that he wished to dominate
the organization and depose those representing other views. The
more direct-action minded were displeased by his frequent ad-
monition that "the rejection of political action would throw the
IWW back upon the methods of barbarism." [46] They even began
to doubt his loyalty to radicalism when he repeatedly stressed the
desirability of having opposing class views find their expression
in the peaceful process of political agitation and balloting.[47]

At the 1907 IWW convention, DeLeon's influence was not
formally challenged though an undercurrent of hostility towards
the SLP leader and his supporters was evident. The factionalism
and the purges of IWW's first two years of existence had left the
IWW seriously weakened. Therefore the St. John-Trautman leadership managed to control themselves and postpone the showdown
with DeLeon until the organization had grown strong enough to
withstand another departure.

In keeping with previous conventions, the political clause of
the preamble produced another lengthy debate. Some of DeLeon's
direct-actionist opponents again tried to delete from it the appeal
to workers to "come together on the political . . . field." But once
more the majority of the convention delegates upheld the political

clause. As the next year's convention was to show, however, the 1907 IWW convention was DeLeon's last victory.

The 1908 IWW convention was an epochal one in the life of the IWW, for DeLeon was ousted, the controversial political clause was eliminated from the preamble, and the direct-actionists gained undisputed control of the organization. All this could happen because the membership had changed since 1905 from that mainly composed of veteran trade-unionists of Socialist political convictions to that of the migratory, unskilled "Overall Brigade" with little knowledge of Socialist political theory. Against the limited education, rebellious temperament, and grim social experiences of such a group, the professorial socialism of DeLeon could make little headway.

On the other hand, Vincent St. John, who had been a delivery boy, farm hand, tinner, printer, upholsterer, and an organizer for the Western Federation of Miners, had a framework of activist experience which enabled him to recognize and give expression to the aspirations of this new element. They in turn, had confidence in him because his background was similar to theirs. Counting on their support, St. John, by 1908, felt strong enough to press for DeLeon's expulsion from the IWW. He considered it necessary to drive out DeLeon because of the differences that existed between them on principles and methods that should dominate the IWW. And he knew well that DeLeon was not one whose political views could be altered.

Two essential differences underlay the thinking of St. John and DeLeon: First, St. John advocated "the use of militant tactics to the full extent of its power to make good." [48] In essence, this meant direct action, sabotage, the breaking of any laws, and violence. The philosophy sanctioning such behavior, St. John told the Senate Industrial Relations Commission in 1914, rested on the premise that anything which aided the workers in their struggle against capitalism was permissible. In the last analysis, St. John's theory meant that the end justifies the means.[49] DeLeon opposed such a theory along with the tactics that resulted from its application. Although he firmly believed in the theory of the class struggle and unremittingly opposed the reformist trends among Socialists, he was convinced that tactics employing violence would do damage to the character and discipline standards of the workingman.

The second fundamental difference between St. John and De-Leon concerned their attitude toward political action. The former was an inherent believer in direct action while the SLP leader maintained that political organization was as necessary as industrial organization for the workers to overcome capitalism.

St. John discounted the effectiveness of working-class political action for a number of reasons. First, many workers, aliens, women, Negroes in southern states, migratory laborers, persons under twenty-one, and persons not paying a poll tax were deprived of the franchise. Secondly, the Democratic and Republican parties already had the allegiance of a large part of the working class who were able to vote. But the most important factor, as St. John saw it, was that "with the working class divided on the industrial field, unity anywhere else—if it could be brought about—would be without results. The workers would be without power to enforce any demands." [50] St. John held that power alone ultimately decided momentous social questions between conflicting forces. And since the basis of all power stemmed from economic power, he wanted the workers to devote all their efforts to acquiring this essential power. It was futile for the workers to exert political pressure on the present lawmaking bodies, he told the Senate Industrial Relations Committee in 1914, because under capitalism the government "was a committee to look after the interests of the employers." [51] Therefore was it not natural to expect that the government would only help the workers as much as the employers were willing for them to be helped? Should a workers' party manage to secure control of the government, they would find then, as history had repeatedly shown, that a ruling class did not peacefully surrender its privileged position. Superior force alone, he contended, always had and always would determine which class would triumph. Superior force rested, he concluded, with those who controlled the means of production, not with those who sat in lawmaking chambers.

The only admission that St. John made for the value of political activity was a wry tribute. He declared that political activity had educational merit which consisted "solely in proving to the workers its utter inefficacy to curb the power of the ruling class and therefore forcing the workers to rely on the organization of their class in the industries." [52]

As already noted, DeLeon urged both political and economic action. He valued political action as a legal mechanism by which the workers "may demand the unconditional surrender of the capitalist" and "may preach and teach the reasons thereof." [53] Yet, although he desired to see the workers capture control of the state power through their own political party, he also warned them of the limitations inherent in politics. Working class politicians, he declared, are apt to become corrupt in the company of capitalist politicians and from the various allurements held out to them in a capitalist society. If they do not become overtly corrupt, their routine as politicians, removed as it is from contact with the workers, often has the result of causing their revolutionary ideals to fade into reform notions. Working class political parties, too, in order to obtain the votes of a wider electorate so that they can secure office, usually tone themselves down into parties of reform. And finally, like St. John, DeLeon thought the capitalist class would not peacefully acquiesce in their expropriation by a workers' government. However, he proposed meeting these limitations of political action by a revolutionary industrial organization of the working class, whose power would be respected because of its ability to cause a general production stoppage. This class-conscious union would use its strength to keep its political representatives mindful of their class duties and to prevent the capitalist class from rejecting proposals of the workers' political party and from initiating counterrevolutionary action.

The result of the contest between DeLeon and St. John at the 1908 convention determined the principles that were to henceforth govern the IWW. St. John and his followers had decided that the simplest and surest way of eliminating DeLeon's ideological influence within the IWW was to declare him ineligible for a seat in the convention because he was not a member of the existing local in the industry in which he worked. The Credential Committee's recommendation to this effect led to a debate indicating that more than a constitutional issue of membership was at stake. Delegate Williams charged that at the Socialist Labor Party convention DeLeon had accused all the IWW national officers except the SLP members of adopting anarchism. Suspicion that DeLeon was seeking to permeate the IWW with his interpretation of Socialist theory and tactics ruled the entire argument against him.[54]

SLP figures like delegate Yates who argued for DeLeon praised his devotion to the cause of the working class and condemned his critics for motives more personal than the resolution against DeLeon suggested. In his own defense, the SLP leader contended that the crux of the issue responsible for the move to bar him from the convention was his concept of the proper theory for the organization. He reviewed the efforts he had made and the activities he had undertaken during his connection with the IWW to have the organization accept the theory that capitalism could not be destroyed without a workers' political and economic organization. This espousal of political action, he charged, had gained him the enmity of the IWW's direct-actionists who now sought to expel him.

St. John, convention chairman, refuted DeLeon's arguments. He challenged DeLeon's contention that political action was essential because it gave dignity to the workers. DeLeon's view of dignity, St. John declared, was "a false dignity, by which he has placed the life of workingmen below the dignified law of property rights, and capitalist class rules and ethics." [55] As long as such ideas dominated the labor movement, it would make no progress. Labor political action pleased the capitalists for it presented them with no danger to their privileges. It was a danger, however, to labor, for it wasted their efforts in an activity that could not gain them their emancipation. DeLeon's ideas and actions, St. John felt, were "at variance with the adopted principles of industrial unionism" and would, if followed, change the IWW from a revolutionary organization into an instrument of his will. For these reasons, St. John averred, it was the delegates' duty not to allow him "to take a seat as delegate to this convention." [56]

The motion to adopt the recommendation of the Credentials Committee and refuse to seat DeLeon was carried by a roll call vote of 40 to 21. Following this action, DeLeon and his small group of followers set up an organization as a rival to the IWW. They, too, called themselves the IWW (Detroit) but they never were anything more than a vocal sect. Until his death in 1914 DeLeon remained a fanatic devotee of Marx, refusing to accept any revisions of his revolutionary principles and tolerating no doctrinal differences of opinion.

DeLeon's defeat now suggested that a change would be made

in the preamble to bring it more in line with the antipolitical views of St. John and his supporters. As the Constitution Committee could not unanimously concur in a recommendation on the preamble, it offered a majority and minority report. Following a hectic debate, the minority report which completely eliminated the political clause and added provisions more adequately displaying the anarcho-syndicalist views of the DeLeon opposition was adopted by a roll call vote of 35 to 32.

The victory of the direct-actionists was now complete. They had purged the IWW of the Socialist Labor Party leader, Daniel DeLeon, and they had stricken from the preamble the political clause which he had always strongly insisted was necessary. The second paragraph of the new preamble now read:

> Between these two classes a struggle must go on until the workers of the world organize as a class, take possession of the earth and the machinery of production, and abolish the wage system.[57]

Two additional paragraphs were also added at this time to the preamble. These two paragraphs read as follows:

> Instead of the conservative motto, "A fair day's wages for a fair day's work," we must inscribe on our banner the revolutionary watchword, "Abolition of the wage system." . . . It is the historic mission of the working class to do away with capitalism. The army of production must be organized, not only for the everyday struggle with capitalists, but also to carry on production when capitalism shall have been overthrown. By organizing industrially we are forming the structure of the new society within the shell of the old.[58]

Besides casting out DeLeon and changing the preamble, St. John gained another victory at the 1908 convention through his election as general secretary-treasurer of the IWW—a position which he was to retain until 1915. Throughout his period of office he was animated by the conviction that the class struggle was not merely a Marxist incantation which explained "the history of all hitherto existing society." It was also a brutal fact of present day society—a fact long observed by him and vividly illustrated by his experience as a worker under capitalism and as an organizer for the Western Federation of Miners. Explaining to the 1914 Senate Industrial Relations Committee why he had no respect for capitalist property, he said of the employer class:

> They take us into the mills before . . . we have even seen the semblance of an education, and they grind up our vitality, brain and muscular energy into profits, and whenever we can not keep pace with the machine speeded to its highest notch, they turn us out onto the road to eke out an existence as best we can, or wind up on the poor farm or in potter's field.[59]

Convinced as he was that the capitalist system heartlessly exploited working people and that existing laws and institutions were the creation and citadel of the capitalist class, his program of action was rooted in the imperative necessity of the workers to destroy this entire vicious, economic-political system.

The ascendency of the St. John faction in 1908 now placed the IWW in the role of a militant propagandist organization seeking the overthrow of capitalism. On the subject of tactics, St. John wrote that the IWW aimed "to use any and all tactics that will get results sought with the least expenditure of time and energy. The tactics used are determined solely by the power of the organization to make good in their use." [60] What did concern the new IWW leaders, however, as well as the real results they sought, was to agitate and propagandize in such a manner that the class struggle would be dramatized for the workers. Any overt demonstration of the workers was considered a success if it promoted their class consciousness. It also was valuable for what the French called "revolutionary gymnastics." In the words of an IWW propagandist:

> Strikes are mere incidents in the class war; they are tests of strength, periodic drills in the course of which the workers train themselves for concerted action. This training is most necessary to prepare the masses for the final 'catastrophe,' the general strike, which will complete the expropriation of the employers.[61]

By continually resuming the industrial conflict with the employing class and encouraging such methods as sabotage, property destruction, and violence to persons, the IWW leaders believed that they were fostering in the workers the revolutionary spirit and intensifying that spirit as well. Such measures, they maintained, not only trained the workers in class warfare but also made them conscious of their own might. When these militant steps inevitably resulted in retaliatory repressive measures by the capitalist class and government, the class nature of the capitalist state would be unmasked and the solidarity of the workers increased. Simply put, the IWW leadership claimed they exalted direct action because it educated the workers by training them in tactical maneuvers, it revealed the class struggle, it infused them with greater solidarity and it gave them an awareness of their own power. Such an education was considered essential before the IWW could achieve its ultimate purpose—"Complete surrender of industry to the organized workers." [62]

The dramatic, aggressive IWW vocabulary alone gives cause for speculating if the IWW found acceptance by some not for the intellectual content of its social analysis but rather for the emotional impact of its message. How much does "the eye see what it takes to the seeing" and how much do the emotions find the philosophy the individual needs?

8.

Thought and Action of the Industrial Workers of the World, 1908–1918

> "I want to die a martyr," he said. The words were like the striking of a light, for having said them he knew that they were true, and had been true from the beginning.
>
> *Joe Hill in Wallace Stegner's* THE PREACHER AND THE SLAVE

THE philosophy of direct action advocated by the group that had won complete control of the IWW in 1908 soon began to express itself in the organization's activities throughout the country. In 1909 the IWW riveted national attention upon itself by its free speech demonstrations in western cities and its strike leadership of unorganized and unskilled workers in eastern cities.

The first major IWW encounter with city authorities over the issue of free speech occurred in Spokane, Washington, a city where the IWW had a strong local and where many migratory laborers congregated. As a feature of its organizing drive, the IWW organizers spoke in front of the Employment Agency Offices. The IWW speakers' purposes were to persuade the workers not to pay the employment agencies a fee for a job, because the agencies had bribed foremen to fire a large number of newly hired workers. This understanding between the agencies and the foremen led to a large labor turnover and a profitable business for the fee-taking agencies.

One result of the IWW's speaking campaign was that the employment centers formed a group called the Associated Agencies of Spokane. This organization got the city council to pass an ordinance forbidding all street meetings, and the IWW was informed

176

that street meetings would be illegal after January 1, 1909. During the winter months the IWW violated the ordinance but not on a massive scale. When the ordinance was amended to exempt religious bodies like the Salvation Army, the IWW in Spokane decided that they would vigorously defy the ordinance because of the amendment's discriminating feature.

Beginning November 2, 1909, the Spokane IWW local began harassing the city to allow IWW street meetings. The plan of the local was to inform the IWW general office that free speech volunteers from other cities were needed in Spokane. The general office then would notify all its affiliated unions to advise their unemployed members that they help out in Spokane. The IWW arrivals from many parts of the country would then hold street meetings in Spokane in defiance of the ban. Of course this would result in the free-speech volunteers going to jail but ultimately it might cause the city to repeal the ordinance rather than to continuously combat the IWW.

On November 2, more than 100 arrests were made in Spokane, but this was offset by the arrival of 40 volunteers from Portland and about the same number from other cities. Because the finances of the general organization were not adequate enough to aid those who answered the call for volunteers at public demonstrations, those who travelled to Spokane came by freight cars and the rods of passenger trains, a method of travel familiar to many IWW members. As soon as they arrived in Spokane they took to street speaking and in short order they were arrested on charges of disorderly conduct and usually given thirty days in prison. Frank Little, IWW western organizer, used the Declaration of Independence for his street speech and was sentenced to thirty days. This incident was used as a propaganda argument by the IWW to illustrate that the reading of the Declaration of Independence in a capitalist-dominated community could lead to a jail sentence.

The results of this clash with the Spokane authorities, "Big Bill" Haywood told the 1915 Senate Investigating Committee, were that "between 500 and 600 men and women, members of the organization, were thrown into prison. Several of them were killed. They were put in the hot box and then moved and put in a cold cell. Several died from pneumonia." [1] On the other hand, the IWW was responsible for the fatal shooting of Chief of Police Sullivan. The struggle concluded early in March, 1910, when the mayor and law enforcement officials informed an IWW committee that the organization could carry on its propaganda meetings, although the anti-free speech ordinance would not be repealed.

The next outstanding example of the revolutionary spirit and direct action methods of the IWW occurred in a 1909 strike of 6,000 unskilled, unorganized, and mixed-nationality workers at the Pressed Steel Car Company at McKee's Rock, Pennsylvania. In spite of these handicaps for united action the severity of the workers' grievances compelled them to strike. Their outstanding complaint was the introduction of a new method of payment by which earnings became dependent on the total production of a group of workers. By this method errors of any member in the section could reduce the earnings of the entire section. What further irritated the men was the company refusal to announce its wage rates.

By the middle of July, 1909, after 40 men had been discharged for refusing to work unless informed of their pay scale, all but 500 of the employees went out on strike. In mid-August the IWW made its appearance in defense of the strikers. To protect their plants, give safe conduct to strikebreakers, and awe the strikers, the employers had the help of the local police force, over 100 armed deputies, and the Pennsylvania State Constabulary or "American Cossacks" as the strikers called them. Testifying before the United States Industrial Commission in 1915, William Haywood said of this strike:

> There was the first time that we went up against what were called the Cossacks, the black plague of that State. The Industrial Workers met them on a different basis to what other labor organizations had done, and told them for 'every man you kill of us, we will kill one of you' and with the death of one or two of the Cossacks their brutality became less.[2]

During the strike the IWW displayed an unusual strike tactic. It provided for no committee to do collective bargaining with the company. It simply sought to maintain the strike until the company gave in. Unable to break the militancy of the strikers and recognizing that public sympathy was with the strikers, the company in early September acknowledged its defeat.

The scene of the IWW's most notable direct action activity in 1910 was at Fresno, California. The organization had been conducting a campaign among the thousands of unskilled fruit workers in the San Joaquin Valley. When street meetings were banned by law, the same mass agitation tactics used in Spokane were adopted by the local IWW organization. Haywood told the Senate Industrial Relations Committee in 1915, that "between 150 and 200 men were thrown into prison there. They were crowded to more than the capacity of the prison. The hose of the fire department was turned on them . . . one night they were compelled to stand up to their knees in water." [3] The arrested IWW members were not represented by counsel and often continued their defiance of the law by making revolutionary speeches in the courtroom. The extent to which IWW members went in their speeches before the courts is seen from the following excerpt of a speech by an IWW member—perhaps a fairly typical example of IWW court-behavior —noted by a labor scholar:

> I have seen you, Judge ————, and others of your kind send them [the workers] to prison because they dared to infringe upon the sacred rights of property. You have become blind and deaf to the rights of man to pursue life and happiness, and you have crushed those rights so that the sacred rights of property should be preserved. Then you tell me to respect the law. I don't. I did violate the law, and I will violate every one of your laws and still come before you and say: "To hell with the courts," because I believe that my right to live is far more sacred than the sacred right of property that you and your kind so ably defend. [4]

Meanwhile as spring was nearing, and the IWW general office call for volunteers in Fresno threatened to win a formidable response, the Fresno city officials rescinded their ban against street meetings.

The most prominent of the IWW free speech fights in 1912 took place in San Diego, California. In this city, employers' antagonism toward organized labor was reflected in a petition, first presented in November, 1911, for the prohibition of street meetings and speeches. The San Diego city council acceded to these demands, and on January 8, 1912, passed an ordinance suppressing street speaking in the main areas of the city. The action of the council was probably affected by a general hysteria against labor following the courtroom confession of the McNamara brothers, AF of L Structural Iron Workers, to the dynamiting of the anti-union Los Angeles *Times*. Various left wing elements, such as the IWW, Socialists, anarchists, and Single-taxers, combined to form the California Free Speech League and inaugurate a program of public defiance of the ordinance. As in previous IWW free speech campaigns, members of the IWW from other cities joined in the struggle at San Diego. Soon more than two hundred violators of the ordinance were jailed. Besides the usual mistreatment of prisoners, this struggle was notable for the activities of an extra-legal patriotic citizens' group known as Vigilantes whose vicious-ness toward left wing agitators illustrates how possible it is for the latent, sadistic impulses within human beings to erupt. Emma Goldman, famed anarchist, participated in the San Diego free speech fight and recorded the behavior of the IWW's extralegal opposition.

> The Vigilantes raided the I.W.W. headquarters, broke up the furniture, and arrested a large number of men found there. They were taken to Sorrento to a spot where a flag-pole had been erected. There the I.W.W.'s were forced to kneel, kiss the flag, and sing the national anthem. As an incentive to quicker action one of the Vigilantes would slap them on the back, which was the signal for a general beating. After these proceedings the men were loaded into automobiles and sent to San Onofre, near the county line, placed in a cattle-pen with armed guards over them, and kept without food or drink for eighteen hours. The following morning they were taken out in groups of five and compelled to run the gauntlet. As they passed between the double line of Vigilantes, they were be-laboured with clubs and blackjacks. Then the flag-kissing epi-sode was repeated, after which they were told to "hike" up the track and never come back. They reached Los Angeles after a tramp of several days, sore, hungry, penniless, and in deplorable physical condition.[5]

Ben Reitman, anarchist friend of Goldman's, relates his gruesome experience with the San Diego Vigilantes.

"As soon as we got out of town, they began kicking and beating me. They took turns pulling my long hair and they stuck their fingers into my eyes and nose. 'We could tear your guts out,' they said, 'but we promised the Chief of Police not to kill you. We are responsible men, property-owners, and the police are on our side.' When we reached the county line, the auto stopped at a deserted spot. The men formed a ring and told me to undress. They tore my clothes off. They knocked me down, and when I lay naked on the ground, they kicked and beat me until I was almost insensible. With a lighted cigar they burned the letters I.W.W. on my buttocks; then they poured a can of tar over my head and, in the absence of feathers, rubbed sage-brush on my body. One of them attempted to push a cane into my rectum. Another twisted my testicles. They forced me to kiss the flag and sing *The Star Spangled Banner*. When they tired of the fun, they gave me back my underwear for fear we should meet any women. They also gave me back my vest, in order that I might carry my money, railroad ticket, and watch. The rest of my clothes they kept. I was ordered to make a speech, and then they commanded me to run the gauntlet. The Vigilantes lined up, and as I ran past them, each one gave me a blow or a kick. Then they let me go." [6]

The pathology of the Vigilantes did not put an end to the direct action tactics of the IWW. New replacements arrived in San Diego, and the free speech campaign continued. National attention was drawn to the struggle, and criticism of the cruelty of the Vigilantes led the governor of California to appoint Colonel Harris Weinstock, a businessman, to investigate and report upon the free speech disturbances in San Diego. His report issued in May, 1912, substantiated the charges made by the victims of the Vigilantes and added that "local commercial bodies have encouraged and applauded the acts of these so-called vigilantes." It also disclosed that public meetings were not allowed unless the Police Chief granted a permit, although no law existed requiring a permit. Considerable testimony revealed that there had been "needless brutality on the part of police officers while meetings were being dispersed." [7]

This condemnation of citizens and authorities of San Diego did not give rise to a new democratic spirit, although it may have been partly responsible for the apparent drop in violence directed against the IWW street meetings held in the summer and autumn of 1912. From the point of view of establishing the right of free speech, Haywood and St. John, in retrospect, acknowledged that the IWW had not gained a victory in San Diego.

The most widely publicized IWW conflict acquainting America with the organization's revolutionary unionism and direct action tactics was the textile workers' strike at Lawrence, Massachusetts, in the winter of 1912. Of the total 85,000 population of Lawrence, almost one half of its inhabitants of fourteen years of age and over were employed in the woolen and cotton mills. The great majority were unskilled workers of Italian, Polish, French, Belgian, French-Canadian, Jewish, German, Lithuanian, Russian, English, Portuguese, and Syrian descent. For a number of years before 1912, the IWW had been organizing in Lawrence along nationality lines, and, at the time of the strike, it had on its rolls some three hundred paid-up members. Approximately twenty-five hundred English-speaking skilled workers were organized by craft and affiliated with the AF of L's United Textile Workers. The four largest mills at Lawrence were owned by the American Woolen Company, which also employed the greatest number of workers there, half of whom were females between the ages of 14 and 18. The average rate of earnings was 16 cents an hour. When the mills were running full time, employees' average weekly wages came to $8.76.[8]

The strike was precipitated by a reduction in take-home pay when the Massachusetts legislature lowered the working hours for women and children from 56 to 54 a week, effective January 1, 1912. Workers had hoped that the American Woolen Company would readjust its time and piece rates so that weekly earnings could be kept at the old level before the revised law was passed, but their hopes were in vain.

The first mill workers to be affected by the new hour law were the weavers employed in the Everett cotton mills. On January 11, 1912, when these weavers, mostly Polish women, were paid and noticed a decrease in their wages, some of them immediately stopped their looms. In response to demands for an explanation, officials of the mill were told through an interpreter that one Polish woman weaver had answered, "Not enough pay." A similar stoppage involving about one hundred workers occurred in the spinning department of the Arlington mill that same afternoon. On the following morning the workers of the Washington and Wood mills joined the strike, and a strikers' meeting that afternoon agreed to telegraph Joseph J. Ettor, a member of the IWW executive board, asking him to come to Lawrence and furnish strike leadership. Two days later, on Sunday, another meeting was held at which Ettor was elected chairman of the strike committee. The workers' demands, as announced by the strike committee, called for a 15 per cent increase in wages on the 54-hour-work-week basis, double pay for overtime work, the abolition of all bonus or premium systems, and no discrimination against any workers for their activities during the strike.

From the strike's outset violence stemming from both sides to the conflict was a common feature. The first clash between strikers and Lawrence law enforcement authorities occurred as early as January 15, when the strikers attempted to molest the employees of the Pacific and Atlantic mills who had not joined the strike. On January 29, a particularly large strikers' demonstration resulted in another battle between them and the police in the course of which Anna Lo Pezzi, a young Italian woman striker, was shot and killed. Joseph Ettor and the IWW leader and poet, Antonio Giovannitti, were arrested as accessories to the murder on the charge that they "did incite, procure and counsel or command the said person whose name is not known, as aforesaid, to commit the said murder." [9] If the arrest of Ettor was intended to deprive the strikers of IWW national leadership, it failed in its purpose inasmuch as "Big Bill" Haywood, called to Lawrence by the strike committee, assumed Ettor's place.

Throughout the strike the IWW brought into vogue many militant tactics characteristic of syndicalism. The acting head of the Lawrence police testified in Washington before a House Investigating Committee that when his men attempted to stop demonstrations by prohibiting "meetings in the city hall and on the public commons," the strikers "were instructed by their leaders to have sidewalk parades. . . . They would go in groups of 20, 30, or 50 and lock arms on the sidewalks . . . and pass along our main business streets and sweep everybody off the sidewalk or against the wall." When this tactic was disrupted by the police and "people found that they could not carry on that sort of parading they were instructed in another phase of the warfare—to pass in and out of our stores; not to buy anything but to go in in great crowds in the stores, walk around and walk out again, and to do that along our streets, and they did do it, and they had our shopkeepers in a state of terror. It was a question whether or not they would shut up their shops." [10] Another variation of picketing and street demonstrations called for women, child-bearing women, and women with young children to be in the forefront of strikers' demonstrations.

The IWW also freely distributed in various languages their propaganda literature among the working people of Lawrence. Proclamations of the strike committee reminded the workers of their exploitation by the "millionaire mill owners." The leaflets said that the actions of the militia, police, and local judge during the strike showed that these forces served the millowners' interests. Working class solidarity was urged to defeat the power of capitalist oppression. The general strike was exalted as labor's victorious weapon.

As a further innovation in strike methods in America, the IWW borrowed a custom originating with strikers in Europe; strikers' children were sent to the homes of sympathizers in nearby cities. This strategy of locating their children away from the dangerous areas of the strike aided the morale of the strikers as well as easing the problem of feeding their families. Moving the children from their homes also attracted sympathetic national publicity. John Golden, president of the AF of L United Textile Workers, while testifying before the House Investigating Committee claimed the children were exploited for IWW propaganda purposes. The strike committee, however, had seen to it that the homes which the children were to visit had been inspected by members of a committee and a report of the conditions furnished to the strike committee. The strike committee also had been careful to obtain the parents' consent for all children leaving the city.

On February 10, 119 children were sent to New York and the following week another 150 children left Lawrence. Anticipating a further departure, assistant marshal Sullivan of Lawrence, prompted by Lawrence priests and Massachusetts business and press interests, stated on February 22, 1912, that henceforth children would be prohibited from leaving Lawrence. A strong protest was raised against this announcement and the strike committee decided to continue with its preparations for sending 150 more children to Philadelphia on February 24. But when the time came for the children to leave, they were prevented from boarding the train by a number of policemen gathered at the railroad station. Many mothers who came to watch the departure of their children became anxious when they saw them being handled and detained by the police. Consequently, they sprang into the disturbance with the result that they were roughly handled by the police and in some instances were clubbed. Fifteen children were arrested and brought before the Lawrence court on complaints that they were "growing up without salutary control," but after several weeks their cases were dismissed.[11] The police made no other efforts to prevent a renewed emigration.

The clash between the police and strikers' families spotlighted national attention and drew protests from sources sympathetic to the strikers. Congressmen William Wilson and Victor Berger introduced resolutions in the House of Representatives asking for the federal government to investigate conditions in Lawrence. Hearings before the House Committee on Rules, in early March, gave testimony of many women and children employed at the Lawrence mills, some of whom were children under sixteen brought to Washington by famed Margaret Sanger. The workers told the committee many heartbreaking stories about their employment conditions and the poverty they endured which aroused the public's sympathy to their situation. The American Woolen Company concerned over the public's reaction to the hearings acceded on March 12, 1912, to the strikers' demands. A short time later the other mills also capitulated.

The trial of Ettor and Giovannitti as accessories to the murder of the young woman striker began at the end of September, 1912. On September 30, the four hundred-strong IWW local in Lawrence called out 15,000 workers for a twenty-four hour general strike as a forewarning of their determination to stand behind their IWW leaders. After a trial lasting almost two months in which the two accused IWW'ers made use of the courtroom as a forum for expounding on their radical ideology, the jury returned an acquittal.

Less than a year after the Lawrence strike ended, the IWW was leading another strike, this time of twenty-five thousand unskilled foreign-born mill workers in the silk mills of Paterson, New Jersey. The principal grievance of the Paterson strikers was the employers' introduction of four looms to replace the customary two which workers had heretofore operated. During the course of the strike, about eighteen hundred picketing workers were arrested on charges of "disorderly conduct" or "unlawful assembly" and about fifteen hundred of them were found guilty by the court. Most of the strikers on being given the option of paying a fine or going to jail chose the latter IWW-approved course.

In the interest of publicizing the strike, raising funds, and increasing class consciousness, the IWW conceived the novel idea of using the strikers as actors to perform scenes of their lives before a paid audience. This production, known as the "Paterson Pageant," was presented by twelve hundred strikers early in June, 1913, at Madison Square Garden in New York City. Although the auditorium was filled to capacity for the performance, the entire affair was not a financial success. One of the enthusiastic producers of the "Paterson Pageant" was John Reed, dramatic editor of the *American Magazine,* whose later eye-witness account of the Russian Revolution, *Ten Days That Shook the World,* became a universal classic. Reed's unwarranted arrest for disorderly conduct in Paterson while simply observing the strike influenced his conversion to Marxism.

The position of the Paterson strikers by late spring, 1913, appeared hopeless. They had been on a general strike since February, and since the employers showed no signs of yielding to their terms, the economic position of the workers and their families was desperate. When the "Paterson Pageant" failed to replenish the strike treasury, it became increasingly difficult to maintain the morale of the strikers.

Less hardy workers began drifting back to their jobs and as this movement gained momentum in July, the IWW was compelled to terminate the strike. Two years later, however, Adolph Lessig, secretary of the IWW National Industrial Union of Textile Workers, claimed before the Senate Industrial Relations Commission that the strike had never actually ceased because the IWW tactic of "passive resistance" had been put into practice "on the job." [12]

A much-publicized IWW strike in the West took place, shortly after the Paterson strike, among hop-pickers on the Durst brothers' ranch in Wheatland, California. This particular hop ranch exemplified the harsh conditions usually encountered by migratory workers. The men, poorly paid and fed, lived in overcrowded, badly-worn tents and most of them slept outdoors on hop vines or straw. There were about eight inadequately-made toilets for almost three thousand men. Sanitary conditions were indescribably primitive causing many of the workers to suffer from malaria, typhoid, dysentery, and diarrhea. But it was the lack of drinking water in the mid-summer California heat that caused the workers under the prodding of Wobbly card holders to finally rebel. On August 3, 1913, the strike began. This threat to the harvest and agricultural profits almost immediately brought out the state militia. The inevitable violence that accompanied the tense situation led to deaths on both sides. The strike leaders, Richard Ford and Herman Suhr, were arrested as accessories to murder and sentenced to life imprisonment. While the strike was officially broken, following the leaders' arrest, the publicity afforded by the strike led to a state investigation of the migratory workers' camps that produced the first installments of much-needed legislation for casual laborers in California.

While the Socialist party gave some help to the IWW in its biggest strikes, like that of Lawrence and Paterson, the leaders of the Socialist party, as previously noted, had not allowed their organization to endorse the IWW, and, with the exception of Eugene Debs and A. M. Simons, remained consistently hostile to the IWW. Nevertheless, a good many in the rank and file of the Socialist party as trade-unionists were affiliated with the IWW and supported the direct action body in its free speech and strike activities. After the direct-actionists won control of the IWW in 1908, members of the Socialist party who were also members of the IWW found themselves in a paradoxical situation. Although their loyalty to the existing principles of the Socialist party required an enthusiasm for political action and a corresponding repudiation of direct action tactics, such as sabotage and violence, their loyalty to the leadership of the IWW called for support of these direct action measures. By 1912 it was apparent that this anomalous position in which many left wing trade-unionists found themselves was becoming increasingly difficult to maintain, because both organizations, instead of reconciling their basic differences, only managed to emphasize the polarity of their views. In short, the Socialist party was placing greater faith in the political action method of peacefully and gradually transforming capitalistic society, whereas the IWW was emphasizing revolutionary action through sabotage, violence, and a disregard for law.

As the "inevitability of gradualness" more and more became the philosophy of the Socialist party, it naturally followed that revolutionary issues had to be toned down in order to attract the votes of people who did not consider themselves part of a revolutionary proletariat but who would vote for a respectable reform party. Without the support of this element there was little chance of the Socialist party candidates having the successes on election day upon which the "inevitability of gradualness" depended.

Consequently, the Socialist party from the time of its first convention in 1901 adopted platforms with respect to such issues as immediate demands, trade-unions, immigration, and collectivization of land that would appeal to a large reformist electorate, rather than only to extreme, class-conscious Socialists. This opportunist attitude is well evidenced in the party's position on immediate demands. A spirited debate on this subject at the party's first convention in 1901 resulted in the adoption of the position consistently held from then on—that of subscribing to and working for immediate demands. On the question of the kind of structure favored for the trade-unions, the opportunist outlook also was consistently followed. Attempts of the radical wing to pass resolutions denouncing craft unionism or the conservative policies of the AF of L were regularly defeated, and in convention the Socialist party never antagonized the AF of L unionists by declaring itself solely in favor of industrial unionism. On the matter of immigration many of the moderate leaders in the Socialist party also fought for a party stand that would carry favor with the bulk of the AF of L membership. Contrary to decisions of the Socialist International Congress, the Committee on Immigration led by Victor Berger at the party's first national congress in 1910 and at the 1912 national convention reported a resolution to the delegates in favor of excluding Asiatics from the United States. The party's 1910 national congress also sought to reassure the farmers that the Socialist party had no intention of nationalizing their land. It stated that "even to declare in any dogmatic manner that all the land must eventually become social property is somewhat utopian." [13]

Interestingly, all of the above compromises of orthodox Socialist principles were strongly opposed by Eugene Debs. Debs constantly expressed his opposition to opportunism within the Socialist party in articles and speeches, but he was unable to direct the party toward his view. In response to the party's adopting the immigration restriction resolution in 1910, Debs wrote in the *International Socialist Review* of July, 1910, "It is utterly unsocialistic, reactionary, and in truth outrageous. . . . Away with the 'tactics' which requires the exclusion of the oppressed and suffering slaves who seek these shores with the hope of bettering their wretched condition and are driven back by the cruel lash of expediency by those who call themselves Socialists. . . . If Socialism, international revolutionary Socialism, does not stand staunchly, unflinchingly, and uncompromisingly for the working class and for the oppressed masses of all lands, then it stands for none and its claim is a false pretense and its profession a delusion and a snare."

Debs's basic disagreement with the moderate position being taken by the Socialist party was contained in an article "Danger Ahead" in the *International Socialist Review* of January, 1911.

> I cannot but feel that some of the votes placed to our credit this year were obtained by methods not consistent with the principles of a revolutionary party, and in the long run will do more harm than good.

> .   .   .   .

> The truth is that we have not a few members who regard vote getting as of supreme importance, no matter by what methods the votes may be secured, and this leads them to hold out inducements and make representations which are not at all compatible with the stern uncompromising principles of a revolutionary party. They seek to make the Socialist propaganda so attractive—eliminating whatever may give offense to bourgeois

sensibilities—that it serves as a bait for votes rather than as a means for education, and votes thus secured do not properly belong to us and do injustice to our party as well as to those who cast them.

These votes do not express Socialism, and in the next ensuing election are quite apt to be turned against us, and it is better that they be not cast for the Socialist party representing a degree of progress the party is not entitled to and indicating a political position the party is unable to sustain.

.   .   .   .

Not for all the vote of the American Federation of Labor and its labor-dividing-and-corruption-breeding craft unions should we compromise one jot of our revolutionary principles; and if we do we shall be visited with the contempt we deserve by all real Socialists, who will scorn to remain in a party professing to be a revolutionary party of the working class while employing the crooked and disreputable methods of ward-heeling and politicians to attain their ends.

Of far greater importance than increasing the vote of the Socialist party is the economic organization of the working class. To the extent, and only to the extent, that the workers are organized and disciplined in their respective industries can the Socialist movement advance and the Socialist Party hold what is registered by the ballot. The election of legislative and administrative officers, here and there, where the party is still in a crude state and the members economically unprepared and politically unfit to assume the responsibilities thrust upon them as the result of popular discontent, will inevitably bring trouble and set the party back, instead of advancing it.

The moderate leadership in control of the Socialist party did not agree with Debs's interpretation and were pleased that their method of appealing for the votes of a broader electorate was showing desired ballot and membership results. As the party's candidate for President of the United States, Debs's vote steadily increased from 96,116 in 1900 to 901,062 in 1912. In 1910, Victor Berger became the first Socialist to be elected to Congress, and his home city of Milwaukee also elected the Socialist candidate, Emil Seidel, as mayor. By 1912, Socialists held fifty-six important city offices which included the mayoralty of Butte, Montana, the victory of George R. Lunn, Presbyterian minister as mayor of Schenectady, New York, and the election of J. Stitt Wilson, a Protestant minister, as mayor of Berkeley, California.[14] In all, the year 1912 saw 1,039 Socialists holding office in more than three hundred municipalities in the United States. Socialist party membership, too, showed impressive gains, having gone from 41,000 in 1909 to 140,000 in 1912.

While these Socialist electoral victories and membership growth cheered the opportunist faction in the party, they did not succeed in convincing the party's members who were also IWW'ers that the party's reformist tendencies and its emphasis on political action were preferable to the revolutionary principles and direct action methods of the IWW. Towards the close of 1909 the left wing journal, *International Socialist Review,* began to express the dissatisfaction that many militant members of the Socialist party had with the Parliamentary Socialist leadership in the party. Its editor in the November, 1909, issue called the Socialist party's attention to the rising of "a new type of unionism, revolutionary as Marx himself, ruthless as capitalism, strong in the thought, learned not from Marx but from grim experience" that the workers have nothing "to lose but their chains, and all the world to gain." It was in such industrial unions that the Socialist party could thrive. Socialism, he wrote, would not grow permanently strong by its present policy of seeking the votes of people who were interested in "immediate demands." Socialist leaders of the middle-class intellectual type who advocated "immediate demands" must be replaced by workers ready "to spread the propaganda of revolution and the new industrialism." [15]

Articles in the *International Socialist Review* disapproved of the political tactics and reformist policies of the Socialist party and propagandized for revolutionary unonism and the IWW conception of the ideal state. Under this conception, capitalist property would be confiscated and the workers would jointly own the industries. As Bill Haywood told the Senate Industrial Relations Commission in 1914, "there will be no such thing as the state or states. The industries will take the place of what are now existing states." No one would be "a subject of state or nation, but a citizen of industry, moving from place to place, belonging to his union, wherever he went he would step in the union hall, show his card, register, and he at once would have a voice in the conduct of the affairs pertaining to his welfare." [16]

The Socialist ideal of government ownership intended for the state to remain built on the same geographical plan as under capitalism. In opposition to this the IWW leadership contended, "Government ownership can never lead to Socialism. It is not a step toward Socialism. It has nothing Socialist about it, because all political government is administration from the top." The IWW, if successful "would abolish practically every office existing under the present form of government and would then establish . . . the legislature of the workers [that] would be composed of men and women representing the different branches of industry." The industrial unions deriving their power from the workers would be the ruling authority in the new society.[17] One of the reasons why the evolutionary Socialists opposed this system was that it ultimately would result in a situation where the workers in the most essential industries would dominate the country by virtue of the strategic positions they held in the nation's economy.

By 1912 the objections of the opportunist Socialist leaders to those militants in the party who favored the principles and tactics of the IWW reached its climax. The underlying cause of the crisis was the moderates' disagreement with IWW ideology and especially with IWW tactics of sabotage and violence. "Big Bill" Haywood and Vincent St. John, undisputed leaders of the IWW, were both increasingly emphasizing direct action in their speeches and writings and the moderates had little tolerance for this revolutionary type of socialism. Haywood's added stress on direct action was partly an outgrowth of his European visit as a Socialist party delegate to the Labor and Socialist Congress of the Second International at Copenhagen in 1910. In the course of his European tour he conferred with Tom Mann, British syndicalist, with leading French syndicalists of the French Confederation of Labor, and arranged for the later American publication of several syndicalist writings.

In a pamphlet published in 1911 Haywood expressed his militancy in clear and simple terms. He wrote that if the worker correctly interprets his experience under capitalism and makes a proper study of socialism, "He retains absolutely no respect for the property 'rights' of the profit takers. He will use any weapon which will win his fight. He knows that the present laws of property are made by and for the capitalists. Therefore he does not hesitate to break them." [18] The biggest Wobbly of them all condemned the kind of agitation by the parliamentary Socialists which secured old age pensions and free meals for poor school children because it "kills the fighting spirit" of the workers. He was for industrial socialism which was "Socialism with its working clothes on." [19] Under this kind of socialism "the government of the Nation will be an industrial government, a shop government." [20] The labor union will be the legislature. "Its purpose will be to manage production and to establish and conduct the great social institutions required by civilized humanity. Political government will then, of course, have ceased to exist." [21] The major purpose of the Socialist party itself is to gain control of the government so that it can prevent the government from being used by the capitalists against "the industrial organization of the workers." [22]

Early in 1912 before a mass meeting at Cooper Union Hall in New York City, Haywood went further in clarifying his position on direct action. His talk took on particular significance because it was sponsored by New York's Socialist local and because a few days before the meeting Haywood had been elected to the Socialist party's National Executive Committee. In a none-too-subtle reference to right wing Socialists who were attacking him from the party's press and platform, Haywood began his speech by saying that he intended to present his views on the class struggle and that he was "going to make it so plain that even a lawyer [and] a preacher . . . the mouthpieces of the capitalist class" would understand his meaning.[23] His conception of political action, he pointed out, differed from that of the parliamentary Socialists. He did not want Socialists in political office to work for immediate demands. Their task was to hamper the ruling class in its struggle against the trade-unions and obstruct the power of the capitalist state from being used against the workers. He asserted that wherever the forces of government came into the control of the IWW they would not be used "to continue to uphold and advance this present system." [24]

... we will use the forces of the police power to overthrow this present system. (*Applause.*) And instead of using the powers of the police to protect the strike breakers, we will use the powers of the police to protect the strikers. (*Applause.*) That's about as far as I go on political action. (*Applause.*) But that's a long way. And the reason that I don't go into the halls of parliament to make laws to govern the working class is because the working class is working with machines, and every time some fellow has a thought, inspiration, the machine changes, and I don't know that laws can be made quick enough to keep up with the changing machinery.

.   .   .   .

I believe in direct action. If I wanted something done and could do it myself I wouldn't delegate that job to anybody. (*Applause.*) That's the reason I believe in direct action. You are certain of it and it isn't nearly so expensive. (*Applause.*)

.   .   .   .

So you understand that we know the class struggle in the west. And realizing, having contended with all the bitter things that we have been called upon to drink to the dregs, do you blame me when I say that I *despise the law* (*tremendous applause and shouts of* "No!") and am not a law-abiding citizen. (*Applause.*) And more than that, no Socialist *can* be a law-abiding citizen. (*Applause.*) When we come together and are of a common mind, and the purpose of our minds is to overthrow the capitalist system, we become conspirators then against the United States government. And certainly it is our purpose to abolish this government and establish in its place an industrial democracy. (*Applause.*) Now, we haven't any hesitation in saying that that is our aim and purpose. Am I correct! (*Tremendous applause.*) Am I absolutely correct when I state this as being the position of the Socialist Party not only of New York, but of the United States and of every nation of the world. (*Applause.*)

.   .   .   .

I know that some of you members here will think that this is not patriotic (*laughter*); that really you ought to fight for the flag; that you ought to live up to your obligations and fulfil your duties. But let me say to you that that isn't being a traitor. If it is it, it's better to be a traitor to your country than it is to be a traitor to your class. (*Applause.*) (*A shout:* "The working man has no country at all!") That's very well said. Not only that, but there are no foreigners in the working class. (*Applause.*)

. . . .

I am not going to take the time tonight to describe to you the conditions in France, though I would like to do so, because I again want to justify direct action and sabotage. You have plenty of it over there. (*Applause.*) I don't know of anything that can be applied that will bring as much satisfaction to you, as much anguish to the boss as a little sabotage in the right place at the right time. Find out what it means. It won't hurt you, and it will cripple the boss.[25]

"Big Bill" had swung hard and like many a swing it left the attacker open to a counterpunch. For an IWW'er to urge lawbreaking, violence, and conspiracy was not unusual. For a National Executive Committeeman of a reformist party to speak in such a manner was an act exceedingly threatening to the party's more prudent leaders. The proponents of evolutionary socialism feared the possibility that Haywood's direct action, revolutionary, and antipolitical views might secure an increased following within the Socialist party. They were worried, too, about the effect of Haywood's speeches on the public's opinion of the Socialist party. If the public should begin to look upon the IWW and the Socialist party as allied organizations, the party would alienate many nonrevolutionary middle-class and working-class voters. Besides wanting to remove the taint of the IWW's radicalism for winning election day votes, Socialist party leaders also thought that the elimination of IWW influence was an essential step for winning AF of L convention support for a Socialist candidate against Gompers. Moreover, there was always the ominous possibility that some IWW member, overwhelmed with zeal for direct action, might commit a major, publicized act of violence, which, if identified in the national mind with the Socialist party, would seriously retard the party's progress among many working-class people.

Lastly, the humanistic ethics of many Socialist party leaders caused them to disagree with militant, direct action tactics. They considered that those who supported violence in the solution of social problems were lacking in moral and intellectual strength. Such persons who would not present their cause to the arbitration of reason must doubt the validity of their cause. Implicit in a belief in volence and sabotage was the belief that education is a farce. Furthermore, immoral means also inevitably endangered right ends. Should socialism be born with violence as its midwife, it was scattering seeds that would produce a tyranny of a new kind.

At its 1912 convention the Socialist party squarely faced the problem posed by members who held a dual allegiance to the Socialist party and to the IWW. The Constitution Committee reported a clause aimed to disqualify for membership in the Socialist party any militant, direct-actionist IWW'er. The clause, Article II, Section 6, of the Socialist party's constitution, after being amended by the delegates, before it was passed, finally read:

> Any member of the party who opposes political action or advocates crime, sabotage, or other methods of violence as a weapon of the working-class to aid in its emancipation shall be expelled from membership in the party. Political action shall be construed to mean participation in elections for public office and practical legislative and administrative work along the lines of the Socialist Party platform.[26]

IWW'ers and their sympathizers at the convention argued that the amendment would have precluded the Boston Tea Party, would compel obedience of the restrictions set on union activities by anti-labor courts, and would tame the working class into accepting the violence imposed by a capitalist class through its capitalist-created laws and state power.

In favoring the clause, the convention moderates claimed that it was necessary "because men have come into the Socialist Party and instead of advocating the principles and tactics of the Socialist political organization, they have advocated the tactics of an economic organization—sabotage." [27] Delegate Goebel further believed that "when a man speaks for the Socialist Party, in a hall which is paid for by Socialists, that he ought to talk what we mean by Socialism." [28] Speaking of sabotage, the Reverend W. H. Gaylord said: "We do not want any of it. None of it. We don't want the touch of it on us. We do not want the hint of it connected with us." [29] Morris Hillquit warned that "if there is one thing in this country that can now check or disrupt the Socialist movement it is not the capitalist class, it is not the Catholic Church, it is our own injudicious friends from within" who are advocating crime, sabotage and violence.[30] Victor Berger charged that the IWW was "anarchism by a new name" and that "articles in the *Industrial Worker* of Spokane, the official organ of the IWW breathe the same spirit, are as anarchistic as anything John Most has ever written." IWW members could not be tolerated within the Socialist party, he held, because "There is no bridge between Socialism and Anarchism." Any Socialist who believed in sabotage, "who is willing to commit such insane acts for his industrial organization should quit our party. I would rather have such a man belong to the Militia of Christ, like the McNamara's. I would prefer that a man committing murder should have a membership card of the Knights of Columbus than show the 'red card.' " [31]

Haywood himself became the first notable IWW figure to be expelled from the Socialist party under the provisions of the new clause. A resolution charging him with being an advocate of sabotage was submitted to a referendum vote of the membership, and in February, 1913, he was recalled from his post on the National Executive Committee. The entire controversy that finally led to the adoption of Article II, Section 6, and the expulsion of Haywood probably weakened the general Marxist movement. The Socialist party lost almost forty-five thousand members, about one-third of its membership, between June, 1912, and June, 1913, and its internal conflict was partly the cause of this huge loss. The left wing Socialists who quit the party following Haywood's expulsion undoubtedly improved the hold of the reformists on the party. In turn, the departure of Socialist party members from the IWW meant the loss of many who had furnished the IWW with intellectual ability, theoretical insights, and common sense restraint on reckless activity. In March, 1914, Debs, who had previously declared his opposition to violence and sabotage as well as to party expulsion for differences of opinion, and who continued to oppose such tactics, wrote in the *International Socialist Review* that he favored the deletion of Article II, Section 6, from the party's constitution. He thought this clause restricted free speech and attempted to curry "favor in bourgeois eyes." If direct action tactics were lawless, a party should not provide "constitutional penalties of expulsion" but it should be left to the state to penalize it like "theft or any other crime." [32]

The IWW's strength and membership declined during 1914 and 1915. Several factors may have been responsible, including the execution in 1915 of IWW song writer and organizer Joe Hill for a grocery holdup and murder in Salt Lake City; the publicity given to sabotage; the rift with the Socialist party; internal friction caused by western affiliates who favored decentralization to restrict the powers of the general officers and executive board; and, finally, the industrial depression of 1914 which brought large-scale unemployment among IWW members.

The IWW's program to meet the 1914 depression was characteristic of its direct action approach. The 1914 IWW convention condemned the food merchants and the government for shipping bread to the warring countries in Europe while no attention was being shown to the needs of hungry American workers. The workers were urged to plunder the granaries and warehouses and feed themselves. The *Chicago Daily News* on September 22, 1914, reported that Haywood told the delegates: "Where machinery is lying idle, use it for your purposes, where houses are unoccupied, enter them and sleep." At this same convention a resolution was unanimously approved which in effect suggested that IWW speakers advocate the tactics of slow down and sabotage. In an article in December, 1914, on "How to Make Work for the Unemployed," Joe Hill wrote that in several industries "men are hired" when the employer has work to be done and they are fired when the work is completed. "Consequently," he advised, "it is to the interest of the workers to make the job last as long as possible." Slowing down the job was a weapon *"without expense* to the *working class* that will *reduce the profits of the exploiter"* and at the same time *"create more work for the wage earners."* [33]

Renewed IWW free speech and strike activity occurred in 1916. While attempting to organize the lumber industry of the northwest, IWW Lumber Workers' Union No. 500 opened a union hall in August, 1916, in Everett, Washington, about thirty miles from Seattle. Attempts, however, to hold meetings aroused the savage opposition of the local police authorities led by Sheriff Donald McRae who repeatedly arrested, beat, and deported the IWW organizers. As in previous instances, an organizing drive developed into a free speech movement.

In Seattle an IWW free speech committee was established to operate the campaign that would win Everett for free speech and organizational activity. On October 30, forty-one free speech crusaders arrived in Everett by boat from Seattle intending to conduct a street meeting. They were met at the dock by Sheriff McRae and his deputies who escorted them to the outskirts of the town where they were forced to run the gauntlet between the deputies lined up on either side with spiked sticks. This exhibition of Everett brutality infuriated the local IWW union and made them more determined about the righteousness of their campaign. Therefore, following a call for volunteers, almost three hundred IWW loggers and lumber workers embarked in two boats from Seattle on November 5, determined to inaugurate free speech in Everett. As the first boat approached the Everett dock, "with everyone on board singing 'Hold the Fort for we are coming, union men be strong,'" the song was interrupted by shooting from the shore where Sheriff McRae and about two hundred armed Vigilantes lay in wait.[34] After ten minutes of shooting from both sides the boats left for Seattle with five IWW members killed and thirty-one wounded. The casualties of the Everett Vigilantes were two killed and nineteen wounded. At Seattle the IWW boats were met by police who arrested several leaders for murder. The men were found guilty and given long prison sentences.

Conditions underlying the strike of iron miners on the Mesabi Range, Minnesota, in 1916 were similar to ones that had culminated in the IWW's leadership of earlier strikes. Workers were of immigrant stock, mostly unorganized, and subjected to long hours of work, low wages, and a piece system or contract method of payment which produced an entrenched system of graft utilized by the foremen. In this particular strike, the mining companies had the benefit of a private police force, deputized citizens, and the state militia, while outside help for the strikers was answered only by the IWW. The strike lasted from June, 1916, until September, with killings occurring on both sides. Four miners were arrested and charged with the murder of a deputy while IWW strike leaders, Joseph Schmidt, Samuel Scarlett, and Carlo Tresca were placed in the Duluth prison for "inciting murder." These IWW leaders were freed but three of the miners received long prison terms. For breaking solidarity and allowing the three miners to plead guilty, Schmidt, Scarlett, and Tresca were expelled from the IWW. The IWW national office also accused IWW leaders Elizabeth Gurley Flynn and Joseph Ettor of being outsmarted by the lawyers who "fixed the case." Therefore they, too, were dropped from the organization.

The disturbance in the Mesabi Range produced hearings before the Minnesota legislature which led to an investigation of conditions in the mines by a commission appointed by Governor Burnquist. Since the commission's report on August 25, 1916, was favorable to the strikers' cause, and at the same time there were signs of weakening in the ranks of the strikers, the strike committee called off the strike on September 19. Two months later the miners received a 10 per cent increase in pay that Bill Haywood bragged in his autobiography was "granted by the Steel Trust without a conference, a settlement or an agreement of any kind." [35]

All during its turbulent period of revolutionary expression and direct action methods, the IWW had provoked the extreme antagonism of business interests and the nation's press. The outbreak of World War I not only intensified this hostility but also resulted in a campaign by the federal government to destroy the IWW. This decision was fanned by the IWW's open antipatriotic and antimilitaristic stand which caused the government to believe that the organization weakened the country's production and conscription efforts.

The foundation for the IWW's antimilitarist position had been laid at its first convention in 1905, when it had gone on record as unalterably opposed to militarism "in all its forms." [36] At its 1914 convention the IWW approved a resolution which, in substance, denounced patriotism and charged the European working class as ignorant for continuing the war which had just started. Social Democratic movements like those in Germany were blamed for instilling "a spirit of patriotism within political boundary lines." As opposed to such political movements, the industrial movement would wipe out national boundaries and "establish an international relationship between all races engaged in industry."

The resolution specifically stated that IWW "members of the industrial army will refuse to fight for any purpose except the realization of industrial freedom." [37]

The 1914 IWW convention also unanimously adopted "A DECLARATION" offered by the General Executive Board which denounced the war as designed to aid capitalist conquest of lands and exploitation of workers, and to delay the day of capitalism's overthrow. The IWW declaration declared that with

> the ever-growing agitation for military preparedness clouding the main issues and delaying the realization of our ultimate aim with patriotic and, therefore, capitalistic aspirations, we openly declare ourselves determined opponents of all nationalistic sectionalism, or patriotism, and the militarism preached and supported by our one enemy, the capitalist class. We condemn all wars, and for the prevention of such, we proclaim the anti-militarist propaganda in time of peace, thus promoting class solidarity among the workers of the entire world, and, in time of war, the General strike in all industries. We extend assurances of both moral and material support to all workers to unite themselves with us that the reign of the exploiters may cease and this earth be made fair through the establishment of the Industrial Democracy.[38]

It was also unanimously agreed at the 1914 convention that this declaration be given publicity through the capitalist press and through the publication of IWW leaflets. Such a leaflet was extensively circulated by the IWW throughout the country as a part of its propaganda campaign against the war. A sticker issued for posting read "Don't be a soldier, be a man. Join the IWW and fight on the job for yourself and your class."

A pamphlet published by the IWW in 1915 further enunciated the organization's antipatriotic position and later was used by the United States government as evidence that the IWW was disloyal to the nation. The pamphlet proclaimed:

> We are international in scope and recognize but one nation, the nation of those who work. . . . The Industrial Workers of the World is an INTERNATIONAL movement; not merely an American movement. We are patriotic for our class, the working class. We realize that as workers we have no country. The

flags and symbols that once meant great things to us have been seized by our employer. Today they mean naught to us but oppression and tyranny. As long as we quarrel among ourselves over differences of nationality we weaken our cause, we defeat our purpose. . . . In our organization, the Caucasian, the Malay, the Mongolian and the Negro are all on the same footing. All are workers and as such their interests are the same. An injury to them is an injury to us.[39]

Despite America's entry into the war on April 6, 1917, the IWW continued its antimilitarist, unpatriotic agitation. In an IWW publication, Haywood wrote that the organization was against war not for religious reasons, like those of the Quakers, but because its belief in the common interests of the workers in all countries precluded killing workers of other countries. The only war it did believe in, he said, was the *class war.*

Nevertheless, the IWW did not advise its members to disregard the draft, inasmuch as such a move would invite government prosecution. A general executive board meeting was called in July, 1917, to decide the organization's formal position on conscription and it was agreed that Ralph Chaplin, editor of *Solidarity,* would write a militant antiwar statement over his own signature, thus technically relieving the organization of any responsibility. Published in the July 28, 1917, issue of *Solidarity,* the article denounced the war as a conflict to enrich capitalists, instructed IWW members to register for the draft but indicate their right to exemption because they were IWW'ers, and implied that any IWW member who joined the military forces would be expelled from the organization. The article, "Were You Drafted?" read in part:

Members joining the military forces of any nation have always been expelled from the organization. . . . The IWW has placed itself on record regarding its opposition to war, and also as being bitterly opposed to having its members forced into the bloody and needless quarrels of the ruling class of different nations. . . . The principles of the international solidarity of labor to which we have always adhered makes it impossible for us to participate in any and all the plunder squabbles of the parasite class. . . . Our songs, our literature, the sentiment of the entire membership—the very spirit of our union, give evidence of our unalterable opposition to both capitalism and its wars. . . . All members of the IWW who have been drafted should mark their claims for exemption: 'IWW, opposed to war.'

Actually, the IWW did not merely preach evasion of conscription, but also practiced it. Individually, there were IWW'ers who did not register and even hid out at home or in Mexico. By covert action, the IWW was aiding such individual behavior.

In several instances the IWW was connected with draft evasion. In June, 1917, 136 IWW members and Socialists in Rockford, Illinois, refused to register as required by the Conscription Law. However, they voluntarily surrendered themselves to the authorities at the county jail and were then imprisoned. At their trial Judge Kenesaw Mountain Landis found them guilty and sentenced them to prison terms. In the Mesabi Iron Range of Minnesota, Finnish IWW miners openly went on strike against conscription.

Like the IWW, the Socialist party of America was antimilitarist from the year of its founding. Antimilitarist declarations were a regular feature of its conventions and congresses. After the outbreak of the war in Europe, its executive committee issued several manifestoes condemning the war as an imperialist conflict. In 1915, a party referendum vote sanctioned the expulsion of any Socialist party office holder who supported a military appropriations bill. The 1916 platform and presidential candidates vigorously denounced preparedness and war. On April 7, 1917, a party convention vote in St. Louis proclaimed, "The Socialist Party of the United States in the present grave crisis solemnly reaffirms its allegiance to the principle of internationalism and working class solidarity the world over, and proclaims its unalterable opposition to the war just declared by the government of the United States." [40] This action resulted in many prominent Socialists breaking with the party and announcing their support of the government.

In addition to the IWW's antimilitarist, antipatriotic principles, and its draft evasion tendencies, the wartime strike activities of the organization increased the government's fears that the IWW's intentions were to obstruct the war effort. The largest IWW strikes in 1917 occurred in the Pacific Northwest lumber fields and in the Arizona and Montana copper regions. Since the materials from both of these industries were essential to the nation's war production effort, these IWW strikes particularly aroused the anxiety of government authorities. At the same time, workers' grievances in these industries were very real. While war contracts for materials were bringing a windfall of immense profits to owners, workers were bothered because their increased wages often failed to keep pace with the rising cost of living. In addition, they desired the eight-hour day, better working conditions, an improvement in company-provided living quarters, and the end of the blacklist and the speedup.

Beginning in April, 1917, IWW strikes became frequent in the northwest lumber districts and by mid-August the logging industry of Washington was pretty much shut down. Many arrests of IWW leaders connected with IWW Lumber Workers' Union No. 500 were made throughout Idaho and in Spokane but the unrest in the lumber industry continued. Because of limited finances, the IWW local made use of a favorite tactic—the strike on the job. The men would either quit work after putting in eight hours instead of the ten expected by their employers, or they would work slowly during these ten hours intending to do the equivalent of eight hours work. On May 1, 1917, a number of IWW lumber workers burned their employer-provided blankets so as to draw attention to the unclean condition of their bedding. Unrest in the northwest lumber industry did not subside until March, 1918, when Colonel Disque of the Spruce Division of the United States Army Signal Corps, acting on the report of *The President's Mediation Commission,* established the eight-hour day for the lumber industry of the northwest. The government's arrest of over three hundred IWW leaders throughout the country in the fall of 1917 also had the effect of scaring rank-and-file workers from engaging in any activities that might cast any suspicion on their loyalty to the government.

In late 1916 and in 1917 the IWW was trying to organize the copper mining areas of Arizona where almost one-third of the total copper output of the United States was produced. The copper workers, composed of many nationalities, were restive because of the common grievances peculiar to the worst-off elements of wage labor, aggravated by the fact that they often had no union to bargain collectively for them. As *The President's Mediation Commission* report pointed out in January, 1918, after having investigated industrial disturbances in the west, "the industry was conducted upon an autocratic basis . . . the final determination of every issue was left with the company. In place of orderly processes of adjustment the workers were given the alternative of submission or strike." Labor difficulties, in these mining areas, the Commission further stated, were also complicated by the antimilitarist, international doctrines of the local IWW leadership who held "the conviction that all wars are capitalistic." This IWW influence in the Globe District of Arizona "led to resolutions of opposition to the war by the miners' local at the outbreak of the war. The situation was further intensified by refusal to display the flag at union headquarters." [41] The Commission also reported that while the IWW took advantage of unjust working conditions in the copper areas to propagate its doctrine the IWW itself did not "account for these strikes. The explanation is to be found in unremedied remedial industrial disorders."

From May, 1917, until October, 1917, there were intermittent strikes in the copper mining districts of Arizona in which various locals of the IWW Metal Workers' Industrial Union No. 800 prominently figured. A Jerome citizens' committee, disturbed by the strikes and IWW principles, arrested several hundred striking miners on July 10, placed seventy of the ringleaders on cattle cars and sent them to California. The California authorities on hand were equally hostile and compelled the group to return to Arizona territory, where it disbanded at Kingman.

An even sharper example of deportation violence perpetrated against the IWW is found in the treatment of strikers at Bisbee, Arizona. In the early hours of July 12, a Loyalty League sponsored by the business elements and deputized by the sheriff, raided the homes of suspected IWW members and sympathizers who were on strike. Over one thousand arrested men were placed under guard at a local baseball park, where they were offered the choice of returning to work or being deported. When only a few agreed to return to work, the rest were herded into cattle and freight railroad cars—many of whose floors were deep with manure—shipped out of Bisbee, and eventually unloaded in desert country without food or water. The federal government, after thirty-six

hours had passed, arranged for these men to be taken to a deten-
tion camp in Columbus, New Mexico, and quartered there until
the middle of September, when the camp closed because the
government would no longer furnish it with rations. Although the
employers' hostility shown by the Jerome and Bisbee deporta-
tions broke the strikes, the abuses suffered by workers also furnished the IWW with material for anticapitalist propaganda and
proof, to their satisfaction, of capitalist tyranny.

Another example of extralegal violence perpetrated against
the IWW during the World War I period took place in Butte,
Montana. A disastrous fire in the Speculator mine during June,
1917, resulted in the death of 164 men. This calamity spurred a
strike by the Metal Mine Workers' Union, which then demanded
the observance of mining laws and an increase in pay. The strike
dragged on throughout the summer of 1917 and spread until it
reached the proportions of a general mine strike in Butte. Assisting
the IWW local was Frank Little, veteran IWW organizer and chairman of the IWW general executive board. Late in the night of July
31, 1917, he was seized in his room at the Finn Hotel by six
armed men who beat him, tied him behind their automobile with a
rope, and drove to the outskirts of Butte. He was then murdered
by hanging on the Milwaukee Railroad trestle, and a card was
pinned on his coat reading: "First and last warning" followed by
the numbers 3 + 7 — 77, the sign of the old Vigilantes.[42] This
terrorism failed to drive the strikers back to work; the effect of
the nationwide mass arrests of over three hundred IWW leaders
by the federal government in September, 1917, however, accomplished this purpose. By mid-December, 1917, the Butte strike
officially terminated.

The IWW's antimilitarist, antipatriotic pronouncements and
beliefs, its suspected opposition to conscription, and its wartime
strike activities, made the organization extremely vulnerable to
suppression by a government seeking the modern wartime require-
ments of a citizens' fighting force and a steady flow of materials
for the military forces. Deciding that tolerance was a virtue too
expensive for a war, the government planned to wipe out the
IWW through a campaign of mass arrests of its leaders. About
one hundred special agents of the Department of Justice trailed
and spied on IWW leaders during 1916 and 1917. On September

5, 1917, federal officers acting in unison throughout the country raided various IWW headquarters and union offices and seized all available records, documents, correspondence, and literature. In another mass raid on September 28, 166 IWW leaders were arrested and indicted in Chicago for violation of the Espionage Act of June, 1917. For several months thereafter raids and arrests continued, mainly in the states of California, Washington, Oregon, Idaho, Kansas, Oklahoma, and Nebraska until practically every important leader connected with the IWW was rounded up. So thoroughgoing were the results of the government's campaign of mass arrests that the IWW lacked the leadership by the end of 1917 to maintain itself as a going concern.

The government's wartime persecution and imprisonment of people strongly antimilitarist extended beyond the IWW to an- archists, "independent" radicals, religious pacifists and antiwar Socialist party members. The Socialist party, its press, and meet- ings were virtually suppressed by the government.

The IWW by 1918 was too weak to carry on any organizing or strike activity, but its surviving members did try to aid their imprisoned leaders. According to the IWW revolutionary philos- ophy, an occasion such as the arrest of its leaders should have served as the signal for a general strike in all industries where the organization had sufficient strength. In 1917, the IWW reputedly was at the height of its all-time strength, having a membership of seventy thousand. But no general strike was called or threatened, for the secondary leaders well knew that the organization was far too feeble for such an undertaking. Ironically, the imprisonment of-its leaders compelled the antipolitical IWW to resort to politi- cal activity. A General Defense organization was established with committees in various cities to create publicity, arouse sympathy, and raise funds for the arrested officials. To aid in these endeavors, those leaders released on bail addressed audiences in many cities.

On April 1, 1918, the largest mass trial of prominent IWW leaders began in the Chicago court of Judge Kenesaw Mountain Landis. One hundred prominent IWW leaders, including Haywood and St. John, faced four indictments, which, in effect, charged them with conspiring to hinder the prosecution of the war. The government attorney, Frank Nebeker, contended that the defend- ants in conducting strikes were not seeking to better the conditions of the workers but that their purpose was to interfere with the war effort. He further charged that the IWW believed in and practiced a philosophy that destroyed patriotism and loyalty. The IWW's pronounced hostility to capitalism and emphasis of itself as an international movement, Nebeker charged, meant that the organization held a higher loyalty to the working class of foreign countries than it did to the business class in its own country.

The defense attorneys, George F. Vanderveer and Otto Christensen, admitted that many of the defendants disapproved of conscription and of the war but claimed that disapproval did not constitute conspiracy. The attorneys contended that the government had failed to prove that the accused had conspired against the government. The defendants sought to place capitalism on trial by discussing the exploitation of labor they had witnessed during their days as IWW organizers. The defendants also described the brutalities they had suffered at the hands of legal authorities and citizens' committees. But as Ralph Chaplin, one of the defendants, later wrote in his autobiography, "The jury was unimpressed. Our most persuasive facts and arguments did not move it nor did the harrowing details of atrocities committed against our members." [43] Undoubtedly the atmosphere of patriotism engendered by the war could hardly provide a judicious background for weighing the IWW's loyalty to the nation by a jury of middle-class Americans, who even in periods of peace were repelled by radical doctrines. After a trial lasting more than four months, the jury on August 7, 1918, deliberated for twenty-five minutes and found ninety-eight defendants guilty on all four counts, an average of less than a half a minute for each verdict. Fifteen of the most important IWW leaders received sentences of twenty years in prison, thirty-five others received ten years, and the remainder lesser sentences.

In the case of forty-six IWW leaders being tried in Sacramento, California, forty-three of the defendants decided to acknowledge the class bias of the court by refusing to participate in its proceedings. While such a gesture had some noble tradition behind it elsewhere in the world, it was considered offensive by the California court. The silent defendants received more severe prison sentences, extending from one to ten years, than those who testified. Other mass trials conducted at Wichita, Kansas; Omaha,

Nebraska; and Spokane, Washington, resulted in imprisonment of thirty-eight IWW defendants in Wichita, twenty-eight in Spokane, and twenty-seven in Omaha. Several hundred IWW members were also tried and convicted under criminal syndicalist laws passed in a number of states. In California alone, 164 persons were found guilty.

One of the few non-IWW voices to speak out for the IWW while its leaders were undergoing the wartime trials was Eugene Debs. As part of a larger talk in Canton, Ohio, June 16, 1918, Debs said:

> There are few men who have the courage to say a word in favor of the IWW. I have. Let me say here that I have great respect for the IWW. Far greater than I have for their infamous detractors . . . In every age the pulpit has been on the side of the rulers and not on the side of the people. That is one reason why the preachers so fiercely denounce the IWW. . . . The IWW in all its career never committed as much violence against the ruling class as the ruling class has committed against the IWW. Just whisper the name of the IWW and you are branded as a disloyalist. And the reason for this is wholly to the credit of the IWW, for whatever may be charged against it, the IWW has always fought for the bottom dog. And that is why Haywood is despised and prosecuted while Gompers is lauded and glorified by the same [Wall Street] gang.[44]

For this speech Debs himself was arrested, convicted in September, 1918, of having violated the Espionage Law, and sentenced to ten years in prison.

The IWW General Defense Organization, the Socialist party, and the National Civil Liberties Bureau, now the American Civil Liberties Union, kept up a steady agitation for the release of all World War I political prisoners. President Woodrow Wilson rejected all such requests, but on December 23, 1921, Debs and the last of the Socialist party members in prison, 23 in number, were granted amnesty by President Harding. Most of the IWW federal prisoners refused the offer of applying for individual clemency, preferring to maintain their solidarity and be freed collectively or not at all. Fourteen, however, including Ralph Chaplin, accepted the commutation of their sentences in mid-1923. The remainder were freed in the Christmas amnesty later that year.

As previously noted, the revolutionary principles of the IWW had caused established trade-unionism and the Socialist party to isolate themselves from its fold and had seriously limited the IWW's growth. This revolutionary philosophy, spurning as it did political action and trade-union policies based on immediate and gradual improvements for the workers, held no attraction for most wage earners who derived greater satisfaction from "more, here and now," than from hope of future fulfillment of the revolutionary ideal. The pathetic irony of the IWW's revolutionary ideal was that the very elements it directed its appeal to and was understood by—the unskilled foreign workers and migratory Americans—were unable to further the cause. By virtue of their exploitation and the fact that they were struggling for a bare existence, the workers of this kind were incapable of furnishing the IWW with the qualities and resources needed for a union to thrive. Although workers in the most economically and socially impoverished group truly needed betterment, they lacked the time, education, finances, emotional security, and physical energy to build a lasting union devoted to their needs.

Having been rejected by organized labor, the Socialist party, and the working class itself, the IWW found its struggle for survival, while continuously embroiled in internal factional disturbances, a most precarious and frustrating experience. The amount of physical punishment its members absorbed from legal authorities, Vigilantes, and citizens enrolled as deputies, would alone have been enough to break the spirit of less courageous and perhaps less masochistic men. The organization's revolutionary thought and the neurotic-motivated radicalism of some of its leaders was largely responsible for its meager growth and for the physical and legal assaults meted out to its followers and led to the crushing campaign of suppression by the federal government, a campaign whose emotional intensity carried over into the immediate postwar years and brought further attacks by the state governments.

One additional misfortune was yet to befall the already battered IWW—the organization of the Third International in Moscow in March, 1919, and the establishment of Communist parties in the United States. These events spelled the IWW's final denouncement. Of the few important IWW leaders left in the post-World War I period, some found their needs answered by communism, others found an outlet for their ambivalence in execrating the Communists who were now competing with them for the allegiance of the working class, and others simply grew tired of, or outgrew, the martyr role played by the revolutionist in a prosperous capitalist society and succumbed to the appealing forces of family, business, and middle-class respectability.

9.

The Roman Catholic Church
and American Labor Unions

Basically conservative as an institutional force, American Catholicism had a significant, even though indirect, role as one environmental factor which influenced American unionism's 'economism.'

Father Thomas J. McDonagh, "SOME ASPECTS OF THE ROMAN CATHOLIC ATTITUDE TOWARD THE AMERICAN LABOR MOVEMENT, 1900–1914"

To the very end of the pre-war era, despite efforts to strike a positive and constructive note, warring upon socialism seemed to most people, perhaps the main social interest of the American Catholic.

Professor Aaron I. Abell (Notre Dame University), "THE RECEPTION OF LEO XIII'S LABOR ENCYCLICAL IN AMERICA, 1891–1919"

LEFT wing political groups customarily have seen the labor unions as a covetous prize to be captured for immediate and long-range purposes. They have intrigued, propagandized, agitated, and bored from within to seduce and win the leaders, rank and file, and organization to their ideology and program. In America their successes have been less notable than elsewhere, but still their theories, practices, and programs have contributed to organized labor's political development. Less well-known and realized is that conservative theory in general, and Catholic social philosophy in particular, have also had a formative influence on the character and behavior of American labor unions. One of America's leading labor scholars, David J. Saposs, pointed in this direction when he informally wrote in the 1930's, "The significant and predomi-

212

nant role of the Catholic Church in shaping the thought and aspirations of labor is a neglected chapter in the history of the American
labor movement. Its influence explains, in part at least, why the
labor movement in the United States differs from others." [1] Along
these lines, too, aged Florence Thorne, Gompers' secretary and
editorial assistant, made the conversational observation to the
author in 1948 that there was no independent Catholic labor union
movement in America, as in many European countries, because
the AF of L had been made safe for catholicism.

The Catholic Church's maintenance of its religious and moral
values and the preservation of its social and economic doctrines
makes necessary its opposition to social doctrines in conflict with
its basic postulates. Above all, the Church is concerned with the
salvation of souls, and in a world where it sees heresy present, it
recognizes the obligation to propagate its own doctrines. Self-
defense, as well as the salvation of souls, requires no less. Further,
the Roman Catholic Church is practical enough to desire as allies
other political and economic institutions whose doctrines are most
nearly in agreement with its own. Conversely, those institutions
which represent dissimilar doctrines and which, in attempting to
advance these doctrines, threaten the religious and moral values
of catholicism inevitably find the Church as their adversary.

The writings and teachings of the fathers of the Church, the
theologians of the Middle Ages, and of the sixteenth and seven-
teenth centuries, show that the Roman Catholic Church seeks to
inculcate its social and economic doctrines into the minds of its
people. Professor R. H. Tawney has written in *Religion and the
Rise of Capitalism,* "The criticism which dismisses the concern
of Churches with economic relations and social organization as a
modern innovation finds little support in past history. What requires explanation is not the view that these matters are part of
the province of religion, but the view that they are not." [2] Cardinal
Manning acknowledged the Catholic Church's concern for the
Catholic as a citizen when he wrote, "The political conscience of
Catholics is not left to the individual judgment alone. It is guided
by the whole Christian morality, by the greatest system of ethical
legislation the world has ever seen, the Canon Law and the Moral
Theology of the Catholic Church." [3] An explanation from a British
Catholic layman, Henry Somerville, tells that "The Church can-

not profess neutrality in social questions and allow her members to form their political and economic affiliations as their sympathies and interests dictate unembarrassed by religious or moral considerations. By declaring the social question to be moral, the Church precludes her abdication from this realm." [4]

In the nineteenth century the Roman Catholic Church was an opponent of many of that century's liberal and revolutionary doctrines. The application of these doctrines as first expressed in the French Revolution had dealt the Church its strongest blows since the Reformation. To the Church, republicanism could mean the separation of Church and State, the suppression of religious orders, the confiscation of Church property, and the abolition of Church control of education. In addition democracy's exaltation of individual sovereignty and rights was at variance with the Church's spiritual values of humility and the discipline of one's impulses. The Church viewed with alarm the nineteenth-century spirit of rationalism and of liberalism because they overemphasized materialistic values and human reason at the expense of the supernatural. Nineteenth-century secularism negated the fundamental doctrine of divinely-instituted natural law and substituted a pseudo freedom from restraints. The Church regarded restraints as essential in perfecting the salvation of souls—its main duty.

The policies of Pius IX (1846–1878) were designed to protect the Church from many of the dangers inherent in nineteenth-century principles of social change. In 1864 he issued an encyclical, *Quanta Cura,* accompanied by a *Syllabus of Errors.* The encyclical condemned the abuses arising from liberty of conscience, freedom of the press, and rationalism. The syllabus, too, denounced many civil activities such as civil marriages, divorces, and freedom of religion. The Pope clearly rejected any notion that catholicism could acquiesce in the direction that modern liberalism was headed.

The strongest response to any questioning of papal authority was given by the Vatican Council when it met at Rome in 1869. The Council declared it to be a dogma "divinely revealed" that when the Pope presented his views upon a question of "faith or morals," he was endowed with "infallibility." [5] By declaring the Pope infallible, the bishops had thereby increased the authoritative nature of papal words henceforth uttered for the protection of Catholics from dangerous institutions and ideas.

Leo XIII, who became Pope in 1878, reconciled the Church to many modern ideas without compromising any of the Church's basic principles. In 1878 he bitterly condemned the "hateful sect" of socialism; in 1885 he said that "the integrity of the Catholic faith cannot be reconciled with opinions verging on Nationalism or Rationalism"; and in 1890 he declared that there must be "complete submission and obedience of will to the Church and to the Roman Pontiff as to God himself." [6]

The famous pronouncement of Leo's regarding labor, was his encyclical letter, *Rerum Novarum*—the most thorough and explicit exposition of the Church on the modern labor question. [7] At the outset, the letter said of socialism:

> Let it be laid down, in the first place, that humanity must remain as it is. It is impossible to reduce human society to a level. The *Socialists* may do their utmost, but all striving against nature is in vain. There naturally exist among mankind innumerable differences of the most important kind; people differ in capability, in diligence, in health, and in strength; and unequal fortune is a necessary result of inequality in condition. . . . To suffer and to endure, therefore, is the lot of humanity; let men try as they may, no strength and no artifice will ever succeed in banishing from human life the ills and troubles which beset it. . . .
>
> The great mistake that is made in the matter now under consideration, is to possess oneself of the idea that class is naturally hostile to class; that rich and poor are intended by nature to live at war with one another. So irrational and so false is this view, that the exact contrary is the truth. . . . [8]

> . . . the *Socialists,* working on the poor man's envy of the rich, endeavor to destroy private property, and maintain that individual possessions should become the common property of all, to be administered by the State or by municipal bodies. They hold that, by thus transferring property from private persons to the community, the present evil state of things will

be set to rights, because each citizen will then have his equal share of whatever there is to enjoy. But their proposals are so clearly futile for all practical purposes that if they were carried out the workingman himself would be among the first to suffer. Moreover, they are emphatically unjust, because they would rob the lawful possessor, bring the State into a sphere that is not its own, and cause complete confusion in a community. . . . The Socialists, therefore, in endeavoring to transfer the possessions of individuals to the community, strike at the interests of every wage earner, for they deprive him of the liberty of disposing of his wages, and thus of all hope and possibility of increasing his stock and of bettering his condition in life.

What is of still greater importance, however, is that the remedy they propose is manifestly against justice. For every man has by nature the right to possess property as his own.[9]

The Pope continued with his views on property:

. . . the common opinions of mankind, little affected by the few dissentients who have maintained the opposite view, has found in the study of nature, and in the laws of nature herself, the foundations of the division of property, and has consecrated by practice of all ages the principle of private ownership, as being pre-eminently in conformity with human nature, and as conducing in the most unmistakable manner to the peace and tranquility of human life. The same principle is confirmed and enforced by the civil laws—laws which, as long as they are just, derive their binding force from the law of nature. The authority of the Divine Law adds its sanction, forbidding us in the gravest terms even to covet that which is another's. . . .[10]

.   .   .   .

Thus it is clear *that the main tenet of Socialism, the community of goods, must be utterly rejected;* for it would injure those whom it is intended to benefit, it would be contrary to the natural rights of mankind, and it would introduce confusion, and disorder into the commonwealth. Our first and most fundamental principle, therefore, when we undertake to

alleviate the condition of the masses, must be the inviolability
of private property.[11]

As for the workers, Pope Leo XIII was against grinding men
"down with excessive labor as to stupefy their minds and wear
out their bodies"; he opposed the labor of children "until their
bodies and minds are sufficiently mature"; and he favored "just"
wages, defined as "enough to support the wage-earner in a reasonable and frugal comfort." [12] Finally, Leo XIII gave his views
on trade-unionism itself:

> In the first place—employers and workmen may themselves
> effect much in the matter of which we treat, by means of those
> institutions and organizations which afford opportune assist-
> ance to those in need, and which draw the two orders more
> closely together. . . .
>
> The most important of all are Workmen's Associations;
> for these virtually include all the rest . . . It is gratifying to
> know that there are actually in existence not a few societies
> of this nature, consisting either of workmen alone, or of work-
> men and employers together. . . .[13]

.   .   .   .

> . . . But there is a good deal of evidence which goes to prove
> that many of these societies are in the hands of invisible lead-
> ers, and are managed on principles far from compatible with
> Christianity and the public well-being; and that they do their
> best to get into their hands the whole field of labor and to
> force workmen either to join them or to starve. Under these
> circumstances the Christian workmen must do one of two
> things: either join associations in which their religion will not
> be exposed to peril or form associations among themselves;—
> unite their forces and courageously shake off an unjust and
> intolerable oppression. . . .
>
> Those Catholics are worthy of all praise—and there are
> not a few—who, understanding what the times require, have,
> by various enterprises and experiments, endeavored to better
> the conditions of the working people without any sacrifice of
> principle. . . . We find it in the grounds of the most cheering
> hope for the future; provided that the Associations we have

described continue to grow and spread, and are well and wisely administered. . . .[14]

.   .   .   .

As far as regards the Church, its assistance will never be found wanting. . . . Every minister of holy Religion must throw into the conflict all the energy of his mind, and all the strength of his endurance . . . they must never cease to urge upon all men of every class upon the high as well as the lowly, the Gospel doctrines of Christian life.[15]

In essence, then, *Rerum Novarum,* issued by the highest authority of the Roman Church, called for strong support of the doctrine of private property, unqualified rejection of and opposition to socialism, and acceptance of trade-unions, if, and when, the unions were dedicated to Catholic social principles. Devout Catholics were accordingly affected by this important encyclical which made clear the Catholic method and solution for the labor-capital conflict. Catholics were not to shun unions, but to see to it that unions fulfilled the moral values implicit in catholicism.

One of catholicism's leading social action priests, Father John A. Ryan, declared that *Rerum Novarum* had given "a clear challenge to and condemnation of all those selfishly interested persons and all those sincerely ignorant persons who say or think that the Church ought to keep to spiritual matters and not meddle with business or industrial matters." [16]

American-Catholic historian Professor Aaron Abell has told of the new era of Catholic labor relations ushered in by *Rerum Novarum.* Writing in the *Review of Politics* for October, 1945, on "The Reception of Leo XIII's Labor Encyclical in America, 1891–1919," Professor Abell says that prior to the advent of *Rerum Novarum* if "American Catholic leaders, ecclesiastical for the most part had not in many instances, or to a conspicuous degree, deferred to great wealth, as a group they had seen in the struggling labor movement little more than a revolutionary uprising, a projection on these shores of the Socialist and Anarchist movements of the Old World." [17] As a safeguard against and substitute for labor unions, Catholic Church opinion, Abell says, looked with favor upon the growth of various Catholic social societies. But the appearance of Leo XIII's labor encyclical inaugurated a new Catholic approach for the Church's devout to follow. Unions were to be supported, as long as they functioned in the conservative manner outlined by *Rerum Novarum*. In fact *Rerum Novarum,* by defining the Church's concept of the proper theory and practices of labor unions, enabled those devoted to their Church and interested in working people and the labor movement to work at the task of establishing Catholic social principles in the labor unions.

Leo XIII's successors maintained the theoretical direction set by *Rerum Novarum*. In 1912, Pius X's encyclical, *Singulari Quadam Caritate,* warned workers of the Catholic faith that "if Catholics are to be permitted to join the trade unions, these associations must avoid everything that is not in accord, whether in principles or in practice, with the teachings and commandments of the Church, or of the proper ecclesiastical authorities; similarly, everything is to be avoided in their literature or in their public utterances or actions which in the above views would incur censure." [18]

The reception of the above-noted encyclicals in the United States led Father Vincent McQuade to observe in his doctoral thesis that "Encouraged and inspired by the Pontiff, opposition to socialism was acknowledged by devout Catholics to be the fundamental issue" within the labor unions.[19] Father William J. Kerby of Catholic University noted in 1907 the extent of Catholic efforts to combat socialism. He wrote:

> The Church has entered the conflict as the avowed enemy of Socialism. Our colleges teach against it, we lecture and write, preach and publish against it, and an anxious Capitalistic world looks to the Church, nervous with gratitude for the anticipated setback that Catholicism is to give to socialism.[20]

Father Kerby's confidence of catholicism's success over socialism was not only a projection of his own dedicated service to the definitions of his Church. He knew, too, that in structure and administration the Church had the unity and strength to gain widespread Catholic support for matters having a vital bearing on faith or morals. This viewpoint was well stated by Father Heuser in the *Ecclesiastical Review* of March, 1906:

No careful observer of things can have a doubt that the Catholic Church possesses an organization which can secure unequaled order of action or that she possesses a unique power to control mind, heart and external conduct of that proportionately large majority of religious believers in our Country, who claim her name. Her unity of doctrine and the stability of her hierarchical government; with a chief pontiff who not only teaches and rules, but also advises with an absolutely directing and restraining effect, are recognized on all sides. It is equally clear that her authority reaches through the closely bound lines of pastoral administration every individual member of the Church.

Besides the influence that the Catholic Church as a religious institution directly has on its membership, a host of Catholic social bodies operate as adjuncts of the Church to carry its message to a Catholic populace. For example, there are Catholic universities and labor schools, Catholic newspapers and magazines, Catholic trade-union associations, Catholic war veterans' groups, Catholic professional societies, Catholic pious associations, Catholic fraternal organizations, and Catholic nationality groups striving in the common purpose as Pope Pius XI urged in his 1931 encyclical, *Quadragesimo Anno,* "to play their part in the Christian reconstruction of human society which Leo XIII inaugurated in his immortal Encyclical Rerum Novarum." [21]

Practical results that can be obtained from the organizational strength and unity of catholicism were explained by Bishop Ignatius Horstman of Cleveland to a convention of Catholic Societies in 1901. He remarked:

I have secured from every parish priest in my diocese the names of his two best men. Whenever I want the men together for their advice and support, I simply touch a button and in 24 hours my men are together ready to oppose any anti-Catholic legislation. Now if so much can be done in this state, what can the representatives from Catholic Societies in every part of the United States do? [22]

The fact that the Roman Catholic Church adopted a position on trade-unions and that it possessed an effective religious and social organization to proclaim and work for its labor principles was not enough to affect the development of American trade-unionism. The successful Catholic permeation of the labor movement would depend on the number of Catholics who were leaders and rank-and-file members of the unions. Simply put, the Church's influence mainly extended to members of its faith. What then was the extent of Catholic numerical strength in the early twentieth-century American labor movement? While no statistics are available on the religious affiliations of trade-unions' members, interviews with people who had firsthand contact with the trade-union movement of that period lead to one conclusion.[23] The Irish-Catholics were the largest nationality group in the American Federation of Labor. Another sizable nationality group in the AF of L in this period was the German-American, a large segment of which was also Catholic. As late as 1928, Professor Selig Perlman wrote that it is "the Catholics who are perhaps in the majority in the American Federation of Labor." [24] Father Peter Dietz wrote in 1909 that "We are told that more than fifty per cent of the members of the American Federation of Labor are Catholics and we believe the statement to be true." [25] Father Marshall I. Boarman, S.J., said in 1908 that "the great majority of the members of the American Federation [of Labor] are Christians and Catholics." [26] Peter W. Collins, prominent lay Catholic Secretary of the International Brotherhood of Electrical Workers in the early twentieth century, wrote that "almost one half of the men of organized labor are Catholic workingmen." [27] Dr. David J. Saposs also acknowledges that during this period, "Since the majority of individual members of unions were Catholics, the Church was in a position to render valuable assistance." [28]

Of the eight vice-presidential offices on the Executive Board of the AF of L, Catholic unionists held at least four in any year during the period under study. The American historian, Samuel Orth, wrote in a chapter on "The Irish Invasion" that "the labor unions are led by them." [29] Professor Norman J. Ware wrote that the AF of L was controlled by "predominantly Irish leadership of the national unions." [30] The following incomplete list of Catholics who held the presidency of international unions in the AF of L (1906–18) reveals the extent of the Irish-Catholic leadership of AF of L unions in this period: [31]

John R. Alpine:	International Association of Plumbers and Steam Fitters
Paul Bennett:	Powder and High Explosive Workers
James F. Brock:	Laundry Workers International Union
John P. Burke:	Pulp, Sulphite, and Paper Mill Workers
J. T. Carey:	International Brotherhood of Paper Makers
James Cullen:	Roofers Union, International Slate and Tile
John F. Curley:	Wavers' Protective Association
Thomas J. Curtis:	International Tunnel and Subway Constructors
T. M. Daly:	Metal Polishers, Brass and Silver Workers
T. M. Doherty:	Pavers, Rammersmen, Asphalt Workers
M. J. Donnelly:	Amalgamated Meat Cutters and Butcher Workmen of North America
Thomas J. Duffy:	National Brotherhood of Operative Potters
Frank Feeney:	International Union of Elevator Workers
James W. Fitzpatrick:	White Rats Actors Union
P. J. Flannery:	Brotherhood of Railroad Freight Handlers
Edward J. Gainor:	Letter Carriers' National Association
John Golden:	International Textile Workers
Fred H. Grahame:	Laundry Workers' International Union
Michael Green:	United Hatters of America
John F. Hart:	Meat Cutters and Butcher Workmen
Frank T. Hawley:	Switchmen's Union of North America
Denis A. Hayes:	International Association of Glass Bottle Blowers
S. C. Hogan:	Marble, Slate and Stove Polishers, Rubbers and Sawyers
Andrew C. Hughes:	Coopers International Union
Jeremiah Hurley:	Roofers, Composition, Damp, and Waterproof Workers
John F. Hynes:	Amalgamated Sheet Metal Workers
Daniel Keefe:	International Longshoremen
David Kirby:	Hodcarriers' and Building Laborers' Union
James W. Kline:	International Brotherhood of Blacksmiths

Joseph S. Leach:	Printers' Union of North America
James M. Lynch:	International Typographical Union
Peter J. McArdle:	Amalgamated Association of Iron, Steel and Tin Workers
Edward McGivern:	International Association of Plasters Operative
Matthew McGivney:	Printers and Color Mixers of the United States
James F. McHugh:	Journeymen Stonecutters' Association of North America
F. J. McNulty:	Brotherhood of Electrical Workers
William J. McSorley:	Lathers' International Union, Wood, Wire and Metal
W. D. Mahon:	Amalgamated Association of Sheet and Electric Railway Employees
Thomas J. Mahoney:	Glove Workers of America
John Mitchell:	United Mine Workers
John Moffat:	International Association of Hatters of North America
Joseph A. Mulaney:	Heat and Frost Insulators and Asbestos Workers
D. D. Mulcahy:	International Woodworkers of America
Patrick F. Murphy:	Bill Posters and Billers of the United States
John R. O'Brien:	Retail Clerks International Protective Association
James O'Connell:	International Association of Machinists
T. V. O'Connor:	International Longshoremen
James F. Riley:	International Brotherhood of Railway Clerks
E. J. Ryan:	Railway Mail Association
Martin F. Ryan:	Brotherhood of Railway Carmen of America
Charles C. Shay:	Stage Employees and Moving Picture Machine Operators
C. P. Shea:	Brotherhood of Teamsters
Charles B. Stillman:	American Federation of Teachers
M. O. Sullivan:	Sheet Metal Workers International Alliance

T. J. Sullivan:	Hotel and Restaurant Employees and Bartenders International League
Dan Tobin:	Brotherhood of Teamsters
John F. Tobin:	Boot and Shoe Workers' Union
Joseph F. Valentine:	Molders International Union
John A. Voll:	Glass Bottle Blowers
Edward Ward:	Brewery Workers
John T. Wilson:	International Brotherhood of Stationary Firemen
Matthew Woll:	Photo-Engravers' Union of North America

The answer to the question of what strength the Catholics held in American trade-unions 1900–1918 may be generalized as follows:

Irish-Catholics were in large strength among the rank and file of the AF of L unions, among the officers of the international unions that comprised the American Federation of Labor, and on the executive board of the AF of L. They were not represented in any appreciable numbers in the rank and file or in the officers of the unskilled trades that composed the IWW, and made up only a very small part of the American trade-union movement. Because of the large Irish-Catholic membership in the AF of L, understandably the message of *Rerum Novarum* would be given serious consideration.

The devotion of the Irish to the Catholic Church was not a new thing. To Bishop Spalding the Irish had "been more loyal" to the Church "than any other people on the broad earth." It was his conviction that "of all peoples the Irish are the most ready to accept the advice of God's minister." [32] Cardinal Gibbons declared in 1914 his agreement with an eminent archbishop who had said, "the Irish people have ever been the chief mainstay of our Church during the trials and difficulties of the past hundred years." [33]

The American clerical figures who would carry the greatest weight with Catholic workers, Irish or otherwise, would be America's cardinals—Cardinal Gibbons of Baltimore, Cardinal O'Connell of Boston, and Cardinal Farley of New York. Each of them, in sermons and writings, vigorously espoused the doctrines set forth in Leo XIII's *Rerum Novarum*.

Monsignor John T. Ellis writes in his biographical work that Cardinal Gibbons gave approval to trade-unions at a time when many "Catholic Bishops and Priests were highly conservative in their social views." His understanding of the need for unions "from the time he first espoused the Knights in the autumn of 1886 through the many pronouncements he made on labor in the succeeding thirty-five years" helped gain Catholic approval for the natural right of the workman to organize for his own protection. At the same time, Cardinal Gibbons "frequently spoke against the [Socialist] movement in addressing himself to labor questions." [34] An earlier biographer writes that Cardinal Gibbons was quick to sense that socialism would be a growing movement and therefore "the Church must be aroused to resist the threatened danger. His position in the Church in America was such that if counter action against Socialism was to come, he must lead it in order to give it effectiveness." [35] When the Socialist candidate for President, Eugene Debs, "polled 402,283 votes in the election of 1904, Gibbons read the signs of the time and prepared to throw the whole force of the Church against the further progress of the movement." [36] In a Baltimore sermon in the cathedral, February 4, 1906, he declared his position and that of the Church with regard to socialism in a manner which riveted the attention of the nation. Inequality of rank, station, and wealth, he said, were inevitable. The Socialist "has not the capacity to discern" that this condition must result from "a law of life established by an overruling Providence." [37]

In an article discussing "The Claims of the Catholic Church in the Making of the [American] Republic" Cardinal Gibbons reiterated Leo XIII's view that social organizations must be based on Catholic ethics. He stated that it was the Catholic Church's "duty to see to it that all schemes devised" to solve social disorders "are founded on Christian principles and do not antagonize the law of nature and the law of God." [38]

The cardinal's view on trade-unions was entirely in accord with the dicta of *Rerum Novarum*. The employers' Anti-Boycott Association reprinted in pamphlet form, with his permission, the text of one of his addresses. In it he declared that trade-unions needed leaders who would not infringe "on the rights of their employers." He advised the unions to avoid strikes, to select conservative leaders, and to be on guard against Socialists who would make the organization "subservient to their own selfish ends, or convert it into a political engine." [39]

Cardinal O'Connell was equally definite and outspoken in making known his views on trade-unions. In a pastoral letter read in all the churches of the archdiocese of Boston, on Sunday, December 1, 1912, he announced that Catholic principles must dominate trade-unions and that employer-employee problems could only be adjusted through the media of Catholic ideals. He denounced the Socialists who "fomented and intensified" the workers "natural discontent" with work. The Socialists were:

> . . . the enemies of God and man, who would overturn the foundations upon which human society is built, and exile God from His universe.
>
> This singular set of men, who seek to conceal the malice of their real principles, but who cannot, are a brood of disturbers. Their doctrines are an abomination striking at the foundations of family life and religion.
>
> There is not, and cannot be a Catholic Socialist. Leo XIII has rejected such a fellowship in his immortal encyclical. The principles of Socialism are utterly opposed to the principles of Christianity. They are mutually destructive of each other. Certain misguided Christians may call themselves Socialists, but objectively, a Catholic Socialist is an utter impossibility.

> .   .   .   .

> We exhort all, both employers and workmen, to enter upon this holy crusade of Christian emulation, to make every effort for a lasting peace, to shut out from their ranks Socialistic disturbers, to be loyal adherents to the Church, faithfully following and carrying out in their daily lives the teachings of the illustrious Leo, that, human passion laid aside and put out of the lives of the Church's children, the Prince of Peace may reign over a tranquil and contented people.[40]

Cardinal O'Connell urged the Holy Name Societies and the Catholic clergy to instruct Catholic workingmen in the social doctrines of their church and the errors and evil of socialism.

> Let the Societies of the Holy Name, now so well established and so flourishing throughout this diocese, serve as the

great spiritual centers where shall radiate this spirit of religious, domestic and social peace and harmony. Let the doctrines of the Church and the principles of her Pontiffs and Bishops, elucidating the economic conditions of her children and their corresponding duties be studied and learned well at the meetings of this Confraternity.

When our people have begun to understand better the malice of those who, under the cover of friendship, stir up strife, and when they realize that the law of Christ alone can make them all free, and that not dollars, but peace and contentment, are the richest and most precious possessions in life, then will the clamor of these noisy hawkers of poisonous social panaceas appear what it is in very truth, the vicious propaganda of enemies of the Christian faith, and deceitful disturbers of the peace of States.

During the Holy Season of Advent we charge those having care of souls to instruct their people in the true doctrine of the Church concerning their duties in the realm of labor; to proclaim again to the workman that the consolations which religion holds out to him are the only real and lasting foundations of true happiness below; and that the envy, the jealousy and hatred of class only render more and more bitter the contest which, even were it victorious, would end only in the ashes of disillusionment.[41]

Cardinal Farley of New York also closely followed the authoritative intention of *Rerum Novarum*. At the annual convention of the Confraternity of Christian Doctrine in 1909, he referred to socialism as "the heresy of the hour—a rampant heresy" which was a serious obstacle to the success of Catholic teachers in keeping Catholic workers true to the faith. He concluded by suggesting methods for Catholics to "combat the common enemy." [42] In a letter of approbation on July 28, 1911, to a Catholic group discussing labor problems at Fordham University he wrote that it was "of utmost importance that the fallacy underlying socialism be pointed out." [43]

The bishops in America equally gave their attention to spreading the precepts of *Rerum Novarum*. They were unanimous in denouncing socialism in their written and spoken words and in recommending Catholic social principles for the labor union movement.

In Kansas City, Missouri, in 1912, Bishop Thomas F. Lillis reiterated the Catholic conflict with socialism before a congregation of 110 priests of the Kansas City diocese who were meeting in a diocesan synod. The *Kansas City Journal* of April 10, 1912, quoted Bishop Lillis as telling the priests that "at present there is a nervous unrest in all nations caused by a school that appeals to the masses to destroy private property . . . inviolability of private property is a fundamental principle of ownership not to be lost sight of, if the welfare of all is to be attained."

One of the more lengthy attacks on socialism was made by Bishop William Stang of Fall River, Massachusetts, in his book, *Socialism and Christianity*. The Bishop endlessly examined and condemned socialism and claimed that, "Yes, the Catholic Church will save America from the devastations of radical Socialism." [44] "Indeed many thoughtful men outside the Catholic Church have come to the conviction that nothing can prevent the spread of Socialism or save society from destruction except the Church of Rome." [45] Bishop Stang considered it "a consoling fact that few Catholics in America have joined the ranks of real socialists." [46]

In the same tone, one of the Midwest's and America's famed bishops, Archbishop John Ireland of St. Paul, in an essay titled "Socialism and Labor," published in 1902, said of socialism that "It is today the peril of lands." He forbade Catholics to accept any doctrine "which ruins private property—the foundation stone upon which rests the social structure." [47] In a Labor Day sermon before the trade-unionists of St. Paul, in 1903, the Archbishop repeated that, "the most sacred right of man is his right to private property," and therefore he was "opposed to the state socialism that is now and then preached as the panacea of labor grievances." [48]

The social views of Bishop Spalding of Peoria, a close friend of United Mineworkers president John Mitchell and a member of a national committee appointed by President Roosevelt to investigate the 1902 anthracite coal strike, were summarized by Sister Agnes Schroll in her doctoral thesis as follows:

. . . labor unions, with wise foresight, Spalding thinks, should foster the spirit of moderation, sobriety and frugality among the workmen. In addition he urges them to discourage the introduction of socialistic and anarchistic doctrines among the laborers, since the spirit of these doctrines is one of revolution and not of reform. It is to the best interest of the laborer that the unions insist on morality and right living. Many of the evils from which the workers suffer are due, not to the competitive system, but to their own improvidence and wastefulness. 'The foe of labor is not capital but ignorance and vice,' says Spalding in 1902.[49]

Sister Schroll also wrote that "Spalding urges the unions to foster the spirit of religious faith among their members." [50]

In an address in 1910 Archbishop Glennon of St. Louis elaborated on Catholic principles for labor unions. Unions should honor trade agreements, oppose violence, and reject social principles that threaten existing social institutions. Unions should not encourage their members to hope for paradise "because there is no paradise for any of us in this world." [51]

Bishop James A. McFaul of Trenton established a Labor Day Sunday in his diocese and directed "the priests of each parish on this day to speak to their people on the Relations between Capital and Labor." He announced that "thousands of Catholics listen to the question of the day [capital and labor] discussed by the most eminent ecclesiastical and laymen in the country." [52] In a pastoral letter he urged the "15,000,000 Catholics in the United States [to be] arrayed in their combined strength against the forces of evil and in the creation of a public opinion that will be irresistible." [53] He accused socialism of being opposed to marriage, to private ownership of property, and to religion. He recalled that "from time to time in public addresses delivered in our large cities, we have referred to Socialism and warned Catholics of its danger. . . . It would abolish the existing order of society, administer to the greed, the lust and the baser passions of humanity." [54]

Bishop Quigley of Buffalo issued a pastoral letter in 1902 to the churches in his diocese in which he exhorted the priests "to warn their people against the theories advocated by the socialists through the means of the labor unions." [55] *The Catholic Union and*

Times of Buffalo in retrospect declared that " 'the bold pronounced views of Bishop Quigley made a profound impression not only upon the Catholic workingmen of Buffalo, but also upon the Catholic workingmen and labor unions throughout the country.' " [56]

Sometimes Catholic clerics were able to speak directly to AF of L convention delegates or to Catholic workers attending AF of L conventions. For example, Bishop John Carroll of Helena, Montana, told the AF of L delegates in 1913:

> Unionism should welcome the help of the Church. The Church is strong. She has existed for 2000 years. . . . Her patronage, her help, her favor are much to be desired by unionists. . . . It would be very impolitic for labor to favor any theory of economics . . . that must incur the enmity of the Church. Millions there are of the laboring class that belong to the Catholic Church and they are the staunchest friends of labor. These men love their religion as their very lives . . . it would be a sad thing for unions to disaffect the rank and file. . . .
>
> .   .   .   .
>
> The Church would have the unions so permeated with religious principles that differences between labor and capital would be easily solved.[57]

Bishop Francis W. Howard of Covington, Kentucky, was also closely related to the union movement. Father McDonagh writes that the Bishop gave many Labor Day addresses, was published in the *Columbus Labor News* and the *Moulder's Journal* and addressed workers on labor topics at their national convention.[58]

A number of bishops also advocated systematic and organized work that would give practical application to Catholic social theory. As early as 1901 Bishop James A. McFaul of Trenton advocated the organization of a Catholic Federation of existing Catholic societies to "assist in forming correct Catholic opinion on the prominent subjects of the day, by their discussion in our assemblies, in the extensive dissemination of Catholic thought and of the Christian solution of the important problems attracting the minds of the age." [59] The following year, Bishop S. G. Messmer of Green Bay pointed out at the first convention of the American

Federation of Catholic Societies that it could perform a great service by making known the Catholic Church's stand on the question of "Capital and Labor." [60] In 1917 Bishop Messmer announced that "the Archbishops assembled in meeting in Washington, the annual meeting, have given their formal approval of Catholic Federation," a Federation that represented over three million members in forty affiliated societies.[61]

Some bishops urged the formation of Catholic workingmen's associations. Bishop James E. Quigley of Buffalo stated in 1902:

The spread of Socialistic principles among the workingmen has convinced the clergy and the thinking men among the laity that the time has come for an organization under the auspices of the Church for the insistence upon the settlement of social questions according to Christian principles. A portion of the clergy and laity of the diocese of Buffalo is already organized along these lines, and it has been suggested that it will be an easy matter to extend the organization.[62]

The Buffalo *Catholic Evening News* of July 5, 1902, wrote that Bishop Quigley planned to "organize circles in every parish in the diocese, to which both workingmen and employers shall belong."

Archbishop John Glennon, of St. Louis, on May 19, 1909, gave his approval to Catholic Workingmen's Associations. In a letter to a St. Louis foreman, Mr. G. Gramann, who became president of the association, Glennon wrote:

. . . I would strongly recommend the formation of Catholic Labor Associations in each parish. I would recommend the same to the various parish priests and I wrote them to give you their constant encouragement, support and sympathy. The most pressing problem of today is that one of capital and labor and it will be properly solved if the solution is set on Catholic principles, but if otherwise, the results are liable to be disastrous to both religion and civilization.[63]

In November, 1910, Archbishop Glennon gave the Church's blessing to the Militia of Christ for Social Service, an organization of Catholic Workingmen, discussed later in this chapter.

Archbishop James J. Keane of Dubuque, Iowa, also gave his
approbation on September 14, 1913, to a local branch of a Catholic Workingmen's Association. He wrote:

Gentlemen:
I heartily approve of the Catholic Workingmen's Union of
Holy Trinity Parish, its aims and methods. Academic denunciations of Socialism and Syndicalism interest comparatively
few of the unsettled multitude. Constructive reform of the individual through a deeper knowledge and love of Catholic
principles is what is needed. Your union for bringing together
Catholic men for a free and frequent study by statement and
discussion of such principles in their relations with actual conditions, deserves every encouragement. I hope and pray that
you will arouse hundreds of our Catholic men from their dis-
couraging lethargy to a live and enduring zeal for the worth
of your union.[64]

The effort to promote Catholic ethics within the trade-unions
at the highest level originated with the Pope and, as noted, received the full support of the cardinals and bishops. This endeavor,
however, would have to receive the unqualified support of the
priests if Catholicism were adequately to utilize its human resources. Fortunately for the Catholic Church, the devotion of the
American priest to Church authority was beyond question. One
Catholic priest concludes his book with this tribute to the loyalty
and diligence of that branch of the hierarchy:

For the one who reads history aright there can be but one
judgment passed on the quality of the American Priest: his
apostolic zeal, his Christlike spirit, his God-given tenacity of
purpose, have made possible that modern miracle, the Catholic Church of the United States.[65]

In November, 1911, the Reverend Albert Muntch editorialized
in the American-German Catholic journal, *Central Blatt and
Social Justice,* on "The Priest's Attitude Towards Social Questions." He recommended to all his brother priests a book by the
Bishop of Rottenberg, Paul Wilhelm von Keppler, and republished
one of its chapters as part of his editorial. The chapter's message
to the priests was:

"Certainly the preacher of the twentieth century must closely watch the social movement; he must study it thoroughly and see carefully how it reacts on his parish. But this movement he must meet not with Socialistic, but with Christian preaching, with the preservation of Christian, Catholic truth, which is needed more and more by the workman than by others."

In keeping with such advice and with official Church teaching on this subject the priests in America appealed for and carried on practical organizational work for Catholic ethics in the trade-unions. The Reverend Marshall I. Boarman, S.J., for example, indicated his approval of AF of L's political principles and his concern lest these conservative principles give way to socialism. In a pamphlet he wrote:

The American Federation of Labor has been conducted on sane and conservative principles, and stands, universally respected today, as the bulwark of labor's defense.

Who for twenty years has tried to kill the American Federation? Socialists.

.   .   .   .

But the American Federation of Labor still speaks in the name of the vast majority of workmen, and is respected, because of its independence of political parties. At present it shows some favor to the Democratic party; but were it to fall down before Socialism, it would immediately burst asunder. The great majority of the American Federation are Christians and Catholics; and President Gompers, the English Hebrew, knows it.[66]

.   .   .   .

The bulwark of morality is religion; and the bulwark of religion is Christianity; and the bulwark of Christianity is the Catholic Church. The Church conquered the pagan world, not by force of arms, but by force of a charity that expended itself upon workingmen and the poor. She never beguiled them with illusive hopes of unjust wealth and an earthly Utopia. The principles by which the Church sprang into life are the principles by which she still lives.

Religion is the best asset of the workingman. It is his hope in life, his consolation in death. . . . The Church is his best friend; and the workingman knows it. . . . Socialists will still continue to make the night hideous bawling on the streets that the Church is allied to capital, and is not the friend of the workingman. Socialism will continue an enemy to all patriotism. The old lie will still travel that the workingman has no home; and that this government is managed for the rich.

It is a fair and a just government, but it is not paternalism. It must do justice to the poor, and to labor, and it must do justice to property. It cannot utterly stamp out man's inhumanity to man. But all just measures for the alleviation of workingmen can be secured by legislation. Organized labor, purged of Socialism, will always meet with the heartfelt cooperation of religion, and of popular sentiment, which, in our land, are invincible.

The rank and file of the Socialist following are not "native here and to the manner born." The majority are bankrupt in character and patriotism. And they have yet to learn, that our Stars and Stripes, as they float over the land and over the sea, are an emblem of strength, a palladium of liberty, an assurance of Christian civilization, and the pledge of a country that is truly "the land of the free and the home of the brave." [67]

Another priest endeavoring to enlighten Catholics on the social question was the Reverend Joseph Husslein, associate editor of the Jesuit journal, *America*, and lecturer at Fordham University. In his book, *The Catholic's Work in the World*, Reverend Husslein cautioned Catholic trade-unionists against the evil committed by reading Socialist publications, and he also urged Catholic workmen to enter the trade-union political struggle on the side of their Catholic faith:

Here therefore is a great apostolate for our Catholic laborers, to fight off the encroachments of radicalism in the labor movement and to substitute true Catholic principles. . . . There is great opportunity in our day for the lay apostolate on the part of our Catholic workingmen. For this they must be perfectly instructed in the bearings of religion upon the social question and deeply imbued with the principles of their holy faith. They must be clear sighted to see not only the dangers that threaten them, but the perils they involve for the entire labor movement.[68]

This plea for Catholic social study and Catholic social leaders was also made by other distinguished Catholic priests and professors. Among them, Catholic University's Father William J. Kerby, personal friend of Samuel Gompers, was early on record as an advocate of this view. In 1900, he outlined a plan for educating the clergy in social studies. He proposed a comprehensive, systematic training which would yield a small number of priests outstanding in the field of economics and social science:

> The dozen great minds which shall furnish us a safer leadership in uncertain social conditions, and show to the world what the Gospel really means to society, and the greater number of Priests who were so taken up with the active care of souls that they could afford no time for social study would thereby profit by the guidance of those better equipped.[69]

Father John A. Ryan was another socially minded Catholic priest of this period who believed in the value of Catholic social education and social action. His closeness to AF of L leaders and interest in the AF of L led Samuel Gompers to introduce him to the delegates of the AF of L national convention in Minneapolis in 1906. In his autobiography Father Ryan says that "In the years between 1908–1915 I made many public addresses on labor unions, their economic justification, their moral aspects and their practices . . . on Socialism I spoke more frequently and more fundamentally." Father Ryan described socialism as a philosophy, a movement, and an economic program. "Its philosophy I contended was historically false and ethically wrong, the Socialist movement was anti-religious and the proposed re-organization of economic society was impractical and unjust. In all the addresses on Socialism, however, I had a great deal to say about social reform." [70] Around 1914 Father Ryan contemplated a weekly Catholic journal to stress social doctrines. Three years later he founded the *Catholic Charities Review* and became its first editor. Matthew Woll, veteran vice-president of AF of L, said of him that he "worked on and for us. As we won our battles, he rejoiced with us." [71] Unlike most of his fellow clergymen in the early twentieth

century, Father Ryan did not dissipate his energies merely attacking socialism, but he earnestly crusaded against poverty, advocated
minimum wage legislation, opposed monopolistic practices of
business, and attempted to broaden Catholic social philosophy so
it would enable Catholics to push for major social reform. "The
failure of Catholics to lead or support reform movements was always regretted by Father Ryan." [72]

One of the more simple and direct examples of clerical propa-
gation of the Church's social precepts to union members was an
address by Father Charles Bruehl, sociology professor in St.
Charles Seminary, Philadelphia. Speaking to the Catholic delegates
who had come to Philadelphia for the 1914 convention of the
American Federation of Labor, Father Bruehl reminded the audience that they, as good Catholics, wanted God's blessing, but before they could get this they needed the Church's approval of
trade-unionism and its activities. In the father's words:

> You wish to implore God's blessing on the activities emanat-
> ing from your organizations, and as loyal sons of the Church,
> you are looking for some token of approval by which she might
> endorse and sanction your movement. For dear as this move-
> ment for economic betterment is to your hearts, I know you do
> not want it to be in conflict with your holy faith, which is still
> more sacred and dear to your hearts. . . . It is well that you
> look for orientation in this matter to your Church for she alone
> possesses unchangeable standards of right and wrong, she
> alone weighs things in balances that are not tipped by fear or
> favor, she alone sets the right value on objects. . . .
>
> It is prudent that you seek the approbation of your Church.
> For your Church is a great power in this world. A cause is the
> stronger for having her support. . . . The Children of the
> Church are especially anxious to have her approval, for they
> know that what the Church cannot approve, God will not bless
> and prosper.

Father Bruehl then informed the Catholic unionists of the
views held by the Church on trade-unionism:

> . . . We wish to hear at this solemn occasion what the Church
> thinks of this spreading and growing movement. . . . We wish

to analyze in detail the attitude of the Church toward labor unions. When I speak of the Church, I mean, and this goes without saying in this magnificent temple, the great historical Church of Christ, which alone bears the surname of Catholic, which alone presents to the world a united front, alone possesses an inalienable capital, alone speaks with a voice of authority. And thus do I define—myself an obedient subject of her authority, most anxious not to deviate from her teachings—her position with regard to the unions. My assertions are based on the utterances of her sovereign pontiffs and her hierarchy and on her practice in former ages and at the present times.

. . . The Church strongly advocates the principles of association. . . . As long as the unions pursue just ends with legitimate means, they enjoy the approval of the Church.

But if the unions are to enjoy permanently the approval of the Church they must be conducted in a spirit of justice, fairness, moderation and equity.

Father Bruehl praised his audience of Catholic trade-unionists for their conservative social doctrines which were akin to those of their Church:

Gentlemen, you are men of sound common sense and of practical judgment. Your daily work brings you into contact with the stern realities of life. You are not dreamers of dreams and not seers of visions. You are not thinking of overturning the existing structure of society. Your purposes are not revolutionary. You admit and accept the existing wage system. Under this system you are satisfied to obtain by collective bargaining a fair share of remuneration for your services. You are conservative, pillars of order, and a bulwark against revolution. It is good that the public knows this, for that knowledge will dispel its distrust and misgivings. We hail labor organizations as one of the conservative forces of this community. To crush labor unions means to open the flood gates of the revolutionary spirit. . . . And here you find yourselves in harmony with the Church. She also loves order and prefers to preserve rather than to destroy.

Father Bruehl continued by enumerating specific attitudes and rules which should govern the trade-union and the conduct of its Catholic members:

> Sweet reasonableness and a willingness to oblige should govern the relations between wage earner and employer; what savors of extortion and resentment should be avoided. Let us not forget that the employer does not stand outside the pale of charity.
>
> The public is deserving of some consideration. It is the innocent third party who in many cases has to shoulder the costs of labor troubles. In its quality as consumer it is also affected by any increase in wages, since generally the manufacturer is able to pass on the additional costs of production. The public accordingly suffers unjustly if wages are unreasonably high and working hours unduly short or if the supply of skilled workmen is kept insufficient by artificial and arbitrary limitations of the number of apprentices admitted to learn the trade.

In concluding this address Father Bruehl stressed that since there was no class conflict between labor and capital, these two classes should co-operate with each other. Socialism, he averred, was the enemy of both classes and could be defeated only by the application of Catholic doctrines in the trade-unions:

> A religious leaven, a Christian tone is indispensable to the unions if they are not to degenerate. . . . Without the Catholic element the trade unions cannot overcome the contagion of socialism; it acts like the salt which preserves from disintegration. Socialism is the enemy of unionism. The leaven of socialism injects a disturbing and dissolvent ingredient into the unions: it does not make for peace and moderation, but leads to unjust and exceeding demands thus precipitating a clash of the classes.

.   .   .   .

> The unions, therefore if they are not to become a danger and menace to the public good, must cultivate the higher social

virtues. They must not be built purely and solely on class interest, they must not be inspired by class hatred. . . . No class
should exploit the others, neither should the labor class attempt
to exploit the others. . . . Especially is there no fundamental
antagonism between labor and capital. They suffer together,
they prosper together.[73]

Such pronouncements as that of Father Bruehl were directed
to the AF of L leadership, as well as to the Catholic unionists'
rank and file. In essence, they reminded the AF of L leaders that
the Catholic workmen were the backbone of AF of L membership. The Church indicated that it was quite willing for Catholic
trade-unionists to participate in the AF of L. In fact, the Church
offered to assist the AF of L in its struggle for survival. On the
other hand, it could only be a friend as long as the AF of L
operated along the general lines of Catholic social philosophy.
Church leaders often pointed out that should the AF of L ever
depart from Catholic principles for labor organizations, and veer
toward a Socialist ideology, the Church would be obliged to withdraw its support of the AF of L and, in fact, would instruct the
large body of Catholic workmen in the AF of L to leave the organization. Because Socialists had gained control of unions in
Belgium and Germany in the late nineteenth century separate
Catholic labor unions had been established in these countries.[74]

This threat to the Federation's existence is a major factor in
evaluating the influence of the Catholic Church on the Federation.
Samuel Gompers may not have been in complete accord with all
of the precepts of *Rerum Novarum,* but as a practical man, he
probably concluded that an AF of L oriented in the direction of
Catholic ethics was better than a weak, or left wing, AF of L.
Even if the AF of L could withstand an exodus of much of its
Catholic membership, Gompers assuredly realized that this would
end his tenure of office, for he could not expect any ballot support
from the large block of remaining Socialists to whom he was
anathema.

Whether or not a tacit agreement existed between Gompers
and the dominating Catholic leadership of AF of L unions, the
fact is that the political philosophy advocated for labor by the
Roman Catholic Church was quite similar to the philosophy fol-

lowed by the AF of L. This similarity is apparent from material in a book of Father William Kress of Cleveland. This work, *Questions of Socialists and Their Answers,* written at the request of Archbishop Messmer of Milwaukee, contained certain extremely significant material showing the kinship of Catholic and AF of L political theory and practice.

> *Question:* Can the working class secure protection without going into politics?
> *Answer:* The law knows no distinction of rich and poor; its protection can be invoked by the one as well as by the other. Labor unions have gained many notable concessions from employers and have secured a considerable amount of legislation without going directly into politics, or what is the same thing, forming a district political party.
> *Question:* What political principles would you advise the working class to adhere to?
> *Answer:* To vote for capable and honest men, whom no amount of money can corrupt.[75]

Many other priests also did more than talk and write in favor of Catholic principles in the trade-unions. Some began the practical work of creating Catholic workingmen's associations or exerting their influence directly within unions. German priests in Buffalo and St. Louis were forerunners in the direction of welding Catholic workers into associations conscious of Catholic social principles. In Buffalo in 1901 Father Herman Maeckel, S.J., founded the St. Anne's Arbeitverein to influence Catholic workmen through a Catholic Society.[76] Around 1902 Father Heiter also of Buffalo devoted his efforts "to form Catholic Workingmen's Associations where the Catholic laborer and employer would be instructed in ethical principles as applied to industry," as well as safeguarded "from socialistic propaganda." [77] Three thousand workmen turned out for a mass meeting sponsored by Father Heiter and attended by Buffalo's Bishop Quigley.[78]

In 1909 German-American Catholics of St. Louis formed the Arbeiterwohl, The Catholic Workingmen's Welfare Association. Specifically, this society was the result of the priests' fear of the influence of Socialists on the brewing industry. The Arbeiterwohl's paper, *Amerika,* according to its editor, Frederick P. Kenkel,

" 'was read by every German speaking priest in St. Louis and could be found in most of the taverns frequented by German speaking workingmen.' " [79] Father Albert Mayer became an enthusiastic promoter of Catholic Workingmen's Unions in St. Louis.[80] In addition in many cities, says Frederick P. Kenkel, there were "priests who were members of Labor Unions affiliated with the A.F.L.; such Priests were quite influential at times." [81]

A priest well known in California and on the West Coast for his work within the early twentieth century union movement was Father Yorke of San Francisco. His biographer, Father Bernard Cronin, writes that Father Yorke was "an influential figure in the entire state, a prominent speaker and journalist" whose inspiration to participate in the labor movement came from Pope Leo XIII's encyclical. In 1901 Father Yorke helped the teamsters in a waterfront strike secure their objective of union recognition. He also spent much of his time "in conference with labor leaders in lectures and in the pages of the *Leader,* the Union-Labor journal which he established in 1902," discussing the application of Catholic principles to the labor problems of his area. Father Cronin writes that throughout the period 1900–1910 Father Yorke accounted for the practical implementation of *Rerum Novarum* in California's unions.[82]

"Examples of priests acting as labor mediators in time of strikes were not wanting," writes Sister Mary Fox.[83] Throughout the industrial areas many priests kept in close contact with union leaders in their locality. In Pittsburgh, Pennsylvania, Father Lawrence O'Connell maintained a close association with the union movement because "nearly all the local labor leaders were Catholic." Father O'Connell, pastor of the Epiphany Church, marched in the Labor Day parades and occasionally addressed workers' meetings in the nearby Labor Temple.[84] In the Wilkes Barre, Pennsylvania, mining areas, Fathers Curran and O'Donnell frequently counseled and travelled with UMW president and AF of L vice-president, John Mitchell. During such tours the priests spoke to groups of miners.[85]

The priest who above all others devoted himself to the organizational tasks necessary for the principles of *Rerum Novarum* to be put into daily practice was Father Peter E. Dietz. Shortly after being assigned to his first parish in 1905 at Elyria, Ohio,

Father Dietz began to make known his concern with American labor unions and his desire to see them develop in ways that would not endanger the faith and morals of their Catholic membership. In a Labor Day address to a working class audience he endorsed unions but advised them to be moderate in their behavior, to cooperate with their employers and their church, and to "beware of agitators." [86] During the next few years Father Dietz found a compatible outlet for his social action needs by working with the German Roman Catholic Central Verein, a socially conscious, national organization of German Roman Catholics. Some of his time was given to lobbying before the Ohio legislature for the Catholic viewpoint and conferring with the Ohio Federation of Labor on its legislative program. In 1909 he led a defeated minority of AF of L delegates out of the Ohio Federation of Labor convention in Toledo because "the socialists carried the convention." He continued to fight the Socialists for several years in the Ohio Federation of Labor and later wrote that he had helped to bring about their defeat.[87]

In April, 1909, Father Dietz persuaded the German Roman Catholic Central Verein to convert their official journal, *Central Blatt and Social Justice,* into a bilingual publication and he became editor of the English language section. This position afforded him an opportunity to bring to his readers the views of many leading Catholic spokesmen—unionists and clerics. He also used the journal's pages for stating his own viewpoint on trade-unions and labor problems. In March, 1908, he wrote that "If Socialism succeeds in America, it will be because labor unionism failed. . . . Therefore the Catholic has a most important and responsible share in the industrial readjustment of society. By his intelligent Christian membership he will be the only solid guarantee that the labor unions will not become socialistic." [88] In July he wrote that "it is eminently proper that Catholics at large identify themselves, *actively* and effectively, with the labor union movement in order to vanquish the secret conspiring forces that are sapping its vitality from within and to lead it to new and larger successes." He pointed out that "in the Catholic bosom," in contrast to the Socialist, "there is no necessary conflict between the rich and the poor; the employer and the employee." [89] Several months later Dietz wrote that "there is an urgent need for the establishment of

Catholic societies for workingmen . . . where the religious principles of Catholicism might be practically applied to the many burning questions that confront the workingman." [90] In the *Central Blatt's* final issue for 1909 Dietz wrote an article on "The American Federation of Labor" stating that "Catholic Workingmen's Societies will prove indispensable to the trade union movement for they ought to form the natural focus from which to project the rays of Catholicity into its heart." [91]

Probably Dietz's most significant accomplishment for translating *Rerum Novarum* into effective daily action was his organization of a Catholic workers' association known as the Militia of Christ for Social Service. The initial steps for the organization were taken when he attended his first AF of L national convention in November 1909 in Toronto. During a reception at the Knights of Columbus Toronto Clubhouse for the visiting labor delegates Dietz's contacts with officers of AF of L unions convinced him that they were receptive to social education along Catholic lines. Through his initiative a temporary organization of Catholic workers was established and Peter J. McArdle, president of the Iron, Steel, and Tin Workers, and Thomas J. Duffy, president of the Operative Potters, were chosen as temporary president and secretary. An understanding was reached that at the next convention of the AF of L this temporary organization would become a permanent one. Sister Mary Fox writes that "The esprit de corps at Toronto was greatly heightened by attendance in a body at Sunday Mass in St. Michael's Cathedral. Father Dietz made this 'Labor Mass' a feature of every Federation convention that he attended from 1909 to 1922." [92]

Prior to the AF of L St. Louis convention of 1910, Dietz wrote to Father P. P. Crane who had a large church central to downtown St. Louis and to Archbishop Glennon of St. Louis in regard to a Catholic celebration in connection with the AF of L meeting. He also wrote to prominent Catholic union officials reminding them of their mutual intention to get together and found a Catholic workers' organization. T. J. Duffy, president of the Operative Potters answered that he was "pleased to hear of the arrangements you are making for the St. Louis program." [93] T. V. O'Connor, president of the Longshoreman's Association wrote, "I am convinced that the time has arrived when the Church should take a definite stand on the question of socialism in the labor unions." [94]

At the AF of L St. Louis convention of 1910 Father Dietz was introduced by Samuel Gompers to the assembled delegates. In a brief address Father Dietz told the delegates that catholicism approved of the conservative brand of trade-unionism espoused by the AF of L. Father Dietz's notable work for Catholic social action was done outside the convention hall. He met in the Knights of Columbus clubhouse with outstanding Catholic trade-union leaders and they put the finishing touches on the constitution and program for the Catholic workers' organization that Dietz had envisaged since the Toronto convention. Their next action was to create a committee consisting of Dietz and trade-union executives to call on the Archbishop of St. Louis, John J. Glennon, for his official blessing. Once this was received on November 22, 1910, the Militia of Christ for Social Service had become an actuality.[95] Father Dietz was named executive secretary, and other officers and the directorate included an imposing array of prominent Catholic trade-union leaders in America at that time. About one hundred Catholic trade-unionists became charter members.

The stationery of the Militia listed the following trade-union leaders as the directorate: Denis A. Hayes, president, International Association of Glass Bottle Blowers (and AF of L vice-president); James O'Connell, president, International Association of Machinists (and AF of L vice-president); John R. Alpine, president, International Association of Plumbers, and Steam Fitters (and AF of L vice-president); John Moffat, president, International Association of Hatters of North America; John Mitchell, chairman, Trades Agreement Department, National Civic Federation (and AF of L vice-president and former president, United Mine Workers); T. V. O'Connor, International President of the Longshoremen; John Golden, International President of the Textile Workers.

The general officers of the Militia of Christ were listed as follows: president, Peter J. McArdle (president, Amalgamated Association of Iron, Steel, and Tin Workers); vice-president, John S. Whalen (ex-secretary of the state of New York); second vice-president, Peter Collins (secretary, International Brotherhood of Electrical Workers); third vice-president, John Mangan (editor of the Steamfitters' journal); recording secretary, Thomas Duffy (president, National Brotherhood of Operative Potters, and Ohio State Deputy, Knights of Columbus); executive secretary, the Reverend Peter E. Dietz.

As its motto, the Militia of Christ for Social Service adopted the precept, "Thy Will Be Done." Its object, according to its Constitution, was "The defense of the Christian order of society and its progressive development." The Militia's platform read: "The economic, ethical, sociological and political doctrines of Christian philosophy as developed in the course of history—the legacy of tradition, interpreted to modern times in the letters of Leo xiii and Pius x."

To implement this platform, a twofold method was to be followed: first, "The Promotion of Social Education," and second, "The Compelling of Social Action."

"Social Education" was to be furthered by "(*1*) syndicate letters to the Catholic and Labor Press; (*2*) social lectures and conferences; (*3*) student apostolates in the colleges and universities; (*4*) lyceum co-operation with diocesan apostolates, mission bands, K. of C. lectureships, societies, and parishes; (*5*) social emphasis upon Confirmation sponsorship; (*6*) a social reference bureau, social science libraries, social centers; (*7*) the publication of leaflets, pamphlets, monograms, and a Journal of Social Service."

Social Action was to be spurred by "(*1*) personal propagandist service and volunteer distribution of literature; (*2*) the advocacy of Christian principles in trade-unions; (*3*) intelligent and active interest in the problems of labor legislation; municipal reform, civil service and general administration, industrial education, prevention of industrial accidents and diseases, workmen's compensation, workshop, factory and mine inspection, and uniform state legislation; (*4*) the cultivation of fraternal relations with all Catholic societies and conservative social movements; (*5*) yearly programmatic convention conjointly with the convention of the American Federation of Labor; (*6*) a Catholic celebration of Labor Day; (*7*) a policy of conciliation, trade agreements, arbitration of industrial difficulties."

Executive membership was "limited to practical Catholics who accept as an axiom, the principle of trade unionism, uncommitted, however, to every special application of the theory."

Archbishop Glennon's letter of approval to Father Dietz (November 22, 1910) read:

> I have before me the programme yourself and the gentlemen of the committee handed me yesterday. I cordially give my approval to the same. I regard the time opportune for its inauguration and I pledge you my continuous interest and cordial support.
>
> You may inscribe my name as an applicant for membership in the society, and accept now and at all times my best wishes.

The Apostolic Delegate, His Excellency, the Most Reverend Diomede Falconio wrote to Dietz, "I am happy to add my commendation to that of Archbishop Glennon of St. Louis in regard to the work undertaken by the Militia." [96]

Other bishops who wrote Dietz that they regarded the Militia's birth as timely and worthy were James H. Blank of New Orleans, Louisiana; Thomas Grace of Sacramento, California; Joseph J. Fox of Green Bay, Wisconsin; James A. McFaul of Trenton, New Jersey; Joseph M. Koudelka of Cleveland, Ohio; Joseph Schrembs of Grand Rapids, Michigan; John E. Gunn of Natchez, Mississippi; J. F. Regis Canevin of Pittsburgh, Pennsylvania; James J. Keane of Dubuque, Iowa; Henry Moeller of Cincinnati, Ohio; and Patrick J. Donahue of Wheeling, West Virginia.[97] Father John A. Ryan thought the Militia was "a splendid idea" and had "great possibilities for good," though he was pessimistic about its possible success.[98] He wrote Dietz that "when your journal is started I shall want to be a subscriber." [99] The United States Commissioner of Labor, Charles O'Neil, wrote Dietz that he was "thoroughly in sympathy" with the Militia's aims and that if the "men and means necessary to carry it on" could be secured, "it cannot but be productive of good." [100]

The postconvention reaction of AF of L trade-union leaders to the Militia of Christ's birth was a favorable one. T. J. Duffy, president of the Operative Potters, wrote Dietz less than a month after the convention, "Since coming home and having had time to reflect, I feel more pleased than ever with what progress was made at St. Louis. I am also of the opinion that such a program is a vital necessity." [101] Two months later he wrote Dietz, "I think I can make things a little disagreeable here for the comrades. . . . I can prevent them from misleading many others." Duffy concluded his letter by hoping that "the Militia will grow and prosper." [102]

John Mitchell, United Mine Workers' president, wrote Dietz in early February, 1911, that "Later on I may be able to send you the names of men I could recommend" for the Militia of Christ.[103] James O'Connell, president of the Machinists wrote about the same time, "I am enclosing a list of a few names I have just recalled whom I believe will be interested in the work and I may be able to get up a larger list later on . . . my best wishes for the success of the movement." [104]

P. J. Flannery, president of Railroad Freight Handlers, informed Dietz at the beginning of February, 1911, that he had received his Militia of Christ membership card, was "proud to be recorded as a charter member" and would exert his "best effort to increase the membership of said society." [105] In May, 1911, T. V. O'Connor, president of the Longshoremen, forwarded Dietz the application of John J. Joyce, secretary-treasurer of the Longshoremen who "desires to become a member of the Militia of Christ in Social Service." [106] Frank L. Rist, AF of L District Organizer in Cincinnati sent in his application and that of two other AF of L men in May of 1911 also.[107] In September, 1911, Edward J. Fliller, secretary of the Photo-Gelatin Workers, requested membership in the Militia from Dietz.[108] Two other prominent union leaders who joined the Militia in 1911 were James M. Lynch, president of the Typographical Union, and Andrew C. Hughes, president of the Coopers Union. Probably Dietz took great pleasure a few months after the Militia's founding in the letter of John Voll, vice-president of the Glass Blowers, which wished him luck in the Militia's work and said "you will find enclosed a commission as Organizer of the A.F. of L. which is an honor to bestow as well as pleasure upon one whose influence is so far reaching." [109]

Father McDonagh in his doctoral dissertation says that the Militia was endorsed generally by the solicited members of the Catholic hierarchy and clergy and looked upon with favor by the majority of Catholic leaders of the AF of L because of its intended

identification of the Catholic Church with the principles of conservative trade-unions.[110]

In a circular letter announcing a meeting to form a Milwaukee
chapter of the Militia in early 1913 Dietz explained the Militia's
value:

> the strengthening of the Catholic trade union sentiment will do
> much for the preservation of legitimate trade union ideals; it
> will enlist the great influence of Catholic public opinion in the
> cause of labor; it will elevate the conditions of industrial peace
> while it stands opposed to the false doctrine of class antago-
> nism, which regards all employers alike as enemies of labor; it
> will cultivate the possibilities of conciliation, conferences,
> trade agreements, to the fullest extent, consistent with honor
> and the proper dignity of labor.[111]

In a letter of March 15, 1913, seeking Cardinal O'Connell's
approval of a Militia chapter in Boston, Dietz justified the Militia's
existence as follows:

> The *ratio existendi* is this: there is no bridge between the
> Church in America and the labor movement. The pulpit and
> the press speak to the individual only and existing Catholic
> societies are an imperfect medium. It is not possible to *take
> hold* of the labor movement in these ways. At a critical mo-
> ment it would be very difficult for the Church to influence a
> given situation. The Militia of Christ would have a disciplined
> array of responsible Catholic Trade-unionists, prepared to act
> in concert at a moment's notice.[112]

Dr. David Saposs has been the lone labor historian to pay
more than a passing word to the Militia until the 1940's when
Catholic scholars brought out their works. In his opinion it was an

> organization of Catholic labor leaders designed to combat
> radicalism. It counted among its members the leading Catholic
> labor leaders, and had the approval of Gompers and the hand-
> ful of other non-Catholic conservative labor leaders. The
> Militia of Christ was an auxiliary of the Church. It had large
> funds at its disposal. It was manned by an able staff. It imme-
> diately became a formidable factor in the fight against radi-

calism. It issued literature and retained a corps of propagandists and lecturers. In addition it routed outstanding labor leaders, and priests who had distinguished themselves in labor affairs, on tours where they spoke to working class audiences against radicalism and for the conservative brand of laborism.[113]

The opinion of Professor Aaron Abell on the purpose and influence of the Militia is quite similar to that of Dr. Saposs. He has written: "Members of the Society, mostly Catholics in key positions in labor unions, helped conservative trade unionists, 'the pure and simplers,' to thwart the continuous endeavors of the Socialists to capture the American Federation of Labor." [114]

The reaction of the Socialists to the Militia's birth was bitter and fearful. Victor Berger, Milwaukee Socialist editor and Congressman, wrote in the *Milwaukee Leader,* June 14, 1913, that the Militia was intended to "bring existing unions under the domination of the Roman Catholic hierarchy." He wrote as follows:

One can understand how the Reverend Peter Dietz can engage in such an enterprise, but how John Mitchell, Peter McArdle and other Irish-Catholic labor leaders who have subscribed to the Constitution of the order of the Militia of Christ can look their fellow-workers of Protestant and non-Catholic belief in the eye without feeling the shame of Judas, is a mystery which may be revealed when the workers that they are seeking to betray into the hands of their enemies come to realize the full extent of their perfidy.[115]

The Chicago *Daily Socialist* wrote, "From the literature of the Militia of Christ it can be seen that trade unions are being shamefully betrayed by their leaders who are organized to fight the honest political beliefs of the progressive members of their respective organizations and are in league with the ever reactionary and conservative Catholic Church. The members of the Militia of Christ are required to be Catholics first and, perhaps, trade unionists after that. In other words, trade unionists are all right, so long as they do not attack the system of society under which we live." [116]

A news story in the *Schenectady Daily Union,* January 9, 1911, relating that "the work of getting Schenectady Catholic union men into the Militia will begin at once by the men in charge here," brought forth a vituperative editorial by DeLeon in his *Daily People,* January 14, 1911. Richard Perrin wrote in the January, 1914, issue of the IWW-orientated monthly, *International Socialist Review,* that: "Every American Unionist knows how bitterly the Catholic Church has fought Socialism in the labor unions through its servile tools, such as the Militia of Christ and similar secret alliances." *The Masses,* the Socialist party journal, in an editorial on AF of L and Catholic Church opposition to socialism, in its July, 1912, issue declared: "The A.F. of L. is getting more and more into the hands of the Militia of Christ." [117]

John M. O'Neill, editor of *The Miners Magazine,* wrote an article, "Something to Think About," in the December 4, 1913, issue about Father Dietz's activity at the 1913 AF of L convention. O'Neill declared, "One of the busiest men in the hotel lobbies of Seattle during the convention was one Father Peter E. Dietz of the Militia of Christ. Father Dietz was in conference with a number of delegates who are members of the Catholic Church, and it is said that when Catholics as delegates in the convention showed by their expressed convictions that they were advocates of political and industrial solidarity and favored co-operation with the Socialist party in the advancement of the interests of the exploited class, the Reverend Dietz became indignant and demanded to know why Catholics as delegates gave their support to any resolution that looked with favor on blending the forces of the labor movement with the Socialist party to uplift the cause of labor.

"It is said that Father Dietz in angry tone declared: 'If you try anything that will tend to aid the Socialists, the Catholic church will be compelled to disown the American Federation of Labor and begin organizing Catholic unions.'" [118]

The editors of *International Socialist Review* in an article titled "The Catholic Threat and The A.F. of L." in January, 1914, wrote, "Who will prevail in the A.F. of L.? Shall the Catholic Church succeed in driving out all Socialists or shall Socialists be given a place in the organization?" The editors added that the Catholic Church was nearly "controlling the A.F. of L." and "it looks bad for us." [119]

Actually it was hard going for the Militia. A correspondence between Father Dietz and John Mitchell, United Mine Workers president and AF of L vice-president, furnishes a glimpse of the Militia's brief history.[120] In April, 1911, Dietz wrote Mitchell that he was preparing a membership magazine for the Militia to be called *Social Service*. By correspondence, he said, he had secured the support of "quite a number of professional men, too, the approval of a number of bishops, and of the Apostolic delegate" Archbishop Diomede Falconio. "But there is much prejudice among the upper ranks against unionism that it will require hard work to drive it out." [121]

After a visit to Father Dietz, Mitchell expressed his approval of the Militia and his readiness to co-operate with it. He said:

> Since my return home I had read with much care, first, the declaration or interpretation of the principles enunciated by the "Militia of Christ for Social Service" and second, the introduction signed by you. I have read also, but with less critical attention, the other articles contained in the magazine. And I have no hesitancy—not even a mental reservation—in saying that you have presented a program of constructive social service that is sound and progressive; a program that is calculated to meet the requirements of our people and our time, and while I do not desire to urge you to make a great sacrifice in carrying forward the movement which you have so well inaugurated, yet it must be done by someone and perhaps if you don't take the lead, someone else not so well equipped will do it in your stead.

> .   .   .   .

> I shall be in Washington attending a meeting of the Executive Council of the American Federation of Labor all of the week beginning June 12th. Inasmuch as three members of the Executive Council, in addition to myself, are members of the Directorate of the Militia of Christ, could it not be arranged for Messrs. McArdle and Duffy to visit Washington during that week? And if you could make the trip there we could probably have a more representative gathering than we should be able to arrange at any other time.[122]

At the Washington meeting arranged by Mitchell, it was decided that Father Dietz should give his full time to the Militia.

The latter explained, however, that it would be necessary for him to receive the permission of his superior, Bishop John P. Farrelly of Cleveland. Upon Dietz's request, Mitchell and John Alpine, AF of L vice-president, wrote to the bishop as follows:

> We, the undersigned, interested in the work outlined by the Militia of Christ, see in it a promise of good both for church and country, and are desirous of its growth and extension.
>
> Father Peter E. Dietz would be able to devote himself to this work more effectively if given a larger opportunity, and we ask your Lordship to make it possible for him to give more of his time and effort to the extension of the Militia of Christ until such a time when the progress of the work shall hold the promise of self-support.[123]

After sending the letter, Mitchell informed Dietz that if James O'Connell, AF of L vice-president, had not been called away from Washington, he, too, would have added his signature. Mitchell also enclosed a check for five dollars to help the Militia's work.[124] Dietz was grateful for the letter to his bishop and for the financial contribution, and he felt sure that his superior would release him so that he could concentrate completely on the Militia.[125] On August 30, 1911, Father Dietz reported to Mitchell on the progress he was making. He said:

> Does the trend of the second issue [Social Service Journal] strike you as allright? I put in a good week at the Convention of the American Fed. of Cath. Societies in Columbus. They endorsed the work—resolved to co-operate with it—provide an organ in the way of a commission of five, viz. Bishop Muldoon, Dr. Cavanaugh, rector of Notre Dame University, Prof. James Hagerty of Ohio State University, Charles I. Denechaud, Esq., of New Orleans and myself. I have all the moral backing now that I will need and it is of a very substantial character. I have added many good names to the roll and the Archbishop of St. Louis is so well pleased as to recommend the holding of a social conference to which the best Catholic minds are to be invited.
>
> My resignation takes effect next week, that is as pastor of

Oberlin—and I am going on the road. The Ohio K. of C. and the two state branches of the Federation will help me to get up a lecture-circuit. But the biggest question for the next few months—may in reality be a financial one. Do you think that you could help me with some of your moneyed friends to procure a gift of one or two thousand dollars—to tide us over well into the next year? The thing will take care of itself once it has gained expansion and it seems to me the prospects for a big and lasting movement are very good. I am going to start out with a Labor Day speech at Youngstown.[126]

At the end of one year's work with the Militia, Father Dietz announced that "The earliest hopes of the Militia of Christ are not fulfilled, yet I am equally sure that the movement has justified itself." He acknowledged that the Militia had several hundred subscriptions, but he was not yet satisfied. He hoped to establish a school of social service which would turn out a trained corps of priests who could devote themselves entirely to Social Service as defined in the pronouncements of Church authority. Since he estimated it would take ten or fifteen thousand dollars "for the foundation of the school" he suggested to Mitchell that "if we could talk the matter over with some men of means, who are glad of your acquaintance and friendship, matters would soon be arranged." [127] Mitchell answered, however, that it would be wiser to issue a circular letter of appeal for "small subscriptions from a large number of men." [128]

The lack of hoped for growth of the Militia and the criticism of union people like Mitchell for its failure to endorse specific labor legislation led to the appearance of a revised edition of the Militia's Constitution in 1912. The new constitution though much longer than the original one, essentially differed little from the old.[129]

The attitude of several top AF of L international union presidents continued to be sympathetic toward the Militia following the adoption of the revised constitution. James O'Connell wrote Dietz that he had received the constitution "and have read the same with much pleasure and it meets with my full approval. I should be glad to continue as a director as suggested by you." [130] John Golden, president of the Textile Workers informed Dietz, "I shall also only be too pleased to continue on the Board of Directors if you think my humble services in that capacity will tend to further the success of the movement." [131]

After two years of existence the Militia had grown to over seven hundred members. Dietz now engaged Peter W. Collins, who had resigned as secretary of the Electrical Workers, to enter the struggle against socialism. But Dietz declared that he could not "supply Collins with sufficient lectures—so he went to the Central Verein." [132]

In 1913 Dietz's biggest step to put life into the Militia was to hire a full time national organizer, William Frances Keates, who felt it was his mission to arouse catholicism "to fighting this slimy octopus," socialism.[133] Keates visited the cities where charter members lived in the hope of establishing or increasing local chapters. His best work was done in Evansville, Indiana, where he claimed in December, 1913, he had secured 100 members.[134] In March, 1914, Dietz dispensed with his services which he regarded as unsatisfactory.

By 1914 it was clear that the Militia had little life left. It had not received the two thousand members that Dietz considered necessary for its survival. It was faced with financial difficulties and Dietz could not give it sufficient time because he was devoting himself more and more to the Social Service Commission of the American Federation of Catholic Societies since its establishment in 1911. One of his last acts to save the Militia was to send a letter to its members stating that the Milwaukee chapter was submitting to a referendum a name change for the organization. The suggested new name, which would be less subject to misrepresentation than Militia, was the American Conference of Catholic Trade Unionists.[135] Though the latter name was adopted, for all practical purposes the American Conference was stillborn. Yet the Militia did not really die because much of its purposes and work were being fulfilled by the Social Service Commission. Dietz had recognized this as early as 1912 when he wrote to John Mitchell that he would be "satisfied to relinquish the title 'Militia of Christ' " to the older and well-established American Federation of Catholic Societies. "You are aware that for years I have been trying to influence Catholic Federation into this field. The Militia of Christ was organized largely as a lever for that body." [136] The first published Catholic paper on Father Dietz holds that "the continuance of Dietz's work of conducting lectures, attending conventions, and issuing a weekly syndicated letter to the Catholic Press, seems to indicate that the Commission became a kind of enlargement of the Militia." [137]

Although the Militia's history show it to have had a brief four year life, a peak membership of seven hundred, and only a handful of functioning chapters, Dietz's biographer, Sister Fox, suggests that the Militia's effectiveness cannot be adequately evaluated by considering the surface records alone. She writes that "such a judgment would ignore the intangibles that are hard to evaluate." The Militia provided "Catholic solidarity" for its "individual members scattered throughout the various labor organizations" and gave them the conviction of its "founder, that Socialism, the insidious enemy of trade unionism, must be defeated at all cost." [138]

Just as Dietz's work with the Militia had emphasized personal service, social service, and press service, so did his work as secretary of the Social Service Commission. His personal service was given on so many innumerable occasions to speaking formally and informally about Catholic social thought that he could not estimate, in his words, the many "friendships made, the enemies disarmed, the reconciliations effected, the policies considered and reconsidered." Samuel Gompers once informed him that he held "the unique distinction of having secured a reversal of decisions by the Executive Board of the A.F. of L." [139] His social service consisted, in part, of establishing fraternal relations with the Knights of Columbus, Catholic organizations generally, attending AF of L conventions and arranging meetings of the Social Service Commission with other groups. His constant purpose, as he wrote in 1914, was to "build up among the Catholic workingmen a school of thought which will bring about unity of action." [140] A large part of his time was spent on press work—on editing the Social Service *Bulletin* and the *Weekly Newsletter* to the Catholic and labor press, preparing pamphlets on social problems and writing articles for the journals of other Catholic groups. As Sister Fox writes, "During the life of the commission, from 1911 to 1918, Father Dietz was its power house of action." [141]

Denis Hayes, Glass Bottle Blowers Union president, AF of L

vice-president, and a member of the seven man Social Service Commission, complimented Dietz's Social Service Commission in a 1916 talk to the American Federation of Catholic Societies. He said he was pleased to see that the Catholic federation was taking "such an active and practical interest in the welfare of the Catholic" workers. He also said the Commission's Press Service was making "a very good impression" on "a number of acquaintances in the labor movement." [142] In 1917, Dietz's last full year with the Social Service Commission, he reported that the Commission was sending out about ten thousand news letters to both the Catholic and the Labor Press, and about an additional four thousand other letters annually.[143]

An example of the closeness between Father Dietz and the AF of L is apparent in two distinct incidents that occurred in 1922. Early in that year Dietz established a National Labor College at Ault Park, Ohio, where, according to Sister Fox, "His lectures, conferences, and retreats gave him the opportunity to imbue trade unionists with correct social principles, which exerted a mellowing influence on labor relations. The importance of this school to the trade union movement was recognized officially by the A.F. of L. when it made the Academy its first National Labor College. No greater mark of confidence has ever been conferred by that organization." [144]

Unfortunately, Dietz's hopes of establishing a permanent National Labor College went unfulfilled because Archbishop Moeller with whom he was not on good terms ordered the closing of the school and the withdrawal of Father Dietz from Cincinnati in late 1922.[145] Archbishop Moeller's announcement that he would no longer support Dietz's labor activities in Ohio brought forth a remarkable tribute to Dietz from the AF of L. More than sixty labor union leaders led by Samuel Gompers, Matthew Woll, Dan Tobin, and Frank Duffy petitioned His Grace to allow Dietz to continue his work in the labor field. Their letter to Archbishop Moeller read as follows:

> Having learned that influences, inimical to organized labor, have been conspiring against the maintenance of the American Academy of Christian Democracy, conducted by Reverend

Peter E. Dietz, at Ault Park, this city, we beg to be permitted to ask the kindly consideration of Your Grace for the following petition:

The adjustment of the relations between Capital and Labor, on principles of justice, is one of the most vitally important questions now demanding solution by the American people, as well as by the world at large.

Delay in settling this question is threatening the very existence of civilized society. It is recruiting the armies of Anarchism and all other radicalisms.

It is now pretty generally recognized that the solution of the Social Question cannot be brought about by civil laws. Practical men on both sides realize that only through mutual confidence, good will, friendly conference and free agreement can the difference between Capital and Labor be settled satisfactorily. This was the advice of Leo XIII.

The logical, practical procedure, therefore, would seem to be to dissipate the prevailing distrust, and replace it with sincere trust on both sides, with a disposition to be mutually fair and just.

To start this procedure it is necessary to obtain the services of devoted men, personally disinterested from a viewpoint of either wages or profits, and dominated with a keen sense of justice and a strong love of humanity, who can mediate between the opposing parties, bring them to the point of composing their differences in a spirit of mutual forbearance, and engender in them a willingness to make mutual concessions and sacrifices for the general good of the community.

Father Dietz is pre-eminently one of these devoted men. He has consecrated his life to precisely this kind of service. He has made an intensive study of the Social Question for more than fifteen years, and has settled a number of industrial disputes satisfactorily to both sides. He is intimately acquainted with all the prominent leaders of the A.F. of L., and is known to many of the officials of organized labor in Europe. These men have the utmost confidence in his sincerity, his judgment and his integrity; and his conscientious regard for his vocation as a priest should be a guarantee, sufficient for employers, that he would not allow his sympathy with labor to lead him to connive at the violation of the just rights of Capital. There is not another man in the entire country as well qualified as Father Dietz to aid in the solution of the Social Question.

Even handicapped as he has been since his advent here, Father Dietz has been a power for good in Cincinnati. He has been a tower of strength against the advances of impractical and dangerous radicalism; and he has labored unceasingly for a more widespread knowledge of correct ethical principles.

May we not, therefore, respectfully petition Your Grace to permit Father Dietz to continue his important work in this community, as we feel certain that such action will conduce toward industrial peace and order, and to general prosperity and happiness.

We might mention that Cincinnati is the logical center for Father Dietz's activities, because two-thirds of the national and international officials of organized labor are residents of this city or of Indianapolis.[146]

But Moeller's views of Dietz would not change and he insisted that Dietz return to his Milwaukee diocese. In April, 1923, Dietz departed from Cincinnati and the active life he had led with the labor movement. The AF of L gave him a gift of $2500 "In token of their friendship and esteem for a priest who had attended their annual conventions since 1909, and whom they had 'known and admired and heeded.' " [147]

Unlike Bishop Moeller, Dietz's bishop, Archbishop Messmer, who had adopted him in 1912 was impressed with his contribution to the Catholic social movement. In a letter to Senator Irwine Lenroot recommending Dietz for a position with the Harding government, Messmer said of Dietz, "He has had remarkable success with a number of American labor organizations in holding them aloof from the more radical and socialistic influences." [148]

As previously noted, the Social Service Commission of the American Federation of Catholic Societies played a vigorous role for Catholic principles in the labor unions. The Commission had strength because by 1912 the American Federation of Catholic

Societies was firmly established and had a strong voice in Catholic circles. The AFCS had first started in 1901 for the purposes of uniting existing Catholic organizations into a federation to defend the Church's interests and to promote social reform as set forth by Leo's encyclical. It had received the approbation and blessing of Leo XIII and Pius X and its advisory board included members of the Catholic hierarchy. The constitution of the AFCS stated that the organization intended to spread Catholic principles in "social and public life, in the State, in business, in all financial and industrial relations." [149] This could be done as seen by the first president of the AFCS, T. B. Minahan, through the development of a Catholic public sentiment. The AFCS president declared that millions of Catholics, united "would be able to wield a power," for "public opinion is the power behind the throne." [150] By 1917 over forty Catholic societies representing three million Catholics were affiliated with the AFCS.

The Catholic federation was a constant supporter of trade-unions that observed Catholic social principles. Its first convention in 1901 adopted a resolution recommending the study of *Rerum Novarum* for all Catholics. At its 1904 convention it gave approval to trade-unionism but advised Catholics to form special associations for moral instruction and Catholic solutions.[151]

A resolution on Industrial Relations at the 1913 Milwaukee convention of the American Federation of Catholic Societies declared:

> *Trade Unions:* We further sympathize with the aspirations of the workers to better their condition by organized effort in conservative trade unions . . . we urge upon all Catholics in the organized trade union movement to use all their influence against the propaganda of class hatred and against any illegitimate social unrest in the trade union movement of America. . . .
> We recommend to Catholics to attend meetings of their local unions faithfully and to take an active part in their deliberations. Catholic members of trade unions should oppose the use of their trade journals as handbooks of socialism; the endorsement of socialist candidates for political office; appropriations for political campaigns, socialist newspapers and legislators.

They should oppose the use of trade union meetings for socialist propaganda.

.   .   .   .

Militia of Christ Trade Union Service: In order to encourage
the application by trade unionists of the sociological principles
outlined in the Encyclicals of Pope Leo XIII and Pope Pius X to
the affairs of trade union organization, we recommend the
establishment of branches of the Militia of Christ.[152]

In January, 1915, Father Peter E. Dietz, as a fraternal delegate
to the American Federation of Labor from the American Federation of Catholic Societies, forwarded a "Memorial" to the AF of L
executive board requesting that the two organizations more closely
affiliate. The "Memorial" stated that "It may be truly said that
the aims, policies, and achievements of the American Federation
of Labor have received at the hands of the American Federation
of Catholic Societies a wholehearted sympathy and often time
practical co-operation that challenges comparison with every
movement outside of the American Federation of Labor itself.
This has contributed not a little to the growth of the American
Federation of Labor in numbers and moral influence both within
the labor movement and outside it." [153] But Gompers answered
that the affiliation Dietz desired was not appropriate to the AF of
L's purposes.

A resolution at the last convention of the AFCS in 1917 recommended to Catholic workers "their faithful attendance to trade-
union duties, active participation in the affairs of their unions, and
unceasing opposition to the abuse of their organizations by the
destructive propaganda of Socialism." [154] The outbreak of World
War I necessitated a more highly centralized federation and the
bishops of the Church created the National Catholic War Council.
In 1919 the War Council was succeeded by a permanent organization called the National Catholic Welfare Council, now known as
the National Catholic Welfare Conference.

Probably the most socially conscious of all the Catholic societies affiliated with the AFCS was the German Roman Catholic
Central Verein, an association of Catholic men of German extraction, founded in 1855. The verein in 1908 established a Central

Bureau so that Catholic ethics could be more widely and effectively interpreted to the United States. The bureau sponsored study
courses and discussion clubs for considering the Church's principles as applied to social reconstruction and for training Catholics
as social leaders to represent their Church's social views. It also
issued *Central Blatt and Social Justice,* a widely circulated monthly
published in German and English for the benefit of clergy and laymen and devoted to the discussion of social problems and the application of Catholic principles for these problems. In addition, it
issued weekly press bulletins in both German and English to about
one hundred Catholic newspapers.[155]

The fear of socialism and the call to social action given by
Leo XIII's *Rerum Novarum,* writes Sister Mary Brophy, led the
Central Verein and the local vereins "to take an active interest in
the labor movement." [156] Mr. Gonner, the president of the German Roman Catholic Central Verein, in an address to the delegates
at the annual convention in 1909, said that the "social reform
movement in the Central Verein" intended "to be an obedient response to the call of a motto of our gloriously-reigning Pontiff Pius
X." He explained that the verein could have a strong influence on
Catholic workmen and on trade-unions through utilizing a Catholic social reform program, an effective organization, and zealous
Catholic leaders. The verein president explained that the Catholic
social reform program "becomes clear when we say that for us
the words 'To Restore All Things in Christ' means the promotion
and defense of Christian Order in society, especially against the
dangers of Socialism and Anarchy in any form." [157] He asserted
that the duty of verein members was to contact Catholic unionists
in the AF of L, to arouse them against Socialist penetration, and
to teach them Catholic social principles. In addition, he proposed
the establishment of Catholic workers' associations:

> The Central Society is urging its more influential members
> in the various cities of the U.S. to gather around themselves in
> groups and circles, Catholic laboring men, members of the
> American Federation of Labor, to instruct them on their
> duties and the Christian principles in the Labor Question, to
> enable these to counteract the baneful activity displayed by
> Socialistic agitators among the laboring men of the United

States and thus while leaving intact American organized labor yet safeguarding Catholic religious and civic rights. . . . As a permanent solution of the problem of safeguarding Catholic laboring men, the Central Society advocates the formation of Catholic laboring-men's organizations, of course, without detriment to the American Federation of Labor.[158]

Resolutions adopted at the Central Verein's 1909 convention also testify to the organization's views on labor unions. One resolution recommended "faithful cooperation with the American Federation of Labor guided as it is by conservatism." Another resolution, "based on the Encyclical of Pope Leo XIII" recommended "as a crying necessity the founding of Catholic Workingmen's Welfare Associations." [159]

As the proceedings of the Central Verein's 1909 meeting suggest, the AF of L was well regarded by this socially alert body. That fact was confirmed by a letter in 1911 from F. P. Kenkel, the Central Bureau's director, to Samuel Gompers. Mr. Kenkel wrote that the verein was interested in the AF of L because one of its objects was "the furtherance of the real interests of the working class." The AF of L president was informed that the Central Verein's 1910 Newark convention, " 'in faithful compliance with the directions laid down in the Encyclical Letters of Pope Leo XIII and Pius X,' " had urged " 'Catholic workingmen to join the Trade Unions wherever possible [and] to combat the propaganda of Socialism in the Unions.' " Mr. Kenkel wrote that the verein's policy "had been to spread a proper understanding of the rights and duties of Capital and Labor and we flatter ourselves in having been instrumental in molding public opinion in certain circles in a manner favorable to the real interests of Labor." Mr. Kenkel added that the verein was pleased with Gompers' ideological leadership of the AF of L because it was in consonance with the social teachings expounded by the Catholic Church. Gompers was extended the verein's "best wishes for the success of organized Labor along the lines most conducive to its real welfare, to the real good of the working classes, to the good of society, of which you are so important a factor in conformity with Christian principles." [160]

The editors of the verein's monthly journal effectively popularized papal letters and the Church's position on unions. Pope

Pius x's encyclical, *Singulari Quadam Caritate,* brought forth two editorials by the Central Verein which with clarity and forcefulness interpreted the encyclical for those interested in and involved in the American labor unions. The first editorial, after quoting important parts of the encyclical, summarized the letter by declaring:

> Briefly, then, we see that the first endeavor must be to form Catholic unions, but that practical reasons may force Rome to tolerate interdenominational unions, since these are not necessarily evil, nor a source of immediate danger. In order to make the danger remote, yea, as remote as possible, the ecclesiastical authorities must watch over them closely and through Catholic labor societies they must warn their subjects and make sure of their loyal obedience.[161]

A second editorial a month later explicitly interpreted *Singulari Quadam Caritate* as a guide to the position that American Catholic workers could take towards trade-unions. It said that Pope Pius's

> words alone would exclude from the ranks of unions to which Catholics might belong all organizations influenced by and fostering socialism. . . . In short, in socialistic organizations we must behold a danger to society, morality and faith. Catholics therefore cannot be members of organizations founded and directed by Socialists for Socialistic purposes as e.g., The Industrial Workers of the World, the American Railroad Union, The Western Labor Union, The American Labor Union, The Western Federation of Miners, the Socialistic Trades and Labor Unions, the Knights of Labor, etc., if they are what they are said to be. . . .
>
> Similarly, to give briefly an example of another kind, the Farmers Educational and Co-operative Union of America is not in conformity with the above teaching. From the '*Amerika*' of November 26, 1912, we learn that this union is interdenominational; advocates—these are the objectionable points —religious interdenominationalism, and puts aside the true standards of morality by declaring its aim and purpose to be 'to secure equity, establish justice and apply the Golden Rule.'

These objectionable features make it fall under the unions censured by the Pope.[162]

The American Federation of Labor was also commented on by the Central Verein editor. He wrote that the AF of L "has not adopted these pernicious and morally unsound principles. It intends to be a purely economic organization." He warned, however, that should the minority radical element, who were advocating such dangerous views as revolutionary strikes, free public school text books, and women suffrage, gain in influence in the AF of L, the Catholics would have no alternative but to quit. If this radical element "ever, as some fear, come into power then the movement will be *near* the danger line, at which all Catholics will have to halt and at which they would have to leave the Federation." Catholics could only remain in interdenominational unions "provided the latter are not positively opposed to the moral laws as regards membership and action. But, we repeat it, this makes the adoption of safeguards, yea, of special assistance peremptory." [163]

The social diligence of the Central Verein in translating the Church's doctrines to the American people earned the praise of Father John A. Ryan. He commended the verein for recommending "that Catholic workingmen take an active part in the regular trade union instead of forming separate organizations. In this way the Catholic workers will be able to oppose most effectively Socialism, unwise Radicalism, and every other tendency or method that is hostile to genuine reform. They will not only be of great service to their fellow unionists, and to the laboring classes generally, but will reflect honor upon their Church as the safeguard of social order and the advocate, inspirer and teacher of economic justice." [164]

In 1955 the Central Verein declared that one of "the two most promising young men" ever employed at the Central Bureau as an assistant to the director Mr. Kenkel and the Committee on Social Action was Louis F. Budenz.[165] Although Budenz' devotion to catholicism was later marred by a ten-year period of membership in the Communist party that included a position as managing editor of the *Daily Worker* from 1940 to 1945, he returned to the Catholic cause in 1945 as a lecturer on economics at Fordham University.

Before coming to work for the Central Verein in late 1913, Budenz was active in the Catholic social movement in Indianapolis. He was a member of several Catholic societies and vice-president and an organizer of the Indiana Federation of Catholic Societies. His paid position was as an associate editor of *The Carpenter,* the official journal of the United Brotherhood of Carpenters and Joiners. The carpenters in those days were the largest union in the AF of L. His own union was the stenographers' union.

Budenz never saw the social struggle in terms of grey, no matter what side he was on, but always in black or white. Writing to his friend, Father Dietz, in January, 1913, he said: "The Catholic people need awakening and particularly do they need to be shown the right side of the Social Question." He told Dietz that president Duffy "has turned the whole magazine over to me" and therefore he was writing most of the editorials for *The Carpenter.* He was "very glad to know" that Dietz was "pleased" with his work and urged Dietz to inform him, "should I at anytime make a slip or important omission." [166]

After attending the 1912 AF of L convention Budenz wrote an article for *Central Blatt and Social Justice* analyzing the progress of socialism in the union movement. He noted that the Socialist, Max Hayes, had received almost five thousand votes to Gompers' twelve thousand for the AF of L presidency. He also listed the various AF of L unions where control had passed into Socialist hands and the union journals that were vehicles for Socialist propaganda. Only Catholic action, he declared, could be the successful adversary to socialism. There was, he wrote, "great and urgent necessity for immediate positive Christian action within" the AF of L.

> Our Catholic Christian laboring men must boldly raise their standard within the labor movement. They must bring our Christian Social program to their meetings—our Solidaristic conception of society and industry—even as the revolutionists bring their ideas. They must fearlessly enunciate their doctrines in the correspondence columns of their trade papers. They must be as unceasing in their activities as the Socialists are in theirs, opposing Socialistic teachings not alone with destructive criticism, but with a constructive plan of action. They

must keep in touch with each other, so as to profit by each other's experiences, and especially remain close to their pastors and recognized leaders, so as not to go astray, but to retain the truth. In order to do this in an efficient and practical manner, they must associate together in Catholic organizations. There are many means, no doubt, at hand to effect this purpose, one of the most satisfactory of which is the formation of Catholic workingmen's associations. In fact, bearing the words of our Holy Father, Pius x, in mind, this is not merely a matter of choice or expedience, but of obligation, from which we cannot easily escape. The Catholic workingman who imagines that there is no danger to himself or to his fellows from Socialistic poison will, in the not far distant future, find that he has been most grievously deceived. Education, of course, is needed in this work—thorough education—but while we are learning and educating we must also be doing. We have no time to lose.[167]

Budenz agreed in particular with Father Dietz's activities about the need for a Catholic workers' organization and for Catholic political lobbying. In a letter to Dietz who requested his help in establishing an Indianapolis chapter of the Militia, he wrote that the Militia was "a very efficient way of putting into practice our Catholic idea of Solidarism." He said he could be relied on to "mention the Militia in all his talks before Catholic groups." [168]

Under his title as vice-president of the Indiana Federation of Catholic Societies, Budenz sent out a circular letter to all affiliated Catholic societies in Indiana urging them to lobby for such Catholic-approved labor measures before the Indiana legislature as a minimum wage for women, an eight-hour workday bill, and a workmen's compensation bill. His letter said, "The day has arrived when it is the duty of the Catholic laymen and laywomen of this country to exercise their energies and influence in behalf of their religion and their beloved land. . . . Act immediately on these matters and send a letter to your Senator and Representative." [169] To Dietz he wrote, "I was very glad you were pleased with our action in regard to labor legislation." He promised Dietz, too, that he would strive to get busy on the Militia in a short time.[170] He also informed Dietz in a following letter that he was "preparing an

article for the May *Carpenter*" which would show the "fundamental difference between Socialism and Christian reform." This
subject "should be brought in every way possible squarely before
our working people." [171]

In answer to a letter from Dietz in April, 1913, Budenz wrote,
"In regard to Keegan . . . I might say this: He is emphatically no
Socialist nor is he in sympathy with them. He is on the other hand a
sincere and submissive Catholic . . . when the Catholic viewpoint
on any particular question is authoritatively pointed out to him,
he immediately takes that side of the question and champions
it." [172] In the same letter Budenz told Dietz:

> I am paving the way for some action on the Militia of Christ.
> . . . I prefer to start with younger men . . . [who are more re-
> sponsive to] the acceptance of Catholic ideals. At this meeting
> I shall have a boiler maker, a pattern maker, a metal polisher
> or more, a machinist, a carpenter, and one or two other crafts
> represented. Those whom I have approached on the subject
> are enthusiastic but prefer to work quietly. . . . When the time
> of crisis comes in the American labor organization (as it is
> sure to come, to be decided one way or the other) I believe
> that the fact that I have even from my earliest days been a
> spokesman for the laboring man will be a great asset in show-
> ing my sincerity in taking the Catholic and consequently anti-
> Socialist view.

Impressed by Budenz' dedicated Catholic spirit, Father Dietz
proposed that Budenz join him in his Milwaukee office and activities. Budenz answered that he "would certainly be pleased if
we could make such an arrangement" and would like to discuss
the matter when they meet at the next AF of L convention. He
added that the "Chautauqua Managers Association and their field
agent has made me an offer to go with them" but he was delaying
accepting because he was "reluctant to leave the real Catholic
field." [173] The prospect of being wanted by Dietz led Budenz to
write of himself, "I am glad to take up Catholic work . . . my whole
ambition has been to further the Catholic social movement in particular and to add to the glory of the Church thereby." He hoped
that Dietz and he could settle the question of his job before long
so that he could "lay plans for getting some strong right-thinking

man in this place." [174] As it turned out, Budenz did not go to work for Father Dietz. He "most unexpectedly received a letter from Mr. Kenkel asking me to join the Central Bureau of the Central Verein" and after giving the matter some thought made up his "mind to accept the offer." [175]

From 1913 to 1917 Budenz worked as the assistant to the director of the Central Bureau of the Central Verein, Mr. Kenkel. His duties consisted of editing *Central Blatt and Social Justice,* teaching courses concerning the social problem at study institutes, lecturing on the social problems, attending the conventions of AF of L and of Catholic societies, meeting with individual Catholic laymen and clergy, and, in general, planning and implementing the Bureau's campaign for furthering the Catholic social movement, particularly in the labor unions. As a Catholic, he sought for the AF of L to stay oriented in Catholic social principles; as a trade-unionist, he sought for catholicism, clergy, and laity, to befriend the union movement.

Following his attendance at the AF of L 1914 convention he wrote in the Central Verein journal with satisfaction that "the conservatism which has in the main marked the course of the American Federation of Labor during the thirty-four years of its existence was characteristic in an especial manner of its last convention." He noted in particular that the meeting had not approved industrial unionism, the eight-hour day for men by legislation, nor the efforts of the machinists to absorb the Elevator Constructors. He warned, however, that it was "most foolish to imagine that Socialism within the Federation was at all dead or that every act of the labor body was governed by the correct point of view. The radical element is strengthened in some cases, as in that of the machinists, by its being upheld and supported by a Masonic clique whose representatives wield at the present time more influence in the labor movement than their natural abilities would give to them because of their close union and cooperation." For the AF of L administration he, like other crusaders for the Catholic cause, had high praise.

> One thing was clearly demonstrated at the convention and that was that the one man to properly direct the Federation at the present time, with the possible exception of John Mitchell, is

the present executive, Samuel Gompers. He thoroughly understands the people and problems with which he has to deal.

.   .   .   .

That the American labor movement will continue to wisely solve its problems as it has in the past is to be certainly desired. It can, by pursuing such a policy, be of good not alone to the working classes, but to all the members of our American society. Upon Catholic workingmen rests a great responsibility in this regard. They should be active in this movement, maintaining in their local unions even more so than they have been doing, the principles for which they stand. They should be as ready to defend their standards as the radical is eager to push forward his ideals and views. In this way will their trade unionism be re-enforced, their hold on their religion strengthened and their whole view of life made better and more consistent.[176]

Budenz was utterly opposed to a minority opinion occasionally heard in Catholic circles that favored the establishment of an independent Catholic trade-union movement. He believed that catholicism could win over socialism in the AF of L; for Catholics to form their own union would be to abdicate and give the AF of L to the Socialists. When the Right Reverend Joseph Busch of the diocese of Lead, South Dakota, publicly called for the forming of a Catholic trade-union, the Verein's Central Bureau sent Budenz to visit with Bishop Busch and persuade him of the ultimate danger to catholicism posed by dual unionism.[177]

Besides the work done for Catholic social principles within the labor movement by the individuals and organizations thus far described, there were two Catholic laymen who labored for many years to bring about Catholic-oriented labor unions. These two men were Peter W. Collins, an Irish-Catholic and International Secretary of the Electrical Workers; and David Goldstein, a convert from Judaism and one-time Socialist Labor Party supporter. Within the period 1900–1918 these men gained national attention in promoting the Catholic social cause among America's laborers. Father Peter E. Dietz claimed credit for being "instrumental in bringing Peter Collins and David Goldstein to the Catholic platform," but even without his encouragement they were devoting themselves to perpetuating Catholic principles in the American trade-union movement and to attacking Socialist theory and activity.[178]

As a trade-unionist, international secretary of the Brotherhood of Electrical Workers from 1905 to 1912, editor of the organizations' official journal, *The Electrical Worker,* and president of the Boston Central Union, Peter W. Collins had a background of trade-union experience and this, coupled with his known anti-Socialist position, made him a coveted speaker for Central Verein, Holy Name, Knights of Columbus, and Militia of Christ audiences. His contacts, too, with Catholic organizations were furthered because he himself was a member and officer of several Catholic societies.

The evidence of Socialist growth in Massachusetts and in the union movement during the first years of the twentieth century seriously alarmed Collins. At first his reaction was to work with others in the fight against socialism in his union, in the state conventions of the AF of L, and in the national AF of L convention. But his anti-Socialist feelings required even more activity and he became a veritable one-man crusade against socialism—writing, lecturing, and teaching.

Writing in the December, 1909, issue of the *Electrical Worker* on the "Menace to Labor" he charged that socialism was the menace. Workers sympathetic to socialism, he declared, did not understand its doctrines "are against the fundamentals of American institutions, doctrines which are opposed to the maintenance of the home and the sanctity of the family." He suggested that "the men of labor" must drive from the ranks "these disrupters and their false and iniquitous doctrines and methods." [179]

His reputation reached the Central Verein by 1909. In their desire to spread the Catholic social movement they had Collins come to Belleville, Illinois, in January, 1910, to conduct a study course in conjunction with Father Dietz that might counter the growth of socialism among the Belleville miners.[180] For several years thereafter the Verein's Central Bureau called in Collins to give brief courses on socialism as part of a wider social science program presented in various places. During the years 1911 through 1913 the Central Bureau also sponsored Collins on extensive anti-Socialist lecture tours in many states.

Collins availed himself, too, of the opportunity to use the pages of the *Central Blatt and Social Justice* for carrying his message to Catholic priests and workers. In the February, 1910, issue he discussed the possibility of the Socialists capturing the American trade-union movement. He reviewed the four methods they were using with some success: (*1*) controlling the local unions; (*2*) using local union's funds for Socialist party purposes; (*3*) operating labor publications; (*4*) persuading state federations of labor in Wisconsin, Iowa, Colorado, and Minnesota to declare in favor of public ownership. Collins was satisfied, however, that the AF of L itself "has taken a firm and positive stand against socialism" and that Socialist "influence has been small" in the AF of L. He was confident that "a thorough campaign of education within the [union] movement" could prevent "the socialistic propaganda from adding to its forces." His article concluded:

> The work which the Catholic men have to do is an important one and to a large extent it rests with them whether or not the pernicious and insidious propaganda of socialism will succeed within the trade-union movement. The influence of our people in the movement is large and it may be surprising to know that almost half of the delegates to the conventions of the American Federation of Labor are loyal members of the church, loyal citizens and loyal trade-unionists. These men and their fellows are a factor in the labor movement and while they have never organized as a body for the purpose of fighting the socialists, their every individual effort has been directed against its progress.
>
> To me it seems that organization among our Catholic men in the labor movement would be of great advantage for they could direct their influence against the spread of socialism and aid tremendously the progress of labor.[181]

Collins' writings and talks concentrated almost entirely on attacking socialism. Some of his pamphlets and articles were titled, "What is Socialism," "Why Socialism is Opposed to Trade Unionism," "Why Socialism is Opposed to the Catholic Church," "The Truth About Socialism," and "Why a Christian Cannot Be a Socialist." The Verein's Central Bureau or the Knights of Columbus often published his writings for mass distribution. Sometimes

Catholic publications in America ran his pamphlets as a series of articles.[182]

One of his typical lecture tours booked by the Verein's Central Bureau, the Minnesota tour under the auspices of the Minnesota State Council, Knights of Columbus, listed his lecture subjects for this tour as: *1*. Social Problems and Social Reform, *2*. Socialism, *3*. Socialism and Christianity, *4*. Why Socialism is Opposed to the Labor Movement, *5*. The Ideals of the Labor Movement, *6*. The Workers in Industry and Their Protection.[183]

About late 1911 Collins felt that his anti-Socialist cause was limited by his connection and work with the Electrical Workers. He weighed the matter of resigning as secretary of the Electrical Workers and devoting himself entirely to arousing Catholic resistance to socialism. He wrote to Dietz, "What is your advice, Father? Give it without reserve. . . . I am going to depend a great deal on your advice." [184] Earlier in this year Collins, as a vice-president of the Militia for Christ, had been on a special lecture tour of industrial areas. Sister Fox writes that "wherever he went he talked about the Militia of Christ, left subscription blanks with the Council of the Knights of Columbus, urging them to interest their members in the organization." [185]

The time and feelings Collins gave to anti-Socialist activities produced some friction between Collins and other leaders of the Electrical Workers. He expressed his irritation to Father Dietz, "I want to be free to do the work against socialism and I really can't do much service by being tied down in Springfield and hampered and hindered by 'four flushing' labor politicians." His "heart and soul" was "in the movement for real *Catholic Social Action and the Militia of Christ*" and he wanted to "go into the battle *now* and fight socialism" rather than be hampered by "some of these yellow men who call themselves Catholic." [186]

Encouraged by Dietz, Collins resigned from the Electrical Workers in April, 1912, and occupied himself entirely with Catholic social action. Throughout 1912 he lectured for the Militia. In the summer of 1912 he advised Dietz, "I believe there ought to be a few retreats for Catholic Trade Unionists and an education of Catholic Labor leaders as to their responsibilities . . . we could sweep socialism and all the other heresies off the earth." [187] In

January, 1913, "he went to the Central Verein" because Dietz had not been able to furnish him "with sufficient lectures." [188]

Collins' general solution for the social question was the formation of Catholic Workers Association.

In this age of perverted ideals and lax conceptions of duty to God and Country, it is indeed assuring to look to the Catholic Church and see how proudly and majestically she stands as the conservator of Christian destination. . . . Not alone do those within the fold of the Church appreciate the service that she has rendered for constructive service, but great numbers of those without look to her as the guide in the progress of civilization. . . . It is necessary, however that in this great work of Christian democracy she should receive not the passive but the active support of every Catholic working-man and indeed the co-operation and support of those workers not within the fold who should look to her for guidance and protection. . . . The Catholic workingman therefore not only to protect his own interests as a worker and to raise his intellectual and material condition, but to protect his moral and spiritual welfare against the insidious influence manifesting itself in our own day, must co-operate in the Catholic Workingmen's Societies for these interests. As Leo XIII well said in his Encyclical on *The Condition of Labor,* 'We approach the subject with confidence and in the exercise of our rights which belong to Us: For no practical solution of this question will ever be found without the assistance of Religion and of the Church. It is we who are the chief guardians of religion and the chief dispenser of what belongs to the Church and we must not by silence neglect the duty which lies upon Us.'

Catholic workers were reminded that since they had the numerical strength to defeat socialism, the moral guilt would be theirs if socialism captured the trade-unions.

One has but to know the unceasing and continuing efforts of Socialists in this country to make the workingmen's organizations a means for the advancement of socialism and against God, country and Trade Unions, to realize how grave the danger, and realizing this, the Catholic workmen can be a factor of more than passing moment in the maintenance and progress of society. [They should combat] the destructive tendencies the socialist and other radicals are attempting to foist upon the trade union movement. . . . Almost one half of the men of organized labor are Catholic workingmen.

.   .   .   .

It rests with them whether or not the pernicious and insidious campaign of socialism will succeed with the organizations of workers.

Collins' positive solution for securing the triumph of Catholic social principles and the defeat of socialism in the unions was to reintroduce Father Dietz's Militia of Christ without its formal name.

We advocate Catholic workingmen's societies to be founded in each parish, whose members shall be instructed as to their special duties to church and society according to precepts laid down by Leo XIII . . . only when so instructed and fortified will Catholic laboringmen be able to do their full share in preventing the insidious enemy from capturing the Trade Union Movement and turning it into a recruiting ground for Socialism, into an appendix of the Socialist Party of the United States.[189]

In the Preface to one of his pamphlets, *Triplets of Destruction: Socialism, Bolshevism and the I.W.W.,* published by the Knights of Columbus in 1919, Collins claimed that his national campaign against the left wing movement had taken him over two hundred and fifty thousand miles into more than two thousand communities and before millions of people.[190] He was known far and wide in American Catholic organizations and had become a legendary figure in labor circles too. Professor Aaron Abell has rated him second only to Father Dietz in his influence in extending Catholic principles into the American labor union movement.[191]

Less influential than Collins in promoting Catholic social principles but more sensational was David Goldstein. How could one be regarded as less than sensational who had early in life embraced the Socialist Labor Party, renounced it in 1903, changed

from the Jewish religion to catholicism in 1906, and finally taken
to the public platform to preach Catholic ethics to others? Such
twists and turns led to a variety of speculation about Goldstein's
motives. The Socialists alleged that Goldstein became a spokesman of the Catholic church because he could obtain a lucrative
living from his talks and increase the profits from the sales of his
writings, too. They alluded also to his personal involvement with
Martha Moore Avery, a Protestant and Socialist who had converted to catholicism in 1905, a year before Goldstein, and who
was his professional associate in Boston and on his lecture tours.
Catholic sources, on the other hand, accepted Goldstein's explanation of the spiritual change he had undergone. *The Pilot,* the official organ of the Boston diocese announced on November 5,
1910, "Mr. David Goldstein is a constant reminder of Catholic
truth as glowing in the heart of a sincere convert." Goldstein stated
his secular reason for embracing catholicism in his book, *Socialism: the Nation of Fatherless Children,* which was sold at his
lectures and was endorsed by Samuel Gompers in 1904.[192] He
wrote in the Preface that socialism must be destroyed and catholicism alone had the strength to accomplish the task.

> It is my personal conviction which I may say I have arrived
> at without association or affiliation with the institution—that
> upon the religious aspects of this great issue the fight now cen-
> ters around the Catholic Church—which is the first and only
> church that has boldly taken up the gauntlet thrown down with
> scorn and defiance by Socialism. This Church is not only in-
> ternational, or rather universal, and so equipped to meet the
> power of the international enemy, but it is erected upon a
> basis—upon religious service—which gives it the strength to
> cope with the aggressions of the approaching foe. There are,
> I am aware, many persons who would rather see Hell reign
> than the Catholic Church should be the victor in so great, so
> masterful a struggle—for such I have but sympathy for they
> but veil themselves in darkness. They may be assured that if
> this institution falls in the fight (if that were possible) all
> religious sects and cults would collapse in its ruins.[193]

Goldstein emphasized that the battle over socialism was growing more keen within the trade-unions. Since it had become clear

to him that socialism destroyed individual liberty, he would aid
the AF of L to destroy socialism:

> There is marked evidence to show that upon economic
> grounds the battle to sustain the individual progress made by
> the race will come to issue between the American Federation
> of Labor and the Socialist propaganda organization. It will no
> doubt be a long drawn series of hand to hand fights upon the
> floor of trade unions—and in the halls of trade union conven-
> tions, state and national. Having fought desperately in the
> glare of its false light, at last the truth was revealed to me that
> socialism is the cause of the damned—not the cause which
> maketh men free—and now within the strength of reason
> rather than in the excitement of fanaticism I shall hope to add
> somewhat to the victories of the American Federation of
> Labor.

Goldstein did his best to foster antisocialism within the AF
of L. Either as a delegate from the Massachusetts Cigarmakers,
or as an observer, he attended annual conventions of both the
Massachusetts State Federation of Labor and the American Federation of Labor. At the conventions he worked with other zealous
anti-Socialists plotting their strategy to defeat Socialist resolutions
and to discredit socialism among the delegates. In his autobiography he quotes two Boston newspapers which tell of his activity
at the 1903 AF of L convention.[194] The Boston *Post* of November 9, 1903, wrote that he "was actively at work among the Federation delegates at the Revere house yesterday" circulating his
writings against socialism and "haranguing different groups of
delegates" about the "danger that confronts the A.F. of L. if Socialism is endorsed." The Boston *Pilot* of November 22, 1903,
said of the convention, "We believe that no little credit for this
memorable defeat of socialism is due to 'Socialism: The Nation
of Fatherless Children,' which was widely circulated and read during the convention! We are glad that the American Federation of
Labor has proved alike its patriotism and its Christianity by antagonizing the would-be destroyers of home, country, and Church."

Goldstein's main work against socialism was more than a convention affair. From 1910 on he lectured throughout the country
under Catholic auspices.[195] Although a rather evangelical atmos-

phere prevailed among the ensemble that toured and gathered on the lecture platform with him the words of this converted Catholic himself provided for his audience a straightforward exposition of the ideological struggle occurring within the American Federation of Labor. As a former Socialist and member of the Cigarmakers Union he claimed familiarity with the techniques and methods of ideological infiltration used by the Socialists. He announced that the Socialists were "battering from without and boring from within" in their effort to gain control of the AF of L. The Socialists, by attacking the "time tried and true officials" of the AF of L, hoped this would lead to their defeat and replacement with Socialist leaders.

Writing in the Central Verein journal at the close of 1910, Goldstein called on the trade-unionists to prize what their unions had gained for them and to avoid political action in their unions. From this advice it is clear once again that the AF of L policy of pure and simple unionism was in conformity with the policy catholicism desired unions to follow:

> There is no graver danger lurking about than when trade unionists themselves fail to appreciate what their unions have done for them. It is then that the devils of disruption get in their underhanded, their hellish work.
>
> There is one other grave danger threatening us as trade unionists. Its onward march should meet with determined resistance. No politics in trade unions may be trite but it is a true guide to safe conduct. The attempt to commit our unions to a specific political party should not be tolerated in our midst, neither by resolution, by financial aid, by giving politicians special privileges to carry on a campaign in our unions or in our office journals.

> .   .   .   .

> No, Socialists must not be allowed to commit us to their program which is nothing more nor less than political atheism.
>
> To be true unionists our work must be confined to such efforts upon the political field as lead only to the enforcing of our economic demands. Our business is not politics but economics. The friends of labor are the men for unionists to sup-

port and the policy of unionists is well expressed in the shibboleth that 'we should reward our friends and punish our
enemies.' [196]

As previously noted, Catholic spokesmen occasionally suggested that devout Catholics would be obliged to leave the AF of L
if that organization departed from Catholic social principles.
Goldstein similarly warned the AF of L leadership:

> If the fall of the A.F. of L. [to socialism] should become a
> matter of history—which I have no fear will be the case—it is
> certain that the trade union movement cannot hold the respect
> which it has gradually forced from a reluctant public opinion
> by its years of hard and intelligent work. And it is equally cer-
> tain that were so disastrous a fate to befall the A.F. of L., its
> best support, those great masses of men who stand for the
> moral principles which are the bulwark of the family, the
> church and the state would stand from under and let it sink
> to its death. The trade union that declares for socialism must
> be met on the same ground as socialist parties are met—they
> must be recognized as the enemies of society—whipped off the
> political arena.[197]

Nevertheless, the Catholic Church's spokesmen were confident
that catholicism had good friends among the leaders of the AF
of L and that these conservative officials were in agreement with
the Church on the principles that should govern trade-unions. It
was Goldstein's view that there was no reason to fear that the AF
of L would succumb to socialism. Optimistically, Goldstein declared to his Catholic audiences, "Fear not! Such men as Samuel
Gompers and John Mitchell stand as good security against so
dreadful a fate" as socialism.[198]

Goldstein's public relations campaign for his tours were clever
appeals to the emotional side of people. He was billed as the nation's foremost opponent of socialism and excerpts from press
stories praising his previous lectures were abundant. His advertising literature carried testimonials of distinguished Catholic
clergy and many Catholic organizations about his abilities, experience, and value. A large part of Goldstein's advertising material
quoted from the attacks made on him and his lectures by Socialists

and their press. His advance publicity also referred to the public-confessional aspect of an ex-Socialist who would discuss such matters as the free love and atheistic practices of Socialists. The net effect of Goldstein's advertising campaign was to emotionally arouse the interest of a wider audience than would have been attracted had his appeal been more intellectual and restrained.[199]

Though Goldstein's approach to carrying the Catholic message had melodramatic overtones his work was deeply satisfying to influential Catholic clergy and laymen. Most of his tours were sponsored either by the Militia of Christ, the Social Service Commission of the American Federation of Catholic Societies, state branches of the American Federation of Catholic Societes, The Knights of Columbus, the Central Bureau of the German Roman Catholic Central Verein, or a combination of these groups. In 1910 Cardinal O'Connell invited him to participate in a series of educational meetings to expose socialism. He complied with His Grace's wishes by undertaking sixteen meetings. Goldstein was particularly occupied with lecture tours in the years 1910 to 1914, years when the Socialists were at the height of their strength in the American Federation of Labor, as well as the nation at large. He described one of his 1911 tours in a letter to director Kenkel of the Central Bureau of the German Roman Catholic Central Verein. The tour which had taken him 102 days in all began in Lewistown, Maine, on September 12, 1911, and concluded in Albany, New York, on December 22, 1911. He had covered 9750 miles and had been generously received by bishops, priests, and laymen in nearly every state in the union. He had addressed forty-eight meetings in thirty-seven different cities with fourteen meetings under the auspices of the Central Bureau of the German Roman Catholic Central Verein and ten sponsored by the Knights of Columbus. In nearly every place that he spoke about two hundred and fifty copies of his book, *Socialism: The Nation of Fatherless Children,* had been put into circulation. He estimated that in the few months since Cardinal O'Connell had given the second edition of his book his imprimatur, in October, 1911, the sales of the book had reached twenty-two thousand.[200]

The proceeds from the sales of Goldstein's books at his lecture were often used, by prearranged plan, to pay him for his lecture. His honorarium was either fifty dollars plus expenses or

the sale of two hundred and fifty copies of his book. The organizations sponsoring his tours urged local federated bodies to choose
the book plan for Goldstein's fee. A circular of the Ohio Branch
of the American Federation of Catholic Societies to its county
organization said, "The book plan is a good one and will be of
much service to the community in which it is adopted, as it not
only defrays the expenses of the speaker and the lecture, but it also
sets into circulation 250 books filled with up-to-date facts and
arguments showing why Catholics may not be Socialists." [201] The
circular listed Goldstein as lecturing from December 31, 1913, to
January 15, 1914, in the Ohio cities of Columbus, Portsmouth,
Ironton, Cincinnati, Hamilton, Springfield, Dayton, Toledo,
Cleveland, Akron, Youngstown, Canton, Martins Ferry, Zanes-
ville, and Newark.

In addition to selling books at his lectures, Goldstein advertised that he was secretary for Mrs. Avery's Boston School of
Political Economy, a Catholic source of opposition to socialism,
which published pamphlets on the attitude of the Church toward
the social problems of the day. The pamphlets, he said, were published "upon so large a scale as to render feasible a liberal distribution of them." The Boston School had available "a half
million 16-page pamphlets on the four following subjects": *Leo
XIII on the Labor Question, Windthorst: The Little Giant of the
German Center Party* by Father Robert Swickerath, S.J., *Socialism: A Menace to Religion and Family* by Father C. J. Kluser,
and *A Socialist Scheme Factory Exposed* by Martha Moore
Avery.[202]

In January, 1914, Goldstein wrote Father Dietz that the Board
of Directors of the Knights of Columbus had called in Peter Collins
and himself to lecture against socialism in the Socialist strongholds
in the country. Collins was assigned the Eastern states while Goldstein was to tour the Pacific Coast and include Oklahoma on his
trip west.[203] "For six months a year, during a period of ten years,"
Goldstein later wrote, he "addressed about 1500 audiences in all
parts of the United States and the Dominion of Canada on various
phases of Socialism." [204] Some of the subjects of his specific lectures were *Socialism From an Economic Standpoint; Socialism
and Religion; Socialism and the Family; Trade Unions: Their
Foundation, Achievement, Dangers and Prospects; From Social-*

ism to the Church; Why I Am A Catholic; and *Leo* XIII *and the Labor Problem.*[205]

Cardinal O'Connell had urged Goldstein for a series of lectures in 1910 "to give workingmen an understanding of the basic principles that underlie the problems that affect their interests, to show them the value of the remedies the Church proposes, as well as to point out the shallowness and deceit of the proposals handed out by charlatans." [206] Many years later when the Church had won its battle and could look in retrospect on those who had aided her in the fight, Goldstein was not forgotten. He was made a Knight of St. Gregory.

The Catholic newspapers and journals during the period 1900–1918 were conscientious and effective media disseminating the principles laid down in *Rerum Novarum.* Leo XIII had reminded the hierarchy of the importance of the press when he said, "All your work will be destroyed, all your efforts will prove fruitless if you are not able to wield the defensive and offensive weapon of a loyal and sincere Catholic press." [207] The wisdom of these words was not lost on the American hierarchy and in the "plenary councils, the bishops of the country have time and again pronounced on its importance, furthered it by every means within their power, urged and commanded and pleaded with the Catholic laity for its support." [208] A pastoral letter of Bishop McFaul of Trenton early in the twentieth century urged:

> Every Catholic family should subscribe for a Catholic newspaper and a Catholic magazine. . . . Catholics should therefore ask their newsdealers for such newspapers as *The Freemen's Journal* of New York, *The Catholic Standard and Times* of Philadelphia, *The Catholic News* of New York, *The Pilot* of Boston, *The Pittsburgh Observer,* and other religious newspapers published in their respective localities. They should also seek the inestimable Catholic periodicals like *The Messenger* and *The Catholic World* of New York, "The Ave Maria," "America" and a host of others.

.   .   .   .

No better example of the power and influence of the press can be given than the results achieved in Germany. It was due to public opinion created by the Catholic press that the Center Party remained undivided and steadfast, triumphed over Kulturkampf, brought Bismark to Canossa, and organized the Catholics of Germany so that they presented an unbroken front to their enemies.

.   .   .   .

We will never attain the position due to us in the civil and religious life of America, unless we employ this powerful lever in the creation of public opinion.[209]

Besides drawing attention to Catholic publications, Church leaders also pointed out improper reading material. Father Husslein, S.J., editor of *America,* cautioned "in particular Catholic trade unionists" that, if they were to remain "men of clear insight and strong Catholic principles," they would not "endorse the socialist publications which were recommended to them." To accept Socialist publications, he declared, meant bringing "into the house of the laborer a weekly apostle of radicalism in almost every shape condemned by the Church. . . . It means to pollute the well springs of pure and wholesome thought by sentiments that are anti-Catholic. . . . It means in fine to substitute for a manly and Catholic insistence upon justice and right the mean and diabolic spirit of envy and hatred." [210]

The period 1900–1918 saw the birth of about fifty Catholic newspapers, of the famed periodical edited by the Jesuits, *America,* and of several publications specifically dedicated to combating socialism. Some of the more noted newspapers founded in these years were *The Pilot* (1908), *The Tablet* (1909), and *The Messenger* of Belleville, Illinois (1908).[211] The Catholic Press Association was established in August, 1911, at Columbus, Ohio, by Catholic editors convening in that city and was incorporated in the state of New York on February 14, 1913. In 1920 the National Catholic Welfare Conference took over the news service of the Catholic Press Association.

In New York City two anti-Socialist publications were founded shortly before World War I by devoted Catholic sources. One was a newspaper, *The Live Issue,* the other a journal, *The Common Cause. The Live Issue*'s "Declaration of Principles," featured above its editorial page, stated that the paper "utterly repudiates and fearlessly combats Socialism." In consideration of the spirit and purposes of *Rerum Novarum,* the editor saw his duty was to teach the workers the values of the Catholic social movement. *"The Live Issue's* mission," he announced, "was to make our workingmen conscious factors in the moulding process which society is now undergoing. And it is to achieve this result that true social enlightenment is an imperative necessity no less than to expose the dangers and fallacies of Socialism." [212]

The Common Cause likewise proclaimed itself a journal which "comes to the defense of right-reason in things economic as against the theories of Socialism." [213] Its issues regularly contained indictments against socialism, and it periodically republished anti-Socialist articles originating elsewhere. The appearance of *The Common Cause* not only elicited an enthusiastic reception from a number of Catholic publications, but its editors also received a letter from Samuel Gompers complimenting its purpose and adding that he took "pleasure in placing your paper on our exchange list." [214]

The weakness of socialism in the American Federation of Labor at the close of World War I was, in part, a testimonial to the success of the Catholic Church's opposition to this doctrine. The Church could credit itself with having waged an effective campaign in checking socialism within the trade-union movement. Labor historians have correctly advanced many explanations for the weakness of socialism within American trade-unions, but have bypassed one explanation that should be included on their list—the strong opposition of the Catholic Church to socialism. Professor Selig Perlman was somewhat aware of this when he wrote in 1928 that for the American labor movement "to make socialism or communism the official 'ism' of the movement, would mean, even if the other conditions permitted it, deliberately driving the Catholics, who are perhaps in the majority in the American Federation of Labor, out of the labor movement, since with them an irreconcilable opposition to socialism is a matter of religious principle." [215] A labor party in an industrialized country can only take shape and grow if it can secure the support of the trade-union movement. A trade-union movement that has neither Socialist leadership nor a Socialist political consciousness among its rank and file will not possess the ideology that would find its political expression in a labor party. The important generalization which Perlman suggested, and which the present chapter's research confirms, is that the failure of socialism and a political labor party to evolve in America were in some measure due to the efforts made by the Catholic Church to prevent such a development. As Father Dietz wrote to Cardinal O'Connell on March 15, 1913, Catholic social action could create a "bridge between the Church in America and the labor movement" enabling it to "take hold of the labor movement." [216]

Catholicism engaged in this task during a period when American trade-unionism, still in its infancy, was developing its institutional traditions. Like all traditions, these would prevail during future generations and tend to become almost conditioned responses. Furthermore, this period also began as one in which the Socialist movement seemed on the threshold of becoming a major American political force. The awareness of these two facts on the part of the Catholic Church was evident in the extent of its exertions against Socialist penetration of the trade-unions. The victory achieved by catholicism at the close of this period was shown by the weakness of the Socialists in the AF of L and the dominance of an anti-Socialist administration. At the conclusion of World War I, considerable similarity between the AF of L's *Reconstruction Program* and the *Bishops' Program of Social Reconstruction* was not a coincidence.[217] It was to some degree the result of the intensive efforts made by the Catholic Church to permeate the AF of L with its social views and the agreement of Catholic leaders like John A. Ryan and Peter Dietz with AF of L leadership on trade-union principles. Aided by the predominantly Catholic officers of the international unions and by the large Catholic rank and file in the AF of L responsive to their Church's views on socialism, catholicism had helped to account for the moderate political philosophy and policies of AF of L, for socialism's weakness in the AF of L, and, therefore, for the absence of a labor party in the United States.

10.

An Interpretation of the Politics

of American Labor Unions

> Unionism is the strongest bulwark in the body politic today
> against the encroachments of socialism.
>
> *Wall Street Journal, November 20, 1903*
>
> The trade union is an obstacle in the path of the socialists.
> While it lives and thrives their destructive doctrines will
> have but comparatively few followers and can do
> little harm.
>
> *Chicago Tribune, November 20, 1903*

AS SHOWN in previous chapters, the political development of
the American Federation of Labor from 1900 to 1918 was a gradual and moderate one. From its almost nonpolitical beginnings
the AF of L's political methods by the close of World War I were
those typical of American pressure groups; it lobbied for legislation necessary for its self-interest and informed its membership of
the results. Like other pressure groups, it hoped that on election
day its rank and file would support the friends and oppose the
enemies to which it had drawn attention. Although the AF of L
alleged that its politics were nonpartisan, its support during political campaigns was given mostly to candidates of the Democratic
party because its experience was that this party was more receptive to organized labor's demands than was the Republican party.
The Federation's political philosophy clearly rejected Socialist doctrine. It accepted the fundamentals of the capitalist system and
denied both in theory and in practice that the class struggle was the
basis of social development. It steadily opposed the formation of
an independent labor party and consistently labeled the Socialists

and their programs as the enemies of trade-unionism. In fact, it viewed the idea of the welfare state with suspicion and actively lobbied only for legislation that would permit trade-unionism to make effective use of its economic power through organizing, through collective bargaining, and through the use of the strike. Its racial and nationalistic policies were indistinguishable from the prejudices of the nation in general. The Federation created no workers' education movement, it hired no academically and professionally trained people for specialized staff work in its offices and it made no serious effort to increase its political strength by alliances with progressive groups outside its fold.

Although organized labor's political position today has developed into that of a moderate reform group giving vigorous support for the electoral success of a liberal Democratic party committed to a regulated capitalism, its traditional repudiation of socialism remains basically unaltered. American trade-unionism stands as a glaring exception to the alliance between trade-unions and Socialist political parties in most of the world. Democratic lands like Britain, France, Norway, Sweden, Denmark, Australia, New Zealand, India, and Israel have strong Socialist parties whose political victories are made possible by labor union support. Why is "the cloth not cut from the same pattern" in the United States?

The following characteristics of twentieth century America will help explain the weakness of socialism within organized labor and the absence of an American labor party: (1) The vitality of American capitalism, (2) The middle-class psychology of American workers, (3) The American's faith in individual rights, (4) The conservative features of the American political system, (5) The anti-Socialist position of the Roman Catholic Church, (6) The anti-Socialist leadership of Samuel Gompers.

The foremost reason for the inability of socialism to attract American workers is the resiliency of the American system of private ownership of production. Although American capitalism historically has been hostile to the presence of unions, nevertheless, in retrospect, an expanding American capitalism has been financially capable of meeting the unions' continual economic demands. The quarrel between trade-unionism and business over the apportionment of profits has not been an insoluble problem in a period of general prosperity especially when business has been able to increase the price of its products following an increase in benefits to the workers. The increased purchasing power which unions have secured for their membership actually has tended to stabilize the economic cycle, rather than threaten the capitalist system.

The trade-unions themselves, once their struggle for survival was finished, acquired a vested interest in capitalism. Unions today own banks, credit unions, co-operatives, summer camps, office buildings, medical centers, and investments in various forms of business enterprise. Why should a union favor a doctrine like socialism, when the operation of capitalism has helped the union achieve its financial strength? Why destroy the goose that lays the golden egg? The trade-unionists look upon themselves as property owners, or at least potential property owners, as well as workers. The conflicts which American trade-unions have with business do not arise because the workers as a class are antagonistic to the private profit system but rather because most workers want a higher standard of living under capitalism. As long as capitalism is able to satisfy the economic expectations of the trade-union membership, Socialist thought will hold little attraction for the bulk of the trade-unionists and the unions will pose no threat to the American capitalistic structure.

A familiar plaque in taverns frequented by American workers reads, "If you're so smart why ain't you rich?" This question suggests the essence of the confidence that most workers have in capitalism. They see it as a system in which they have materially bettered themselves. When they make comparisons of their standards of living with others, they select their parents and grandparents, previous generations of Americans, and workers in other lands at the present time. Recognizing that they have more material benefits than those to whom they have compared themselves, they attribute this to the superior functioning of the present economic system.

Steadily over the years the number of trade-unionists owning their own homes has increased. These homes contain such modern manufactured consumer goods as electric washing machines, radios, high fidelity phonographs, refrigerators, television sets, and the family probably owns a late model automobile. Although these products may be cheaper imitations of the more expensive models owned by the employers of labor, this does not lessen the worker's enjoyment and satisfaction. Where this appreciation of the operation of the capitalist system exists, motivation from within the worker for a labor-socialist party will be lacking.

A new political party's rise is usually a symptom of discontent with existing institutions. But a worker not overwhelmingly displeased with what life appears to offer him is uninterested in changing the system under which he lives. An employed, self-satisfied, politically-indifferent worker does not conceive of himself as a victim of capitalist exploitation.

The Marxist appeal, "workers of the world, unite, you have nothing to lose but your chains," is ludicrous to most American trade-unionists. They are much more susceptible to capitalistic mythology and more prepared to believe slogans about free enterprise, though theirs is an age of billion dollar corporations. But mostly it is the economic facts of the worker's own experiences that nurture his loyalty to the existing economic system. American trade-unionists have seen their economic status improve even in such times as the past two world wars which brought so much economic distress to European workers.

The operation of the American economic system has not destroyed the individualistic philosophy which accompanied its birth nor has the system produced class-consciousness and an awareness of class struggle. Objectively, a labor party is the derivative of class-conscious workers determined to utilize their political power and change society more to their advantage. Unless there is a widespread discontent among workers with their economic situation, Socialist theory will make no appeal, socialism will not take root, nor a labor party develop. Socialists are not made by ethical appeals for the creation of a co-operative society, or by economic forecasts of capitalistic contradictions and weaknesses. Men as a group are more moved to action by their own emotional and material needs rather than by the lofty visions or rational explanations of others.

Another factor hindering Socialist growth in America is the psychology of the union members. By and large, American trade-unionists are motivated more by their American psychology—largely middle class in its origin—than by working-class feelings. The failure to understand the psychological nature of the American worker has led socialism to waste its recruiting energies. Marxist philosophy, too often expressed in technical jargon, explains economic phenomena in terms of rational men making choices. The serious errors in this method are that it assumes that men are more rational than they are and it grossly disregards the emotional factors influencing human behavior. The politicians of the two major parties have been much shrewder judges of human motivation in this respect. Their propaganda has been directed to the workers' biases, fears, and hopes.

The psychology of the American worker is an inevitable and unconscious result of American culture as well as a result of the deliberate cultivation of middle-class social values within the entire population by business sources. Because the governmental authority and the opinion-forming organs are under considerable obligation to advance the views and interests of big business, American people are constantly presented with concepts favorable to the capitalistic system.

The task of propagandizing has been made easier by the techniques of mass indoctrination particularly available in as industrialized a country as the United States. The movies, television, radio, and the press, all big-business owned, are major examples of propaganda instruments presenting a middle-class psychology for American workers through the content of their subject matter and the value system transmitted through their advertising. In addition, the churches, the educational system and the social and professional clubs, for the most part, reflect capitalistic mores, because they are financed or operated by men of business.

Most polls and surveys of American workers have disclosed that the large majority of Americans in unions consider themselves as middle class. The Socialist may retort that since the workers do not own the means of production and since their labor is bought by those who do own the means of production, this role of the worker within capitalism makes him a member of the working class. But the worker does not accept this definition of class. If there is a class system he concludes, he is in the middle class. Probably, it is the Negro, he feels, who is in the lower class.

The study *When Labor Votes* by Kornhauser, Sheppard, and Mayer, interestingly reports that two-thirds of the United Auto Workers in Detroit identify themselves as working class, in spite of their social and economic successes. Evidently a union that earnestly and constantly seeks to politically educate its membership to their working-class interests, can be effective also in influencing workers' social values.

To the Marxist theoretician most American workers lack class consciousness because they refuse to accept the view that wage labor under the private profit system is inherently exploited. But a person's feelings are psychological, not logical, and his ways of living are affected by subjective as well as objective factors. When Socialists criticize the self-interest and acquisitive spirit of capitalism, the worker feels under attack for within himself, he knows, burns the capitalistic spirit. A worker can feel gratitude and loyalty to his union and at the same time have an allegiance to the company and its owners who represent the realization of the worker's phantasies of "making good" and getting to the "top of the heap." The American worker feels middle-class and behaves middle-class. To understand his politics, one must recognize his psychology, a large part of which is middle-class derived.

The absence of a feudal tradition with its accompanying class stratification has enabled American workers to participate in American life as first-class citizens. Assembly line production and standardization make available products for a mass market and all people with purchasing power to avail themselves of these products thereby rid themselves of the stigma of any working-class origins they may have had. The working man in America feels himself accepted and integrated by an American society that is on the move upward. The clothes he wears, the nationally advertised goods he buys, the mechanical appliances in his home, the car he drives, the newspaper and magazine he reads, the comic strip he enjoys, the movie he attends, the television program he follows, and the national ball team he favors, instill in the worker the feeling that his life as a consumer is not different in kind from those more wealthy than he. An American worker enjoys, also, the social mobility available in a country not affected by a feudal tradition. He may belong to veterans' organizations, social clubs, recreational groups, nationality associations, and religious units which give him the satisfying feeling of acceptance by existing society. Such multiple loyalties, also, lessen his emotional need for a strong involvement in politics. In addition, through the social organizations he joins and the relationships he has with business and professional people, the worker absorbs middle-class experiences. Furthermore, his formal education is a democratic intermingling in the public schools with middle-class students under the supervision of middle-class teachers and administrators. Consciously and unconsciously, the molding process goes on and the worker's middle-class psychology inevitably increases with his age and affluence.

Precisely what is this American middle-class psychology? It is above all the desire to identify with those above in the social scale whose values dominate the culture. It is a search for social approval and acceptance by others who are regarded as important and popular. The tragicomedy of it is illustrated in a cartoon in a popular magazine as one family says to another, "You mean all the time we were trying to keep up with you, you were trying to keep up with us?" It is an intense need to be given the value of acceptance by another or others. It is the quest to "make the team." Even observing a television show provides a feeling of entry and participation with the screen characters. To avoid the blow of rejection by others, Americans will wear the current styles, keep up with the latest gossip, strive for social invitations, hold conventional opinions, and adjust their feelings and behavior to the demands of leaders of their peer group.

Emotional insecurity is a prominent feature of middle-class psychology. The person's opinion of himself rests on what he thinks others think of him. He never comes to grips with his own true feelings but represses them in order to be compatible with the feelings of those whose approval he wants. The conversation between two workers in Paddy Chayefsky's motion picture academy award winner *Marty* well illustrates the emptiness, loneliness, and acceptance-needs of many people. "What do you feel like doing tonight?" "I don't know, Angie, what do you feel like doing?"

Thus American workers are vulnerable to this American psychology which has grown out of bored lives lacking in community, out of the vastness and loneliness of America, out of the weakened family structure, the competitive and materialistic spirit of the economic system, and the anxiety of a fast-changing technological age. The effect of this psychology on politics is that Americans have become a people who accept and imitate, conform and fit into the fears and fashions, the pleasures and prejudices of those whose approval raises their own sense of self-esteem. American workers are prone to accept the political stereotypes that their town and national leaders furnish them. And these leaders, like all people, rationalize their self-interest as the public good.

Thomas Wolfe with the poet's insight in *You Can't Go Home Again* describes the strength of the identification appeal that America's successful leaders make for the peoples' support:

> "See, I am one of you—I am one of your children, your son, your brother, and your friend. Behold how sleek and fat I have become—and all because I am just one of you, and your friend. Behold how rich and powerful I am—and all because I am one of you—shaped in your way of life, of thinking, of accomplishment. What I am, I am because I am one of you, your humble brother and your friend. 'Behold,' cries enemy, 'The man I am, the man I have become, the thing I have accomplished—and reflect. Will you destroy this thing? I assure you that it is the most precious thing you have. It is yourselves, the projection of each of you, the triumph of your individual lives, the thing that is rooted in your blood, and native to your stock and inherent in the traditions of America. It is the thing that all of you may hope to be,' says enemy, 'For—humbly— 'Am I not just one of you? Am I not just your brother and your son? Am I not the living image of what each of you may hope to be, would wish to be, would desire for his own son? Would you destroy this glorious incarnation of your own heroic self? If you do, then,' says enemy, 'you destroy yourselves—kill the thing that is most gloriously American, and in so killing, kill yourselves.' " [1]

A political movement's success or failure will very much depend on how well its advocates recognize and articulate the emotional needs of those to whom its appeal is directed. A labor party appeal is a threat, not an aid, to the emotional security system of an American worker. A labor party carries a connotation of a class movement. It reintroduces the fears of a past when workers had less rights and status than today. It is reminder of an age of class conflict and a time of economic insecurity, preferably forgotten, not resurrected.

Justification for a labor party arouses a worker's doubts of his entire value system—doubts which repressed, keep him feeling more comfortable. He wants to be accepted as an American and being an American, he feels, is to be loyal to family, God, and country. A labor party has overtones of a working-class movement, a working-class movement suggests socialism, and socialism, to him or to those he needs for emotional support, is synonymous with un-Americanism.

The exaltation of the nation is a frequently encountered symptom of emotional insecurity. The greater the doubt of one's own worth, the greater the need for identification with something which raises one's own sense of worth. The nation, for some, becomes a socially acceptable parental-image substitute. The excessive attachment of many workers to the nation presents a difficulty for the proponents of a labor party. A labor party requires its followers to critically examine national policy that may be influenced by private business interests. The parental-substitute has to be judged for shortcomings, mistakes, and failures. But resistance to an objective examination of an emotional involvement is deep rooted. The country—right or wrong—is thus beyond objective judging, like the parents—good or bad—have been beyond objective examination. In fact, a serious critic of the nation arouses considerable hostility in others, who need to see the nation as a good parent. Psychology has its explanation for the intensity of the hostility encountered by orthodox Marxists in the Western democracies. Marxist propaganda and activities in non-Marxist states flagrantly violate concepts like private property, religion, and nation which provide deep psychological gratification for many human beings.

A study of early twentieth-century American unionism demonstrates that the nationalism of the American worker frequently affects his behavior. The AF of L's persistent activity for immigration restriction, its racial attacks on Asiatics, its discrimination against American Negroes, its coolness toward the International Federation of Trade Unions, its frequent criticism of socialism as a European importation, its super-patriotic support of the government during World War I, and its efforts to Americanize foreign-born workers through the American Alliance for Labor and Democracy are examples of the presence of nationalism in merely one period of American labor history. The American worker's nationalism is a powerful sentiment which continues to reject political movements not in consonance with traditional values associated with America. Interestingly, nationalism is one of the forces that the Marxist fathers did not adequately evaluate. The support given by Socialists to their governments during World War I, the nationalistic emphasis of fascism, the nationalistic quarrels between Communistic Russia and other Communistic nations, and the continued appeals to nationalism evident in Socialist countries illustrate the psychological naïveté of Marx and Engels who wrote in the *Communist Manifesto* that the "workers have no country."

There is another psychological characteristic of the American, trade-unionist or not, hindering the development of a labor political party. Most Americans shy away from theoretical speculation. This represents an American tradition that has regarded action and achievement as superior to intellectual thought and reflection. On a deeper psychological level, the glorification of non-intellectual pursuits is a compensation for long-held feelings of worthlessness and fears of one's masculinity. Intellectualizing is often threatening because it is associated with weakness or femininity. Doubts of one's worth lead to a fear that one is incapable of intellectual learning. Anxiety arising from the inability to pursue theorizing has caused intellectual activity to be referred to as only for misfits who cannot gain material or social status. Once, German and Jewish trade-unionists in America were strongly drawn to theoretical reflection but the process of Americanization overcame this tendency. The Germans in the Brewers, Printers, Bakers, Painters and Cigarmakers unions and the Jews in the Garment and Needle Trades Unions accounted for a large part of the Socialist strength formerly existing within the trade-union movement.

Today unions offer members athletic activities, recreational programs, social entertainments, and educational courses. Like the general American educational system, unions usually feature specialized educational courses having a cash value rather than broad theoretical courses concerned with an exploration of comparative ideas and of value systems. The educational course work is intended to mechanically convey to workers how to function as a shop steward or a voter but such teaching is not directed to getting workers to think and to ask questions.

The interest of the American trade-unionist in intellectual effort is illustrated by the attendance at a trade-union dance as compared to the turnout for a political lecture or by comparing his knowledge of the roster and record of various ball clubs with his knowledge of the causes accounting for various major social changes in the world.

The two major political parties in America require little mental effort from their supporters. Their political propaganda is not a continuous affair but mainly occurs during the brief campaign preceding an election. Most Republican and Democratic politicians make their appeal to the voter's emotions through the use of word-symbols. They enliven their message by attacks on the personalities of the opposition candidates. Promises of immediate benefits are made to the exclusion of long range considerations. By the mid-twentieth century, the Republican and Democratic parties were hiring advertising agencies to furnish political propaganda scientifically exploiting the voters' psychological needs. Politics, more so than ever, was turned into a comic strip of villains and heroes, the voters' anxieties were aroused, and father figures offered to make everything well.

A labor party, by comparison, in accord with its ideological basis, offers a serious examination of the total social order, explains its basic principles, and proposes its ultimate goals. In a land where the people's psychology rejects an intellectual approach, the style of a labor party campaign is unattractive. Since the political psychology of the American worker revolves around status, nationalism, and anti-intellectualism, a labor party's appeal is in conflict with his existing psychological needs.

Another difficulty in the way of Socialist success in the United States is America's ideological heritage—the belief in individual rights. In Europe, the legacy of feudalism's severe class system produced a working-class sentiment that found socialism's hostility to privilege an attractive creed. The American worker's legacy, however, was not feudalism, but an age of individualism which nourished doctrines based on individual success, not on class-conflict movements.

The major philosophical source for individual rights came

from the seventeenth-century political theories of John Locke. He wrote that man at birth is the possessor of natural rights. These are the rights of life, liberty, and property. They were not socially granted or determined but were God-given. To maintain and realize his rights the individual entered into a social contract and formed a body politic. Since governments, until Locke's time, had shown little respect for the rights of the individual, the age of individualism was more concerned with what government should not do than with what government should do. Governmental interference with the individual was to be kept at a minimum. A clear statement of Locke's philosophy of individual rights was written into the Declaration of Independence by Thomas Jefferson with the added provision that the pursuit of happiness was also man's natural right. The American Revolution was justified in the Declaration of Independence because man's *individual* rights had been violated by the British government. Similarly, American labor unions—though social in structure and action—arose later out of the same motivation as the colonial revolt against England— the protection of *individual* rights.

The American Constitution—whose conservative spirit differs in some instances with the revolutionary spirit of the Declaration of Independence—nevertheless unites with the Declaration to produce for Americans a central creed. This political tradition is expressed in the faith that government is something to be feared and the greater the power that government possesses the more there is to fear. This nation was born in rebellion against a tyrannous British government, the Declaration of Independence says to every school child, and the debates of the Calvinistic founding fathers at the Constitutional Convention abound with proof that power granted to government must be carefully divided, lest a new governmental tyranny result. The significance of this historical tradition is that Americans are well alerted to the dangers that government can be to their liberties but they do not realize that a democratically operated and controlled government may be a positive force for their individual benefit. Thus a Socialistic appeal to Americans runs counter to American political theory, for socialism, after all, is synonymous with more government, not less. Americans react more favorably to political ideas that increase the individuals' rights over the government, like the suffrage, the direct primary, the initiative, referendum, recall, and the long ballot, than to ideas extending the government's authority over individual activity.

The social theory of individual rights in America reached incredible heights, because it found support from other sources besides politics. Individual rights was the secular application of the lessons of theology. Each individual man had free will and responsibility. He had the right to choose for himself, good or evil, and receive grace or otherwise. In Protestant theology, especially, the individual's right of conscience was his final guide to conduct. The individual's right of conscience gave him the opportunity to be a moral being. Wealth, in fact, was cited as an evidence of individual morality. "In the long run, it is only to the man of morality that wealth comes," declared Bishop Lawrence, Harvard's great fund raiser.[2] John D. Rockefeller justified the gigantic growth of Standard Oil as "merely the working out of a law of nature and a law of God."[3] George F. Baer, president of the Pennsylvania and Reading Railroad said in 1902, "The rights and interests of the laboring man will be protected not by the labor agitators, but by the Christian men to whom God has given control of the country."[4] Religion encouraged the belief in an individual outlook, in individual effort, in individual dignity and salvation. These beliefs were transferred into political, economic, and social life with some adaptation and became a secular creed in these areas. Like salvation, earthly success could be achieved by acts of individual will. Horatio Alger stories became the secular bible. Social status or the lack of it became the reward or punishment for material success or failure. Every American-born boy had the right to set Wall Street or the White House as his cherished goal.

In the economic area of American life the theory of individual rights found a remarkable opportunity and displayed its greatest application. It is no coincidence that Adam Smith's *Wealth of Nations* and the Declaration of Independence were both published in the same year. American workers grew up within an economic system in which the doctrine of individual rights was central to the system's purpose and existence. The economic activity of farmer or robber baron, shop-keeper or stock speculator had this in common—each individual was exercising his right to promote his own interest and judge his own advantage. A mass of rationalizations were used that included Darwin's theory of the survival of the fittest and "freedom of contract" to raise the aggressive self-interested spirit of the businessman into a national philosophy. The philosophy has been insistent in its claim that any governmental interference with the individual's right to do business as he pleases struck at the core of this nation's freedom. This hymn to individualism, business ambition, and laissez faire government was repeated as an endless chorus in all the social institutions of American life in which the businessman had influence. The incantation of individual freedom and property rights expressed by the justices of the Supreme Court in the late nineteenth and early twentieth centuries led to the familiar reproach of Justice Holmes, "That the fourteenth amendment does not enact Mr. Herbert Spencer's *Social Statics*." [5] American law, as taught, practiced, and interpreted has seemed to be overwhelmingly concerned with safeguarding the individual's right to private property from invasion by the government or by labor unions.

Thus the common roots that individual rights had in capitalist economics, political democracy, and Christian theology, combined to strengthen it as an American social ideology. Programs for social progress may be in accord or in contradiction with his social theory. If an appeal caters to individual rights, that appeal will win greater acceptance than if its emphasis is on group need. The public's support of programs and treatment for mentally ill individuals as contrasted to the lack of interest in civil air defense are cases in point.

Individual rights also have deep meaning for people because they fill basic human needs like love for oneself, self-development, the enjoyment of power, and selfishness. Where institutions do not exist or are weak in involving man with others as a moral person, individual rights enter the vacuum created by the absence of community. The theory of individual rights was more successful in America than elsewhere in the world and attained exalted height because of certain conditions peculiar to America, to wit—the absence of a feudal tradition, frontier conditions, an abundance of land and natural resources, a shortage of labor, and a geographical position providing a long period of security from outside aggression. What need was there for Americans to doubt the ideology of individualism when in their mind its operation was responsible for their obtaining bigger and better material rewards than any nation had ever bestowed upon its people? Their personal successes made them optimistic of the future and confident that individual rights was a satisfactory philosophy of life.

The American workers' rejection of socialism was not that they were hostile to the Socialist idea of man's right to a better life, but that their needs in this uplifting direction were being met by their own social, economic, and political experiences. The *equalitarian* idea of socialism, however, was viewed with apprehension. Americans wanted individual rights so they could become equal to those above them, but they were not seriously concerned for those below to become equal to them.

Another hinderance to the successful development of a labor party is the structure and functioning of the American political system. With sufficient worker desire for a labor party such political difficulties probably would not be insurmountable. Labor leaders, in fact, have often justified their opposition to the formation of a labor party by emphasizing the difficulties. In some instances, this emphasis was probably a rationalization of conclusions based on other nonarticulated factors. Yet it is true that there are features of the American political system that make the venture of a labor party a high risk.

The American Constitution was written by propertied men seeking to establish legal sanction for individualism and private property and to prevent a popular majority from securing control of the government. The Constitution provides for a bicameral legislature; a check and balance system controlling the executive, legislative, and judicial branches of government; a federal system with powers divided between the national and state governments; the election of the President by a majority of the electoral votes of the states; and a difficult process for amending the Constitution. These conservative features of the Constitution have discouraged any party from trying to secure complete control of the national government and to enact and enforce legislation limiting the rights of private property. Nevertheless, should a political party gain control of the national government, it would still face limitations in asserting its will and imposing its policies on the nation, as evidenced by the Supreme Court's invalidation of considerable socioeconomic legislation in American history. Even if the courts presented no problem to a political party challenging private property, such a party's program would be handicapped because the national government shares sovereignty with the forty-eight states. The constitutional decentralization of the American political system means the nation's domestic policies are not settled in Washington alone but are made on individual state levels, too. In fact, the control of political parties resides primarily in the states and many state election laws make it very difficult for a new party to organize and get on the ballot. Furthermore, the single member district system as the unit for determining Congressional representation and the electoral college severely handicaps all parties but the two major parties. A party with a sizable minority vote in many districts can be seatless in the legislature because it failed to gain a majority of the vote in any one district. Such a party may have accumulated an impressive total national vote yet under the operation of the single member district system as the basis for Congressional representation, this party will have no membership in Congress nor opportunity to share in the responsibility of political power. A labor party as a new minority party would face this difficulty as well as the problem of an American electorate long and emotionally attached to the Republican or Democratic party.

The idea of the two major American parties has a long pedigree. When disagreement with the economic policies of Washington's first administration produced an opposition led by Thomas Jefferson, two parties developed to challenge each other concerning the economic policies the nation should adopt. This two-party system gradually became characteristic of American politics. By the time of the development of the industrial revolution and modern trade-unionism, the workers had been supporters for many years of one or the other of the two parties, and their traditional attachments to the old parties made it difficult to gain their support for a new party. The extension of the suffrage to white males in the early nineteenth century did more than win the workers' votes for the existing parties. It also robbed the workers of a common grievance—their disfranchisement—that could give them solidarity through a shared discrimination. In early nineteenth-century Britain, workers' feelings of class status were reinforced because, as a class, they were denied the ballot. The extension of the franchise to the American workers, however, prevented the emergence of the suffrage as an issue around which worker-class feeling could thrive. The foresight, too, of the two major parties occasionally incorporating into their platforms the more popular planks of the minor parties, took away the appeal that a third party had for many possible supporters.

As the preceding chapter shows, Roman Catholicism seriously concerned itself with combating Socialist growth in the labor union movement. In evaluating the influence of the Catholic Church in its struggle against socialism it is important to recognize that strong organization and human will can affect social development. Ideas alone unaided by individuals or institutions cannot socially triumph. True, an idea that has validity because it satisfies man's basic needs, cannot be permanently beaten, no matter how strong the organization and leadership opposing it. However, the political successes in the twentieth century of such diverse systems as communism, fascism, and socialism indicate that social development is not predestined nor independent of human will. The Catholic Church, recognizing the importance of will and organization, has been participating with all the power at its command in the social struggle taking place in this century. It has astutely understood that the labor movement is one of the vital areas wherein this struggle occurs.

The activity of the Catholic Church within the American trade-union movement became even more organized and vigorous as the twentieth century continued. The work it had earlier accomplished in the AF of L helped to make that organization quite immune from radical political infiltration, but the emergence of the CIO in 1935 in the mass production industries presented the Church with a new challenge. For one thing the workers were unskilled and were organized industrially, a fact which made them more prone to radical political doctrine than had been the skilled and craftminded AF of L members. The fact that the CIO was also a child of the depression period of the 1930's and the discovery that hard-working Communist leadership had gained control of many union positions further increased the Church's concern and its efforts. One factor that again worked to the advantage of the Church, however, was the religious composition of the CIO. Although Catholics probably did not quite constitute a majority

in the CIO, they were the largest religious group. The Irish were
not as powerful as they were in the AF of L, but Italian and Polish
Catholics made up for much of this loss. The national leadership
of the CIO for most of its twenty years was held by president
Philip Murray and secretary-treasurer James Carey, both devout
Catholics.

In its objective of eliminating Communist influence in the CIO,
the Church has made effective use of an affiliated organization
patterned after the Militia of Christ for Social Service. The new
organization, the Association of Catholic Trade Unionists, is an
arm of Catholic Action, the world organization of militant lay
Catholics created by Pope Pius XI to defend and spread Catholic
thought in all economic, social, and political matters as directed
by the hierarchy. The Association of Catholic Trade Unionists
was founded in 1937 to see that Catholic trade-union principles
were carried into the American labor movement. ACTU conducts
labor schools to educate Catholic trade-unionists in their Church's
social views and to train them for leadership in the unions, it pub-
lishes a newspaper, the *Labor Leader,* and it conducts a speakers'
bureau comprised of priests and members of ACTU qualified by
background and experience to address Catholic and nonsectarian
groups on the Catholic Church's position relative to labor movement matters. ACTU seeks to bring Catholic workers into the
union movement and into ACTU also. One of ACTU's most apparent activities has been to serve as a clearing house for gathering
and distributing to its members information exposing Communist
influence, leaders, and tactics, in the unions and for directing the
Catholic struggle against the Communists and other extreme left
wing influences in the unions. The Detroit chapter of the ACTU,
for example, has been credited with having played a decisive part
in the defeat of the Communist leadership of the UAW-CIO in
1946.

In the post-World War II period the success of catholicism in
its drive against the Communists in the American trade-union
movement, aided by a strong anti-Communist sentiment existing
throughout America, was of remarkable proportions. Its effectiveness caused some Communist trade-union leaders to resign from
their offices, others to be defeated when standing for re-election,
and still others publicly to renounce their association with com-

munism. Probably the greatest victory won by the Catholic Social
Actionists within the CIO came when the organization withdrew
from its affiliation with the U.S.S.R.-affiliated World Federation
of Trade Unions and when such Communist-dominated CIO international unions as the Electrical Workers, Fur and Leather
Workers, Mine, Mill, and Smelter Workers, Food and Tobacco
Workers, and Public Workers were expelled by the CIO national
office. Finally, the amalgamation of the AF of L-CIO in 1955 was
also a victory for Catholic leaders who saw the conservative influence that the AF of L would have on the more leftist CIO. The
initial all-important eight man executive committee of the AF of L-
CIO contained four Roman Catholics, George Meany, Matthew
Woll, James Carey, and David McDonald. One of the long range
programs extensively developed in recent years by catholicism is
in the field of workers' education. The education of trade-union
members takes place in about one hundred Catholic labor schools
operated either by Catholic universities, the Social Action Department of a diocese, the Society of Jesus, or ACTU. An ultimate objective engaging the attention of Catholic social action sources is
the establishment of Industry Councils in the American labor
union movement.

Because of the political indifference and general alienation of
the average worker from any emotional involvement in his union,
the union leader often finds that political power has come to him
by default. The political policies he approves or disapproves may
account, at certain times, for the political program of trade-unionism. His political behavior is not merely an impersonal result of
economic causes or rank-and-file pressure. His beliefs and behavior are also determined by his own personality. Since union
leaders, as psychological studies suggest, often have aggressive
personalities, the union leader seeks to direct and influence his
organization, politically and otherwise. If he is a devout Roman
Catholic his influence will, directly or indirectly, reflect the labor
policies of his Church; and if he is a Socialist, his union will be
affected differently.

To Samuel Gompers, more than to any other individual, goes
the personal responsibility for establishing the political traditions
of the early twentieth-century American Federation of Labor.
These political traditions have had a formative influence on the

later political development of American labor unions. With the exception of 1895, Gompers was the AF of L's president from its origin in 1886 until his death in December, 1924. He was an aggressive, vain, and gregarious person whose unconscious fears of rejection required him either to assert control over others, or to go to unusual lengths of submissiveness. This basic insecurity was further increased by his feeling that being Jewish, an immigrant, of a poor family, and a labor leader were serious handicaps in gaining the acceptance of the community. Thus his personality not only needed the drama and power of office but he was driven compulsively again and again to prove himself to be correct in the important choices he made for the organization. This meant that AF of L people were subjected to persistent explanation from Gompers and his headquarters concerning the political ideas and activities that had been adopted. In an administrative sense, his personal authority was far-reaching in the AF of L, through his appointments and control of the AF of L general organizers. Most of the other AF of L executive officers of his time lacking his administrative ability, practical education, social vision, and political interests were satisfied to leave the political course of trade-unionism to him. Only if he had swung over to the Socialists would he have given the presidents of the affiliated international unions anxiety, and they had no reason to fear such a development. From his earliest years as AF of L president he was at odds with the Socialists and by the twentieth century he had reached the point where there was an irreparable breach between them. He wore his antisocialism like regimental colors and in convention halls, union meetings, executive sessions, on public platforms, and in the Federation journal he battled the Socialists again and again. In fact, his obsession with the Socialist danger and the frequency and intensity of his attacks appeared at times to be partly motivated by his own internal conflicts and not entirely by the external facts of socialism. But to explore the motivation of a leader and peer beneath the surface phenomena of behavior was not to be expected of early twentieth-century workers.[6] They accepted at face value that Gompers, the head of their organization, was firmly convinced that a Socialist was a traitor to the interests of the working man. Although he did not cause any of the prominent Socialists in the AF of L to forsake their socialism, he did reinforce and increase the hostility toward socialism of those who were already suspicious of it. He probably aroused latent anti-Socialist feelings in others. When Gompers assumed leadership of the AF of L, the Socialists were a vigorous minority within the organization. He rallied the non-Socialists to his side and alerted them to the dangers of socialism. By his forceful and dramatic example of combatting the Socialists, he freed many AF of L members from the inhibition that had governed them in combatting socialism. Many workers felt uneasy about turning on the Socialists for was this not allying themselves with the employers who were also anti-Socialist? The image of the AF of L president as an anti-Socialist settled this doubt for those sensitive on this matter. Gompers made antisocialism respectable for a worker's conscience. By the time of his death, opposition to socialism had become a badge of honor, if not a shibboleth for AF of L members.

The political philosophy and behavior of American labor unions extend today considerably beyond organized labor itself. The membership strength, financial resources, and political influence of American unions have grown to the extent that they help to account for legislation or the lack of legislation seriously influencing consumer prices, employer's profits, unorganized labor's wages, civil rights, national health, public education, in fact all important and controversial public problems. Labor unions and their leaders are also assuming a larger role in international trade-unionism than they have hitherto. Their policies abroad raise or lower American prestige, lose or gain us friends, and help or hinder the achievement of "peace on earth, good will to men." In short, the politics of American labor unions is a force for aiding in the growth of democracy in America and in the world, but also it may unknowingly contribute to retarding progress. The stakes are high and risks are great in the challenging situation in which American unions now find themselves. Do their leaders know how to meet and handle their growing responsibilities?

The top men running America's unions are called labor leaders, but actually most of them are more adept at following than leading. Socially, they follow the prejudices of their members; economically, they follow the values of business; politically, they follow the methods of pressure groups. They see themselves as free men representing free unions made up of free workers but far too many are limited by philosophical and political traditions, by middle-class values, and by bitter, early-life emotional experiences. They want control of unions and they have it. But power to be wisely used requires greatness of character and mind. Most American labor leaders fail to understand and act on the vast social problems of this age. Their consolation can be that whatever the extent of their failure to handle adequately their huge responsibilities, the guilt is not theirs alone. Leaders of other social groups—businessmen, lawyers, preachers, politicians, journalists, and educators—have equally been unable to provide the required leadership. American labor leaders, along with leaders in other fields, have been unable to overcome those defects of material interests, racial prejudice, and moral superiority which have prevented America from exercising the leadership in the twentieth century that the national and world situation requires. Yet mankind has survived in spite of its ignorance, selfishness, and betrayal by leadership because inherently man wants to live, think well of himself, and learn from his mistakes. Mankind will continue to move forward—slowly—and at great cost and pain, but forward to a wider practice of brotherhood.

NOTES

BIBLIOGRAPHY

INDEX

Notes

Full bibliographical information for the following references when not supplied may be found in the Bibliography.

CHAPTER ONE

1. Commons and Associates, 1, 326.
2. Grossman, pp. 229–32.
3. Ware, *The Labor Movement in the United States, 1860–1895,* p. 99.
4. See "Memorial Presented to the Holy See by Cardinal Gibbons on the Knights of Labor," in Ryan and Husselein, pp. 145–58.
5. "Knights of Labor Preamble," quoted in Ely, p. 86.
6. Quoted in Commons and Associates, II, 324.
7. AF of L Convention *Proceedings,* 1895, p. 79.
8. *Ibid.,* 1899, p. 107.
9. Hillquit, *History of Socialism in the United States,* pp. 199–210.
10. Commons and Associates, IV, 221.
11. Hillquit, *Loose Leaves from a Busy Life,* p. 46.
12. *Ibid.*
13. Daniel Bell, "Marxian Socialism in the United States," in Egbert and Persons, I, 246.
14. DeLeon, *Reform or Revolution,* p. 27.
15. DeLeon, *Two Pages from Roman History,* p. 35.

CHAPTER TWO

1. Gompers to John T. Lennon, October 15, 1900, in Gompers manuscripts in AF of L Headquarters, Washington, D.C.
2. AF of L Convention *Proceedings,* 1897, p. 81.

3. *Truax* v. *Corrigan,* 257 U.S. 312, 354, 368 (1921), quoted in Frankfurter and Green, pp. 132–33.
4. *The Congressional Record,* XL, Part I, 94.
5. Perlman, *Labor in the New Deal Decade,* p. 19.
6. Perlman and Taft, p. 152.
7. *American Federationist,* XIII (March, 1906), 156–57.
8. AF of L Convention *Proceedings,* 1903, p. 198.
9. Robbins, p. 19.
10. Gompers, "The Injunction in Labor Disputes Must Go," pp. 228–30.

CHAPTER THREE

1. "Labor's Bill of Grievances," p. 296.
2. *The Nation,* LXXX (March 29, 1906), 254.
3. *New York Daily Tribune,* March 25, 1906.
4. "Labor's Bill of Grievances," p. 296.
5. American Federationist, XIII (May, 1906), 293.
6. "A.F. of L. Campaign Programme," p. 530. Five years later James O'Connell was one of the AF of L leaders on the directorate of the Militia of Christ for Social Service. See Chapter Nine "The Roman Catholic Church and American Labor Unions."
7. "A.F. of L. Campaign Programme."
8. For the liason between corrupt labor officials and city political machines see Harold Seidman, *Labor Czars* (New York: Liveright, 1938), pp. 217–36.
9. Apparently Gompers desired to limit the AF of L's political participation in the 1906 campaign so that it would not be construed that the national office was infringing on the political autonomy of the affiliated unions. For example when John Mitchell, United Mine Workers leader, wrote him and asked "the support of the Labor Representation Committee and whatever assistance can be given" for Mr. John G. McHenry of Benton, Pennsylvania, who, if elected to Congress, "can be depended upon to favor and advocate the legislature demands of organized labor," Gompers answered, "I should prefer not to interfere leaving that to our labor men and friends in each district for you can readily understand there may be several aspirants among the forces of organized labor." (Mitchell to

Gompers, August 13, 1906, in John Mitchell papers located in the Department of Archives and Manuscripts, Mullen Library, Catholic University of America; Gompers to Mitchell, August 17, 1906, in John Mitchell papers.)

Again in desiring the election to the House of Champ Clark of Missouri, Gompers was careful to write to the United Mine Workers and have its president present this to the membership. To Mitchell he wrote, "I respectfully request you to communicate with the officers and members of your unions" in the district of Champ Clark "calling to their attention the favorable record of Mr. Champ Clark, since he has been a member of Congress." (Gompers to Mitchell, October 6, 1906, in John Mitchell papers.)

10. *American Federationist,* XIV (October, 1907), 784–85.

11. Gompers, "Free Speech and Free Press Invaded by Injunction against the A.F. of L.—A Review and Protest," p. 98.

12. *American Federationist,* XV (February, 1908), 113.

13. Gompers, Mitchell, and Morrison were given terms of one year, nine months, and six months, respectively. After lengthy court litigation this decision was reversed by the U.S. Supreme Court in 1914. No prison term was actually served by any of these men. The injunction decision was also dismissed by the same court in 1914 upon the technicality that the statute of limitations applied.

14. *American Federationist,* XV (March, 1908), 180.

15. *Loewe* v. *Lawlor,* 208 U.S. 305.

16. *Adair* v. *United States,* 208 U.S. 174–75. Justice Oliver Wendell Holmes in the famed *Lockner* v. *New York* case (1905) gave the classic reply to judges of Harlan's mind when he wrote, "There can be no freedom of contract where there is not equality of bargaining power."

17. *American Federationist,* XV (April, 1908), 270.

18. Quoted in Samuel Gompers, "Congressional Perfidy—The Responsibility—Labor's Duty," *American Federationist,* XV (July, 1908), 527.

19. Gompers, "Both Parties Have Spoken—Choose Between Them," pp. 599–600.

20. *Ibid.,* p. 600.

21. The labor historians Selig Perlman and Philip Taft (p. 127) have written of the 1908 AF of L campaign that "the Federation refrained from formally endorsing the Democratic Party

and Bryan's candidacy." The author questions this conclusion on the basis of his evidence.

22. *American Federationist* xv (August, 1908), 603.
23. Book ii, Index Card 4, "Press Statements and Interviews," Gompers Collection located in the Economics Division, The New York Public Library.
24. Gompers, "Candidate Taft, Take Notice!" p. 962.
25. Samuel Gompers, "Editorial Notes," *American Federationist,* xv (November, 1908), 972.
26. Gompers to Mack, August 28, 1908, Washington, D.C., in Gompers manuscripts in AF of L Headquarters, Washington, D.C.
27. Gompers, *Seventy Years of Life and Labor,* ii, Book iv, 88.
28. AF of L Convention *Proceedings,* 1908, p. 245.
29. Gompers to Mitchell, July 31, 1908, in John Mitchell papers; Mitchell to Gompers, August 3, 1908, in John Mitchell papers.
30. Book i, Index Card 6, "Press Statements and Interviews," Gompers Collection.
31. Bryan to Gompers, November 10, 1908, quoted in "Correspondence," *American Federationist,* xv (December, 1908), 1095.
32. AF of L Convention *Proceedings,* 1909, p. 32.
33. *American Federationist,* xvii (March, 1910), 224.
34. AF of L Convention *Proceedings,* 1910, p. 17.
35. Gompers, "Elect Trade Union Congressmen," p. 463.
36. Gompers, "Labor's Political Campaign—Its Causes and Progress—Labor's Duty," pp. 801–14.

CHAPTER FOUR

1. Jones, p. 79.
2. Woodrow Wilson to Samuel Gompers, May 6, 1913, in Woodrow Wilson manuscripts in the Library of Congress, Washington, D.C.
3. Samuel Gompers to Frank Morrison, May 20, 1913, in Gompers manuscripts in AF of L Headquarters, Washington, D.C.
4. Gompers, "Russianized West Virginia," p. 827.
5. AF of L Convention *Proceedings,* 1914, p. 105.
6. *Hitchman Coal and Coke Co.* v. *Mitchell,* 202 Fed. 512 (1912).

This decision was overruled by the Circuit Court of Appeals, 214 Fed. 685 (1914). The Hitchman Company then appealed to the United States Supreme Court which in 1917 gave a decision in its favor (245 U.S. 219).

7.   "Minutes of Executive Council Meeting," p. 584.
8.   *Ibid.*
9.   *Ibid.*
10. Gompers, *Seventy Years of Life and Labor,* II, Book IV, 296–98.
11. Gompers, "Labor Not a Commodity," p. 866.
12. *Ibid.,* pp. 866–67.
13. Harvey Wish, *Contemporary America* (New York: Harper, 1945), p. 177.
14. Samuel Gompers, "Labor's Magna Carta—Demand It," *American Federationist,* XXI (October, 1914), 556.
15. Wilson to Gompers, January 7, 1916, in Woodrow Wilson manuscripts.
16. "A. F. of L. Building Dedication," p. 663.
17. *Ibid.*
18. Gompers to H. O. McClurg, August 19, 1916, in Gompers manuscripts.
19. Gompers' address before the Platform and Resolution Committee of the Democratic National Convention, June 14, 1916, in Book II, Index Card E 32, "General Addresses," Gompers Collection located in the Economics Division, The New York Public Library.
20. *Wilson and Labor* (Democratic National Campaign Committee, 1916), in Woodrow Wilson manuscripts.
21. AF of L Convention *Proceedings,* 1916, pp. 306–7.
22. *Ibid.*
23. Gompers to officers of the AF of L, October 14, 1916, in Gompers manuscripts.
24. Gompers' address in Tomlinson Hall, Indianapolis, Indiana, October 25, 1916, in Book II, Index Card E 38, "General Addresses," Gompers Collection.
25. Gompers' address at Powers Theater, Chicago, October 19, 1916, in Book II, Index Card 537, Gompers Collection.
26. Gompers' address under the auspices of the Washington Central Labor Union, August 30, 1916, in Book II, Index Card 58, Gompers Collection.
27. AF of L Convention *Proceedings,* 1916, p. 308.

28. Telegram: Gompers to Woodrow Wilson, November 9, 1916, in Book II, Index Card 105, "Press Interviews," Gompers Collection.
29. Gompers, *Seventy Years of Life and Labor,* I, Book III, 549.

CHAPTER FIVE

1. AF of L Convention *Proceedings,* 1913, p. 362–63.
2. Gompers, "Militarism Must Not Prevail," pp. 862–63.
3. Gompers to Legien, September 30, 1914, Washington, D.C., in Gompers manuscripts in AF of L Headquarters, Washington, D.C.
4. Gompers, "For Effective International Peace," pp. 868–69.
5. *American Federationist,* XXI (November, 1914), 961.
6. AF of L Convention *Proceedings,* 1915, p. 461.
7. Gompers, *Seventy Years of Life and Labor,* II, Book IV, 334–40.
8. Samuel Gompers, *Preparedness for National Defense,* address by Gompers before the annual meeting of the National Civic Federation, Washington, D.C., January 18, 1916 ([64th Congress., 1st sess.; Sen. Doc. 311.] Washington, D.C.: Government Printing Office, 1916).
9. Samuel Gompers, *Address before League to Enforce Peace,* May 26, 1916, located in AF of L Archives, Washington, D.C.
10. Samuel Gompers, *Address before Wilson Eight Hour League,* Washington D.C., October 14, 1916, quoted in Robbins, p. 230.
11. Gompers to Champ Clark, February 10, 1917, in Gompers manuscripts in AF of L Headquarters, Washington, D.C.
12. Samuel Gompers to AF of L Executive Council, Washington, D.C., February 28, 1917, quoted in the *American Federationist,* XXIV (April, 1917), 271.
13. Gompers, "American Labor's Position in Peace or War," p. 280.
14. See Chapter Eight, "The IWW Thought and Action, 1900–1918."
15. AF of L Convention *Proceedings,* 1917, p. 112.
16. Gompers, *Seventy Years of Life and Labor,* II, Book V, 372.
17. *American Federationist,* XXV (May, 1918), 369–71.
18. *Ibid.*
19. Samuel Gompers to AF of L Executive Council, March 29, 1918, Washington, D.C., in Gompers manuscripts.

20. Gompers, "A.F. of L., Of, For, and By Labor," p. 688.
21. Gompers, "United in Spirit and Purpose," pp. 386–87.
22. Gompers to Hutcheson, April 2, 1918, in Gompers manuscripts.
23. AF of L Convention *Proceedings,* 1918, p. 86.
24. Samuel Gompers, *Address before London Trades Council,* London, England, September 22, 1918, quoted in Robbins, pp. 235–36.
25. Gompers, "Labor and Democracy," p. 840.
26. *Ibid.,* pp. 840–41.
27. AF of L Convention *Proceedings,* 1917, p. 305.
28. Letter from Samuel Gompers to George Barnes, Washington, D.C., January 5, 1918, quoted in Gompers, "International Labor Relations," p. 295.
29. Cable: Gompers to Appleton, Washington, D.C., January 9, 1918, quoted in Gompers, "International Labor Relations," p. 295.
30. Letter from Carl Durr to the American Federation of Labor, Berne, Switzerland, March 28, 1917, quoted in "Labor's International Relations," pp. 958–59.
31. AF of L Convention *Proceedings,* 1917, p. 61.
32. Gompers, *Seventy Years of Life and Labor,* II, Book IV, 508.
33. Cables: Samuel Gompers to Jouhaux, Secretary of the French Conference of Labor, Louis Dubreuilh, Secretary of the French Socialist Party, G. J. Wardle, Chairman of the British Labor Party, Washington, D.C., May 8, 1917, quoted in "Labor's International Relations," p. 967.
34. Gompers' address at the Canadian Victory Loan Rally, Toronto, Ontario, Canada, November 28, 1917, quoted in Robbins, p. 233.
35. Cable: Gompers to Appleton, January 9, 1918, in Robbins, pp. 295–96.
36. Gompers' address to the Canadian House of Commons, Ottawa, Ontario, Canada, April 27, 1918, quoted in Robbins, pp. 263–64.
37. Gompers, *Seventy Years of Life and Labor,* II, Book IV, 404–6.
38. *American Federation of Labor: History, Encyclopedia, Reference Book,* p. 6.
39. Gompers, *Seventy Years of Life and Labor,* II, Book IV, 418.
40. *Ibid.,* p. 421.
41. *Ibid.,* p. 429.
42. *Ibid.*

43. *Ibid.,* p. 434.
44. Quoted in "The Nation's Tribute to American Labor's Service Abroad," p. 1085.
45. *Ibid.,* p. 1082.
46. Gompers, *Seventy Years of Life and Labor,* ii, Book iv, 489.
47. *Ibid.,* pp. 491–92.
48. Cable: Gompers to Petrograd Council of Workers and Deputies, Washington, D.C., April 2, 1917, quoted in "Labor's International Relations," p. 955.
49. Gompers, *Seventy Years of Life and Labor,* ii, Book iv, 399–400.
50. Gompers' address at May Day Meeting, Central Labor Union, Faneuil Hall, Boston, May 1, 1918, quoted in Robbins, p. 267.
51. AF of L Convention *Proceedings,* 1919, p. 79.

CHAPTER SIX

1. *Report of the Committee of the Senate upon Relations between Labor and Capital* ([48th Cong., 2d sess.; Sen. Misc. Doc. 49.] Washington, D.C.: Government Printing Office, 1885).
2. Max Hayes, "The World of Labor," *International Socialist Review,* vii (July, 1906), 56.
3. AF of L Convention *Proceedings,* 1906, pp. 34–35.
4. *Ibid.,* p. 184. One of the members of this committee was Peter J. McArdle, president of the Iron, Tin and Steel Workers, who in 1911 became the first president of the Militia of Christ for Social Service. See Chapter Nine, "The Roman Catholic Church and American Labor Unions."
5. AF of L Convention *Proceedings,* 1906, p. 185.
6. *Ibid.,* p. 187.
7. *Ibid.,* pp. 194–95.
8. *Ibid.,* p. 196.
9. *Ibid.,* pp. 197–98.
10. *Ibid.,* pp. 198–99.
11. O'Connell was on the Board of Directorate of the Militia of Christ for Social Service. See Chapter Nine, "The Roman Catholic Church and American Labor Unions."
12. AF of L Convention *Proceedings,* 1906, p. 200.
13. *Ibid.,* p. 201.
14. *Ibid.,* pp. 201–2.
15. *Ibid.,* p. 204.

16. "Statement of Purpose" of Conciliation Department adopted at first annual meeting of National Civic Federation, quoted in Bonnett, p. 389.
17. "The National Civic Federation, Its Method and Its Aim," quoted in Bonnett, p. 393.
18. Gompers, *Seventy Years of Life and Labor,* II, Book IV, 217–18.
19. Ware, *Labor in Modern Industrial Society,* p. 323.
20. AF of L Convention *Proceedings,* 1911, pp. 217–18.
21. *Ibid.,* pp. 218–20.
22. *Ibid.,* p. 220.
23. *Ibid.,* pp. 221–22.
24. *Ibid.,* p. 223.
25. *Ibid.,* p. 235.
26. *Ibid.,* 1915, p. 486.
27. *Ibid.,* p. 492.
28. *Ibid.,* pp. 498–99.
29. *Ibid.,* p. 502.
30. *Ibid.,* p. 501.
31. *Ibid.,* 1913, pp. 314–15.
32. "Testimony of Samuel Gompers," *Industrial Relations: Final Report,* II, 1492–1549.
33. "Testimony of John Mitchell," *Industrial Relations: Final Report,* IX, 6078–8079.
34. John Lennon, "What is Americanism?" *American Journal of Sociology,* XX (March, 1915), 620.
35. "President's Report," AF of L *Proceedings,* 1911, p. 22.
36. Gompers, "Voluntary Social Insurance vs. Compulsory," p. 680.
37. AF of L Convention *Proceedings,* 1913, p. 63.
38. "Testimony of Samuel Gompers," *Industrial Relations: Final Report,* II, 1500.
39. Gompers, "Labor vs. Its Barnacles," p. 270.
40. Gompers, *Address before Conference on Social Insurance,* Washington, D.C., December 8, 1916, in Book II, Index Card 40, Gompers Collection located in the Economics Division, The New York Public Library.
41. Samuel Gompers, "Unemployment, an Illusive and a Real Way Out," *American Federationist,* XXI (April, 1914), 312.
42. Gompers, *Seventy Years of Life and Labor,* II, Book IV, 160.
43. *American Federationist,* VIII (August, 1901), 305–6.
44. AF of L Convention *Proceedings,* 1901, pp. 154–55.

45. *Ibid.,* pp. 19–20.
46. Samuel Gompers and Herman Gutstadt, *Meat vs. Rice, American Manhood against Asiatic Coolieism—Which Shall Survive?* (San Francisco, Calif.: Asiatic Exclusion League, 1908), p. 34.
47. Gompers' address before the Conference on Immigration of the National Civic Federation, December, 1905, quoted in Robbins, p. 83.
48. AF of L Convention *Proceedings,* 1914, p. 364.
49. *Ibid.,* p. 469. According to Dr. Weimar, Asian immigrants did not "constitute an economic challenge" to the AF of L membership "to the extent that A.F. of L. spokesmen alleged they did." The Chinese worked in the cigar, shoe, cotton, and woolen industries, but it was only in the cigar industry that their numbers reached any significant size.
50. Gompers, *Seventy Years of Life and Labor,* ii, Book iv, 165-66.
51. Gompers, "Trade Union Attitude Toward Colored Workers," pp. 118–19.
52. *East St. Louis Riots* ([65th Cong., 2d sess.; H.R. Doc. 1231] Washington, D.C.: Government Printing Office, 1918), p. 15.
53. AF of L Convention *Proceedings,* 1917, pp. 349–50.
54. Taft, p. 314.
55. Spero and Harris, pp. 109–10.
56. Socialist Party Convention *Proceedings,* 1912, p. 136.
57. *American Federationist,* xiii (April, 1906), 233.
58. Taft, p. 158.
59. Kipnis, p. 328.
60. AF of L Convention *Proceedings,* 1918, p. 325.
61. *Ibid.,* 1919, p. 105.
62. *Should a Political Labor Party be Formed?* p. 9. British scholars point out otherwise. G. D. H. Cole, for example, writes in *Fabian Socialism* (London: Routledge, 1946) that the British trade-union movement accounts for the diluting of socialism in the British Labor party program.
63. Gompers, *Labor in Europe and America,* pp. 286–87.
64. Gompers, "The Future Foreign Policy of the United States," pp. 138–40.
65. AF of L Convention *Proceedings,* 1902, p. 72. Dr. Delbert Lee McKee has made a valuable contribution to scholarship by his excellent dissertation, "The American Federation of Labor and American Foreign Policy, 1886–1912."
66. Gompers, *Seventy Years of Life and Labor,* ii, Book v, 304.

67. *Ibid.,* p. 309.
68. AF of L Convention *Proceedings,* 1913, p. 364.
69. Gompers, *Seventy Years of Life and Labor,* II, Book V, 318.

CHAPTER SEVEN

1. "The Chicago Conference for Industrial Unionism," *International Socialism Review,* V (February, 1905), 476–79.
2. "Letter of Max Hayes," IWW Convention *Proceedings,* 1905, pp. 99–100.
3. Socialist Party Convention *Proceedings,* 1904, p. 214.
4. "Editorial," *American Federationist,* XII (March, 1905), 139.
5. Max Hayes, "The World of Labor," *International Socialist Review,* V (March, 1905), 693.
6. IWW Convention *Proceedings,* 1905, pp. 1–2.
7. *Ibid.,* p. 142.
8. *Ibid.,* pp. 142–45.
9. *Ibid.,* pp. 148–51.
10. *Ibid.,* p. 118.
11. *Ibid.,* p. 589.
12. *Ibid.,* p. 163.
13. *Ibid.,* p. 129.
14. *Ibid.,* p. 223.
15. *Ibid.,* p. 229.
16. *Ibid.,* p. 230.
17. *Ibid.,* p. 225.
18. *Ibid.,* p. 232.
19. *Ibid.,* p. 240.
20. *Ibid.,* p. 227.
21. *Ibid.,* pp. 228–31.
22. *Ibid.,* p. 575.
23. *Ibid.,* p. 569.
24. *Ibid.,* p. 154.
25. Debs, "Craft Unionism, Chicago, November 23, 1905," *Writings and Speeches of Eugene V. Debs,* p. 188.
26. *Ibid.,* p. 181.
27. Debs, "Revolutionary Unionism, Chicago, November 25, 1905," *Writings and Speeches of Eugene V. Debs,* p. 210.
28. Debs, "Class Unionism, Chicago, November 24, 1905," *Writings and Speeches of Eugene V. Debs,* p. 204.
29. *International Socialist Review,* VI (September, 1905), 182.

30. DeLeon, *Preamble of the Industrial Workers of the World,* p. 40.
31. *Ibid.*
32. IWW Convention *Proceedings,* 1906, p. 271.
33. "A Statement of Facts," *The Industrial Workers of the World Bulletin,* No. iv (December 1, 1906).
34. IWW Convention *Proceedings,* 1906, p. 610.
35. *Ibid.,* pp. 305–6.
36. *Ibid.,* p. 309.
37. *Ibid.,* p. 311.
38. *Ibid.,* p. 312.
39. *Ibid.,* p. 316.
40. *Ibid.,* p. 241.
41. *Ibid.,* p. 545.
42. *Ibid.,* p. 589.
43. *Ibid.,* "Report of the General Secretary-Treasurer."
44. Socialist Party Convention *Proceedings,* 1908, p. 103.
45. St. John, *The I.W.W., Its History, Structure and Methods,* p. 7.
46. DeLeon, *As To Politics.*
47. *Ibid.*
48. St. John, *The I.W.W., Its History, Structure and Methods,* p. 19.
49. "Testimony of Vincent St. John before Industrial Relations Commission," *Industrial Relations: Final Report,* ii, 1451–52
50. St. John, *The I.W.W., Its History, Structure and Methods,* p. 41.
51. "Testimony of Vincent St. John before Industrial Relations Commission," *Industrial Relations: Final Report,* ii, 1453.
52. St. John, *The I.W.W., Its History, Structure and Methods,* p. 42.
53. DeLeon, *As To Politics.*
54. "Fourth Day Session—Fourth Annual Convention of the IWW," *Industrial Union Bulletin* (Chicago), ii (October 10, 1908).
55. *Ibid.,* p. 4.
56. *Ibid.*
57. "Proceedings of the Fourth Convention," *Industrial Union Bulletin,* November 7, 1908.
58. *Ibid.*
59. "Testimony of Vincent St. John before Industrial Relations Commission," *Industrial Relations: Final Report,* ii, 1452.
60. St. John, *The I.W.W., Its History, Structure and Methods,* p. 17.

61. Tridon, p. 32.
62. St. John, *The I.W.W., Its History, Structure and Methods,*
     p. 17.

CHAPTER EIGHT

1. "Testimony of William Haywood before Industrial Relations
    Commission," *Industrial Relations: Final Report,* III, 10573.
2. *Ibid.*
3. *Ibid.*
4. Quoted in Brooks, p. 103.
5. Goldman, p. 494.
6. *Ibid.,* pp. 500–1.
7. Quoted in Whipple, p. 225.
8. *Report on Strike of Textile Workers at Lawrence, Mass.,* p. 33.
9. *Ibid.,* p. 45.
10. *Hearings on the Strike at Lawrence, Massachusetts,* pp. 294
    and 295.
11. *Ibid.,* p. 250.
12. "Testimony of Adolph Lessig before Industrial Relations
    Commission," *Industrial Relations: Final Report,* III, 2464.
13. Socialist Party National Congress, 1910.
14. In 1908 there were about three hundred Protestant ministers in
    the Socialist party. Some of those who played a more promi-
    nent part in the Socialist party besides George Lunn and J. Stitt
    Wilson were George D. Herrin, Winfield Gaylord, Carl D.
    Thompson, Walter Thomas Mills, Edward Ellis Carr, Bouck
    White, Eliot White, and Robert W. Webster. See David Shan-
    non, *The Socialist Party of America* (New York: Macmillan,
    1955), pp. 59–60.
15. "The Editor's Chair," *International Socialist Review,* X
    (November, 1909), 449–57.
16. "Testimony of William Haywood before Industrial Relations
    Commission," *Industrial Relations: Final Report,* III, 10584.
17. Haywood and Bohn, pp. 50–52.
18. *Ibid.,* p. 57.
19. *Ibid.,* p. 62.
20. *Ibid.,* p. 49.
21. *Ibid.,* p. [4].
22. *Ibid.,* p. 59.

23. Haywood, "Socialism—The Hope of the Working Class," p. 464.

24. *Ibid.,* p. 466.

25. *Ibid.,* pp. 466–69.

26. *National Constitution of the Socialist Party* (Chicago: Socialist Press, 1914), p. 2.

27. Socialist Party Convention *Proceedings,* 1912, p. 123.

28. *Ibid.*

29. *Ibid.*

30. *Ibid.,* p. 135.

31. *Ibid.,* p. 130.

32. "A Plea for Solidarity," *International Socialist Review,* March, 1914, quoted in *Writing and Speeches of Eugene V. Debs,* pp. 372–73.

33. Joe Hill, "How to Make Work for the Unemployed," p. 335.

34. Chaplin, p. 203.

35. Haywood, *Bill Haywood's Book,* p. 292.

36. IWW Convention *Proceedings,* 1905, p. 269.

37. *Solidarity* (Industrial Workers of the World Publication, 1909–17), October 3, 1914, p. 4.

38. Haywood, *Bill Haywood's Book,* p. 294. A number of labor histories have quoted this "Declaration" from *Bill Haywood's Book,* p. 294; for example, see Gambs, pp. 41–42. In so doing they have unknowingly repeated a falsification. Haywood's biography says that this resolution was adopted at the 1916 IWW Convention and was "formulated from the Lenin resolution at the Zimmerwald Conference." Communist editing of Haywood's manuscript after his death in Russia in the 1920's probably explains why Lenin was credited with influencing the "Declaration"—a declaration which, in truth, the IWW had passed long before the Zimmerwald Conference.

39. Perry, p. 10.

40. Quoted in Fine, p. 310. The entire majority and minority reports on the Socialist party attitude toward America's entry into the war is contained in Fine's book, pp. 310–16.

41. *Report of the President's Mediation Commission to the President of the United States,* pp. 4–6.

42. Chaplin, p. 210.

43. *Ibid.,* p. 242.

44. *Debs and the War,* pp. 30–31.

CHAPTER NINE

1. Saposs, "The Catholic Church and the Labor Movement," *Modern Monthly*, VII (May, 1933), 225.
2. R. H. Tawney, *Religion and the Rise of Capitalism* (New York: Harcourt, 1926), p. 278.
3. Cardinal Henry Edward Manning, *The Vatican Decrees and Their Bearing on Civil Allegiance* (New York: The Catholic Publication Society, 1875), p. 40.
4. Somerville, pp. 5 and 6.
5. *The Catholic Encyclopedia* (New York: Encyclopedia Press, 1913), p. 308.
6. See the following encyclical letters of Pope Leo XIII: *Concerning Modern Errors*, December 28, 1878; *The Christian Constitution of States*, November 1, 1885; *Christians as Citizens*, January 10, 1890. These letters appear in Eyre, *The Pope and the People*.
7. Pope Leo XIII, *Rerum Novarum*.
8. *Ibid.*, pp. 11–12.
9. *Ibid.*, pp. 4–5.
10. *Ibid.*, p. 8.
11. *Ibid.*, p. 10.
12. *Ibid.*, pp. 25, 26, and 27.
13. *Ibid.*, p. 29.
14. *Ibid.*, pp. 32–33.
15. *Ibid.*, p. 37.
16. Quoted in Richard Purcell, p. 159.
17. Abell, "The Reception of Leo XIII's Labor Encyclical in America, 1891–1919," p. 464.
18. Vincent Yzermans (ed.), *All Things in Christ: Encyclicals and Selected Documents of Blessed Pius X* (St. Paul, Minn.: Saint Helena's Workshop, 1952), p. 167.
19. McQuade, p. 50.
20. William J. Kerby, "Aims in Socialism," *The Catholic World*, LXXXV (July, 1907), 511.
21. *Selected Papal Encyclicals and Letters 1928–1932* (Rev. ed.; London: Catholic Truth Society, 1933), p. 59.
22. Matre, Vol. X, pp. 38–47.
23. The people interviewed by the author included Frank Morrison, secretary of the AF of L from 1896 until his retirement

in 1929; Florence Thorne, editorial assistant to president of the AF of L Samuel Gompers; William Collins, senior organizer of the AF of L who started as an organizer with the AF of L in 1910; Dr. David Saposs, labor historian; and Nathan Fine, labor historian and AF of L researcher.

24. Perlman, *A Theory of the Labor Movement,* p. 169.
25. Dietz, "The American Federation of Labor," p. 11.
26. Boarman, p. 4.
27. Collins, "Catholic Workingmen's Associations," pp. 35–36.
28. Saposs, "The Catholic Church and the Labor Movement," *Modern Monthly,* VII (June, 1933), 296. Dr. Saposs notes on page 297 of this article that the Knights of Labor which preceded the AF of L "was dominated by native and Protestant working men [but] the A.F.L. was primarily an immigrant organization, and as the second generation Irish who had become the highly skilled workers came into the ascendency, the membership of the Federation's unions became predominantly Catholic."
29. Samuel Orth, "The Irish Invasion," *Our Foreigners: A Chronicle of Americans in the Making* (New Haven, Conn.: Yale University Press, 1921), p. 122.
30. Ware, *Labor in Modern Industrial Society,* p. 35.
31. The author compiled this list in an interview with Frank Morrison (AF of L secretary, 1896–1929), whose personal contact with the men on this list familiarized him with their religious faith. A very small number of Irish Catholic trade-union presidents with Socialist sympathies are not included on the list.
32. Quoted in Sister Agnes C. Schroll, "The Social Thought of John Lancaster Spalding" (Unpublished Ph.D. dissertation, Catholic University of America, 1944), p. 193.
33. *The National Hibernian,* August, 1915, p. 8.
34. Ellis, I, 535–43.
35. Will, II, 670.
36. *Ibid.,* p. 674.
37. *Ibid.,* pp. 676–77.
38. Cardinal Gibbons, *A Retrospect of Fifty Years,* I, 258–59.
39. Cardinal James Gibbons, "Organized Labor," reprinted by the Anti-Boycott Association as part of a pamphlet, *The Morals and Law Involved in Labor Conflicts,* pp. 20–21.
40. Cardinal William O'Connell, "Pastoral Letter on Labor's Rights," quoted in Ryan and Husslein, pp. 177–86.

41. *Ibid.*
42. *America,* II (January 8, 1910), 352.
43. *The Catholic German American,* August 5, 1911.
44. Stang, p. 33.
45. *Ibid.,* p. 27.
46. *Ibid.,* p. 140.
47. Archbishop John Ireland, quoted in *Common Cause,* June, 1912, pp. 109–10.
48. Archbishop John Ireland, *The Church and Modern Society; Lectures and Addresses by John Ireland* (2 vols.; New York: D. J. McBride and Co., 1903–4), II, 343.
49. Sister Agnes C. Schroll, p. 125.
50. *Ibid.,* p. 127.
51. Quoted in McDonagh, p. 164.
52. McFaul, p. 375.
53. *Ibid.,* p. 255.
54. *Ibid.,* pp. 271–75.
55. Leonard, p. 45.
56. Buffalo *Catholic Union and Times,* April 15, 1937, quoted in Leonard, p. 46.
57. AF of L Convention *Proceedings,* 1913, pp. 207–10.
58. McDonagh, pp. 163–64.
59. Matre, Vol. X, pp. 38–47.
60. *Ibid.,* pp. 261–72. Bishop Messmer became Archbishop of Milwaukee in 1903.
61. Archbishop S. G. Messmer, *Bulletin* of American Federation of Catholic Societies, XII (August–October, 1917).
62. *Buffalo Catholic Evening News,* July 5, 1902, quoted in *The Messenger,* XXXVIII (October, 1902), 246.
63. Glennon to G. Gramann, May 19, 1909; copy in the German Roman Catholic Central Verein Library, St. Louis, Missouri.
64. Quoted in McDonagh, p. 114.
65. G. Shaughnessy, *Has the Immigrant Kept the Faith?* (New York: Macmillan, 1925), p. 269.
66. Boarman, pp. 4–5.
67. *Ibid.,* pp. 31–32.
68. Husslein, pp. 112–16.
69. William J. Kerby, "The Priesthood and the Social Movement," *The Catholic University Bulletin,* VI, 24–25.
70. Ryan, *Social Doctrine in Action,* pp. 112–13.
71. Quoted in Richard Purcell, p. 158.

72. *Ibid.,* p. 159.
73. The Reverend Charles P. Bruehl, D.D., Ph.D., "The Conditions of Labor," in *Addresses at Patriotic and Civic Occasions by Catholic Orators,* i, 63–82.
74. For examples of Catholic labor leaders in Belgium and Germany in the late nineteenth century who "separated themselves from unions that had fallen under Socialist domination" and established Catholic trade-unions, see Somerville, pp. 151–54.
75. Kress, pp. 113–14.
76. Leonard, p. 75.
77. *Ibid.,* pp. 45 and 76.
78. *Ibid.,* p. 45.
79. Letter from F. P. Kenkel to Mr. Norman McKenna, April 29, 1940, quoted in Leonard, p. 96.
80. *Ibid.,* p. 95.
81. Letter of F. P. Kenkel to Sister Leonard, June 24, 1940. This letter was generously loaned to the author by Sister Leonard.
82. Cronin, pp. 179–80.
83. Fox, p. 26.
84. Letter from The Reverend Owen Rice to Father McDonagh, April 1, 1950, quoted in McDonagh, p. 159.
85. Stroh, "The Catholic Clergy and American Labor Disputes, 1900–1937."
86. *Elyria Daily Chronicle,* quoted in Fox, p. 34.
87. Dietz to Sister Leonard, July 19, 1940. This letter was kindly loaned to the author by Sister Leonard.
88. "The Social Problem: A Supplement," March 16, 1908, Dietz family papers, quoted in Fox, p. 49.
89. Dietz, "The Metamorphosis," pp. 7–10.
90. Dietz, "Workingmen's Welfare Organizations," pp. 8–9.
91. Dietz, "The American Federation of Labor," p. 12.
92. Fox, p. 49.
93. T. J. Duffy to Dietz, November 7, 1910, in Dietz files, German Roman Catholic Central Verein Library, St. Louis, Missouri.
94. T. V. O'Connor to Dietz, November 9, 1910, in Dietz files.
95. A copy of the Militia's constitution and platform and endorsement of Archbishop Glennon is contained among the John Mitchell papers located in the Department of Archives, Mullen Library, Catholic University of America, Washington, D.C., and in the Dietz files at the Central Bureau of the German Roman Catholic Central Verein, St. Louis, Missouri.
96. Falconio to Dietz, March 21, 1911, in Dietz files.

97. Various letters in Dietz files.
98. Ryan to Dietz, March 25, 1911, in Dietz files.
99. Ryan to Dietz, February 18, 1911, in Dietz files.
100. Neil to Dietz, February 28, 1911, in Dietz files.
101. T. J. Duffy to Dietz, December 10, 1910, in Dietz files.
102. T. J. Duffy to Dietz, February 13, 1911, in Dietz files.
103. John Mitchell to Dietz, February 8, 1911, in Dietz files.
104. James O'Connell to Dietz, February 9, 1911, in Dietz files.
105. P. J. Flannery to Dietz, February 3, 1911, in Dietz files.
106. T. V. O'Connor to Dietz, May 3, 1911, in Dietz files.
107. Frank L. Rist to Dietz, May 9, 1911, in Dietz files.
108. Edward J. Fliller to Dietz, September 25, 1911, in Dietz files.
109. John Voll to Dietz, February 4, 1911, in Dietz files.
110. McDonagh, p. 129.
111. April 4, 1913, in Dietz files.
112. Dietz to O'Connell, March 15, 1913; copy in Dietz files.
113. Saposs, "The Catholic Church and the Labor Movement,"
     Modern Monthly, VII (June, 1933), 298.
114. Abell, "The Reception of Leo XIII's Labor Encyclical in Amer-
     ica, 1891–1919," p. 489.
115. Victor Berger, "Organized Intolerance," *Milwaukee Leader,*
     June 14, 1913, quoted in Fox, p. 87.
116. *The Chicago Daily Socialist,* n.d., quoted in *Social Service,*
     August, 1911, p. 126.
117. *The Masses,* July, 1912, p. 3.
118. John M. O'Neill, "Something to Think About," *The Miners
     Magazine,* December 4, 1913, p. 7.
119. "The Catholic Threat and the A.F. of L.," *International Social-
     ist Review,* January, 1914, p. 415.
120. These letters are located among the John Mitchell papers found
     in the Department of Archives and Manuscripts, Mullen Li-
     brary, Catholic University of America, Washington, D.C.
121. Dietz to Mitchell, Oberlin, Ohio, April 18, 1911, in John
     Mitchell papers.
122. Mitchell to Dietz, June 1, 1911, in John Mitchell papers.
123. Mitchell to John P. Farrelly, June 17, 1911; copy in John
     Mitchell papers.
124. Mitchell to Dietz, June 24, 1911, copy in John Mitchell papers.
125. Dietz to Mitchell, June 26, 1911, in John Mitchell papers.
126. Dietz to Mitchell, August 30, 1911, in John Mitchell papers.
127. Dietz to Mitchell, December 30, 1911, in John Mitchell papers.
128. Mitchell to Dietz, January 3, 1912, in John Mitchell papers.

129. *The Militia of Christ, Constitution and Charter Laws,* Rev. ed., 1912, in Dietz files.
130. James O'Connell to Dietz, July 3, 1912, in Dietz files.
131. John Golden to Dietz, August 30, 1912, in Dietz files.
132. Dietz to Heckenkamp, January 14, 1913, in Dietz files.
133. Keates to Bishop Muldoon, December 25, 1912, in Dietz files.
134. Keates to Dietz, December 17, 1913, in Dietz files.
135. Dietz to members of Militia of Christ, May 5, 1914, in Dietz files.
136. Dietz to Mitchell, August 3, 1912, in John Mitchell papers.
137. Browne, "Peter E. Dietz, Pioneer Planner of Catholic Social Action," p. 454.
138. Fox, p. 114.
139. Dietz to Sister Joan Leonard, July 19, 1940.
140. *Weekly Press Service* of Social Service Commission of American Federation of Catholic Societies, December 21, 1914.
141. Fox, p. 57.
142. *Bulletin* of American Federation of Catholic Societies, XI (October–November, 1916), 1.
143. *Bulletin* of American Federation of Catholic Societies, XII (August–September, 1917), 11.
144. Fox, pp. 386–87.
145. Bishop Moeller was only one of many people who had difficulty in getting along with Father Dietz. Sister Harrita Fox's biography of Dietz contains some illuminating facts which suggest Dietz had a troubled emotional life. Sister Fox writes that in his second year in college he became very melancholy and discontinued "his studies because of ill health." (Sister Fox, p. 3.) Later while studying abroad near Vienna from 1900–1902 Dietz complained "of frequent headaches and nervous disorders which kept him alternating between the depths of despair and the heights of optimism and exaltation. Frequent difficulties with authority added to his disturbances." Back in America in 1904 for study at St. Mary's Seminary in Baltimore, "His Diary recounts his difficulties with Father Dyer, now rector at St. Mary's. Recurring nervous attacks put him in the hospital in April, 1904. Reluctant to return to St. Mary's, Dietz received permission to recuperate in North Carolina." (*Ibid.,* p. 13.)

      Sister Fox sums up her evaluation of Father Dietz's character as follows: "In many respects Father Dietz was a paradox. Lacking many of the social graces, abrupt and often harsh

in manner, he made loyal friends among all types of people—
bishops, priests, trade unionists, students at his school, and pa-
rishioners. That 'sad melancholy' that plagued him as a very
young man seemed to bear the 'dire fruits' in later life which
he predicted. Aggravating his natural tendency to irritability
were the recurring attacks of neuralgia and other nervous disorders. His *Diary* contains frequent references to the ungrate-
ful way he repaid the kindness of others, particularly his
mother and sisters. Those who survived his brusqueness, accu-
sations, suspicions, and harsh criticism, found that he was
honest in his dealings and that his sympathies once aroused
were deep and generous." (*Ibid.,* p. 32.)

Letters in the Dietz files in the Central Verein in St. Louis
added further significant information about Dietz's emotional
problems. In a letter to Bishop Muldoon, January 5, 1916, explaining an earlier resignation as editor of *Central Blatt and
Social Justice,* Dietz said he resigned "because of differences
with Mr. Kenkel which however were not of a philosophical
character but personal, for what reasons I have never known
for the trouble was not on my side." In a letter of December
31, 1915, to Bishop Muldoon, Dietz confided that he "had
'nerves' for about a week." A letter from Anthony Matre, national secretary of the American Federation of Catholic Societies, of September 22, 1916, expresses Matre's amazement
that Dietz would "believe I am your enemy."

The strongest reference made to Dietz about his emotional
difficulties was in a letter of September 9, 1916, from Francis
E. Slattery of Boston, a member of the Social Service Commission of the American Federation of Catholic Societies. Slattery said, "Permit me this suggestion which may help you
personally. I have a feeling that your temperament is such that
you are quick to believe that anyone who differs with you on
any measure is personally somewhat antagonistic. If only you
would realize that men's opinions are separate and apart from
man's emotions and that almost always when intelligent Catholics are conferring they are trying to derive correct solutions
of various problems and think very little of individualities."

146. Fox, pp. 334–35.
147. Browne, "Peter E. Dietz, Pioneer Planner of Catholic Social
Action," p. 456.
148. Messmer to Lenroot, April 19, 1921, in Dietz files.
149. Matre, Vol. IX, pp. 247–59.

150.   *The Messenger,* XXXVIII (October, 1902).
151.   *Sacred Heart Review,* XXXII (August 13, 1904), 97.
152.   Quoted in McDonagh, pp. 146–47.
153.   Fox, p. 195.
154.   *Bulletin* of American Federation of Catholic Societies, XII (August–October, 1917), 11.
155.   *The Central Verein: History, Aims and Scope.* This leaflet was kindly loaned to the author by Sister Leonard.
156.   Brophy, pp. 72–83.
157.   German Roman Catholic Central Verein Convention *Proceedings,* 1909.
158.   *Ibid.*
159.   "The Aftermath of the Indianapolis Convention," *Central Blatt and Social Justice,* II (October, 1909), 8–9.
160.   *Central Blatt and Social Justice,* IV (December, 1911), 204.
161.   *Ibid.,* v (January, 1913), 217–19.
162.   *Ibid.,* v (February, 1913), 243–45.
163.   *Ibid.*
164.   Ryan, "The Central Verein," p. 132.
165.   *Official Program,* Centennial Convention, The Catholic Central Verein of America, Rochester, New York, August, 1955, p. 88.
166.   Budenz to Dietz, January 24, 1913, in Dietz files.
167.   Budenz, "The Present Crisis in the American Labor Movement," pp. 89–91.
168.   Budenz to Dietz, February 28, 1913, in Dietz files.
169.   Budenz to Catholic Societies Affiliated to Indiana Federation of Catholic Societies, February, 1913, in Dietz files.
170.   Budenz to Dietz, February 28, 1913, in Dietz files.
171.   Budenz to Dietz, March 10, 1913, in Dietz files.
172.   Budenz to Dietz, April 28, 1913, in Dietz files.
173.   Budenz to Dietz, May 9, 1913, in Dietz files.
174.   Budenz to Dietz, May 26, 1913, in Dietz files.
175.   Budenz to Dietz, June 4 and 25, 1913, in Dietz files.
176.   *Central Blatt and Social Justice,* VI (December, 1914), 267.
177.   McDonagh, pp. 137–38.
178.   Dietz to Sister Leonard, July 19, 1940.
179.   Peter W. Collins, "Menace to Labor," *Electrical Worker,* December, 1909, quoted in McDonagh, pp. 70–71.
180.   "Der Soziale-Kursus zu Belleville," *Central Blatt and Social Justice,* II (March, 1909), 17.
181.   Collins, "The Labor Movement and Socialism," pp. 7–10.

182. *Peter W. Collins,* published by the Central Bureau of the Central Verein. This is found in the Collins Tours files which are located at the German Roman Catholic Central Verein Library, St. Louis, Missouri.
183. *Ibid.*
184. Collins to Dietz, October 19, 1911, in Dietz files.
185. Fox, p. 95.
186. Collins to Dietz, October 19, 1911, in Dietz files.
187. Collins to Dietz, July 1912, in Dietz files.
188. Dietz to Heckenkamp, January 14, 1913, in Dietz files.
189. Collins, "Catholic Workingmen's Associations," pp. 35–36.
190. Peter W. Collins, *Triplets of Destruction: Socialism, Bolshevism, and the I.W.W.* (New Haven, Conn.: Knights of Columbus, 1919), in Collins Tours files.
191. Abell, "The Reception of Leo XIII's Labor Encyclical in America, 1891–1919," p. 489.
192. Gompers' endorsement, American Federation of Labor, Washington, D.C., May 21, 1904, reads as follows: "I beg to say that I have read with keenest interest your book on 'Socialism, The Nation of Fatherless Children,' and have no hesitancy in saying that the book is not only timely, but an excellent contribution to the literature on the labor question and the labor movement. It tears the mask of hypocrisy from the face of those who have long pretended to be friends of the trade union movement, and yet seek its destruction or diversion to an improper purpose. I have found your book a ready reference to the many hostile utterances and actions of pretended friends."
193. Goldstein, *Socialism: The Nation of Fatherless Children,* p. x.
194. David Goldstein, *Autobiography of a Campaigner for Christ* (Boston: Catholic Campaigners for Christ, 1936), pp. 65–67.
195. *Ibid.,* pp. 117–354.
196. Goldstein, "Trade Unions: Their Foundations, Achievements, Dangers and Prospects," p. 189.
197. Goldstein, *Socialism: The Nation of Fatherless Children,* p. 368.
198. *Ibid.,* p. 369.
199. *An Appeal for Catholic Action* (Boston: Thomas J. Flynn and Co., n.d.), located in the Goldstein Tours files at the German Roman Catholic Central Verein Library, St. Louis, Missouri.
200. David Goldstein to F. P. Kenkel, December 23, 1911, Goldstein Tours files.
201. *Ohio Branch, American Federation of Catholic Societies to*

the County Organizations of the Ohio Federation of Catholic Societies, n.d., Goldstein Tours files.

202. *An Appeal to Catholic Patriotism* (Boston: Boston School of Political Economy, n.d.), Goldstein Tours files.
203. Goldstein to Dietz, January 27, 1914, Dietz files.
204. Goldstein, *Autobiography of a Campaigner for Christ,* p. 143.
205. McDonagh, p. 86.
206. Goldstein, *Autobiography of a Campaigner for Christ,* p. 117.
207. Quoted in Burke, "Convention of Catholic Editors," p. 81.
208. *Ibid.*
209. McFaul, pp. 252 and 255.
210. Husslein, pp. 112–16.
211. Apollinaris W. Baumgartner, *Catholic Journalism in the United States* (New York: Columbia University Press, 1931), pp. 55–64.
212. *The Live Issue* (New York City), April 11, 1914, p. 2.
213. Goldstein, *Socialism: The Nation of Fatherless Children,* p. 368.
214. Gompers to *The Common Cause,* Washington, D.C., December 14, 1911, in Gompers manuscripts, in AF of L Headquarters, Washington, D.C.
215. Perlman, *A Theory of the Labor Movement,* pp. 168–69.
216. Dietz to Cardinal O'Connell, March 15, 1913; copy in Dietz files.
217. *Bishops' Program of Social Reconstruction* (Washington, D.C.: National Catholic Welfare Conference, 1919).

CHAPTER TEN

1. Thomas Wolfe, *You Can't Go Home Again* (New York: Harper, 1940), p. 742.
2. The Rt. Rev. William Lawrence, "The Relation of Wealth to Morals," *The World's Work,* I (1900–1), 287.
3. Quoted in Richard Hofstadter, *Social Darwinism in American Thought* (Philadelphia: University of Pennsylvania Press, 1944), p. 3.
4. Quoted in Ware, *Labor in Modern Industrial Society,* p. 326.
5. *Lochner* v. *New York,* 198 U.S. 75.
6. For a study of subjective motivation influencing workers to join unions, see Marc Karson, "The Psychology of Trade Union Membership," *Mental Hygiene,* XLI (January, 1957), pp. 87–93.

Bibliography

UNPUBLISHED DISSERTATIONS AND THESES

Appel, John C. "The Relationship of American Labor to United States Imperialism, 1895–1906." Ph.D. Dissertation, University of Wisconsin, 1933.

Boyle, John P. "Peter E. Dietz and the American Labor Movement." Master's thesis, Catholic University of America, 1948.

Brophy, Sister Mary L. "The Social Thought of the Central Verein." Ph.D. dissertation, Catholic University of America, 1941.

Carwell, Joseph. "The International Role of American Labor." Ph.D. dissertation, Columbia University, 1956.

Cerny, Karl H. "Monsignor John A. Ryan and the Social Action Department." Ph.D dissertation, Yale University, 1955.

Cronin, Bernard C. "Father Yorke and the Labor Movement in San Francisco, 1900–1910." Ph.D. dissertation, Catholic University of America, 1943.

Fox, Sister Mary Harrita. "Peter E. Dietz: Pioneer in the Catholic Social Action Movement." Ph.D. dissertation, University of Notre Dame, 1950.

Gearty, Patrick W. "The Economic Thought of Monsignor John A. Ryan." Ph.D. dissertation, Catholic University of America, 1953.

Harris, Arvil E. "Organized Labor in Party Politics, 1906–1932." Ph.D. dissertation, University of Iowa, 1937.

Higgins, George G. "The Changing Attitude of American Trade Unionism towards Social and Labor Legislation, 1930–1940." Ph.D. dissertation, Catholic University of America, 1944.

Jones, Dallas L. "The Wilson Administration and Organized Labor, 1912–1919." Ph.D. dissertation, Cornell University, 1955.

Leonard, Sister Joan de Lourdes. "Catholic Attitude Towards American Labor, 1884–1919." Master's thesis, Columbia University, 1955.

McDonagh, The Reverend Thomas J. "Some Aspects of the Roman Catholic Attitude Toward the American Labor Movement,

1900–1914." Ph.D. dissertation, University of Wisconsin, 1951.

McKee, Delbert Lee. "The American Federation of Labor and American Foreign Policy, 1886–1912." Ph.D. dissertation, Stanford University, 1952.

McQuade, The Reverend V. A. "American Catholic Attitude on Child Labor since 1891." Ph.D. dissertation, Catholic University of America, 1938.

Mervis, Leonard J. "The Social Justice Movement of the American Reform Rabbis, 1890–1940." Ph.D. dissertation, University of Pittsburgh, 1951.

Ryan, Sister Mary Timothy. "An Analysis of Modern Socialism by Catholic Journalists." Ph.D. dissertation, St. Louis University, 1952.

Stalvey, James B. "Daniel DeLeon, A Study of Marxian Orthodoxy in the United States." Ph.D. dissertation, University of Illinois, 1946.

Stroh, The Rev. Paul. "The Catholic Clergy and American Labor Disputes, 1900–1937." Ph.D. dissertation, Catholic University of America, 1939.

Weimar, David. "Myth in the American Federation of Labor, 1880–1914." Ph.D. dissertation, University of Minnesota, 1955.

GOVERNMENT PUBLICATIONS

East St. Louis Riots. (65th Cong., 2d sess.; H.R. Doc. 1231.) Washington, D.C.: Government Printing Office, 1918.

Hearings on the Strike at Lawrence, Massachusetts. (62nd Cong., 2d sess.; H.R. Doc. 671.) Washington, D.C.: Government Printing Office, 1912.

Industrial Relations: Final Report and Testimony Submittted to Congress by the Commission on Industrial Relations. 11 vols. (64th Cong., 1st sess.; S. Doc. 415.) Washington, D.C.: Government Printing Office, 1916.

Report of the Committee of the Senate upon Relations between Labor and Capital. (48th Cong., 2d sess.; S. Misc. Doc. 49.) Washington, D.C.: Government Printing Office, 1885.

Report of the President's Mediation Commission to the President of the United States. Washington, D.C.: Government Printing Office, 1918.

Report on the Strike of Textile Workers at Lawrence, Mass. (62nd
Cong., 2d sess.; S. Doc. 870.) Washington, D.C.: Government
Printing Office, 1912.

ARTICLES

Abell, Aaron I. "The Catholic Church and Social Problems in the
World War I Era," *Mid-America,* XXX (July, 1948), 139–51.
———. "Monsignor Ryan: An Historical Interpretation," *Review of
Politics,* VIII (January, 1946), 128–34.
———. "Origins of Catholic Social Reform in the United States:
Ideological Aspects," *Review of Politics,* XI (July, 1949), 294–
309.
———. "The Reception of Leo XIII's Labor Encyclical in America,
1891–1919, *Review of Politics,* VII (October, 1945), 464–95.
"A.F. of L. Building Dedication," *American Federationist,* XXIII
(August, 1916), 658–64.
"A.F. of L. Campaign Programme," *American Federationist,* XIII
(August, 1906), 529–31.
Bates, Ernest S. "The A.F. of L.: Enemy of Labor," *American Mer-
cury,* XXXIV (January, 1935), 52–62.
Blakeley, Paul L. "The Federated Catholic Societies," *America,* XI
(October 10, 1914), 638–39.
Browne, Henry J. "Peter E. Dietz, Pioneer Planner of Catholic Social
Action," *The Catholic Historical Review,* XXXIII (January,
1948), 448–56.
Budenz, Louis F. "The American Federation of Labor Convention,"
Central Blatt and Social Justice, VII (December, 1914), 266–
67.
———. "The Present Crisis in the American Labor Movement," *Cen-
tral Blatt and Social Justice,* VI (July, 1913), 89–91.
Burke, John. "Convention of Catholic Editors," *The Catholic World,*
XCIV (October, 1911), 81–86.
Collins, Peter W. "Catholic Workingmen's Associations," *Central
Blatt and Social Justice,* V (May, 1912), 35–36.
———. "The Labor Movement and Socialism," *Central Blatt and So-
cial Justice,* II (February, 1910), 7–10.
Cooper, Lyle. "The American Federation of Labor and the Intellec-
tuals," *Political Science Quarterly,* XXXIII (1928), 388–427.

Cuniff, M. G. "Labor in Politics," *The World's Work,* xii (October, 1906), 8130–35.

Debs, Eugene V. "The Industrial Convention," *International Socialist Review,* vi (August, 1905), 85–86.

Dietz, Peter E. "American Federation of Labor," *Central Blatt and Social Justice,* ii (December, 1909), 11–12.

———. "The Metamorphosis," *Central Blatt and Social Justice,* ii (July, 1909), 7–10.

———. "Workingmen's Welfare Organizations," *Central Blatt and Social Justice,* ii (November, 1909), 8–9.

Dobbs, Charles. "Eliminating the Anarchist," *The Masses,* July, 1912, p. 5.

Goldstein, David. "Trade Unions, Their Foundations, Achievements, Dangers and Prospects," *Central Blatt and Social Justice,* iii (December, 1910), 189–92.

Gompers Samuel. "A.F. of L. Of, For, and By Labor," *American Federationist,* xxiv (August, 1918), 687–90.

———. "American Labor's Position in Peace or in War," *American Federationist,* xxiv (April, 1917), 269–81.

———. "Both Parties Have Spoken—Choose Between Them," *American Federationist,* xv (August, 1908), 598–606.

———. "Candidate Taft, Take Notice!" *American Federationist,* xv (November, 1908), 960–65.

———. "Elect Trade Union Congressmen," *American Federationist,* xix (June, 1912), 459–64.

———. "For Effective International Peace," *American Federationist,* xxi (October, 1914), 867–69.

———. "Free Speech and Free Press Invaded by Injunction against the A.F. of L.—A Review and Protest," *American Federationist,* xv (February, 1908), 98–105.

———. "The Future Foreign Policy of the United States," *American Federationist,* v (September, 1898), 138–40.

———. "The Injunction in Labor Disputes Must Go," *American Federationist,* xiii (April, 1906), 228–30.

———. "International Labor Relations," *American Federationist,* xxv (April, 1918), 293–97.

———. "Labor and Democracy," *American Federationist,* xxiv (October, 1917), 837–42.

———. "Labor Not a Commodity," *American Federationist,* xxi (October, 1914), 866–67.

———. "Labor vs. Its Barnacles," *American Federationist,* xxiii (April, 1916), 268–74.

Gompers, Samuel. "Labor's Political Campaign—Its Causes and Progress—Labor's Duties," *American Federationist,* XIX (October, 1912), 801–14.

———. "Militarism Must Not Prevail," *American Federationist,* XX (October, 1913), 862–63.

———. "Russianized West Virginia," *American Federationist,* XX (October, 1913), 827–35.

———. "Trade Union Attitude Toward Colored Workers," *American Federationist,* VIII (April, 1901), 118–19.

———. "United in Spirit and Purpose," *American Federationist,* XXIV (May, 1918), 386–87.

———. "Voluntary Social Insurance vs. Compulsory," *American Federationist,* XXIII (August, 1916), 669–81.

Guilday, The Reverend Peter. "The Church in the United States, 1870–1920," *Catholic Historical Review,* VI (January, 1921), 533–47.

Haywood, William. "Socialism, The Hope of the Working Class," *International Socialist Review,* XII (February, 1912), 461–71.

Heuser, The Reverend H. J., D.D. "Catholicizing the United States," *Ecclesiastical Review,* XXV (March, 1906), 236–50.

Hill, Joe. "How to Make Work for the Unemployed," *International Socialist Review,* XV (December, 1914), 335–36.

Hoxie, Robert F. "Gompers and the Labor Vote," *Journal of Political Economy,* XVI (December, 1908), 693–700.

Industrial Union Bulletin (Chicago), Industrial Workers of the World Publication, 1907–9.

"Labor's Bill of Grievances," *American Federationist,* XIII (May, 1906), 293–97.

"Labor's International Relations," *American Federationist,* XXIV (November, 1917), 954–79.

Mandell, Bernard. "Samuel Gompers and Religion," *The Chicago Jewish Forum,* XIII (Fall, 1954), 11–15.

Mann, Arthur. "Gompers and the Irony of Racism," *Antioch Review,* XIII (Summer, 1953), 203–14.

Marcy, Leslie H. "The Class War in Colorado," *International Socialist Review,* XIV (June, 1914), 708–21.

———, and *Frederick Sumner Boyd.* "One Big Union Wins," *International Socialist Review,* XII (April, 1912), 613–30.

Marcy, Mary E. "The Battle for Bread at Lawrence," *International Socialist Review,* XII (March, 1912), 533–43.

Matre, Anthony. "The American Federation of Catholic Societies," *Illinois Catholic Historical Review,* IX, 247–59, and X, 38–47, 267–72.

"Minutes of Executive Council Meeting," *American Federationist*, XXI (July, 1914), 584–89.

Muntch, *The Reverend Albert.* "The Priest's Attitude Toward Social Questions," *Central Blatt and Social Justice*, IV (November, 1911), 169–70.

"The Nation's Tribute to American Labor's Service Abroad," *American Federationist*, XXV (December, 1918), 1073–88.

Nilsson, *B. E.* "Unionism and Socialist Politics," *International Socialist Review*, X (November, 1909), 402–8.

Perrin, *Richard.* "The German Catholic Unions," *International Socialist Review*, XIV (January, 1914), 397–99.

Purcell, *Richard,* "John A. Ryan: Prophet of Social Justice," *Studies*, XXXV (June, 1946), 153–74.

Reed, *John.* "War in Paterson," *The Masses*, June, 1913, pp. 14–17.

Ryan, *John A.* "The Central Verein," *Catholic Forthnightly Review*, XVI (March, 1909), 132.

St. John, *Vincent.* "The Lesson of Ludlow," *International Socialist Review*, XIV (June, 1914), 725–27.

Saposs, *David J.* "The Catholic Church and the Labor Movement," *Modern Monthly*, VII (May, 1933), 225–30.

———. "The Catholic Church and the Labor Movement," *Modern Monthly*, VII (June, 1933), 294–98.

———. "The Immigrant in the Labor Movement," *Modern Quarterly*, III (January–March, 1926), 119–24.

Seidman, *Joel.* "Organized Labor in Political Campaigns," *Public Opinion Quarterly*, III (October, 1939), 646–54.

Semple, *Henry C., S.J.* "Case of Socialism v. the Catholic Church and the United States," *Catholic World*, CVI (February, 1918), 646–53.

Shippey, *Hartwell.* "The Shame of San Diego," *International Socialist Review*, XII (May, 1912), 718–23.

Simons, *A. M.* "The Chicago Conference for Industrial Unionism," *International Socialist Review*, V (February, 1905), 476–79.

———. "The Industrial Workers of the World," *International Socialist Review*, VI (August, 1905), 65–67.

Taylor, *Graham.* "The Industrial Viewpoint," *Charities and the Commons*, XXI (December, 1908), 401–6.

———. "Organized Labor and the Elections," *Charities and the Commons*, XXI (November, 1908), 274–76.

———. "Organized Labor's Political Front Unbroken," *Charities and the Commons*, XXI (October, 1908), 149–50.

BOOKS AND PAMPHLETS

Addresses at Patriotic and Civic Occasions by Catholic Orators, *2 vols. New York: Wagner, 1915.*

Address Before League to Enforce Peace. *Washington, D.C.: American Federation of Labor Headquarters, n.d.*

American Federation of Labor; History, Encyclopedia, Reference Book. *Washington, D.C.: American Federation of Labor, 1919.*

Barbash, Jack. The Practice of Unionism. *New York: Harper, 1956.*

Berman, Edward. Labor and the Sherman Act. *New York: Harper, 1930.*

Bingham, Alfred. The Revolt of the Middle Class. *New York: Holt, 1935.*

Bishops' Program of Social Reconstruction. *Washington, D.C.: National Catholic Welfare Conference, 1919.*

Blum, Fred. Toward a Democratic Work Process. *New York: Harper, 1953.*

Boarman, The Reverend Marshall I. Comedy of Socialism. *St. Louis, Mo.: B. Herder, (1908?).*

Bonnett, Clarence. Employers Associations in the United States. *New York: Macmillan, 1922.*

Boyd, Frederick. The Pageant of the Paterson Strike. *New York: Success Press, 1913.*

Brissenden, Paul Frederick. The I.W.W.: A Study of American Syndicalism. *New York: Columbia University, 1920.*

Brooks, John G. American Syndicalism. *New York: Macmillan, 1913.*

Browne, Henry J. The Catholic Church and The Knights of Labor. *Washington, D.C.: Catholic University Press, 1949.*

Carroll, Mollie R. Labor and Politics. *Boston: Houghton, 1923.*

The Central Verein: History, Aims and Scope. *St. Louis, Mo.: The Central Bureau of the German Roman Catholic Central Verein, n.d.*

Chaplin, Ralph. Wobbly. *Chicago: University of Chicago Press, 1948.*

Coleman, McAlister. The Man Unafraid: Eugene Debs. *New York: Greenberg, 1931.*

Commons, John R., David J. Saposs, Helen L. Sumner, E. B. Mittelman, H. E. Hoagland, John B. Andrews, and Selig Perlman.

History of Labor in the United States. *4 vols. New York: Macmillan, 1935–36.*

Crosser, Paul K. Ideologies and American Labor. *London: Oxford, 1941.*

Daugherty, Carrol R. Labor Problems in American Industry. *Boston: Mifflin, 1941.*

David, Henry. The History of the Haymarket Affair. *New York: Rinehart, 1936.*

Debs, Eugene V. Industrial Unionism. *New York: New York Labor News Co., 1911.*

——. Writings and Speeches of Eugene V. Debs, *ed. Arthur Schlesinger, Jr. New York: Hermitage Press, 1948.*

Debs and the War. *Chicago: National Office of the Socialist Party, n.d.*

DeLeon, Daniel. As to Politics. *New York: New York Labor News Co., 1907.*

——. The Burning Question of Trades Unionism. *New York: New York Labor News Co., 1904.*

——. Preamble of the Industrial Workers of the World. *New York: New York Labor News Co., 1905.*

——. Reform or Revolution. *New York: New York Labor News Co., 1906.*

——. Two Pages from Roman History. *New York: New York Labor News Co., 1903.*

Dulles, Foster Rhea. A History of Labor in America, *New York: Crowell, 1953.*

Egbert, Donald D., and Stow Persons (ed.). Socialism and American Life. *2 vols. Princeton, N.J.: Princeton University Press, 1952.*

Ellis, Monsignor John Tracy. The Life of James Cardinal Gibbons. *2 vols. Milwaukee, Wis.: Bruce Publishing Co., 1952.*

Ely, Richard T. The Labor Movement in America. *London: Heinemann, 1890.*

Evidence and Cross Examination of William D. Haywood in the Case of the U.S.A. v. William D. Haywood. *Chicago: General Defence Committee of the Industrial Workers of the World, n.d.*

Eyre, W. H., S.J. The Pope and the People. *London: Art and Book, 1895.*

Fine, Nathan. Labor and Farmer Parties in the United States, 1828–1928. *New York: Rand School, 1928.*

Foner, Philip S. History of the Labor Movement in the United States. *2 vols. New York: International Publishers, 1947.*

Foster, William Z. American Trade Unionism. *New York: International Publishers, 1947.*

Foster, William Z. Misleaders of Labor. *Chicago: Trade Union Educational League, 1927.*

———. Pages from a Worker's Life. *New York: International Publishers, 1939.*

Fox, Sister Mary Harrita. Peter E. Dietz, Labor Priest. *South Bend, Ind.: University of Notre Dame Press, 1953.*

Frankfurter, Felix, and Nathan Greene. The Labor Injunction. *New York: Macmillan, 1930.*

Gambs, John S. The Decline of the I.W.W. *New York: Columbia University Press, 1932.*

Gibbons, Cardinal James. The Morals and Law Involved in Labor Conflicts. *New York: American Anti-Boycott Assn., 1907.*

———. A Retrospect of Fifty Years. *2 vols. Baltimore: J. Murphy, 1916.*

Ginger, Ray. The Bending Cross. *New Brunswick, N.J.: Rutgers University Press, 1949.*

Ginzberg, Eli. The Labor Leader. *New York: Macmillan, 1948.*

Gluck, Elsie, John Mitchell, Miner. *New York: John Day, 1929.*

Goldman, Emma. Living My Life. *2 vols. London: Duckworth, 1932.*

Goldstein, David. Autobiography of a Campaigner for Christ. *Boston: Catholic Campaigners for Christ, 1936.*

———. Socialism: The Nation of Fatherless Children. *Boston: Union News League, 1902.*

Gompers, Samuel. Labor in Europe and America. *New York: Harper, 1910.*

———. Seventy Years of Life and Labor. *2 vols. in one. New York: Dutton, 1934.*

Grossman, Jonathan. William Sylvis, Pioneer of American Labor. *New York: Columbia University Press, 1945.*

Hardman, J. B. S. (ed.). American Labor Dynamics. *New York: Harcourt, 1928.*

Harris, Herbert. American Labor. *New Haven, Conn.: Yale University Press, 1938.*

Harvey, Rowland H. Samuel Gompers, Champion of the Toiling Masses. *Stanford, Calif.: Stanford University Press, 1935.*

Haywood, William D. Bill Haywood's Book. *London: Lawrence, 1929.*

———, *and Frank Bohn.* Industrial Socialism. *Chicago: C. Kerr and Co., 1911.*

Higgins, George Gilmary. Voluntarism in Organized Labor in the United States, 1930–1940. *Washington, D.C.: The Catholic University of America Press, 1944.*

Hillquit, Morris. History of Socialism in the United States. *New York: Funk, 1906.*

————. Loose Leaves from A Busy Life. *New York: Macmillan, 1934.*

————, *and John A. Ryan.* Socialism: Promise or Menace? *New York: Macmilllan, 1914.*

Hopkins, Charles H. The Rise of the Social Gospel in American Protestantism, 1865–1915. *New Haven, Conn.: Yale University Press, 1940.*

Hoxie, Robert F. Trade Unionism in the United States. *New York: Appleton-Century-Crofts, Inc., 1923.*

Hughan, Jessie W. The Present Status of Socialism in America. *New York: John Lane, 1911.*

Hunter, Robert. Labor in Politics. *Chicago: Socialist Party, 1915.*

Husslein, The Reverend Joseph, S.J. The Catholic's Work in the World, *New York: Benziger, 1917.*

Interpreting the Labor Movement. *Madison, Wis.: Industrial Relations Research Association, 1952.*

Kipnis, Ira. The American Socialist Movement 1897–1912. *New York: Columbia University Press, 1952.*

Kress, The Reverend William. Questions of Socialists and Their Answers. *Cleveland, Ohio: Apostolate, 1908.*

Laidler, Harry W. Boycotts and the Labor Struggle. *New York: John Lane, 1913.*

Laski, Harold J. Trade Unions in the New Society. *New York: Viking Press, 1949.*

Legislative Achievements of the American Federation of Labor. *Washington, D.C.: American Federation of Labor, 1916.*

Lens, Sidney. Left, Right, and Center: Conflicting Forces in American Labor. *Chicago: Regnery, 1949.*

Leo XIII, *Pope.* Rerum Novarum: Encyclical Letter of Pope Leo XIII on the Condition of Labor (With Discussion Club Outline). *New York: The Paulist Press, 1939.*

Lorwin, Lewis. American Federation of Labor. *Washington, D.C.: Brookings Institute, 1934.*

————. Labor and Internationalism. *New York: Macmillan, 1929.*

Lozovsky, A. S. Marx and the Trade Unions. *New York: International, 1935.*

McFaul, The Rt. Rev. James A. Pastoral Letters, Addresses and Other Writings of the Rt. Rev. James A. McFaul, *ed. The Rev. James J. Powers. 2nd ed. New York: Benziger, 1916.*

Madison, Charles A. American Labor Leaders. *New York: Holt, 1952.*

Marot, Helen. American Labor Unions. *New York: Holt, 1914.*

May, Henry F. The Protestant Church and Industrial America. *New York: Harper, 1949.*

Maynard, Theodore. The Story of American Catholicism. *New York: Macmillan, 1942.*

Mills, C. Wright. The New Men of Power. *New York: Harcourt, 1948.*

Mitchell, John. Organized Labor. *Philadelphia, Pa.: American Book and Bible House, 1903.*

Northrup, Herbert. Organized Labor and the Negro. *New York: Harper, 1944.*

O'Connell, Cardinal William. Pastoral Letter on Relations Between Employer and Employee. *A copy of this letter is to be found in the Mullen Library, Catholic University of America.*

An Open Letter to President Harding. *Chicago: Industrial Workers of the World General Defense Committee, n.d.*

Orth, Samuel. The Armies of Labor. *New Haven, Conn.: Yale University Press, 1919.*

Parker, Carleton H. The Casual Laborer and Other Essays. *New York: Harcourt, 1920.*

Parsons, Albert R. Anarchism: Its Philosophy and Scientific Basis. *Chicago: Mrs. Albert R. Parsons, 1887.*

Perlman, Selig. History of Trade Unionism in the United States. *New York: Macmillan, 1923.*

————. Labor in the New Deal Decade. *New York: International Ladies Garment Workers' Union, 1945.*

————. A Theory of the Labor Movement. *New York: Macmillan, 1928.*

————, *and Philip Taft.* History of Labor in the United States, 1896–1932. *New York: Macmillan, 1935.*

Perry, Grover H. The Revolutionary I.W.W. *Cleveland, Ohio: Industrial Workers of the World Publishing Bureau, 1915.*

Peterson, Florence. American Labor Unions. *New York: Harper, 1945.*

Peterson, H. C., and Gilbert C. Fite. Opponents of War, 1917–1918. *Madison, Wis.: University of Wisconsin Press, 1957.*

Proceedings of the . . . Annual Convention of the Industrial Workers of the World. *New York.*

Purcell, Theodore. The Worker Speaks His Mind on Company and Union. *Cambridge, Mass.: Harvard University Press, 1953.*

Record of Senator William E. Borah. *Washington, D.C.: American Federation of Labor Headquarters, 1912.*

Reed, Louis S. The Labor Philosophy of Samuel Gompers. *New York: Columbia University, 1930.*

Report of Proceedings of the . . . Annual Convention of the American Federation of Labor.

Robbins, Hayes (ed.). Labor and the Common Welfare. *New York: Dutton, 1919.*

Rogoff, Henry. An East Side Epic, The Life and Work of Meyer London. *New York: Vanguard, 1930.*

Ryan, John A. Social Doctrine in Action. *New York: Harper, 1941.*
————, *and Joseph Husslein (ed.).* The Church and Labor. *New York: Macmillan, 1924.*

St. John, Vincent. The I.W.W., Its History, Structure and Methods. *Rev. ed.; Chicago: Industrial Workers of the World, 1919.*

Saposs, David J. Left Wing Unionism. *New York: International Publishers, 1926.*

Shannon, David. The Socialist Party of America. *New York: Macmillan, 1953.*

Should a Political Labor Party Be Formed? *Washington, D.C.: American Federation of Labor Headquarters, 1919.*

Somerville, Henry. Studies in the Catholic Social Movement. *London: Burns, Oates and Washbourne, 1933.*

Spargo, John. Social Democracy Explained. *New York: Harper, 1918.*

Spero, Sterling D., and Abram L. Harris. The Black Worker. *New York: Columbia University Press, 1931.*

Stang, Bishop William. Socialism and Christianity. *New York: Benziger, 1905.*

Symes, Lillian, and Clement Travers. Rebel America. *New York: Harper, 1934.*

Taft, Philip. The A.F. of L. in the Time of Gompers. *New York: Harper, 1957.*

Textbook of Labor's Political Demands. *Washington, D.C.: American Federation of Labor Headquarters, 1906.*

Thorne, Florence Calvert. Samuel Gompers—American Statesman. *New York: Philosophical Library, 1957.*

Tridon, Andre. The New Unionism. *New York: Huebsch, 1913.*

Walling, William E. American Labor and American Democracy. *London: Harper, 1926.*

————. Socialism As It Is. *New York: Macmillan, 1912.*

Ware, Norman J. The Industrial Worker, 1840–1860. *Boston: Houghton, 1924.*

————. Labor in Modern Industrial Society. *New York: Heath, 1935.*

————. The Labor Movement in the United States, 1860–1895. *New York: Appleton-Century-Crofts, 1929.*

Wesley, Charles H. Negro Labor in the United States 1850–1925: A Study in American Economic History. *New York: Vanguard, 1927.*

Whipple, Leon. The Story of Civil Liberty in the United States. *New York: Vanguard, 1927.*

Will, Allen Sinclair. Life of Cardinal Gibbons, Archbishop of Baltimore. *2 vols. New York: Dutton, 1922.*

Witte, Edwin E. The Government in Labor Disputes. *New York: McGraw, 1932.*

Yellin, Samuel. American Labor Struggles. *New York: Harcourt, 1936.*

Index

347

Green, William, 129
Gunn, Bishop John E. *See* Bishops

HAGERTY, Professor James, 252
Haiti occupation, 146
Harding, President Warren G., 209, 258
Hat and Cap makers, 131
Hayes, Denis: National Civic Federation supporter of, 127; officer of Militia of Christ, 244; member of Social Service Commission of American Federation of Catholic Societies, 255
Hayes, Max: candidate for AF of L presidency, 130; IWW Convention invitation rejected by, 153; warns Socialists against joining IWW, 154, 162; mentioned, 26, 120, 167, 265
Haywood, William: charged with murder of Governor Steunenberg, 142; chairman first convention of IWW, 154; candidate for governor of Colorado, 166; testimony before Industrial Relations Commission, 177, 178, 179, 191–92; syndicalist philosophy of, 178, 192–95, 198; acknowledges failure of San Diego free speech campaign, 182; leads Lawrence textile strike, 183; delegate to Second International meeting, 192; expelled from Socialist Party executive committee, 197; wartime arrest and trial of, 207, 208
Hearst, William Randolph, 61
Heiter, Father. *See* Priests
Henderson, Arthur, 107, 109, 110, 112
Heuser, Father. *See* Priests
Hill, Joe, 143, 176, 198
Hillquit, Morris: leads group out of Socialist Labor Party, 26; opinion of DeLeon's dogmatism, 26–27; cross-examines Gompers, 117; denounces IWW for advocating violence, 197
Hitchman Coal Company case, 76
Holder, Arthur, 78, 81
Holmes, Justice Oliver Wendell, 298, 311
Holy Name societies, 226, 270

Horstman, Bishop Ignatius. *See* Bishops
Howard, Bishop Francis W. *See* Bishops
Hughes amendment, 68, 75
Hughes, Charles Evans, 85, 87, 88
Husslein, Father Joseph. *See* Priests
Hutcheson, William, 100

IMMIGRATION restriction: sought by AF of L, 43, 71, 81, 115, 136; opposed by Debs, 189
Indiana Federation of Catholic Societies, 266
Individual rights: American political theory based on, 296–97; Protestant theology emphasizes, 297; capitalist philosophy supports, 297–98
Industrial Relations Commission, 82. *See also* Gompers, Samuel; Haywood, William
Industrial Workers of the World: Chicago Manifesto, 152; conventions, 154–59, 163–67, 167–68, 169–74; political ideas at first convention, 154; political clause, 156–58, 164–65, 168–69, 170–73; civil rights constitutional provisions, 158; and education, 158–59; strike philosophy of, 159, 166–67, 174; antimilitarist position of, 159; 200–3, 322; rejects sick and death benefits, 166; opposes Socialist party, 167, 187–89, 191, 192; free speech fights, 176–78, 179, 179–82, 198–99; direct action strikes, 178, 183–85, 186, 187, 204–6; attitude toward law, 179; political philosophy of, 191–92; draft evasion, 203; wartime government campaign against, 204, 206–7; membership, 207; general defense organization, 207, 209; state government trials, 208–9; Criminal syndicalist laws, 209; amnesty for imprisoned, 209–10; Catholics warned against, 263
Injunctions: power of, 31–32; lobbied for, 32; against Chicago Typographical Union, 37; Republican party in favor of, 58; against Mine Workers, 76; mentioned, 30. *See also* Clayton Act